Praise for *Managing Cloud Natve Data on Kubernetes*

This book challenged my notions about storing data on Kubernetes. I no longer fear the loss of data.

—*Jesse Anderson, Managing Director, Big Data Institute*

Managing Cloud Native Data on Kubernetes is a groundbreaking work not only because it is the first to tackle this problem space, but because it simultaneously obviates the need for any other book on the subject. Drawing on their decades of experience, Jeff and Patrick give readers the confidence to run stateful workloads on Kubernetes in production. This book will be the reference on the topic for years to come.

—*Umair Mufti, Director of Product Management, Portworx by Pure Storage*

Kubernetes is notoriously complex, and dealing with persistent data adds to the complexity. This book does an amazing job of taming the complexity of dealing with data using Kubernetes with many useful code examples and architectural diagrams.

—*Noah Gift, Duke Executive in Residence*

Storage is one of the hardest infrastructure layers to master and arguably has the longest innovation cycles. We are at the cusp of one such innovation cycle at the moment with cloud native applications. Jeff and Patrick have tackled this subject head-on, by having the readers understand the evolution of cloud native storage and help transform theirstorage strategy to meet the next gen application demands. Anyone that is working with microservices (which is almost everyone at the moment), must read this book before they have completed their transformation projects.

—*Kiran Mova, Founder, Architect Storage Startups Open Source Advocate/Manager, VMware*

I have learned a lot from reading this book! I have been working full time in the Kubernetes ecosystem for several years at Red Hat but this book touches areas that I haven't had experience with. It was an eye-opener for me to realize that Kubernetes is not only for stateless microservices. I can clearly see where the platform is going and this book definitely helped me see that direction. Industry experts Jeff Carpenter and Patrick McFadin put some very nice articles from other experts in the book and I loved reading how tech evolved into its current state.

—Ali Ok, Principal Software Engineer, Red Hat

This is *the book* you need if doing persistence on Kubernetes is your ultimate goal. Jeff and Patrick do a tremendous job in this comprehensive view of Data on Kubernetes to the point where it doesn't have to be scary, especially if you have this book on your shelf!

—Rick Vasquez, Senior Director,
Strategic Initiatives, Western Digital

Managing Cloud Native Data on Kubernetes

Architecting Cloud Native Data Services Using Open Source Technology

Jeff Carpenter and Patrick McFadin

Beijing • Boston • Farnham • Sebastopol • Tokyo

Managing Cloud Native Data on Kubernetes

by Jeff Carpenter and Patrick McFadin

Published by O'Reilly Media, Inc., 1005 Gravenstein Highway North, Sebastopol, CA 95472.

O'Reilly books may be purchased for educational, business, or sales promotional use. Online editions are also available for most titles (*http://oreilly.com*). For more information, contact our corporate/institutional sales department: 800-998-9938 or *corporate@oreilly.com*.

Acquisitions Editor: Aaron Black
Development Editor: Jill Leonard
Production Editor: Beth Kelly
Copyeditor: Justin Billing
Proofreader: Sharon Wilkey
Indexer: Potomac Indexing, LLC
Interior Designer: David Futato
Cover Designer: Karen Montgomery
Illustrator: Kate Dullea

December 2022: First Edition

Revision History for the First Edition

2022-12-01: First Release

See *http://oreilly.com/catalog/errata.csp?isbn=9781098111397* for release details.

978-1-098-11139-7

[LSI]

Table of Contents

Foreword

You're about to go on an amazing adventure into the heart of the biggest change in the technology industry. In this adventure, you're part of a fellowship led by a brave duo who have dared the mountains, depths, and lakes of data for decades. You'll journey with Patrick McFadin and Jeff Carpenter, along with a band of visionary practitioners, to attain the prize: the power to create the future of data.

After reading this book, you'll be able to create your own new adventures and bring others along with you to go beyond the old world of computation, ruled by infrastructure, into the new world of cognition, ruled by autonomous experiences. It's going to be awesome.

The book you hold is written in a time when we've already seen a significant change in how we imagine, understand, and operate large-scale systems. The act of writing a book about technology in the midst of all this change may itself seem quixotic, but it's essential. It's a moment to stop at the Last Homely House as we gather the cognitive tools, supplies, and artifacts that will help us in the journey ahead.

We need all the help we can gather because change tends to accelerate.

In a few short decades, we've gone from mainframes to networks to data centers to clouds. Each new era feels like a new world with new rules and new opportunities. We build ecosystems of tools to match the era; the tools enable faster progress, and we build even more of them; we grow unsatisfied despite the speed, and suddenly there is a new breakthrough that heralds another new era.

Each era needs to deal with the same concerns: networking, computation, and data. At each leap forward, they all need to transform. Mainframes and terminals, networks and routers, data centers and virtualization, clouds and containers; by architecting for new levels of abundance, each sets a new bar for velocity, scale, and unit economics. We strive to go faster, bigger, and more efficient.

As the tools change, so do the people; mindsets must be rebuilt for each new wave of abundance, from the mainframe high priests to overworked network admins to dutiful datacenter operators to savvy cloud engineers. Infrastructure has always been considered expensive since it's a cost of doing business rather than the business itself; each era's technology teams have needed to focus on what the business values.

Mainframes and transaction processing, networks and file sharing, data centers and ecommerce, clouds and apps—each era's north star reflects the standard business focus of the time. As we look into the near future, we see new nouns: edges, models, predictions, and decisions, collectively powering autonomous businesses.

What's holding us back from the next era? What's the big unlock we're collectively struggling to achieve? It's the one thing that we haven't solved beautifully—yet.

The first half of the cloud era was defined by Amazon's AWS and copied by others: singular global-scale federated datacenters using virtual machines and infrastructure microservices, designed and evolved together as one unique whole. No two of these clouds are alike. They vary by aesthetic, by identity models, by billing systems, by APIs. Just like in the beginnings of the mainframe, network, and datacenter eras, each cloud stack was vertically integrated. This lock-in offered great utility at the price of never leaving.

The second half of the cloud era is defined by Kubernetes and its vibrant ecosystem of tools, all built on the same premise: the unit of work is a container, not a virtual machine, physical server, or mainframe processor. Containers are the law of the land, representing the standard granularity of technology workloads until the next era comes along. It's about transcending single clouds to gain a cloud native stance anywhere. The Kubernetes breakthrough is named *cloud native* to mark the mature state of the cloud era.

What is the magic power we find in containers? It is simply this: we've learned that scaling out our ideas requires scaling down our units of work. Software is made of ideas; fluidity requires scaling down to fit these ideas into more efficient units, and leverage requires scaling out to take advantage of any available infrastructure.

The cloud native manifesto that is so well-represented by Kubernetes and its ecosystem has taken us a long way toward the future, but we now find ourselves pinned in place, short of the summit we aspire to. For all the advances we've made, they are focused on stateless operations. We now face the final stage of the era: cloud native data.

When we conquer this challenge collectively, we'll have created a world where any app or model can run anywhere it's needed, at the speed that users demand, because the data will flow with it. Whether it's on a phone, a car, a metro edge, a cloud, or a satellite, the data will be self-describing, observable, fluid, and accessible. Infrastructure can become invisible and deliver power however developers may dream.

This book is key to unlocking that potential.

Like any epic journey, cloud native data on Kubernetes is a progressive revelation. The ordinary world of storage and StatefulSets leads you to mastery of architecting data infrastructure for any given workload, from applications to analytics and machine learning. The door to the extraordinary world will then be open to you: a vision of the next generation of data management and the open source projects that are advancing the art of the possible. Open communities sharing ideas and code together are the only way we can realize this future.

Looking ahead to the next decade, we don't know exactly what the technologies we use will be named, but we do know that they will be built on the ideas we're making real now. Welcome to the adventure of cloud native data, and take joy in the journey!

— Sam Ramji
Chief Strategy Officer at DataStax
Strategic Advisor to the Linux Foundation

Preface

Is Kubernetes ready for stateful workloads?

This might be the question that got you to open this book. Since cloud computing first emerged, data infrastructure (NoSQL/NewSQL, streaming, analytics) and application infrastructure (Docker, Kubernetes) have been maturing rapidly but on separate tracks. In our view, it's time to formalize bringing these two areas together. This isn't an aspiration for the future; it is already happening with collaboration across multiple communities. Organizations that are trying to manage two distinct stacks for applications and data will soon find themselves at a competitive disadvantage.

For the first few years of Kubernetes' existence after its public launch in 2014, the maxim that it was not ready for data and stateful workloads was rarely questioned. An example of the prevailing wisdom can be found in this Kelsey Hightower tweet (*https://oreil.ly/d4jRU*) from 2018:

> Kubernetes has made huge improvements in the ability to run stateful workloads including databases and message queues, but I still prefer not to run them on Kubernetes.

Over the past few years, the tide has turned. Problem-solving engineers took this challenge from Kelsey and turned it into action. In some sense, the maturation of Kubernetes for stateful workloads was inevitable, as the demand was so great. Those of us who can remember arguments about why a database had to run on a bare-metal machine or why you should never deploy data infrastructure in containers can relate to this concern.

We've also learned that there is a huge difference between "never" and "not yet." Compute, storage, networking are now considered commodities; why not data management? The value proposition of Kubernetes for reducing cost and simplifying application development means that the migration of data infrastructure onto Kubernetes was inevitable. The changes are not just in Kubernetes. As you will see, projects in data infrastructure have been changing as well.

Why We Wrote This Book

We were caught up in the trend of moving stateful workloads to Kubernetes when our "day job" responsibilities at DataStax challenged us to consider how to deploy and operate Apache Cassandra in Kubernetes effectively. In the spirit of open source development, we sought out other practitioners who were attempting similar feats (and succeeding) with databases and other stateful workloads. We found a group of like-minded individuals and helped launch the Data on Kubernetes Community (*https://oreil.ly/WGlmp*) (DoKC) in 2020. DoKC is now an independent organization and has hosted well over 100 meetups and several in-person events. The variety of topics and presenters (*https://oreil.ly/b1imM*) in the DoKC meetup is evidence of a vibrant community, working collaboratively to establish standards and best practices. Most importantly, we are learning together, applying lessons from the past and supporting each other as we build something new.

As we participated in these meetups, a set of common themes began to emerge. We heard, again and again, the virtues of the PersistentVolume subsystem, the pros and cons of StatefulSets, the promise of the operator pattern for making database operations more manageable, and the early hints of ideas for new types of data management. Over time, we developed a strong conviction that this fledgling community of practitioners needed a place for all of the wisdom scattered across multiple presentations and blog posts to be gathered and distilled into a digestible form. This book is the result of that process.

Much work remains to be done in the area of cloud native data, and many areas need further exploration, including operators, machine learning, data APIs, declarative management of data sets, and many more. Our hope is that this book opens the gates for a flood of additional books, blogs, presentations, and learning resources.

Who Is This Book For?

The primary audience for this book comprises the developers and architects who are designing, building, and running applications in the cloud. If that describes you and you're picking up this book, chances are you've heard the thundering herd of organizations adopting Kubernetes and have joined that trend or are at least considering it. However, you may have also heard the reservations about stateful workloads on Kubernetes and are looking for help in how to proceed. You've come to the right place! By reading this book you will gain the following:

- An understanding of basic Kubernetes resources and how they are used to compose data infrastructure
- An appreciation for how tools like Helm and operators can automate the deployment and operations of data infrastructure on Kubernetes

- The ability to evaluate and select data infrastructure technologies for use in your applications
- The knowledge of how to integrate these data infrastructure technologies into your overall stack
- A view toward emerging technologies that will enhance your Kubernetes-based applications in the years to come

A smaller but no less important audience includes core Kubernetes developers and data infrastructure developers, many of whom we've met through the DoKC. We hope to create a common set of principles and best practices that we can use as a framework to drive improvements into the Kubernetes core as well as the data infrastructure built to run in Kubernetes. Together we can push the practice of data on Kubernetes forward.

For everyone, know that our objective in this book is to shoot straight. Where the technology is mature and solid, we'll let you know, but there are also many areas where the technology is still emerging. We'll make sure to highlight those areas where improvement is needed.

How to Read This Book

This book is designed to be read from start to finish, especially by readers who are less experienced with Kubernetes. The first few chapters introduce Kubernetes terminology and concepts that are referenced throughout the remainder of the book as we discuss more advanced topics. Here's how this book is organized:

Chapter 1, "Introduction to Cloud Native Data Infrastructure: Persistence, Streaming, and Batch Analytics"
: This chapter lays out the goal of modernizing your cloud native applications by putting not only stateless but also stateful workloads on Kubernetes. Of course we would say this, but you really should start here, as we define key goals and terms to give all readers a level playing field. Specifically, we propose a definition for the term *cloud native data* and define principles for cloud native data infrastructure that we'll use to measure technologies throughout the rest of the book.

Chapter 2, "Managing Data Storage on Kubernetes"
: In this chapter, we'll look at one of the foundational areas for data infrastructure on Kubernetes: storage. We'll begin with how storage works in containerized systems starting with Docker, then moving to Kubernetes and its PersistentVolume subsystem. We'll discuss the various types of storage available including file, block, and object storage, and the trade-offs of using local versus remote storage solutions.

Chapter 3, "Databases on Kubernetes the Hard Way"
: This chapter introduces Kubernetes compute resources such as Pods, Deployments, and StatefulSets and walks you through the step-by-step process of deploying databases like MySQL and Apache Cassandra using these resources. You'll learn some of the strengths and weaknesses of StatefulSets for managing distributed databases.

Chapter 4, "Automating Database Deployment on Kubernetes with Helm"
: Continuing the themes of the previous chapter, we revisit the deployment of MySQL and Cassandra on Kubernetes, this time in a more automated fashion using the Helm package manager. You'll also learn about Kubernetes resources that help with configuration including ConfigMaps and Secrets. We discuss the role of Helm in your overall DevOps process and CI/CD toolset and some of its shortcomings with respect to managing database operations.

Chapter 5, "Automating Database Management on Kubernetes with Operators"
: This chapter concludes our sequence on database deployment by introducing the operator pattern and demonstrating how operators can help manage "day two" database operations. We'll examine how operators extend the Kubernetes control plane to manage databases, using Vitess (MySQL) and Cass Operator (Apache Cassandra) as examples. Along the way, you'll learn how to assess operators' maturity and even how to build your own operators by using frameworks such as the Operator SDK.

Chapter 6, "Integrating Data Infrastructure in a Kubernetes Stack"
: In this chapter, we begin to expand the focus beyond just deploying and operating databases to consider how databases and other data infrastructure can be incorporated in your overall application stack. We'll look at a project called K8ssandra that integrates Apache Cassandra along with tools for managing monitoring, security, and database backups, and an API layer for easier data access.

Chapter 7, "The Kubernetes Native Database"
: At this point, we take a step back and summarize what you've learned about cloud native data management in the book's first half and use that knowledge to consider the question, "What is a Kubernetes native database?" More than just a debate about industry buzzwords, this discussion is an important one for you who are involved in selecting data infrastructure and those developing that infrastructure.

Chapter 8, "Streaming Data on Kubernetes"
: Moving beyond persistence, we'll start working through the rest of the data infrastructure, starting with streaming technologies. Moving and processing data in cloud native applications is just as prevalent as database persistence, but requires different strategies in deployment: connecting endpoints securely and building in

default resilience and elasticity. In this chapter, Apache Pulsar and Apache Flink will be used to demonstrate those important practices to build.

Chapter 9, "Data Analytics on Kubernetes"
: Ironically, the needs for large-scale analytics deployments are part of the origin story of many of the methodologies we see used in Kubernetes today—namely, orchestration and resource management. Coming full circle, running analytics in Kubernetes is now a top priority in many organizations. We highlight changes in Apache Spark to give you a head start for your use case and look at the leading edge of analytics in Kubernetes with the Dask and Ray projects.

Chapter 10, "Machine Learning and Other Emerging Use Cases"
: The topics of AI and machine learning are already on the cutting edge within infrastructure. Projects that have started in the past few years could start in Kubernetes first, and it's an interesting thing to consider. There are other types of projects thinking in terms of cloud native first and providing some directionality to the future of data. This chapter is meant to be a survey of those projects and offered broadly as ideas and methodologies to consider as you move forward with cloud native data.

Chapter 11, "Migrating Data Workloads to Kubernetes"
: All the knowledge you've obtained in reading the book goes to waste if you don't put it into practice. In this chapter, we highlight the key teachings of the previous chapters and propose a framework of people, process, and technology changes you can make to migrate your stateful workloads to Kubernetes successfully. We conclude with a vision of what your organization's data infrastructure could look like in the near future.

The discipline of managing data on Kubernetes is an emerging one with a lot of change in particular areas. We acknowledge that this, like any technical book, represents a snapshot of available knowledge at a specific point in time—in this case, late 2022. The real danger of writing a book about a fast-moving topic is how quickly irrelevant the information can become.

To best address this reality, you will see a common formula applied in this book: we provide plenty of examples but stress the fundamentals. As we progress through the book, the technology we examine becomes progressively less mature. Rather than looking for the copy-and-paste answer or the one-size-fits-all architecture, we encourage you to extract the core tenets you can apply to your unique use cases.

In particular, since Chapters 2–5 address well-established topics, you'll find more in-depth explanations and hands-on examples in these chapters. Chapters 8–10 get into data infrastructure that is still experiencing quite a bit of change, at least in terms of deployment on Kubernetes. In these cases, we point more frequently to third-party learning resources so that you can be sure to have the most up-to-date experience. In the spirit of this book's inception, we encourage you to share new resources you find with others so we can move forward together.

Conventions Used in This Book

The following typographical conventions are used in this book:

Italic
: Indicates new terms, URLs, email addresses, filenames, and file extensions.

`Constant width`
: Used for program listings, as well as within paragraphs to refer to program elements such as variable or function names, databases, data types, environment variables, statements, and keywords.

`Constant width bold`
: Shows commands or other text that should be typed literally by the user.

`Constant width italic`
: Shows text that should be replaced with user-supplied values or by values determined by context.

This element signifies a tip or suggestion.

This element signifies a general note.

This element indicates a warning or caution.

Using Code Examples

Supplemental material (code examples, exercises, etc.) is available for download at *https://github.com/data-on-k8s-book/examples*.

If you have a technical question or a problem using the code examples, please send email to *bookquestions@oreilly.com*.

This book is here to help you get your job done. In general, if example code is offered with this book, you may use it in your programs and documentation. You do not need to contact us for permission unless you're reproducing a significant portion of the code. For example, writing a program that uses several chunks of code from this book does not require permission. Selling or distributing examples from O'Reilly books does require permission. Answering a question by citing this book and quoting example code does not require permission. Incorporating a significant amount of example code from this book into your product's documentation does require permission.

We appreciate, but generally do not require, attribution. An attribution usually includes the title, author, publisher, and ISBN. For example: "*Managing Cloud Native Data on Kubernetes* by Jeff Carpenter and Patrick McFadin (O'Reilly). Copyright 2023 Jeffrey Carpenter and Patrick McFadin, 978-1-098-11139-7."

If you feel your use of code examples falls outside fair use or the permission given above, feel free to contact us at *permissions@oreilly.com*.

O'Reilly Online Learning

For more than 40 years, *O'Reilly Media* has provided technology and business training, knowledge, and insight to help companies succeed.

Our unique network of experts and innovators share their knowledge and expertise through books, articles, and our online learning platform. O'Reilly's online learning platform gives you on-demand access to live training courses, in-depth learning paths, interactive coding environments, and a vast collection of text and video from O'Reilly and 200+ other publishers. For more information, visit *https://oreilly.com*.

How to Contact Us

Please address comments and questions concerning this book to the publisher:

O'Reilly Media, Inc.
1005 Gravenstein Highway North
Sebastopol, CA 95472
800-998-9938 (in the United States or Canada)
707-829-0515 (international or local)
707-829-0104 (fax)

We have a web page for this book, where we list errata, examples, and any additional information. You can access this page at *https://oreil.ly/cloud-native-data-Kubernetes*.

Email *bookquestions@oreilly.com* to comment or ask technical questions about this book.

For news and information about our books and courses, visit *https://oreilly.com*.

Find us on LinkedIn: *https://linkedin.com/company/oreilly-media*.

Follow us on Twitter: *https://twitter.com/oreillymedia*.

Watch us on YouTube: *https://youtube.com/oreillymedia*.

Acknowledgments

Thanks go first of all to Jess Haberman, who believed in the concept of this book from our first conversation and fought to make it happen, and to our editor Jill Leonard for her continual encouragement and wise counsel.

One of the key features of this book is the inclusion of sidebars based on our conversations with expert technologists and practitioners. We've tried to let their words speak for themselves with as little editing as possible. With that, we offer up our heartfelt thanks to those who shared their time and insights with us: Rick Vasquez, Kiran Mova, Maciej Szulik, John Sanda, Deepthi Sigireddi, Umair Mufti, Irfan Ur Rehman, Dongxu (Ed) Huang, Jake Luciani, Jesse Anderson, Josh van Leeuwen, Holden Karau, Dean Wampler, Theofilos Papapanagiotou, Willem Pienaar, Xiaofan Luan, Josh Patterson, Adi Polak, and Craig McLuckie.

These experts have not only contributed their words, but also influenced the direction of our research and the choice of technologies we discuss here. Deepthi, Jesse, Umair, and Rick also did double duty as technical reviewers of the book. We also appreciate the insights of our other technical reviewers: Wei Deng, Ali Ok, Aaron Morton, and Noah Gift.

The Data on Kubernetes Community (DoKC) has been a huge inspiration for this effort, and we're especially grateful to Bart Farrell, Demitrios Brinkmann, and Melissa Logan for connecting us with many other community members and for their encouragement and support. We'd like to give special acknowledgment to Evan Powell, who birthed the DoKC by finding Demetrios and funding the initial meetups. That was the spark that has lit the forge for so many good things to come.

Sam Ramji was a major influence on this book, not only by writing the foreword but also in challenging our thought processes by reminding us: "You have to do the work to have an opinion." Sam was always willing to get on a call, make an introduction, or share ideas over a beer.

This book was born during the early days of a global pandemic and nurtured throughout seasons of uncertainty, challenge, and renewal, both on a global and personal level. We're so very grateful for the support of many friends and family who walked with us through these times and reminded us of the power of questions like "How's the book going?" or even just a simple "How are you doing?"

CHAPTER 1

Introduction to Cloud Native Data Infrastructure: Persistence, Streaming, and Batch Analytics

Do you work at solving data problems and find yourself faced with the need for modernization? Is your cloud native application limited to the use of microservices and service mesh? If you deploy applications on Kubernetes (sometimes abbreviated as "K8s") without including data, you haven't fully embraced cloud native. Every element of your application should embody the cloud native principles of scale, elasticity, self-healing, and observability, including how you handle data.

Engineers who work with data are primarily concerned with stateful services, and this will be our focus: increasing your skills to manage data in Kubernetes. By reading this book, our goal is to enrich your journey to cloud native data. If you are just starting with cloud native applications, there is no better time to include every aspect of the stack. This convergence is the future of how we will consume cloud resources.

So, what is this future we are creating together?

For too long, data has lived outside of Kubernetes, creating a lot of extra effort and complexity. We will get into valid reasons for this, but now is the time to combine the entire stack to build applications faster, at the needed scale. Based on current technology, this is very much possible. We've moved away from the past of deploying individual servers and toward the future where we will be able to deploy entire virtual datacenters. Development cycles that once took months and years can now be managed in days and weeks. Open source components can now be combined into a single deployment on Kubernetes that is portable from your laptop to the largest cloud provider.

The open source contribution isn't a tiny part of this, either. Kubernetes and the projects we discuss in this book are under the Apache License 2.0 unless otherwise noted, and for a good reason. If we build infrastructure that can run anywhere, we need a license model that gives us the freedom of choice. Open source is both free-as-in-beer and free-as-in-freedom, and both count when building cloud native applications on Kubernetes. Open source has been the fuel of many revolutions in infrastructure, and this is no exception.

That's what we are building: the near future reality of fully realized Kubernetes applications. The final component is the most important, and that is you. As a reader of this book, you are one of the people who will create this future. Creating is what we do as engineers. We continuously reinvent the way we deploy complicated infrastructure to respond to increased demand. When the first electronic database system was put online in 1960 for American Airlines, a small army of engineers made sure that it stayed online and worked around the clock. Progress took us from mainframes to minicomputers, to microcomputers, and eventually to the fleet management we do today. Now, that same progression is continuing into cloud native and Kubernetes.

This chapter will examine the components of cloud native applications, the challenges of running stateful workloads, and the essential areas covered in this book. To get started, let's turn to the building blocks that make up data infrastructure.

Infrastructure Types

In the past 20 years, the approach to infrastructure has slowly forked into two areas that reflect how we deploy distributed applications (as shown in Figure 1-1):

Stateless services
: These are services that maintain information only for the immediate lifecycle of the active request—for example, a service for sending formatted shopping cart information to a mobile client. A typical example is an application server that performs the business logic for the shopping cart. However, the information about the shopping cart contents resides external to these services. They need to be online for only a short duration from request to response. The infrastructure used to provide the service can easily grow and shrink with little impact on the overall application, scaling compute and network resources on demand when needed. Since we are not storing critical data in the individual service, that data can be created and destroyed quickly, with little coordination. Stateless services are a crucial architecture element in distributed systems.

Stateful services
: These services need to maintain information from one request to the next. Disks and memory store data for use across multiple requests. An example is a database or filesystem. Scaling stateful services is more complex since the information

typically requires replication for high availability. This creates the need for consistency and mechanisms to keep data in sync between replicas. These services usually have different scaling methods, both vertical and horizontal. As a result, they require different sets of operational tasks than stateless services.

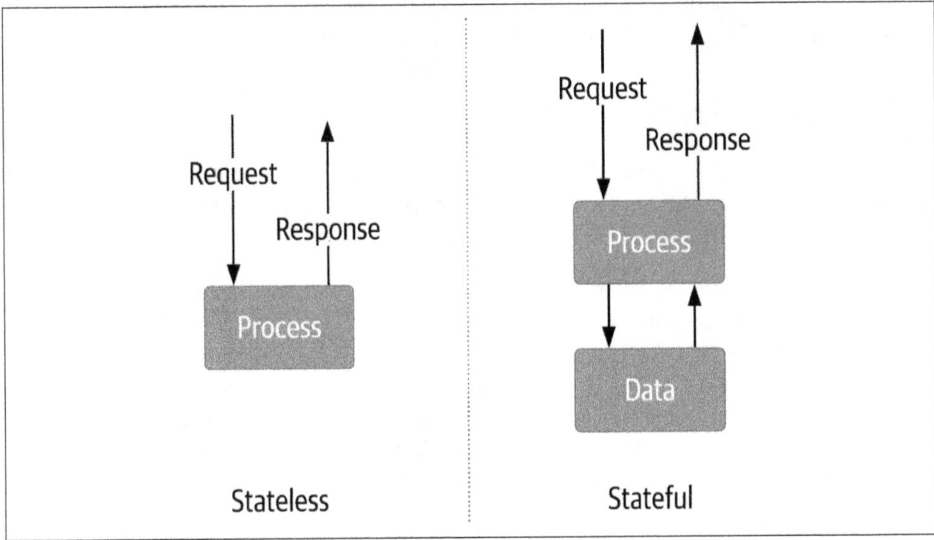

Figure 1-1. Stateless versus stateful services

In addition to the way information is stored, we've also seen a shift toward developing systems that embrace automated infrastructure deployment. These recent advances include the following:

- Physical servers have given way to virtual machines (VMs) that are easy to deploy and maintain.
- VMs have been simplified and focused on specific applications to containers.
- Containers have allowed infrastructure engineers to package an application's operating system requirements into a single executable.

The use of containers has undoubtedly increased the consistency of deployments, which has made it easier to deploy and run infrastructure in bulk. Few systems emerged to orchestrate the explosion of containers like Kubernetes, which is evident from its incredible growth. This speaks to how well it solves the problem. The official documentation (*https://oreil.ly/3WKn4*) describes Kubernetes as follows:

> Kubernetes is a portable, extensible, open source platform for managing containerized workloads and services that facilitates both declarative configuration and automation. It has a large, rapidly growing ecosystem. Kubernetes services, support, and tools are widely available.

Kubernetes was originally designed for stateless workloads, and that is what it has traditionally done best. Kubernetes has developed a reputation as a "platform for building platforms" in a cloud native way. However, there's a reasonable argument that a complete cloud native solution has to take data into account. That's the goal of this book: exploring how we make it possible to build cloud native data solutions on Kubernetes. But first, let's unpack what "cloud native" means.

What Is Cloud Native Data?

Let's begin defining the aspects of cloud native data that can help us with a final definition. First, let's start with the definition of cloud native from the Cloud Native Computing Foundation (CNCF) (*https://oreil.ly/OTdhS*):

> Cloud native technologies empower organizations to build and run scalable applications in modern, dynamic environments such as public, private, and hybrid clouds. Containers, service meshes, microservices, immutable infrastructure, and declarative APIs exemplify this approach.
>
> These techniques enable loosely coupled systems that are resilient, manageable, and observable. Combined with robust automation, they allow engineers to make high-impact changes frequently and predictably with minimal toil.

Note that this definition describes a goal state, desirable characteristics, and examples of technologies that embody both. Based on this formal definition, we can synthesize the qualities that differentiate a cloud native application from other types of deployments in terms of how it handles data. Let's take a closer look at these qualities:

Scalability
: If a service can produce a unit of work for a unit of resources, adding more resources should increase the amount of work a service can perform. *Scalability* describes the service's ability to apply additional resources to produce additional work. Ideally, services should scale infinitely given an infinite amount of compute, network, and storage resources. For data, this means scale without the need for downtime. Legacy systems required a maintenance period while adding new resources, during which all services had to be shut down. With the needs of cloud native applications, downtime is no longer acceptable.

Elasticity
: Whereas *scale* is adding resources to meet demand, elasticity is the ability to free those resources when they are no longer needed. The difference between scalability and elasticity is highlighted in Figure 1-2. Elasticity can also be called *on-demand infrastructure*. In a constrained environment such as a private datacenter, this is critical for sharing limited resources. For cloud infrastructure that charges for every resource used, this is a way to prevent paying for running services you don't need. When it comes to managing data, this means that we

need capabilities to reclaim storage space and optimize our usage—for example, moving older data to less expensive storage tiers.

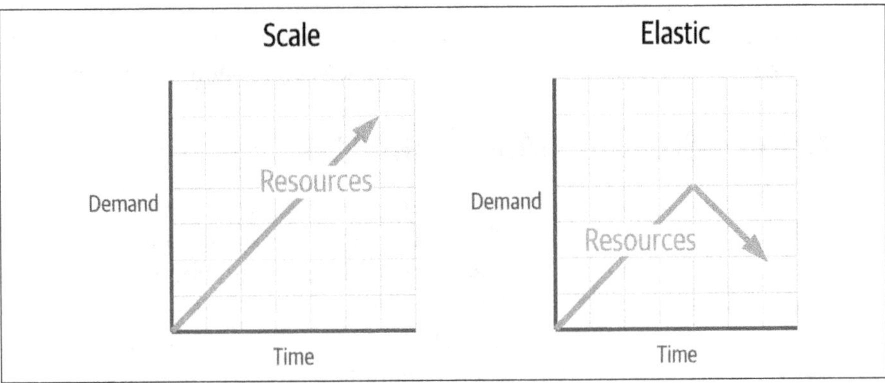

Figure 1-2. Comparing scalability and elasticity

Self-healing
: Bad things happen. When they do, how will your infrastructure respond? Self-healing infrastructure will reroute traffic, reallocate resources, and maintain service levels. With larger and more complex distributed applications being deployed, this is an increasingly important attribute of a cloud native application. This is what keeps you from getting that 3 A.M. wake-up call. For data, this means we need capabilities to detect issues with data such as missing data and data quality.

Observability
: If something fails and you aren't monitoring it, did it happen? Unfortunately, not only is the answer yes, but that can be an even worse scenario. Distributed applications are highly dynamic, and visibility into every service is critical for maintaining service levels. Interdependencies can create complex failure scenarios, which is why observability is a key part of building cloud native applications. In data systems, the volumes that are commonplace need efficient ways of monitoring the flow and state of infrastructure. In most cases, early warnings for issues can help operators avoid costly downtime.

With all the previous definitions in place, let's try a definition that expresses these properties:

> *Cloud native data* approaches empower organizations that have adopted the cloud native application methodology to incorporate data holistically rather than employ the legacy of people, process, technology, so that data can scale up and down elastically, and promote observability and self-healing. This is exemplified by containerized data, declarative data, data APIs, data meshes, and cloud native data infrastructure (that is, databases, streaming, and analytics technologies that are themselves architected as cloud native applications).

For data infrastructure to keep parity with the rest of our application, we need to incorporate each piece. This includes automation of scale, elasticity, and self-healing. APIs are needed to decouple services and increase developer velocity, as well as enable you to observe the entire stack of your application to make critical decisions. Taken as a whole, your application and data infrastructure should appear as one unit.

More Infrastructure, More Problems

Whether your infrastructure is in a cloud, on premises, or both (commonly referred to as *hybrid*), you could spend a lot of time doing manual configuration. Typing things into an editor and doing incredibly detailed configuration work requires deep knowledge of each technology. Over the past 20 years, significant advances have occurred in the DevOps community, both to code and the way we deploy our infrastructure. This is a critical step in the evolution of modern infrastructure. DevOps has kept us ahead of the scale required for applications, but just barely. Arguably, the same amount of knowledge is needed to fully script a single database server deployment. It's just that now we can do it a million times over (if needed) with templates and scripts. What has been lacking is a connectedness between the components and a holistic view of the entire application stack. Let's tackle this problem together. (Foreshadowing: this is a problem that needs to be solved.)

As with any good engineering problem, let's break it into manageable parts. The first is resource management. Regardless of the many ways we have developed to work at scale, fundamentally, we are trying to manage three things as efficiently as possible: compute, network, and storage, as shown in Figure 1-3. These are the critical resources that every application needs and the fuel that's burned during growth. Not surprisingly, these are also the resources that carry the monetary component to a running application. We get rewarded when we use the resources wisely and pay a literal high price if we don't. Anywhere you run your application, these are the most primitive units. When on prem, everything is bought and owned. When using the cloud, we're renting.

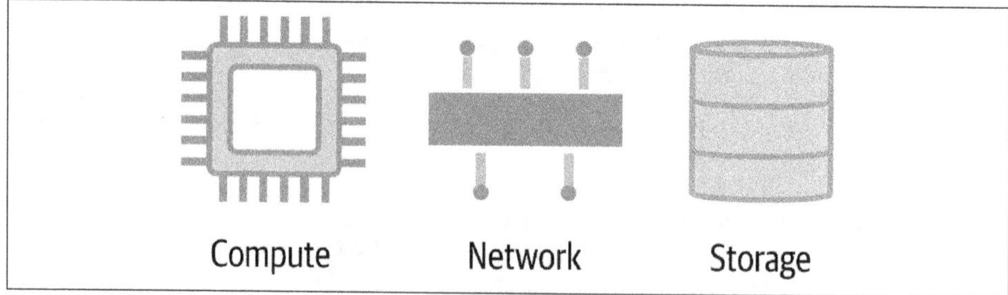

Figure 1-3. Fundamental resources of cloud applications: compute, network, and storage

The second part of the problem is having an entire stack act as a single entity. DevOps has provided many tools to manage individual components, but the connective tissue between them provides the potential for incredible efficiency—similarly to how applications are packaged for the desktop but working at datacenter scales. That potential has launched an entire community around cloud native applications. These applications are similar to what we've always deployed. The difference is that modern cloud applications aren't a single process with business logic. They are a complex coordination of many containerized processes that need to communicate securely and reliably. Storage has to match the current needs of the application, but remain aware of how it contributes to the stability of the application. When we think of deploying stateless applications without data managed in the same control plane, it sounds incomplete because it is. Breaking your application components into different control planes creates more complexity and thus goes against the ideals of cloud native.

Kubernetes Leading the Way

As mentioned before, DevOps automation has kept us on the leading edge of meeting scale needs. Containerization produced a need for much better orchestration, and Kubernetes has answered that need. For operators, describing a complete application stack in a deployment file makes a reproducible and portable infrastructure. This is because Kubernetes has gone far beyond the simple deployment management popular in the DevOps tool bag. The Kubernetes control plane applies the deployment requirement across the underlying compute, network, and storage to manage the entire application infrastructure lifecycle. The desired state of your application is maintained even when the underlying hardware changes. Instead of deploying VMs, we're now deploying virtual datacenters as a complete definition, as shown in Figure 1-4.

The rise in popularity of Kubernetes has eclipsed all other container orchestration tools used in DevOps. It has overtaken every other way we deploy infrastructure and shows no signs of slowing down. However, the bulk of early adoption was primarily in stateless services.

Managing data infrastructure at a large scale was a problem well before the move to containers and Kubernetes. Stateful services like databases took a different track parallel to the Kubernetes adoption curve. Many experts advised that Kubernetes was the wrong way to run stateful services and that those workloads should remain outside of Kubernetes. That approach worked until it didn't, and many of those same experts are now driving the needed changes in Kubernetes to converge the entire stack.

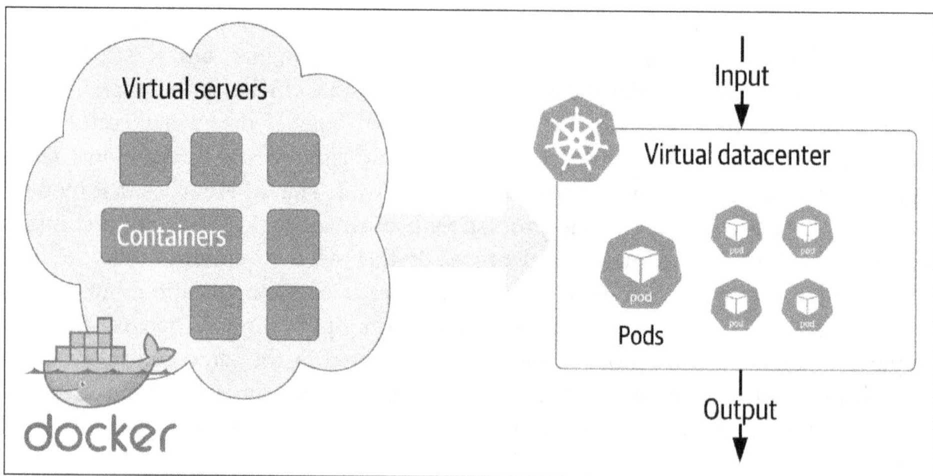

Figure 1-4. Moving from virtual servers to virtual datacenters

So, what are the challenges of stateful services? Why has it been hard to deploy data infrastructure with Kubernetes? Let's consider each component of our infrastructure.

Managing Compute on Kubernetes

In data infrastructure, counting on Moore's law has made upgrading a regular event. Moore's law predicted that computing capacity would double every 18 months. If your requirements double every 18 months, you can keep up by replacing hardware. Eventually, raw compute power started leveling out. Vendors started adding more processors and cores to keep up with Moore's law, leading to single-server resource sharing with VMs and containers, and enabling us to tap into the vast pools of computing power left stranded in islands of physical servers. Kubernetes expanded the scope of compute resource management by considering the total datacenter as one large resource pool across multiple physical devices.

Sharing compute resources with other services is somewhat taboo in the data world. Data workloads are typically resource intensive, and the potential of one service impacting another (known as the *noisy neighbor problem*) has led to policies of keeping them isolated from other workloads. This one-size-fits-all approach eliminates the possibility for more significant benefits. First is the assumption that all data service resource requirements are the same. Apache Pulsar brokers can have far fewer requirements than an Apache Spark worker, and neither are similar to a sizable MySQL instance used for online analytical processing (OLAP) reporting. Second, the ability to decouple your underlying hardware from running applications gives operators a lot of undervalued flexibility. Cloud native applications that need scale, elasticity, and self-healing need what Kubernetes can deliver. Data is no exception.

Managing Network on Kubernetes

Building a distributed application, by nature, requires a reliable and secure network. Cloud native applications increase the complexity of adding and subtracting services, making dynamic network configuration a new requirement. Kubernetes manages all of this inside your virtual datacenter automatically. When new services come online, it's like a virtual network team springs into action. IP addresses are assigned, routes are created, DNS entries are added, the virtual security team ensures that firewall rules are in place, and when asked, Transport Layer Securiity (TLS) certificates provide end-to-end encryption.

Data infrastructure tends to be far less dynamic than something like microservices. A fixed IP with a hostname has been the norm for databases. Analytic systems like Apache Flink are dynamic in processing but have fixed hardware addressing assignments. Quality of service is typically at the top of the requirements list and, as a result, the desire for dedicated hardware and dedicated networks has turned administrators off of Kubernetes.

The advantage of data infrastructure running in Kubernetes is less about the past requirements and more about what's needed for the future. Scaling resources dynamically can create a waterfall of dependencies. Automation is the only way to maintain clean and efficient networks, which are the lifeblood of distributed, stateless systems. The future of cloud native applications will include more components and new challenges, such as where applications will run. We can add regulatory compliance and data sovereignty to previous concerns about latency and throughput. The declarative nature of Kubernetes networks make it a perfect fit for data infrastructure.

Managing Storage on Kubernetes

Any service that provides persistence or analytics over large volumes of data will need the right kind of storage device. Early versions of Kubernetes considered storage a basic commodity part of the stack and assumed that most workloads were ephemeral. For data, this was a huge mismatch—you can't let your Postgres datafiles get deleted every time a container is moved. Additionally, at the outset, the underlying block storage ranged from high-performance NVMe disks to old 5400 RPM spinning disks, and you could not always be certain what type of hardware you'd get. Thankfully, this has been an essential focus of Kubernetes over the past few years and has significantly improved.

With the addition of features like StorageClasses, it is possible to address specific requirements for performance, capacity, or both. With automation, we can avoid the point when you don't have enough of either. Avoiding surprises is the domain of capacity management—both initializing the needed capacity and growing when required. When you run out of capacity in your storage, everything grinds to a halt.

Coupling the distributed nature of Kubernetes with data storage opens up more possibilities for self-healing. Automated backups and snapshots keep you ready for potential data loss scenarios. Placing compute and storage together minimizes hardware failure risks and allows automatic recovery to the desired state when the inevitable failure occurs. All of this makes the data storage aspects of Kubernetes much more attractive.

Cloud Native Data Components

Now that we have defined the resources consumed in cloud native applications, let's clarify the types of data infrastructure that powers them. Instead of a comprehensive list of every possible product, we'll break them into larger buckets with similar characteristics:

Persistence
: This is likely the category you think of first when we talk about data infrastructure. These systems store data and provide access by some method of a query: relational databases like MySQL and Postgres, and NoSQL systems like Apache Cassandra and MongoDB. These have been the last holdouts to migrate to Kubernetes because of their strict resource needs and high-availability requirements. Databases are usually critical to a running application and central to every other part of the system.

Streaming
: The most basic function of streaming is facilitating the high-speed movement of data from one point to another. Streaming systems provide a variety of delivery semantics based on a use case. In some cases, data can be delivered to many clients, or when strict controls are needed, delivered only once. A further enhancement of streaming is the addition of *processing*: altering or enhancing data mid-transport. The need for faster insights into data has propelled streaming analytics into mission-critical status, catching up with persistence systems in terms of importance. Examples of streaming systems that move data are Apache Flink and Apache Kafka, whereas processing system examples are Apache Flink and Apache Storm.

Batch analytics
: One of the first problems in big data is analyzing large sets of data to gain insights or repurpose into new data. Apache Hadoop was the first large-scale system for batch analytics that set the expectations around using large volumes of compute and storage, coordinated in a way to produce the results of complex analytic processes. Typically, these are issued as jobs distributed throughout the cluster, as is common with Spark. The concern with costs can be much more prevalent in these systems because of the sheer volume of resources needed. Orchestration systems help mitigate the costs by intelligent allocation.

Looking Forward

There is a compelling future with cloud native data. The path we take between what we have available today and what we can have in the future is up to us: the community of people responsible for data infrastructure. Just as we have always done, we see a new challenge and take it on. There is plenty for everyone to do here, but the result could be pretty amazing and raise the bar yet again.

A Call for Databases to Modernize on Kubernetes

With Rick Vasquez, Senior Director, Strategic Initiatives, Western Digital

This is something for anyone working with databases in the 2020s. Kubernetes is leading the charge in building cloud native and distributed systems. Data systems aren't leveraging the full capacity and feature set possible if they were better integrated with Kubernetes. I'm a convert from the "you should never run a database in a container" way of thinking. Now, I think we should be pushing everybody to have the main deployment in Kubernetes. My background has always been on scale enterprise use cases. I don't see this as a passing fad. I'm looking at the applicability to global scale for some of the largest companies in the world.

One line of thinking we need to overcome is treating Kubernetes like an operating system that enables other applications to run on it. That's the wrong way to look at running data workloads. If your system runs in a container, then of course it will work on Kubernetes, right? No! It will react to how the control plane deploys and runs your application, and the result may or may not be what you want. What if data systems were more tightly integrated with Kubernetes and could offload functions to be handled by the Kubernetes control plane? Service discovery, load balancing, storage orchestration, automated rollouts and rollbacks, automated bin packing, self-healing, and secret and config management are all powerful things that allow you to have a consistent developer and SRE experience. The name of the game with Kubernetes is driving consistency. You can use Kubernetes to become globally consistent across all your deployments and do them the same way over and over. But that needs to include database systems. Imagine if you have Postgres, MongoDB, MySQL, or Cassandra, and it was built natively on Kubernetes. What would you do?

Having the access to use different storage tiers, either local or remote disk—all of it is declarative in some configuration objects. I want to configure that in and with the database. If I'm using MySQL, I want logs to be on the local disk, because I don't want any bottlenecks. I want certain tables to be on a slower disk that may be over the network. And I want the last seven days of data to be in hot, local NVMe disks, using every single bit of capacity that you have with replicas actually doing things—like offloading reads or multiple write nodes—and one big aggregate for analytics. All of those things should be possible with a Kubernetes-based deployment with a cloud native database.

Databases don't reason about or have a opinions about how big they are. If you make a database bigger, it just needs more resources. You can set up auto-scaling to get bigger, or horizontal scaling. What happens when you want to use the true elasticity that's given to you by Kubernetes? It's not just the scale up and out. It's the scale back and down! Why don't databases just do that? It's so important to maximize the value that you're getting out of a Kubernetes-based deployment or, more broadly, a cloud native–based deployment. We have a lot of work to do, but the future is worth it.

Rick's point is specifically about databases, but we can extrapolate his call to action for our data infrastructure running on Kubernetes. Unlike deploying a data application on physical servers, introducing the Kubernetes control plane requires a conversation with the services it runs.

Getting Ready for the Revolution

As engineers who create and run data infrastructure, we have to be ready for coming advancements, both in the way we operate and the mindset we have about the role of data infrastructure. The following sections describe what you can do to be ready for the future of cloud native data running in Kubernetes.

Adopt an SRE Mindset

The role of site reliability engineering (SRE) has grown with the adoption of cloud native methodologies. If we intend our infrastructure to converge, we as data infrastructure engineers must learn new skills and adopt new practices. Let's begin with the Wikipedia definition of SRE (*https://oreil.ly/lq1rc*):

> Site reliability engineering is a set of principles and practices that incorporates aspects of software engineering and applies them to infrastructure and operations problems. The main goals are to create scalable and highly reliable software systems. Site reliability engineering is closely related to DevOps, a set of practices that combine software development and IT operations, and SRE has also been described as a specific implementation of DevOps.

Deploying data infrastructure has been primarily concerned with the specific components deployed—the "what." For example, you may find yourself focused on deploying MySQL at scale or using Spark to analyze large volumes of data. Adopting an SRE mindset means going beyond *what* you are deploying and focusing more on the *how*. How will all the pieces work together to meet the application's goals? A holistic deployment view considers the way each piece will interact, the required access, including security, and the observability of every aspect to ensure that service levels are met.

If your current primary or secondary role is database administrator (DBA), there is no better time to make the transition. The trend on LinkedIn shows a year-over-year decrease in the DBA role (*https://oreil.ly/4VFc7*) and a massive increase for SREs. Engineers who have learned the skills required to run critical database infrastructure have an essential baseline that translates into what's needed to manage cloud native data. These needs include the following:

- Availability
- Latency
- Change management
- Emergency response
- Capacity management

New skills need to be added to this list to become better adapted to the more significant responsibility of the entire application. These are skills you may already have, but they include the following:

CI/CD pipelines
: Embrace the big picture of taking code from repository to production. There's nothing that accelerates application development more in an organization. Continuous integration (CI) builds new code into the application stack and automates all testing to ensure quality. Continuous delivery (CD) takes the fully tested and certified builds and automatically deploys them into production. Used in combination (pipeline), organizations can drastically increase developer velocity and productivity.

Observability
: DevOps practitioners like to make a distinction between the "what" (the actual service you're deploying) and the "how" (the methodology of deploying that service). Monitoring is something everyone with experience in infrastructure is familiar with. In the "what" part of DevOps, the properties you monitor let you know your services are healthy, and give you the information needed to diagnose problems. Observability expands monitoring into the "how" of your application by considering everything as a whole—for example, tracing the source of latency in a highly distributed application by giving insight into every hop that data takes as it traverses your system.

Knowing the code
: When things go bad in a large, distributed application, the cause is not always a process failure. In many cases, the problem could be a bug in the code or a subtle implementation detail. Being responsible for the entire health of the application, you will need to understand the code that is executing in the provided environment. Properly implemented observability will help you find problems,

and that includes the software instrumentation. SREs and development teams need to have clear and regular communication, and code is common ground.

Embrace Distributed Computing

Deploying your applications in Kubernetes means embracing all that distributed computing offers. When you are accustomed to single-system thinking, that transition can be hard, mainly in the shift in thinking around expectations and understanding where problems crop up. For example, with every process contained in a single system, latency will be close to zero. It's not what you have to manage. CPU and memory resources are the primary concern there. In the 1990s, Sun Microsystems was leading in the growing field of distributed computing and published this list of eight common fallacies of distributed computing (*https://oreil.ly/XAR93*):

- The network is reliable.
- Latency is zero.
- Bandwidth is infinite.
- The network is secure.
- Topology doesn't change.
- There is one administrator.
- Transport cost is zero.
- The network is homogeneous.

Behind each of these fallacies is surely the story of a developer who made a bad assumption, got an unexpected result, and lost countless hours trying to solve the wrong problem. Embracing distributed methodologies is worth the effort in the long run. They allow us to build large-scale applications and will continue to do so for a long time. The challenge is worth the reward, and for those of us who do this daily, it can be a lot of fun too! Kubernetes applications will test each of these fallacies, given its default distributed nature. When you plan your deployment, consider things such as the cost of transport from one place to another or latency implications. They will save you a lot of wasted time and redesign.

Principles of Cloud Native Data Infrastructure

As engineering professionals, we seek standards and best practices to build upon. To make data the most "cloud native" it can be, we need to embrace everything Kubernetes offers. A truly cloud native approach means adopting key elements of the Kubernetes design paradigm and building from there. An entire cloud native application that includes data must be one that can run effectively on Kubernetes. Let's explore a few Kubernetes design principles that point the way.

Principle 1: Leverage compute, network, and storage as commodity APIs

One of the keys to the success of cloud computing is the commoditization of compute, networking, and storage as resources we can provision via simple APIs. Consider this sampling of AWS services:

Compute
: We allocate VMs through Amazon Elastic Compute Cloud (EC2) and Auto Scaling groups (ASGs).

Network
: We manage traffic using Elastic Load Balancers (ELB), Route 53, and virtual private cloud (VPC) peering.

Storage
: We persist data using options such as the Simple Storage Service (S3) for long-term object storage, or Elastic Block Store (EBS) volumes for our compute instances.

Kubernetes offers its own APIs to provide similar services for a world of containerized applications:

Compute
: Pods, Deployments, and ReplicaSets manage the scheduling and lifecycle of containers on computing hardware.

Network
: Services and Ingress expose a container's networked interfaces.

Storage
: PersistentVolumes (PVs) and StatefulSets enable flexible association of containers to storage.

Kubernetes resources promote the portability of applications across Kubernetes distributions and service providers. What does this mean for databases? They are simply applications that leverage compute, networking, and storage resources to provide the services of data persistence and retrieval:

Compute
: A database needs sufficient processing power to process incoming data and queries. Each database node is deployed as a Pod and grouped into StatefulSets, enabling Kubernetes to manage scaling out and scaling in.

Network
: A database needs to expose interfaces for data and control. We can use Kubernetes Services and Ingress controllers to expose these interfaces.

Storage
: A database uses PersistentVolumes of a specified StorageClass to store and retrieve data.

Thinking of databases in terms of their compute, network, and storage needs removes much of the complexity involved in deployment on Kubernetes.

Principle 2: Separate the control and data planes

Kubernetes promotes the separation of control and data planes. The Kubernetes API server is the front door of the control plane, providing the interface used by the data plane to request computing resources, while the control plane manages the details of mapping those requests onto an underlying infrastructure-as-a-service (IaaS) platform.

We can apply this same pattern to databases. For example, a database data plane consists of ports exposed for clients, and for distributed databases, ports used for communication between database nodes. The control plane includes interfaces provided by the database for administration and metrics collection and tooling that performs operational maintenance tasks. Much of this capability can and should be implemented via the Kubernetes operator pattern. Operators define custom resources (CRDs) and provide control loops that observe the state of those resources, taking actions to move them toward the desired state, helping extend Kubernetes with domain-specific logic.

Principle 3: Make observability easy

The three pillars of observable systems are logging, metrics, and tracing. Kubernetes provides a great starting point by exposing the logs of each container to third-party log aggregation solutions. Multiple solutions are available for metrics, tracing, and visualization, and we'll explore several of them in this book.

Principle 4: Make the default configuration secure

Kubernetes networking is secure by default: ports must be explicitly exposed in order to be accessed externally to a pod. This sets a valuable precedent for database deployment, forcing us to think carefully about how each control plane and data plane interface will be exposed and which interfaces should be exposed via a Kubernetes Service. Kubernetes also provides facilities for secret management that can be used for sharing encryption keys and configuring administrative accounts.

Principle 5: Prefer declarative configuration

In the Kubernetes declarative approach, you specify the desired state of resources, and controllers manipulate the underlying infrastructure in order to achieve that state. Operators for data infrastructure can manage the details of how to scale up intelligently—for example, deciding how to reallocate shards or partitions when scaling out additional nodes or selecting which nodes to remove to scale down elastically.

The next generation of operators should enable us to specify rules for stored data size, number of transactions per second, or both. Perhaps we'll be able to specify maximum and minimum cluster sizes, and when to move less frequently used data to object storage. This will allow for more automation and efficiency in our data infrastructure.

Summary

At this point, we hope you are ready for the exciting journey in the pages ahead. The move to cloud native applications must include data, and to do this, we will leverage Kuberentes to include stateless *and* stateful services. This chapter covered cloud native data infrastructure that can scale elastically and resist any downtime due to system failures, and how to build these systems. We as engineers must embrace the principles of cloud native infrastructure and, in some cases, learn new skills. Congratulations—you have begun a fantastic journey into the future of building cloud native applications. Turn the page, and let's go!

CHAPTER 2

Managing Data Storage on Kubernetes

There is no such thing as a stateless architecture. All applications store state somewhere.
—Alex Chircop, CEO, StorageOS

In the previous chapter, we painted a picture of a possible near future with powerful, stateful, data-intensive applications running on Kubernetes. To get there, we're going to need data infrastructure for persistence, streaming, and analytics. To build out this infrastructure, we'll need to leverage the primitives that Kubernetes provides to help manage the three commodities of cloud computing: compute, network, and storage. In the next several chapters, we'll begin to look at these primitives, starting with storage, in order to see how they can be combined to create the data infrastructure we need.

To echo the point raised by Alex Chircop, all applications must store their state somewhere, which is why we'll focus in this chapter on the basic abstractions Kubernetes provides for interacting with storage. We'll also look at the emerging innovations being offered by storage vendors and open source projects creating storage infrastructure for Kubernetes that itself embodies cloud native principles.

Let's start our exploration with a look at managing persistence in containerized applications in general and use that as a jumping-off point for our investigation into data storage on Kubernetes.

Docker, Containers, and State

The problem of managing state in distributed, cloud native applications is not unique to Kubernetes. A quick search will show that stateful workloads have been an area of concern on other container orchestration platforms such as Mesos and Docker Swarm. Part of this has to do with the nature of container orchestration, and part is driven by the nature of containers themselves.

First, let's consider containers. One of the key value propositions of containers is their ephemeral nature. Containers are designed to be disposable and replaceable, so they need to start quickly and use as few resources for overhead processing as possible. For this reason, most container images are built from base images containing streamlined, Linux-based, open source operating systems such as Ubuntu, that boot quickly and incorporate only essential libraries for the contained application or microservice. As the name implies, containers are designed to be self-contained, incorporating all their dependencies in immutable images, while their configuration and data are externalized. These properties make containers portable so that we can run them anywhere a compatible container runtime is available.

As shown in Figure 2-1, containers require less overhead than traditional VMs, which run a guest operating system per VM, with a hypervisor layer (*https://oreil.ly/5gE1u*) to implement system calls onto the underlying host operating system.

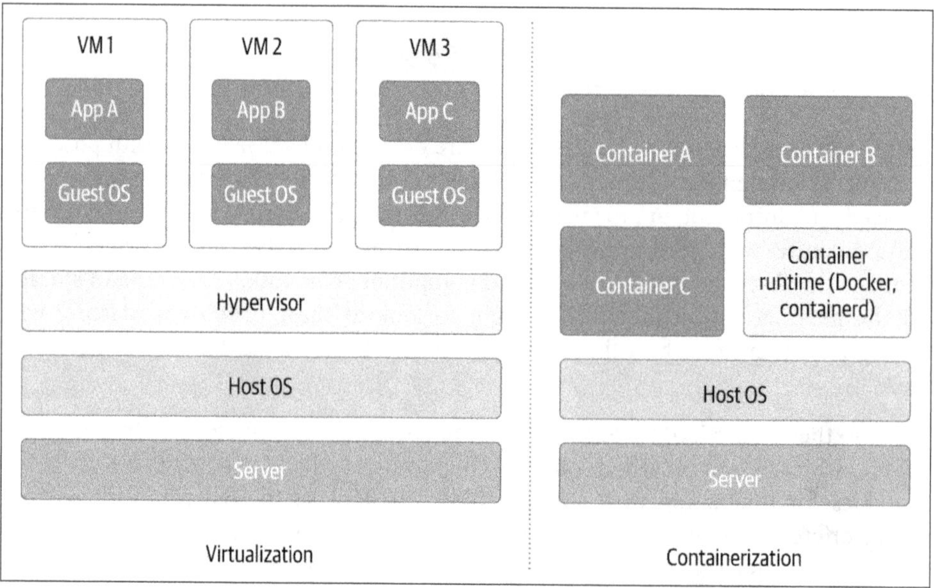

Figure 2-1. Comparing containerization to virtualization

Although containers have made applications more portable, it's proven a bigger challenge to make their data portable. Since a container itself is ephemeral, any data that is to survive beyond the life of the container must by definition reside externally. The key feature for a container technology is to provide mechanisms to link to persistent storage, and the key feature for a container orchestration technology is the ability to schedule containers in such a way that they can access persistent storage efficiently.

Managing State in Docker

Let's take a look at the most popular container technology, Docker, to see how containers can store data. The key storage concept in Docker is the volume. From the perspective of a Docker container, a *volume* is a directory that can support read-only or read/write access. Docker supports the mounting of multiple data stores as volumes. We'll introduce several options so we can later note their equivalents in Kubernetes.

Bind Mounts

The simplest approach for creating a volume is to bind a directory in the container to a directory on the host system. This is called a *bind mount*, as shown in Figure 2-2.

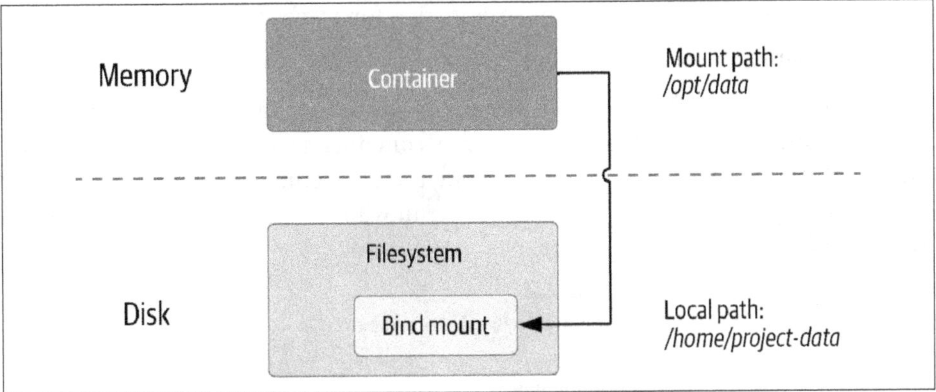

Figure 2-2. Using Docker bind mounts to access the host filesystem

When starting a container within Docker, you specify a bind mount with the `--volume` or `-v` option and the local filesystem path and container path to use. For example, you could start an instance of the Nginx web server and map a local project folder from your development machine into the container. This is a command you can test out in your own environment if you have Docker installed:

```
docker run -it --rm -d --name web -p 8080:80 \
  -v ~/site-content:/usr/share/nginx/html nginx
```

This exposes the web server on port 8080 on your local host. If the local path directory does not already exist, the Docker runtime will create it. Docker allows you to create bind mounts with read-only or read/write permissions. Because the volume is represented as a directory, the application running in the container can put anything that can be represented as a file into the volume—even a database.

Bind mounts are quite useful for development work. However, using bind mounts is not suitable for a production environment since this leads to a container being dependent on a file being present in a specific host. This might be fine for a single-machine deployment, but production deployments tend to be spread across multiple hosts. Another concern is the potential security hole that is presented by opening up access from the container to the host filesystem. For these reasons, we need another approach for production deployments.

Volumes

The preferred option within Docker is to use volumes. Docker volumes are created and managed by Docker under a specific directory on the host filesystem. The Docker `volume create` command is used to create a volume. For example, you might create a volume called `site-content` to store files for a website:

```
docker volume create site-content
```

If no name is specified, Docker assigns a random name. After creation, the resulting volume is available to mount in a container using the form `-v VOLUME-NAME:CONTAINER-PATH`. For example, you might use a volume like the one just created to allow an Nginx container to read the content, while allowing another container to edit the content, using the `ro` option:

```
docker run -it --rm -d --name web \
  -v site-content:/usr/share/nginx/html:ro nginx
```

Docker Volume Mount Syntax

Docker also supports a `--mount` syntax that allows you to specify the source and target folders more explicitly. This notation is considered more modern, but it is also more verbose. The syntax shown in the preceding example is still valid and is the more commonly used syntax.

As we've implied, a Docker volume can be mounted in more than one container at once, as shown in Figure 2-3.

The advantage of using Docker volumes is that Docker manages the filesystem access for containers, which makes it much simpler to enforce capacity and security restrictions on containers.

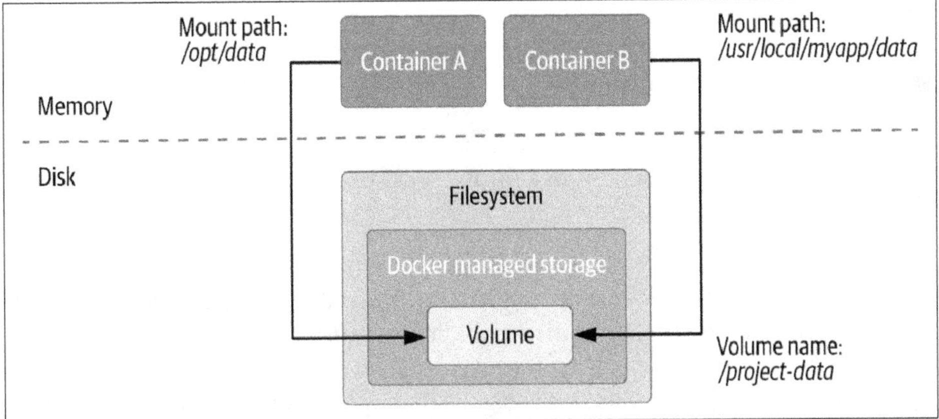

Figure 2-3. Creating Docker volumes to share data between containers on the host

Tmpfs Mounts

Docker supports two types of mounts that are specific to the operating system used by the host system: *tmpfs* (or *temporary filesystem*) and *named pipes*. Named pipes are available on Docker for Windows, but since they are typically not used in Kubernetes, we won't give much consideration to them here.

Tmpfs mounts are available when running Docker on Linux. A tmpfs mount exists only in memory for the lifespan of the container, so the contents are never present on disk, as shown in Figure 2-4. Tmpfs mounts are useful for applications that are written to persist a relatively small amount of data, especially sensitive data that you don't want written to the host filesystem. Because the data is stored in memory, faster access is a side benefit.

Figure 2-4. Creating a temporary volume using Docker tmpfs

To create a tmpfs mount, use the `docker run --tmpfs` option. For example, you could use a command like this to specify a tmpfs volume to store Nginx logs for a web server processing sensitive data:

```
docker run -it --rm -d --name web --tmpfs /var/log/nginx nginx
```

The `--mount` option may also be used for more control over configurable options.

Volume Drivers

Docker Engine has an extensible architecture that allows you to add customized behavior via plug-ins for capabilities including networking, storage, and authorization. Third-party storage plug-ins (*https://oreil.ly/b9P9X*) are available for multiple open source and commercial providers, including the public clouds and various networked filesystems. Taking advantage of these involves installing the plug-in with Docker Engine and then specifying the associated volume driver when starting Docker containers using that storage, as shown in Figure 2-5.

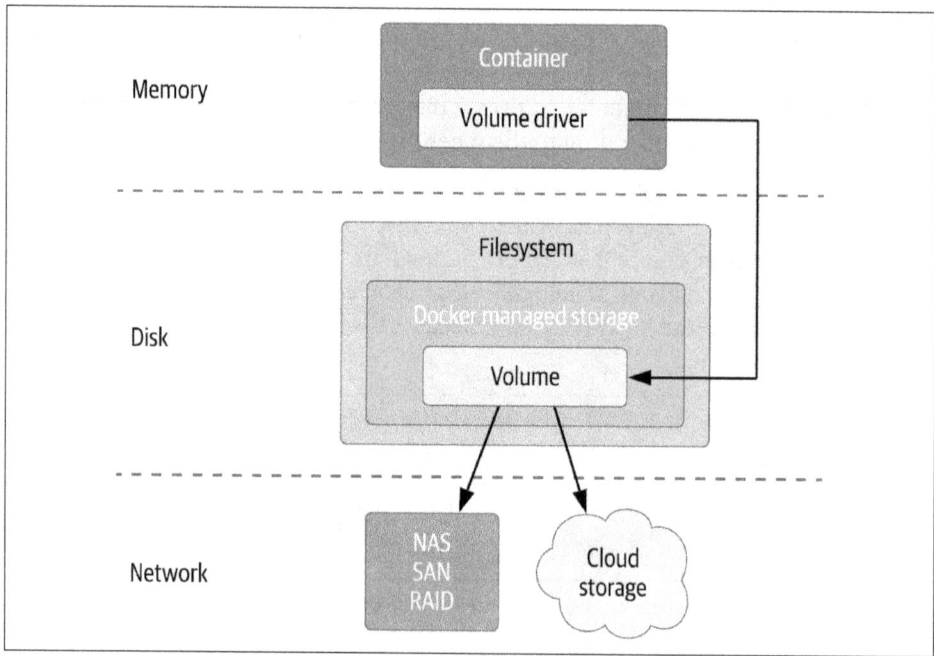

Figure 2-5. Using Docker volume drivers to access networked storage

For more information on working with the various types of volumes supported in Docker, see the Docker storage documentation (*https://oreil.ly/vVPb4*), as well as the documentation for the `docker run` command (*https://oreil.ly/Tj3NT*).

File, Block, and Object Storage

In our modern era of cloud architectures, the three main formats in which storage is traditionally provided to applications are files, blocks, and objects. Each stores and provides access to data in different ways:

File storage
: Represents data as a hierarchy of folders, each of which can contain files. The file is the basic unit of access for both storage and retrieval. The root directory that is to be accessed by a container is mounted into the container filesystem such that it looks like any other directory. Each of the public clouds provides its own file storage (for example, Google Cloud Filestore or Amazon Elastic Filestore). Gluster (*https://www.gluster.org*) is an open source distributed filesystem. Many of these systems are compatible with the Network File System (*https://oreil.ly/yrSWs*) (NFS), a distributed filesystem protocol invented at Sun Microsystems in 1984 that is still in common use.

Block storage
: Organizes data in chunks and allocates those chunks across a set of managed volumes. When you provide data to a block storage system, it divides the data into chunks of varying sizes and distributes those chunks in order to use the underlying volumes most efficiently. When you query a block storage system, it retrieves the chunks from their various locations and provides the data back to you. This flexibility makes block storage a great solution when you have a heterogeneous set of storage devices available. Block storage doesn't provide a lot of metadata handling, which can place more burden on the application.

Object storage
: Organizes data in units known as *objects*. Each object is referenced by a unique identifier, or *key*, and can support rich metadata tagging that enables searching. Objects are organized in buckets. This flat, nonhierarchical organization makes object storage easy to scale. S3 is the canonical example of object storage, and most object storage products will claim compatibility with the S3 API.

If you're tasked with building or selecting data infrastructure, you need to understand the strengths and weaknesses of these patterns. Throughout the rest of the book, you'll learn how each storage type is used by various data infrastructure projects. There are trade-offs to consider when choosing a storage format and whether to use a centralized or distributed storage architecture. For example, in Chapter 7, we'll look at a refactored version of Cassandra that uses object storage for long-term persistence instead of file storage on local disks.

Kubernetes Resources for Data Storage

Now that you understand basic concepts of container and cloud storage, let's see what Kubernetes brings to the table. In this section, we'll introduce some of the key Kubernetes concepts, or *resources* in the API for attaching storage to containerized applications. Even if you are already somewhat familiar with these resources, you'll want to stay tuned, as we'll focus particularly on how each one relates to stateful data.

Pods and Volumes

One of the first Kubernetes resources new users encounter is the *Pod*. This is the basic unit of deployment of a Kubernetes workload. A Pod provides an environment for running containers, and the Kubernetes control plane is responsible for deploying Pods to Kubernetes Worker Nodes.

The *Kubelet* is a component of the Kubernetes control plane (*https://oreil.ly/1ITFv*) that runs on each Worker Node. It is responsible for running Pods on a node, as well as monitoring the health of these Pods and the containers inside them. These elements are summarized in Figure 2-6.

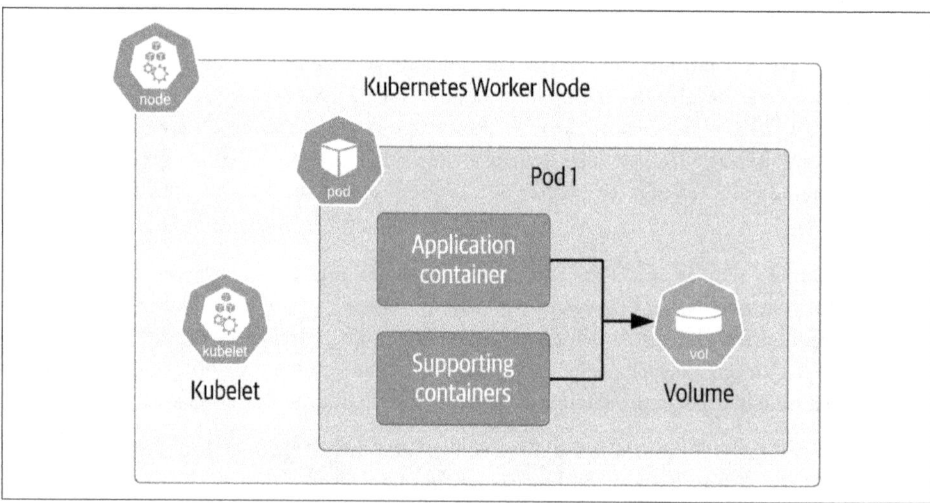

Figure 2-6. Using volumes in Kubernetes Pods

While a Pod can contain multiple containers, the best practice is for a Pod to contain a single application container, along with optional additional helper containers, as shown in Figure 2-6. These helper containers might include *init containers* that run prior to the main application container in order to perform configuration tasks, or *sidecar containers* that run alongside the main application container to provide helper services such as observability or management. In later chapters, you'll see how data infrastructure deployments can take advantage of these architectural patterns.

Now let's see how persistence is supported within this Pod architecture. As with Docker, the "on disk" data in a container is lost when a container crashes. The Kubelet is responsible for restarting the container, but this new container is a *replacement* for the original container—it will have a distinct identity and start with a completely new state.

In Kubernetes, the term *volume* is used to represent access to storage within a Pod. By using a volume, the container has the ability to persist data that will outlive the container (and potentially the Pod as well, as we'll see shortly). A volume may be accessed by multiple containers in a Pod. Each container has its own *volumeMount* within the Pod that specifies the directory to which it should be mounted, allowing the mount point to differ among containers.

In multiple cases, you might want to share data between containers in a Pod:

- An init container creates a custom configuration file for the particular environment that the application container mounts to obtain configuration values.
- The application Pod writes logs, and a sidecar Pod reads those logs to identify alert conditions that are reported to an external monitoring tool.

However, you'll likely want to avoid situations in which multiple containers are writing to the same volume, because you'll have to ensure that the multiple writers don't conflict—Kubernetes does not do that for you.

Preparing to Run Sample Code

The examples in this book assume you have access to a running Kubernetes cluster. For the examples in this chapter, a development cluster on your local machine such as kind, K3s, or Docker Desktop should be sufficient. The source code used in this section is located at the book's repository (*https://oreil.ly/VjIq1*).

Using a volume in a Pod requires two steps: defining the volume and mounting the volume in each container that needs access. Let's look at a sample YAML configuration that defines a Pod with a single application container, the Nginx web server, and a single volume. The source code (*https://oreil.ly/nlBJA*) is in this book's repository:

```
apiVersion: v1
kind: Pod
metadata:
  name: my-pod
spec:
  containers:
  - name: my-app
    image: nginx
    volumeMounts:
```

```
    - name: web-data
      mountPath: /app/config
  volumes:
  - name: web-data
```

Notice the two parts of the configuration: the volume is defined under `spec.volumes`, and the usage of the volumes is defined under `spec.containers.volumeMounts`. First, the `name` of the volume is referenced under `volumeMounts`, and the directory where it is to be mounted is specified by `mountPath`. When declaring a Pod specification, volumes and volume mounts go together. For your configuration to be valid, a volume must be declared before being referenced, and a volume must be used by at least one container in the Pod.

You may have also noticed that the volume has only a `name`. You haven't specified any additional information. What do you think this will do? You could try this out for yourself by using the example source code file *nginx-pod.yaml* or cutting and pasting the preceding configuration to a file with that name, and executing the `kubectl` command against a configured Kubernetes cluster:

```
kubectl apply -f nginx-pod.yaml
```

You can get more information about the Pod that was created by using the `kubectl get pod` command, for example:

```
kubectl get pod my-pod -o yaml | grep -A 5 "  volumes:"
```

And the results might look something like this:

```
  volumes:
  - emptyDir: {}
    name: web-data
  - name: default-token-2fp89
    secret:
      defaultMode: 420
```

As you can see, Kubernetes supplied additional information when creating the requested volume, defaulting it to a type of `emptyDir`. Other default attributes may differ depending on what Kubernetes engine you are using, but we won't discuss them further here.

Several types of volumes can be mounted in a container; let's have a look.

Ephemeral volumes

You'll remember tmpfs volumes from our previous discussion of Docker volumes, which provide temporary storage for the lifespan of a single container. Kubernetes provides the concept of an *ephemeral volume* (*https://oreil.ly/zaiKG*), which is similar, but at the scope of a Pod. The `emptyDir` introduced in the preceding example is a type of ephemeral volume.

Ephemeral volumes can be useful for data infrastructure or other applications that want to create a cache for fast access. Although they do not persist beyond the lifespan of a Pod, they can still exhibit some of the typical properties of other volumes for longer-term persistence, such as the ability to snapshot. Ephemeral volumes are slightly easier to set up than PersistentVolumes because they are declared entirely inline in the Pod definition without reference to other Kubernetes resources. As you will see next, creating and using PersistentVolumes is a bit more involved.

Other Ephemeral Storage Providers

Some of the in-tree and CSI storage drivers we'll discuss next that provide PersistentVolumes also provide an ephemeral volume option. You'll want to check the documentation of the specific provider to see what options are available.

Configuration volumes

Kubernetes provides several constructs for injecting configuration data into a Pod as a volume. These volume types are also considered ephemeral in the sense that they do not provide a mechanism for allowing applications to persist their own data.

The following volume types are relevant to our exploration in this book since they provide a useful means of configuring applications and data infrastructure running on Kubernetes. We'll describe each of them briefly:

ConfigMap volumes
: A ConfigMap is a Kubernetes resource that is used to store configuration values external to an application as a set of name-value pairs. For example, an application might require connection details for an underlying database such as an IP address and port number. Defining these in a ConfigMap is a good way to externalize this information from the application. The resulting configuration data can be mounted into the application as a volume, where it will appear as a directory. Each configuration value is represented as a file wherein the filename is the key and the contents of the file contain the value. See the Kubernetes documentation for more information on mounting ConfigMaps as volumes (*https://oreil.ly/zaiKG*).

Secret volumes
: A Secret is similar to a ConfigMap, only it is intended for securing access to sensitive data that requires protection. For example, you might want to create a Secret containing database access credentials such as a username and password. Configuring and accessing Secrets is similar to using ConfigMap, with the additional benefit that Kubernetes helps decrypt the Secret upon access within the Pod. See the Kubernetes documentation for more information on mounting Secrets as volumes (*https://oreil.ly/mPkMB*).

Downward API volumes

The Kubernetes downward API exposes metadata about Pods and containers either as environment variables or as volumes. This is the same metadata that is used by `kubectl` and other clients.

The available Pod metadata includes the Pod's name, ID, Namespace, labels, and annotations. The containerized application might aim to use the Pod information for logging and metrics reporting, or to determine database or table names.

The available container metadata includes the requested and maximum amounts of resources such as CPU, memory, and ephemeral storage. The containerized application might seek to use this information in order to throttle its own resource usage. See the Kubernetes documentation for an example of injecting Pod information as a volume (*https://oreil.ly/LrOn2*).

hostPath volumes

A `hostPath` (*https://oreil.ly/kjr8P*) volume mounts a file or directory into a Pod from the Kubernetes Worker Node where it is running. This is analogous to the bind mount concept in Docker, discussed in "Bind Mounts" on page 21. Using a `hostPath` volume has one advantage over an `emptyDir` volume: the data will survive the restart of a Pod.

However, using `hostPath` volumes has some disadvantages. First, in order for a replacement Pod to access the data of the original Pod, it will need to be restarted on the same Worker Node. While Kubernetes does give you the ability to control which node a Pod is placed on using affinity, this tends to constrain the Kubernetes scheduler from optimal placement of Pods, and if the node goes down for some reason, the data in the `hostPath` volume is lost. Second, as with Docker bind mounts, there is a security concern with `hostPath` volumes in terms of allowing access to the local filesystem. For these reasons, `hostPath` volumes are recommended only for development deployments.

Cloud volumes

It is possible to create Kubernetes volumes that reference storage locations beyond just the Worker Node where a Pod is running, as shown in Figure 2-7. These can be grouped into volume types that are provided by named cloud providers, and those that attempt to provide a more generic interface.

These include the following:

- The `awsElasticBlockStore` (*https://oreil.ly/CmTCt*) volume type is used to mount volumes on Amazon Web Services (AWS) Elastic Block Store (EBS). Many databases use block storage as their underlying storage layer.

- The `gcePersistentDisk` (*https://oreil.ly/01JEm*) volume type is used to mount Google Compute Engine (GCE) persistent disks (PD), another example of block storage.
- Two types of volumes are supported for Microsoft Azure: `azureDisk` (*https://oreil.ly/pIann*) for Azure Data Disk volumes, and `azureFile` (*https://oreil.ly/kInGC*) for Azure File volumes.
- The `cinder` (*https://oreil.ly/VVLrx*) volume type can be used to access OpenStack Cinder volumes for OpenStack deployments.

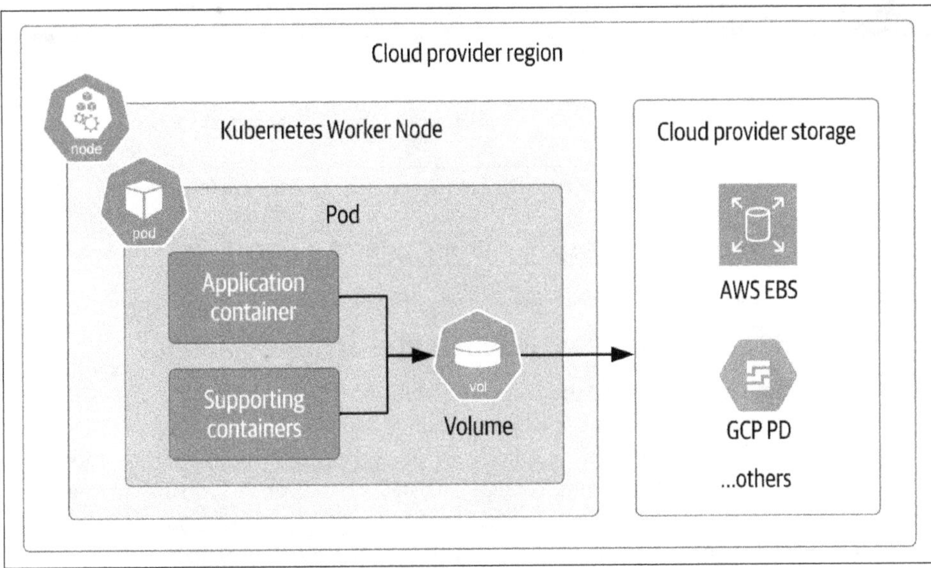

Figure 2-7. Kubernetes Pods directly mounting cloud provider storage

Usage of these types typically requires configuration on the cloud provider, and access from Kubernetes clusters is typically confined to storage in the same cloud region and account. Check your cloud provider's documentation for more details.

Additional volume providers

Numerous additional volume providers vary in the types of storage provided. Here are a few examples:

- The `fibreChannel` volume type can be used for SAN solutions implementing the Fibre Channel protocol.
- The `gluster` volume type is used to access file storage using the Gluster (*https://www.gluster.org*) distributed filesystem referenced previously.

- An `iscsi` volume mounts an existing Internet Small Computer Systems Interface (iSCSI) volume into your Pod.
- An `nfs` volume allows an existing NFS share to be mounted into a Pod.

We'll examine more volume providers that implement the Container Attached Storage pattern in "Container Attached Storage" on page 45. Table 2-1 compares Docker and Kubernetes storage concepts we've covered so far.

Table 2-1. Comparing Docker and Kubernetes storage options

Type of storage	Docker	Kubernetes
Access to persistent storage from various providers	Volume (accessed via volume drivers)	Volume (accessed via in-tree or CSI drivers)
Access to host filesystem (not recommended for production)	Bind mount	`hostPath` volume
Temporary storage available while container (or Pod) is running	Tmpfs	`emptyDir` and other ephemeral volumes
Configuration and environment data (read-only)	(No direct equivalent)	ConfigMap, Secret, downward API

How Do You Choose a Kubernetes Storage Solution?

Given the number of storage options available, trying to determine the kind of storage you should use for your application can certainly be intimidating. Along with determining whether you need file, block, or object storage, you'll want to consider your latency and throughput requirements, as well as your expected storage volume. For example, if your read latency requirements are aggressive, you'll most likely need a storage solution that keeps data in the same datacenter where it is accessed.

Next, you'll want to consider any existing commitments or resources you have. Perhaps your organization has a mandate or bias toward using services from a preferred cloud provider. The cloud providers will frequently provide cost incentives for using their services, but you'll want to weigh this against the risk of lock-in to a specific service. Alternatively, you might have an investment in a storage solution in an on-premises datacenter that you need to leverage.

Overall, cost tends to be the overriding factor in choosing storage solutions, especially over the long term. Make sure your modeling includes not only the cost of the physical storage and any managed services, but also the operational cost involved in managing your chosen solution.

In this section, we've discussed how to use volumes to provide storage that can be shared by multiple containers within the same Pod. While using volumes is sufficient for some use cases, it doesn't address all needs. A volume doesn't provide the ability to share storage resources among Pods. The definition of a particular storage location is tied to the definition of the Pod. Managing storage for individual Pods doesn't scale well as the number of Pods deployed in your Kubernetes cluster increases.

Thankfully, Kubernetes provides additional primitives that help simplify the process of provisioning and mounting storage volumes for both individual Pods and groups of related Pods. We'll investigate these concepts in the next several sections.

PersistentVolumes

The key innovation the Kubernetes developers introduced for managing storage is the PersistentVolume subsystem (*https://oreil.ly/ec8BB*). This subsystem consists of three additional Kubernetes resources that work together: PersistentVolumes, PersistentVolumeClaims, and StorageClasses. These allow you to separate the definition and lifecycle of storage from the way it is used by Pods, as shown in Figure 2-8:

- Cluster administrators define PersistentVolumes, either explicitly or by creating a StorageClass that can dynamically provision new PersistentVolumes.
- Application developers create PersistentVolumeClaims that describe the storage resource needs of their applications, and these PersistentVolumeClaims can be referenced as part of volume definitions in Pods.
- The Kubernetes control plane manages the binding of PersistentVolumeClaims to PersistentVolumes.

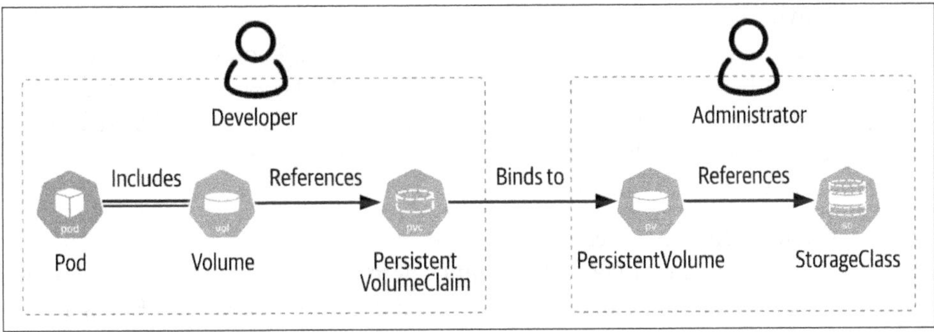

Figure 2-8. PersistentVolumes, PersistentVolumeClaims, and StorageClasses

Let's look first at the *PersistentVolume* resource (often abbreviated *PV*), which defines access to storage at a specific location. PersistentVolumes are typically defined by cluster administrators for use by application developers. Each PV can represent storage of the same types discussed in the previous section, such as storage offered by cloud providers, networked storage, or storage directly on the Worker Node, as shown in Figure 2-9. Since they are tied to specific storage locations, PersistentVolumes are not portable between Kubernetes clusters.

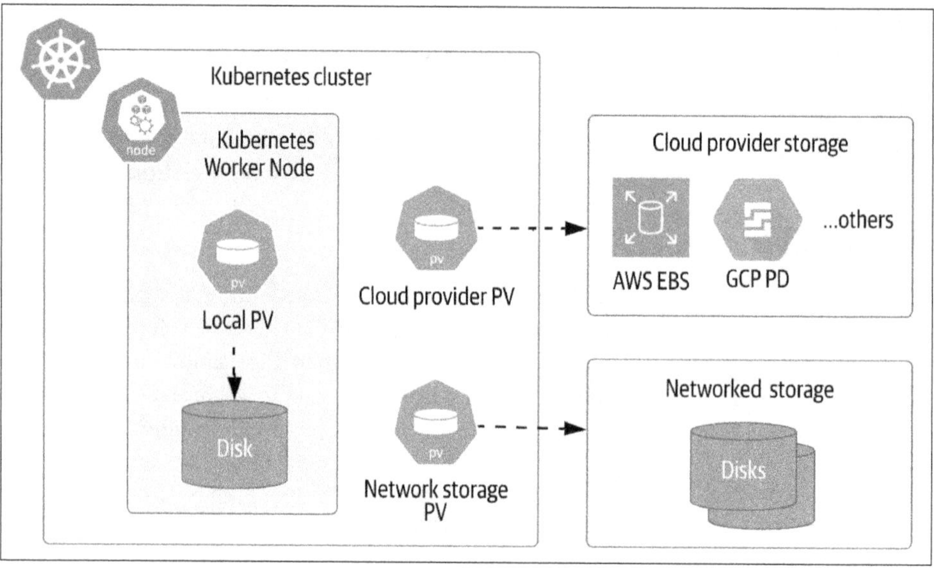

Figure 2-9. Types of Kubernetes PersistentVolumes

Local PersistentVolumes

Figure 2-9 also introduces a PersistentVolume type called `local`, which represents storage mounted directly on a Kubernetes Worker Node such as a disk or partition. Like `hostPath` volumes, a `local` volume may also represent a directory. A key difference between `local` and `hostPath` volumes is that when a Pod using a `local` volume is restarted, the Kubernetes scheduler ensures that the Pod is rescheduled on the same node so it can be attached to the same persistent state. For this reason, `local` volumes are frequently used as the backing store for data infrastructure that manages its own replication, as we'll see in Chapter 4.

The syntax for defining a PersistentVolume will look familiar, as it is similar to defining a volume within a Pod. For example, here is a YAML configuration file that defines a local PersistentVolume. The source code (*https://oreil.ly/b1zHe*) is in this book's repository:

```
apiVersion: v1
kind: PersistentVolume
metadata:
  name: my-volume
spec:
  capacity:
    storage: 3Gi
  accessModes:
    - ReadWriteOnce
  local:
    path: /app/data
```

```
    nodeAffinity:
      required:
        nodeSelectorTerms:
        - matchExpressions:
          - key: kubernetes.io/hostname
            operator: In
            values:
            - node1
```

As you can see, this code defines a `local` volume named `my-volume` on the Worker Node `node1`, 3 GB in size, with an access mode of `ReadWriteOnce`. The following access modes (*https://oreil.ly/mm5HT*) are supported for PersistentVolumes:

`ReadWriteOnce`
: The volume can be mounted for both reading and writing by a single node at a time, although multiple Pods running on that node may access the volume.

`ReadOnlyMany`
: The volume can be mounted by multiple nodes simultaneously, for reading only.

`ReadWriteMany`
: The volume can be mounted for both reading and writing by many nodes at the same time.

Choosing a Volume Access Mode

The right access mode for a given volume will be driven by the type of workload. For example, many distributed databases will be configured with dedicated storage per Pod, making `ReadWriteOnce` a good choice.

Besides capacity (*https://oreil.ly/TSKOD*) and access mode, other attributes for PersistentVolumes include the following:

- The `volumeMode`, which defaults to `Filesystem` but may be overridden to `Block`.
- The `reclaimPolicy` defines what happens when a Pod releases its claim on this PersistentVolume. The legal values are `Retain`, `Recycle`, and `Delete`.
- A PersistentVolume can have a `nodeAffinity` that designates which Worker Node or nodes can access this volume. This is optional for most types but required for the `local` volume type.
- The `class` attribute binds this PV to a particular StorageClass, which is a concept we'll introduce later in this chapter.
- Some PersistentVolume types expose `mountOptions` that are specific to that type.

Differences in Volume Options

Options differ among volume types. For example, not every access mode or reclaim policy is accessible for every PersistentVolume type, so consult the documentation on your chosen type for more details.

You use the `kubectl describe persistentvolume` command (or `kubectl describe pv` for short) to see the status of the PersistentVolume:

```
kubectl describe pv my-volume
Name:              my-volume
Labels:            <none>
Annotations:       <none>
Finalizers:        [kubernetes.io/pv-protection]
StorageClass:
Status:            Available
Claim:
Reclaim Policy:    Retain
Access Modes:      RWO
VolumeMode:        Filesystem
Capacity:          3Gi
Node Affinity:
  Required Terms:
    Term 0:        kubernetes.io/hostname in [node1]
Message:
Source:
    Type:  LocalVolume (a persistent volume backed by local storage on a node)
    Path:  /app/data
Events:    <none>
```

The PersistentVolume has a status of `Available` when first created. A PersistentVolume can have multiple status values:

`Available`
: The PersistentVolume is free and not yet bound to a claim.

`Bound`
: The PersistentVolume is bound to a PersistentVolumeClaim, which is listed elsewhere in the `describe` output.

`Released`
: An existing claim on the PersistentVolume has been deleted, but the resource has not yet been reclaimed, so the resource is not yet `Available`.

`Failed`
: The volume has failed its automatic reclamation.

Now that you've learned how storage resources are defined in Kubernetes, the next step is to learn how to use that storage in your applications.

PersistentVolumeClaims

As we've discussed, Kubernetes separates the definition of storage from its usage. Often these tasks are performed by different roles: cluster administrators define the storage, while application developers use the storage. PersistentVolumes are typically defined by the administrators and reference storage locations that are specific to that cluster. Developers can then specify the storage needs of their applications using *PersistentVolumeClaims (PVCs)*, which Kubernetes uses to associate Pods with a PersistentVolume meeting the specified criteria. As shown in Figure 2-10, a PersistentVolumeClaim is used to reference the various volume types we introduced previously, including local PersistentVolumes, or external storage provided by cloud or networked storage vendors.

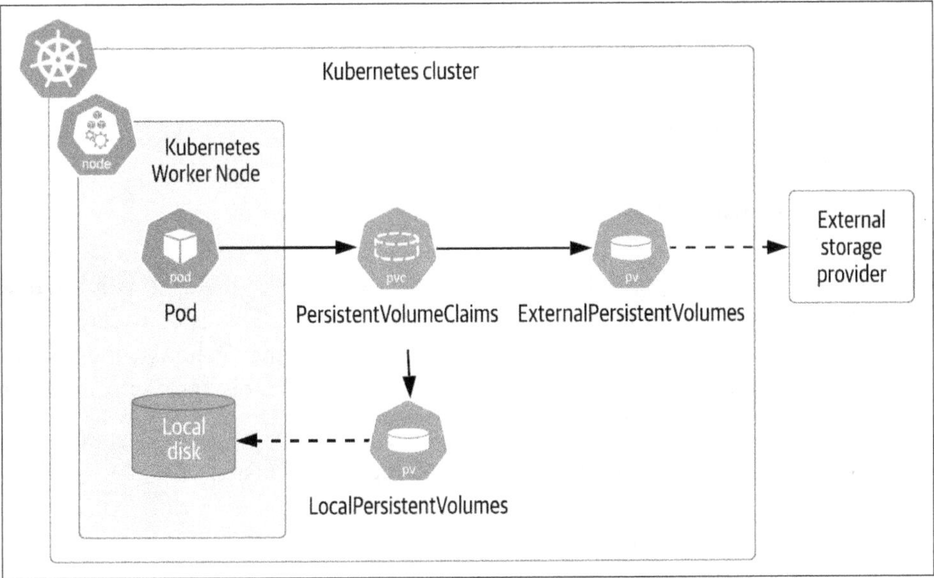

Figure 2-10. Accessing PersistentVolumes using PersistentVolumeClaims

Here's what the process looks like from an application developer perspective. First, you'll create a PVC representing your desired storage criteria. For example, here's a claim that requests 1 GB of storage with exclusive read/write access. The source code (*https://oreil.ly/njKPH*) is in this book's repository:

```
apiVersion: v1
kind: PersistentVolumeClaim
metadata:
  name: my-claim
spec:
  storageClassName: ""
  accessModes:
  - ReadWriteOnce
```

```
    resources:
      requests:
        storage: 1Gi
```

One interesting thing you may have noticed about this claim is that the `storageClassName` is set to an empty string. We'll explain the significance of this when we discuss StorageClasses in the next section. You can reference the claim in the definition of a Pod like this. The source code (*https://oreil.ly/VnJN4*) is in this book's repository:

```
apiVersion: v1
kind: Pod
metadata:
  name: my-pod
spec:
  containers:
  - name: nginx
    image: nginx
    volumeMounts:
    - mountPath: "/app/data"
      name: my-volume
  volumes:
  - name: my-volume
    persistentVolumeClaim:
      claimName: my-claim
```

As you can see, the PersistentVolume is represented within the Pod as a volume. The volume is given a name and a reference to the claim. This is considered to be a volume of the `persistentVolumeClaim` type. As with other volumes, the volume is mounted into a container at a specific mount point—in this case, into the main application Nginx container at the path */app/data*.

A PVC also has a state, which you can see if you retrieve the status:

```
kubectl describe pvc my-claim
Name:          my-claim
Namespace:     default
StorageClass:
Status:        Bound
Volume:        my-volume
Labels:        <none>
Annotations:   pv.kubernetes.io/bind-completed: yes
               pv.kubernetes.io/bound-by-controller: yes
Finalizers:    [kubernetes.io/pvc-protection]
Capacity:      3Gi
Access Modes:  RWO
VolumeMode:    Filesystem
Mounted By:    <none>
Events:        <none>
```

A PVC has one of two status values: `Bound`, meaning it is bound to a volume (as in this example), or `Pending`, meaning that it has not yet been bound to a volume. Typically, a status of `Pending` means that no PV matching the claim exists.

Here's what's happening behind the scenes. Kubernetes uses the PVCs referenced as volumes in a Pod and takes those into account when scheduling the Pod. Kubernetes identifies PersistentVolumes that match properties associated with the claim and binds the smallest available module to the claim. The properties might include a label, or node affinity, as we saw previously for `local` volumes.

When starting up a Pod, the Kubernetes control plane makes sure the PersistentVolumes are mounted to the Worker Node. Then, each requested storage volume is mounted into the Pod at the specified mount point.

StorageClasses

The previous example demonstrates how Kubernetes can bind PVCs to PersistentVolumes that already exist. This model in which PersistentVolumes are explicitly created in the Kubernetes cluster is known as *static provisioning*. The Kubernetes PersistentVolume subsystem also supports *dynamic provisioning* of volumes using *StorageClasses* (often abbreviated *SC*). The StorageClass is responsible for provisioning (and deprovisioning) PersistentVolumes according to the needs of applications running in the cluster, as shown in Figure 2-11.

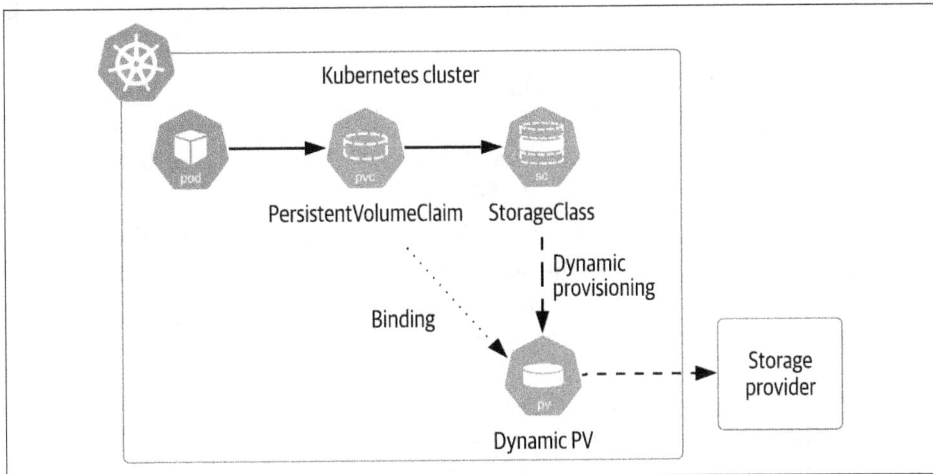

Figure 2-11. StorageClasses support dynamic provisioning of volumes

Depending on the Kubernetes cluster you are using, at least one StorageClass is likely already available. You can verify this using the command `kubectl get sc`. If you're running a simple Kubernetes distribution on your local machine and don't see any

StorageClasses, you can install an open source local storage provider from Rancher with the following command:

```
set GH_LINK=https://raw.githubusercontent.com
kubectl apply -f \
  $GH_LINK/rancher/local-path-provisioner/master/deploy/local-path-storage.yaml
```

This storage provider comes preinstalled in K3s, a desktop distribution also provided by Rancher. If you take a look at the YAML configuration referenced in that statement, you'll see the following definition of a StorageClass. The source code (*https://oreil.ly/nTocI*) is in this book's repository:

```
apiVersion: storage.k8s.io/v1
kind: StorageClass
metadata:
  name: local-path
provisioner: rancher.io/local-path
volumeBindingMode: WaitForFirstConsumer
reclaimPolicy: Delete
```

As you can see from the definition, a StorageClass is defined by a few key attributes:

- The `provisioner` interfaces with an underlying storage provider such as a public cloud or storage system in order to allocate the actual storage. The provisioner can be either one of the Kubernetes built-in provisioners (referred to as *in-tree* because they are part of the Kubernetes source code), or a provisioner that conforms to the Container Storage Interface (CSI), which we'll examine later in this chapter.
- The `reclaimPolicy` describes whether storage is reclaimed when the PersistentVolume is deleted. The default, `Delete`, can be overridden to `Retain`, in which case the storage administrator would be responsible for managing the future state of that storage with the storage provider.
- The `volumeBindingMode` (*https://oreil.ly/iFvrm*) controls when the storage is provisioned and bound. If the value is `Immediate`, a PersistentVolume is immediately provisioned as soon as a PersistentVolumeClaim referencing the StorageClass is created, and the claim is bound to the PersistentVolume, regardless of whether the claim is referenced in a Pod. Many storage plug-ins also support a second mode known as `WaitForFirstConsumer`, in which case no PersistentVolume is provisioned until a Pod is created that references the claim. This behavior is considered preferable since it gives the Kubernetes scheduler more flexibility.
- Although not shown in this example, there is also an optional `allowVolumeExpansion` flag. This indicates whether the StorageClass supports the ability for volumes to be expanded. If `true`, the volume can be expanded by increasing the size of the `storage.request` field of the PersistentVolumeClaim. This value defaults to `false`.

- Some StorageClasses also define `parameters`, specific configuration options for the storage provider that are passed to the provisioner. Common options include filesystem type, encryption settings, and throughput in terms of I/O operations per second (IOPS). Check the documentation for the storage provider for more details.

Limits on Dynamic Provisioning

Local PVs cannot be dynamically provisioned by a StorageClass, so you must create them manually yourself.

Application developers can reference a specific StorageClass when creating a PVC by adding a `storageClass` property to the definition. For example, here is a YAML configuration for a PVC referencing the `local-path` StorageClass. The source code (*https://oreil.ly/Ixwv7*) is in this book's repository:

```
apiVersion: v1
kind: PersistentVolumeClaim
metadata:
  name: my-local-path-claim
spec:
  storageClassName: local-path
  accessModes:
  - ReadWriteOnce
  resources:
    requests:
      storage: 1Gi
```

If no `storageClass` is specified in the claim, the default StorageClass is used. The default StorageClass can be set by the cluster administrator. As we showed in "PersistentVolumes" on page 33, you can opt out of using StorageClasses by using the empty string, which indicates that you are using statically provisioned storage.

StorageClasses provide a useful abstraction that cluster administrators and application developers can use as a contract: administrators define the StorageClasses, and developers reference the StorageClasses by name. The details of the underlying StorageClass implementation can differ across Kubernetes platform providers, promoting portability of applications.

This flexibility allows administrators to create StorageClasses representing a variety of storage options—for example, to distinguish between different quality-of-service guarantees in terms of throughput or latency. This concept is known as *profiles* in other storage systems. See "How Developers Are Driving the Future of Kubernetes Storage" on page 48 for more ideas on how StorageClasses can be leveraged in innovative ways.

Kubernetes Storage Architecture

In the preceding sections, we discussed the various storage resources that Kubernetes supports via its API (*https://oreil.ly/k1Ttm*). In the remainder of the chapter, we'll look at how these solutions are constructed, as they can give us valuable insights into constructing cloud native data solutions.

Defining Cloud Native Storage

Most of the storage technologies we discuss in this chapter are captured as part of the "cloud native storage" solutions listed in the CNCF landscape (*https://oreil.ly/vY3wF*). The CNCF Storage Whitepaper (*https://oreil.ly/bKRi9*) is a helpful resource that defines key terms and concepts for cloud native storage. Both of these resources are updated regularly.

Flexvolume

Originally, the Kubernetes codebase contained multiple in-tree storage plug-ins (that is, included in the same GitHub repo as the rest of the Kubernetes code). This helped standardize the code for connecting to different storage platforms, but there were a couple of disadvantages. First, many Kubernetes developers had limited expertise across the broad set of included storage providers. More significantly, the ability to upgrade storage plug-ins was tied to the Kubernetes release cycle, meaning that if you needed a fix or enhancement for a storage plug-in, you'd have to wait until it was accepted into a Kubernetes release. This slowed the maturation of storage technology for Kubernetes and as a result, adoption slowed as well.

The Kubernetes community created the *Flexvolume specification* to allow development of plug-ins independently—that is, out of the Kubernetes source code tree and thus not tied to the Kubernetes release cycle. Around the same time, storage plug-in standards were emerging for other container orchestration systems, and developers from these communities began to question the wisdom of developing multiple standards to solve the same basic problem.

Future Flexvolume Support

The Flexvolume feature has been deprecated in Kubernetes 1.23 in favor of the Container Storage Interface.

Container Storage Interface

The *Container Storage Interface (CSI)* initiative was established as an industry standard for storage for containerized applications. CSI is an open standard used to define plug-ins that will work across container orchestration systems including Kubernetes, Mesos, and Cloud Foundry. As Saad Ali, Google engineer and chair of the Kubernetes Storage Special Interest Group (SIG) (*https://oreil.ly/JDsVv*), noted in "The State of State in Kubernetes" (*https://oreil.ly/sUzfM*) in *The New Stack*, "The Container Storage Interface allows Kubernetes to interact directly with an arbitrary storage system."

The CSI specification is available on GitHub (*https://oreil.ly/kCOhg*). Support for the CSI in Kubernetes began with the 1.*x* release, and it went general availability (GA) (*https://oreil.ly/AbUpe*) in the 1.13 release. Kubernetes continues to track updates to the CSI specification.

Additional CSI Resources

The CSI documentation site (*https://oreil.ly/KFIXI*) provides guidance for developers and storage providers who are interested in developing CSI-compliant drivers. The site also provides a very useful list of CSI-compliant drivers (*https://oreil.ly/wHkva*). This list is generally more up-to-date than one provided on the Kubernetes documentation site.

Once a CSI implementation is deployed on a Kubernetes cluster, its capabilities are accessed through the standard Kubernetes storage resources such as PVCs, PVs, and SCs. On the backend, each CSI implementation must provide two plug-ins: a node plug-in and a controller plug-in, as depicted in Figure 2-12.

The CSI specification defines required interfaces for these plug-ins using gRPC but does not specify exactly how the plug-ins are to be deployed. Let's briefly look at the role of each of these services:

The controller plug-in
: This plug-in supports operations on volumes such as create, delete, listing, publishing/unpublishing, tracking, and expanding volume capacity. It also tracks volume status including what nodes each volume is attached to. The controller plug-in is also responsible for taking and managing snapshots, and using snapshots to clone a volume. The controller plug-in can run on any node—it is a standard Kubernetes controller.

The node plug-in
: This plug-in runs on each Kubernetes Worker Node where provisioned volumes will be attached. The node plug-in is responsible for local storage, as well as

mounting and unmounting volumes onto the node. The Kubernetes control plane directs the plug-in to mount a volume prior to any Pods being scheduled on the node that require the volume.

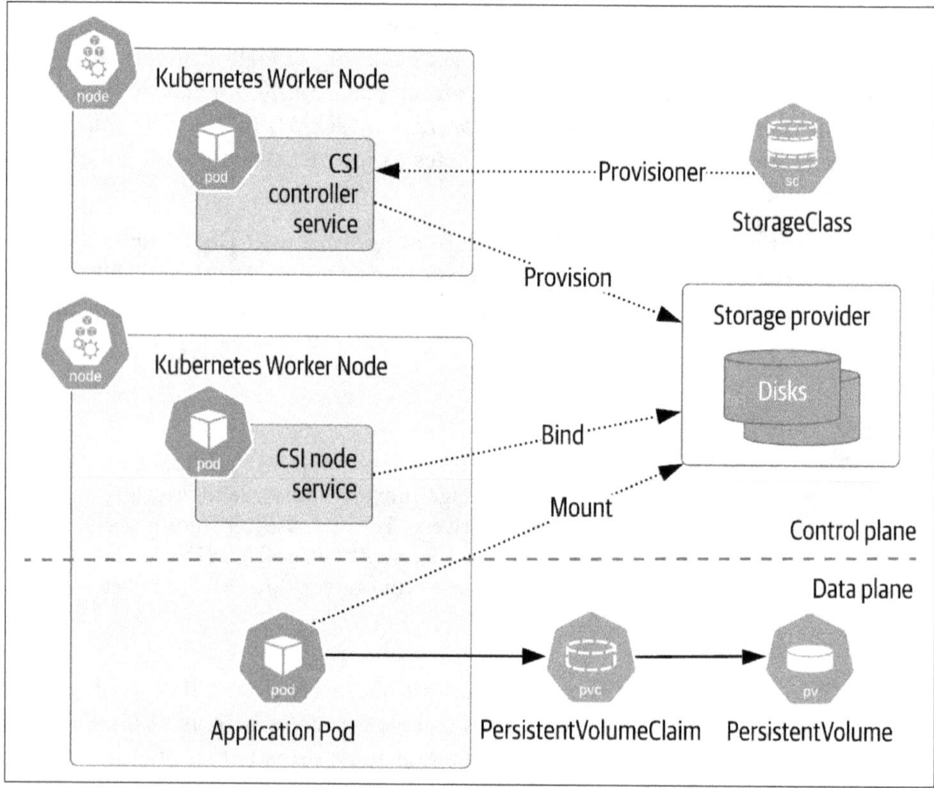

Figure 2-12. CSI mapped to Kubernetes

CSI Migration

The Kubernetes community has been very conscious of preserving forward and backward compatibility among versions, and the transition from in-tree storage plug-ins to the CSI is no exception. Features in Kubernetes are typically introduced as alpha features, and progress to beta, before being released as GA. Introducing a new API such as the CSI presents a more complex challenge because it also involves the deprecation of older APIs.

The CSI migration approach (*https://oreil.ly/qduG8*) was introduced to promote a coherent experience for users of storage plug-ins. The implementation of each corresponding in-tree plug-in is changed to a facade when an equivalent CSI-compliant driver becomes available. Calls on the in-tree plug-in are delegated to the underlying

CSI-compliant driver. The migration capability is itself a feature that can be enabled on a Kubernetes cluster.

This allows a staged adoption process that can be used as existing clusters are updated to newer Kubernetes versions. Each application can be updated independently to use CSI-compliant drivers instead of in-tree drivers. This approach to maturing and replacing APIs is a helpful pattern for promoting stability of the overall platform and providing administrators control over their migration to the new API.

Container Attached Storage

While the CSI is an important step forward in standardizing storage management across container orchestrators, it does not provide implementation guidance on how or where the storage software runs. Some CSI implementations are basically thin wrappers around legacy storage management software running outside of the Kubernetes cluster. While this reuse of existing storage assets certainly has its benefits, many developers have expressed a desire for storage management solutions that run entirely in Kubernetes alongside their applications.

Container Attached Storage is a design pattern that provides a more cloud native approach to managing storage. The logic to manage storage operations such as attaching volumes to applications is itself composed of microservices running in containers. This allows the storage layer to have the same properties as other applications deployed on Kubernetes and reduces the number of different management interfaces administrators have to keep track of. The storage layer becomes just another Kubernetes application.

As Evan Powell noted in "Container Attached Storage: A Primer" (*https://oreil.ly/zplhD*) on the *CNCF Blog*:

> Container Attached Storage reflects a broader trend of solutions that reinvent particular categories or create new ones—by being built on Kubernetes and microservices and that deliver capabilities to Kubernetes-based microservice environments. For example, new projects for security, DNS, networking, network policy management, messaging, tracing, logging and more have emerged in the cloud-native ecosystem.

Several examples of projects and products embody the CAS approach to storage. Let's examine a few of the open source options.

OpenEBS

OpenEBS is a project created by MayaData and donated to the CNCF, where it became a Sandbox project in 2019. The name is a play on Amazon's Elastic Block Store, and OpenEBS is an attempt to provide an open source equivalent to this popular managed service. OpenEBS provides storage engines for managing both local and NVMe PersistentVolumes.

OpenEBS provides a great example of a CSI-compliant implementation deployed onto Kubernetes, as shown in Figure 2-13. The control plane includes the OpenEBS provisioner, which implements the CSI controller interface, and the OpenEBS API server, which provides a configuration interface for clients and interacts with the rest of the Kubernetes control plane.

The OpenEBS data plane consists of the Node Disk Manager (NDM) as well as dedicated pods for each PersistentVolume. The NDM runs on each Kubernetes worker where storage will be accessed. It implements the CSI node interface and provides the helpful functionality of automatically detecting block storage devices attached to a Worker Node.

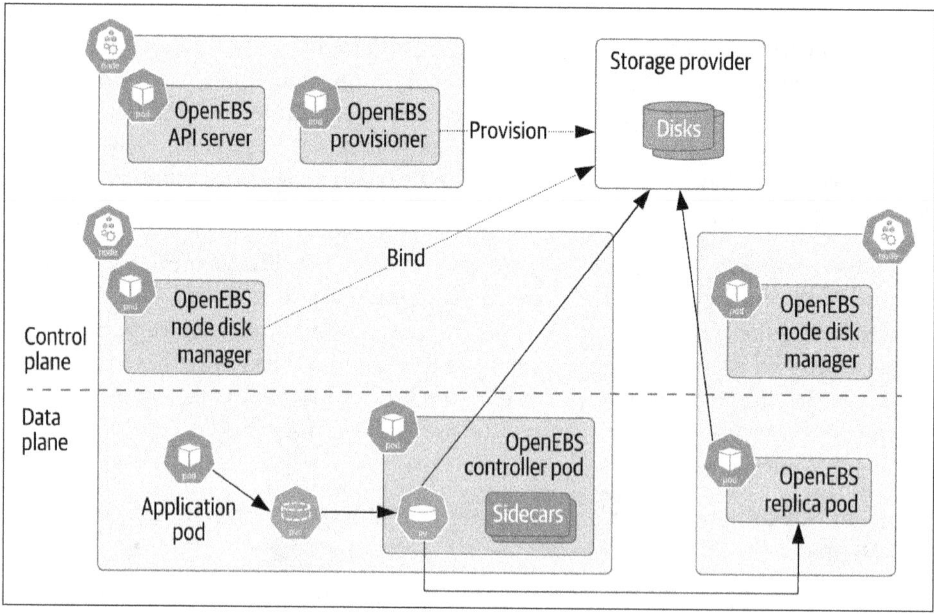

Figure 2-13. OpenEBS architecture

OpenEBS creates multiple Pods for each volume. A controller Pod is created as the primary replica, and additional replica Pods are created on other Kubernetes Worker Nodes for high availability. Each Pod includes sidecars that expose interfaces for metrics collection and management, which allows the control plane to monitor and manage the data plane.

Longhorn

Longhorn (*https://longhorn.io*) is an open source, distributed block storage system for Kubernetes. It was originally developed by Rancher and became a CNCF Sandbox project in 2019. Longhorn focuses on providing an alternative to cloud-vendor storage and expensive external storage arrays. Longhorn supports providing incremental backups to NFS or S3-compatible storage, and live replication to a separate Kubernetes cluster for disaster recovery.

Longhorn uses a similar architecture to that shown for OpenEBS; according to the documentation (*https://oreil.ly/TXTjG*), "Longhorn creates a dedicated storage controller for each block device volume and synchronously replicates the volume across multiple replicas stored on multiple nodes. The storage controller and replicas are themselves orchestrated using Kubernetes." Longhorn also provides an integrated user interface to simplify operations.

Rook and Ceph

According to its website, "Rook is an open source cloud-native storage orchestrator, providing the platform, framework, and support for a diverse set of storage solutions to natively integrate with cloud-native environments." Rook was originally created as a containerized version of Ceph that could be deployed in Kubernetes. Ceph (*https://ceph.io/en*) is an open source distributed storage framework that provides block, file, and object storage. Rook was the first storage project accepted by the CNCF and is now considered a CNCF graduated project (*https://oreil.ly/xmc1i*).

Rook is a truly Kubernetes native implementation in the sense that it makes use of Kubernetes custom resources (CRDs) and custom controllers called operators. Rook provides operators for Ceph, Cassandra, and NFS. We'll learn more about custom resources and operators in Chapter 4.

Some commercial solutions for Kubernetes also embody the CAS pattern. These include MayaData (*https://mayadata.io*) (creators of OpenEBS), Portworx (*https://portworx.com*) by Pure Storage (*https://oreil.ly/3rJuQ*), Robin.io (*https://robin.io*), and StorageOS (*https://storageos.com*). These companies provide both raw storage in block and file formats, as well as integrations for simplified deployments of additional data infrastructure such as databases and streaming solutions.

Container Object Storage Interface

The CSI provides support for file and block storage, but object storage APIs require different semantics and don't quite fit the CSI paradigm of mounting volumes. In Fall 2020, a group of companies led by MinIO (*https://min.io*) began work on a new API for object storage in container orchestration platforms: the *Container Object Storage Interface (COSI)*. COSI provides a Kubernetes API (*https://oreil.ly/BwcKA*) more suited to provisioning and accessing object storage, defining a `bucket` custom resource, and including operations to create buckets and manage access to buckets. The design of the COSI control plane and data plane is modeled after the CSI. COSI is an emerging standard with a great start and potential for wide adoption in the Kubernetes community and potentially beyond.

How Developers Are Driving the Future of Kubernetes Storage

With Kiran Mova, Cofounder and CTO of MayaData and member of the Kubernetes Storage SIG (https://oreil.ly/GRRuD)

Many organizations are just starting their containerization journey. Kubernetes is the shiny object, and everybody wants to run everything in Kubernetes. But not all teams are ready for Kubernetes, much less managing stateful workloads on Kubernetes.

Application developers are the ones driving the push for stateful workloads on Kubernetes. These developers get started with cloud resources that are available to them, even a single-node Kubernetes cluster, and assume they're ready to run that in production. Developers are "Kuberneticizing" their in-house applications, and the demands on storage are quite different from what the platform teams that support them are used to.

Microservices and Kubernetes have changed the way storage volumes are provisioned. Platform teams are used to thinking about data in terms of provisioning volumes with the required throughput or capacity. In the old way, the platform team would meet with the application team, estimate the size of the data, do a month of planning, provision a 2–3 TB volume, and mount it into the VMs or bare-metal servers, and that would provide enough storage capacity for the next year.

With Kubernetes, provisioning has become ad hoc and much easier. You can run things in a highly cost-effective and agile way by adopting Kubernetes. But many platform teams are still working to catch up. Some teams are simply focused on provisioning storage correctly, while others are beginning to focus on "day two" operations, such as automated provisioning, expanding volumes, or disconnecting and destroying volumes.

Platform teams don't yet have a foolproof way to run stateful workloads in Kubernetes, so they often offload persistence to public cloud providers. The public clouds make a strong case for their managed services, claiming they have everything that you'll need to run a storage system, but once you start using managed services for state, you can become dependent on those cloud providers and get stuck.

Meanwhile, innovations in storage technology are happening in parallel:

- The landscape is shifting back and forth between hyperconverged and disaggregated. This rearchitecture is happening at all the layers of the stack, and it's not just the software: it includes processes and the people who consume the data.
- Hardware trends are driving toward low-latency solutions including NVMe and DPDK/SPDK, and changes to the Linux kernel like io_uring to take advantage of faster hardware.
- Container Attached Storage will help us manage storage more effectively—for example, being able to reclaim storage space when workloads shrink. This can be

a difficult problem with data distributed across multiple nodes. We'll need better logic for relocating data onto existing nodes.

- Technologies that bring more automation for compliance and operations are coming into the picture as well.

With all these innovations, it can be a bit overwhelming to understand the big picture and determine how to leverage this technology for maximum benefit. Platform SREs need to learn about Kubernetes, declarative deployments, GitOps principles, new volume types, and even database concepts like eventual consistency.

We envision a future in which application developers will specify their Kubernetes storage needs in terms of the required quality of service, such as IOPS and throughput. Developers should be able to specify different storage needs for their workloads in more human-relatable terms. For example, platform teams could define StorageClasses for "fast storage" versus "slow storage," or perhaps "metadata storage" versus "data storage." These StorageClasses will make different cost/performance trade-offs and provide specific service level agreements (SLAs). We may even see some standard definitions start to emerge for these new StorageClasses.

Ideally, application teams should not be choosing storage solutions. The only thing an application developer should be concerned with is specifying PersistentVolumeClaims for their application, with the StorageClasses they need. The other details of managing storage should be hidden, although of course the storage subsystem will report errors including status and logs via the standard Kubernetes mechanisms. This capability will make things a lot simpler for application developers, whether they're deploying a database or some other stateful workload.

These innovations will guide us to an optimal place with storage on Kubernetes. Today, deploying infrastructure is easy. Let's work together to get to a place where deploying the *right* infrastructure is easy.

As you can see, storage on Kubernetes is an area comprising a lot of innovation, including multiple open source projects and commercial vendors competing to provide the most usable, cost-effective, and performant solutions. The cloud native storage section (*https://oreil.ly/cm4Ms*) of the CNCF landscape provides a helpful listing of storage providers and related tools, including the technologies referenced in this chapter and many more.

Summary

In this chapter, we've explored how persistence is managed in container systems like Docker, and container orchestration systems like Kubernetes. You've learned about the various Kubernetes resources that can be used to manage stateful workloads, including Volumes, PersistentVolumes, PersistentVolumeClaims, and StorageClasses.

We've seen how the Container Storage Interface and Container Attached Storage pattern point the way toward more cloud native approaches to managing storage. Now you're ready to learn how to use these building blocks and design principles to manage stateful workloads including databases, streaming data, and more.

CHAPTER 3

Databases on Kubernetes the Hard Way

As we discussed in Chapter 1, Kubernetes was designed for stateless workloads. A corollary to this is that stateless workloads are what Kubernetes does best. Because of this, some have argued that you shouldn't try to run stateful workloads on Kubernetes, and you may hear various recommendations about what you should do instead: "Use a managed service," or "Leave data in legacy databases in your on-premises datacenter," or perhaps even "Run your databases in the cloud, but in traditional VMs instead of containers."

While these recommendations are still viable options, one of our main goals in this book is to demonstrate that running data infrastructure in Kubernetes has become not only a viable option, but a preferred option. In his article "A Case for Databases on Kubernetes from a Former Skeptic" (*https://oreil.ly/SjQV0*), Christopher Bradford describes his journey from being skeptical of running any stateful workload in Kubernetes, to grudging acceptance of running data infrastructure on Kubernetes for development and test workloads, to enthusiastic evangelism around deploying databases on Kubernetes in production. This journey is typical of many in the Data on Kubernetes Community (DoKC). By the middle of 2020, Boris Kurktchiev was able to cite a growing consensus that managing stateful workloads on Kubernetes had reached a point of viability, and even maturity, in his article "3 Reasons to Bring Stateful Applications to Kubernetes" (*https://oreil.ly/xtm89*).

How did this change come about? Over the past several years, the Kubernetes community has shifted focus toward adding features that support the ability to manage state in a cloud native way on Kubernetes. The storage elements represent a big part of this shift we introduced in the previous chapter, including the Kubernetes PersistentVolume subsystem and the adoption of the CSI. In this chapter, we'll complete this part of the story by looking at Kubernetes resources for building stateful applications on top of this storage foundation. We'll focus in particular on a specific type of stateful application: data infrastructure.

The Hard Way

The phrase "doing it the hard way" has come to be associated with avoiding the easy option in favor of putting in the detailed work required to accomplish a result that will have lasting significance. Throughout history, pioneers of all persuasions are well known for taking pride in having made the sacrifice of blood, sweat, and tears that made life just that little bit more bearable for the generations that follow. These elders are often heard to lament when their protégés fail to comprehend the depth of what they had to go through.

In the tech world, it's no different. While new innovations such as APIs and "no code" environments have massive potential to grow a new crop of developers worldwide, a deeper understanding of the underlying technology is still required in order to manage highly available and secure systems at worldwide scale. It's when things go wrong that this detailed knowledge proves its worth. This is why many of us who are software developers and never touch a physical server in our day jobs gain so much from building our own PC by wiring chips and boards by hand. It's also one of the hidden benefits of serving as informal IT consultants for our friends and family.

For the Kubernetes community, of course, "the hard way" has an even more specific connotation. Google engineer Kelsey Hightower's "Kubernetes the Hard Way" (*https://oreil.ly/xd6ne*) has become a sort of rite of passage for those who want a deeper understanding of the elements that make up a Kubernetes cluster. This popular tutorial walks you through downloading, installing, and configuring each of the components that make up the Kubernetes control plane. The result is a working Kubernetes cluster that, although not suitable for deploying a production workload, is certainly functional enough for development and learning. The appeal of the approach is that all of the instructions are typed by hand. Rather than downloading a bunch of scripts that do everything for you, you must understand what is happening at each step.

In this chapter, we'll emulate this approach and walk you through deploying some example data infrastructure the hard way ourselves. Along the way, you'll get more hands-on experience with the storage resources you learned about in Chapter 2, and we'll introduce additional Kubernetes resource types for managing compute and network to complete the compute, network, storage triad we introduced in Chapter 1. Are you ready to get your hands dirty? Let's go!

Examples Are Not Production-Grade

The examples we present in this chapter are primarily for introducing new elements of the Kubernetes API and are not intended to represent deployments we'd recommend running in production. We'll make sure to highlight any gaps so that we can demonstrate how to fill them in upcoming chapters.

Prerequisites for Running Data Infrastructure on Kubernetes

To follow along with the examples in this chapter, you'll want to have a Kubernetes cluster to work on. If you've never tried it before, perhaps you'll want to build a cluster using the "Kubernetes the Hard Way" (*https://oreil.ly/sLopS*) instructions, and then use that same cluster to add data infrastructure the hard way as well. You could also use a simple desktop Kubernetes, since we won't be using a large amount of resources. If you're using a shared cluster, you might want to install these examples in their own Namespace to isolate them from the work of others:

```
kubectl config set-context --current --namespace=<insert-namespace-name-here>
```

You'll also need to make sure you have a StorageClass in your cluster. If you're starting from a cluster built the hard way, you won't have one. You may want to follow the instructions in "StorageClasses" on page 39 for installing a simple StorageClass and provisioner that expose local storage. The source code (*https://oreil.ly/iV1Tg*) is in this book's repository:

```
apiVersion: storage.k8s.io/v1
kind: StorageClass
metadata:
name: local-path
provisioner: rancher.io/local-path
volumeBindingMode: WaitForFirstConsumer
reclaimPolicy: Delete
```

You'll want to use a StorageClass that supports a `volumeBindingMode` (*https://oreil.ly/rpNyc*) of `WaitForFirstConsumer`. This gives Kubernetes the flexibility to defer provisioning storage until we need it. This behavior is generally preferred for production deployments, so you might as well start getting in the habit.

Running MySQL on Kubernetes

First, let's start with a super simple example. MySQL is one of the most widely used relational databases because of its reliability and usability. For this example, we'll build on the MySQL tutorial (*https://oreil.ly/cY6cv*) in the official Kubernetes documentation, with a couple of twists. You can find the source code used in this section at "Deploying MySQL Example—Data on Kubernetes the Hard Way" (*https://oreil.ly/YfjiG*). The tutorial includes two Kubernetes deployments: one to run a MySQL Pod, and another to run a sample client—in this case, WordPress. This configuration is shown in Figure 3-1.

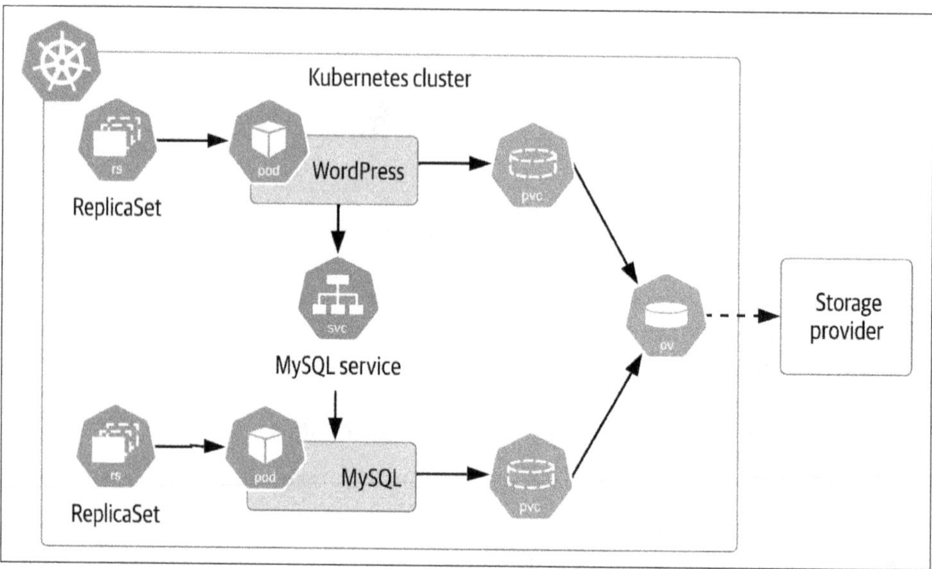

Figure 3-1. Sample Kubernetes deployment of MySQL

In this example, we see that there is a PersistentVolumeClaim for each Pod. For the purposes of this example, we'll assume these claims are satisfied by a single volume provided by the default StorageClass. You'll also notice that each Pod is shown as part of a ReplicaSet and that there is a service exposed for the MySQL database. Let's take a pause and introduce these concepts.

ReplicaSets

Production application deployments on Kubernetes do not typically deploy individual Pods, because an individual Pod could easily be lost when the node disappears. Instead, Pods are typically deployed in the context of a Kubernetes resource that manages their lifecycle. ReplicaSet is one of these resources, and the other is StatefulSet, which we'll look at later in the chapter.

The purpose of a *ReplicaSet* is to ensure that a specified number of replicas of a given Pod are kept running at any given time. As Pods are destroyed, others are created to replace them in order to satisfy the desired number of replicas. A ReplicaSet is defined by a Pod template, a number of replicas, and a selector. The Pod template defines a specification for Pods that will be managed by the ReplicaSet, similar to what we saw for individual Pods created in the examples in Chapter 2. The number of replicas can be zero or more. The selector identifies Pods that are part of the ReplicaSet.

Let's look at a portion of an example definition of a ReplicaSet for the WordPress application shown in Figure 3-1:

```
apiVersion: apps/v1
kind: ReplicaSet
metadata:
  name: wordpress-mysql
  labels:
    app: wordpress
spec:
  replicas: 1
  selector:
    matchLabels:
      app: wordpress
      tier: mysql
  template:
    metadata:
      labels:
        app: wordpress
        tier: mysql
    spec:
      containers:
      - image: mysql:8.0
        name: mysql
        ...
```

A ReplicaSet is responsible for creating or deleting Pods in order to meet the specified number of replicas. You can scale the size of a ReplicaSet up or down by changing this value. The Pod template is used when creating new Pods. Pods that are managed by a ReplicaSet contain a reference to the ReplicaSet in their `metadata.ownerReferences` field. A ReplicaSet can actually take responsibility for managing a Pod that it did not create if the selector matches and the Pod does not reference another owner. This behavior of a ReplicaSet is known as *acquiring* a Pod.

Define ReplicaSet Selectors Carefully

If you do create ReplicaSets directly, make sure that the selector you use is unique and does not match any bare Pods that you do not intend to be acquired. Pods that do not match the Pod template could be acquired if the selectors match. For more information about managing the lifecycle of ReplicaSets and the Pods they manage, see the Kubernetes documentation (*https://oreil.ly/8Bc9D*).

You might be wondering why we didn't provide a full definition of a ReplicaSet. As it turns out, most application developers do not end up using ReplicaSets directly, because Kubernetes provides another resource type that manages ReplicaSets declaratively: Deployments.

Deployments

A Kubernetes *Deployment* is a resource that builds on top of ReplicaSets with additional features for lifecycle management, including the ability to roll out new versions and roll back to previous versions. As shown in Figure 3-2, creating a Deployment results in the creation of a ReplicaSet as well.

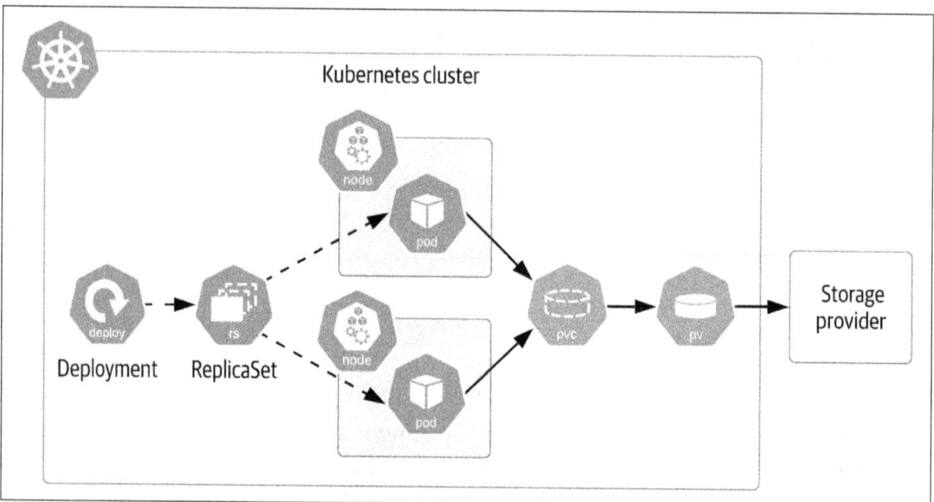

Figure 3-2. Deployments and ReplicaSets

This figure highlights that ReplicaSets (and therefore the Deployments that manage them) operate on cloned replicas of Pods, meaning that the definitions of the Pods are the same, even down to the level of PersistentVolumeClaims. The definition of a ReplicaSet references a single PVC that is provided to it, and there is no mechanism provided to clone the PVC definition for additional Pods. For this reason, Deployments and ReplicaSets are not a good choice if your intent is for each Pod to have access to its own dedicated storage.

Deployments are a good choice if your application Pods do not need access to storage, or if your intent is that they access the same piece of storage. However, the cases where this would be desirable are pretty rare, since you likely don't want a situation in which you could have multiple simultaneous writers to the same storage.

Let's create an example Deployment. First, create a Secret that will represent the database password (substitute in whatever string you want for the password):

```
kubectl create secret generic mysql-root-password \
  --from-literal=password=<your password>
```

Next, create a PVC that represents the storage that the database can use. The source code (*https://oreil.ly/CHccy*) is in this book's repository. A single PVC is sufficient in this case since you are creating a single node. This should work as long as you have an appropriate StorageClass, as referenced earlier:

```
apiVersion: v1
kind: PersistentVolumeClaim
metadata:
  name: mysql-pv-claim
  labels:
    app: wordpress
spec:
  accessModes:
    - ReadWriteOnce
  resources:
    requests:
      storage: 1Gi
```

Next, create a Deployment with a Pod template spec that runs MySQL. The source code (*https://oreil.ly/v9TEt*) is in this book's repository. Note that it includes a reference to the PVC you just created as well as the Secret containing the root password for the database:

```
apiVersion: apps/v1
kind: Deployment
metadata:
  name: wordpress-mysql
  labels:
    app: wordpress
spec:
  selector:
    matchLabels:
      app: wordpress
      tier: mysql
  strategy:
    type: Recreate
  template:
    metadata:
      labels:
        app: wordpress
        tier: mysql
    spec:
      containers:
      - image: mysql:8.0
        name: mysql
        env:
```

```
        - name: MYSQL_ROOT_PASSWORD
          valueFrom:
            secretKeyRef:
              name: mysql-root-password
              key: password
        ports:
        - containerPort: 3306
          name: mysql
        volumeMounts:
        - name: mysql-persistent-storage
          mountPath: /var/lib/mysql
      volumes:
      - name: mysql-persistent-storage
        persistentVolumeClaim:
          claimName: mysql-pv-claim
```

We have a few interesting things to note about this Deployment's specification:

- The Deployment has a `Recreate` strategy. This refers to the way the Deployment handles the replacement of Pods when the Pod template is updated; we'll discuss this shortly.
- Under the Pod template, the password is passed to the Pod as an environment variable extracted from the Secret you created in this example. Overriding the default password is an important aspect of securing any database deployment.
- A single port is exposed on the MySQL image for database access, since this is a relatively simple example. In other samples in this book, we'll see cases of Pods that expose additional ports for administrative operations, metrics collection, and more. The fact that access is disabled by default is a great feature of Kubernetes.
- The MySQL image mounts a volume for its persistent storage using the PVC defined in this example.
- The number of replicas was not provided in the specification. This means that the default value of 1 will be used.

After applying the configuration, try using a command like `kubectl get deployments,rs,pods` to see the items that Kubernetes created for you. You'll notice a single ReplicaSet named after the Deployment that includes a random string (for example, `wordpress-mysql-655c8d9c54`). The Pod's name references the name of the ReplicaSet, adding some additional random characters (for example, `wordpress-mysql-655c8d9c54-tgswd`). These names provide a quick way to identify the relationships between these resources.

Here are a few of the actions that a Deployment takes to manage the lifecycle of ReplicaSets. In keeping with the Kubernetes emphasis on declarative operations, most of these are triggered by updating the specification of the Deployment:

Initial rollout
: When you create a Deployment, Kubernetes uses the specification you provide to create a ReplicaSet. The process of creating this ReplicaSet and its Pods is known as a *rollout*. A rollout is also performed as part of a rolling update.

Scaling up or down
: When you update a Deployment to change the number of replicas, the underlying ReplicaSet is scaled up or down accordingly.

Rolling update
: When you update the Deployment's Pod template (for example, by specifying a different container image for the Pod), Kubernetes creates a new ReplicaSet based on the new Pod template. The way that Kubernetes manages the transition between the old and new ReplicaSets is described by the Deployment's `spec.strategy` property, which defaults to a value called `RollingUpdate`. In a rolling update, the new ReplicaSet is slowly scaled up by creating Pods conforming to the new template, as the number of Pods in the existing ReplicaSet is scaled down. During this transition, the Deployment enforces a maximum and minimum number of Pods, expressed as percentages, as set by the `spec.strategy.rollingupdate.maxSurge` and `maxUnavailable` properties. Each of these values defaults to 25%.

Recreate update
: The other option for use when you update the Pod template is `Recreate`. This is the option that was set in the preceding Deployment. With this option, the existing ReplicaSet is terminated immediately before the new ReplicaSet is created. This strategy is useful for development environments since it completes the update more quickly, whereas `RollingUpdate` is more suitable for production environments since it emphasizes high availability. This is also useful for data migration.

Rollback update
: When creating or updating a Deployment, you could introduce an error—for example, by updating a container image in a Pod with a version that contains a bug. In this case, the Pods managed by the Deployment might not even initialize fully. You can detect these types of errors using commands such as `kubectl rollout status`. Kubernetes provides a series of operations for managing the history of rollouts of a Deployment. You can access these via `kubectl` commands such as `kubectl rollout history`, which provides a numbered history of rollouts for a Deployment, and `kubectl rollout undo`, which reverts a Deployment to the previous rollout. You can also `undo` to a specific rollout version with the `--to-version` option. Because `kubectl` supports rollouts for other resource types we'll cover later in this chapter (StatefulSets and DaemonSets), you'll

need to include the resource type and name when using these commands—for example:

```
kubectl rollout history deployment/wordpress-mysql
```

This produces output such as the following:

```
deployment.apps/wordpress-mysql
REVISION  CHANGE-CAUSE
1         <none>
```

As you can see, Kubernetes Deployments provide some sophisticated behaviors for managing the lifecycle of a set of cloned Pods. You can test out these lifecycle operations (other than rollback) by changing the Deployment's YAML specification and reapplying it. Try scaling the number of replicas to 2 and back again, or using a different MySQL image. After updating the Deployment, you can use a command like `kubectl describe deployment wordpress-mysql` to observe the events that Kubernetes initiates to bring your Deployment to your desired state.

Other options are available for Deployments that we don't have space to go into here—for example, how to specify what Kubernetes does if you attempt an update that fails. For a more in-depth explanation of the behavior of Deployments, see the Kubernetes documentation (*https://oreil.ly/ibjpA*).

Services

In the preceding steps, you've created a PVC to specify the storage needs of the database, a Secret to provide administrator credentials, and a Deployment to manage the lifecycle of a single MySQL Pod. Now that you have a running database, you'll want to make it accessible to applications. In our scheme of compute, network, and storage that we introduced in Chapter 1, this is the networking part.

Kubernetes *Services* are the primitive that we need to use to expose access to our database as a network service. A Service provides an abstraction for a group of Pods running behind it. In the case of a single MySQL node as in this example, you might wonder why we'd bother creating this abstraction. One key feature that a Service supports is to provide a consistently named endpoint that doesn't change. You don't want to be in a situation of having to update your clients whenever the database Pod is restarted and gets a new IP address. You can create a Service for accessing MySQL by using a YAML configuration like this. The source code (*https://oreil.ly/FyR9E*) is in this book's repository:

```
apiVersion: v1
kind: Service
metadata:
  name: wordpress-mysql
  labels:
    app: wordpress
```

```
spec:
  ports:
    - port: 3306
  selector:
    app: wordpress
    tier: mysql
  clusterIP: None
```

Here are a couple of things to note about this configuration:

- This configuration specifies a `port` that is exposed on the Service: 3306. In defining a Service, two ports are actually involved: the `port` exposed to clients of the Service, and the `targetPort` exposed by the underlying Pods that the Service is fronting. Since you haven't specified a `targetPort`, it defaults to the `port` value.
- The `selector` defines what Pods the Service will direct traffic to. In this configuration, there will be only a single MySQL Pod managed by the Deployment, and that's just fine.
- If you have worked with Kubernetes Services before, you may note that there is no `serviceType` defined for this Service, which means that it is of the default type, known as `ClusterIP`. Furthermore, since the `clusterIP` property is set to `None`, this is what is known as a *headless Service*—that is, the Service's DNS name is mapped directly to the IP addresses of the selected Pods.

Kubernetes supports several types of Services to address different use cases, which are shown in Figure 3-3. We'll introduce them briefly here in order to highlight their applicability to data infrastructure:

ClusterIP Service
: This type of Service is exposed on a cluster-internal IP address. ClusterIP Services are the type used most often for data infrastructure such as databases in Kubernetes, especially headless services, since this infrastructure is typically deployed in Kubernetes alongside the application that uses it.

NodePort Service
: A NodePort Service is exposed externally to the cluster on the IP address of each Worker Node. A ClusterIP service is also created internally, to which the NodePort routes traffic. You can allow Kubernetes to select what external port is used from a range of ports (30000–32767 by default), or specify the one you desire by using the `NodePort` property. NodePort services are most suitable for development environments, when you need to debug what is happening on a specific instance of a data infrastructure application.

LoadBalancer
: LoadBalancer Services represent a request from the Kubernetes runtime to set up an external load balancer provided by the underlying cloud provider.

For example, on Amazon's Elastic Kubernetes Service (EKS), requesting a LoadBalancer Service causes an instance of an Elastic Load Balancer (ELB) to be created. Usage of LoadBalancers in front of multinode data infrastructure deployments is typically not required, as these data technologies often have their own approaches for distributing load. For example, Apache Cassandra drivers are aware of the topology of a Cassandra cluster and provide load-balancing features to client applications, eliminating the need for a load balancer.

ExternalName Service
: An ExternalName Service is typically used to represent access to a Service that is outside your cluster—for example, a database that is running externally to Kubernetes. An ExternalName Service does not have a selector, as it is not mapping to any Pods. Instead, it maps the Service name to a CNAME record. For example, if you create a `my-external-database` Service with an `externalName` of `database.mydomain.com`, references in your application Pods to `my-external-database` will be mapped to `database.mydomain.com`.

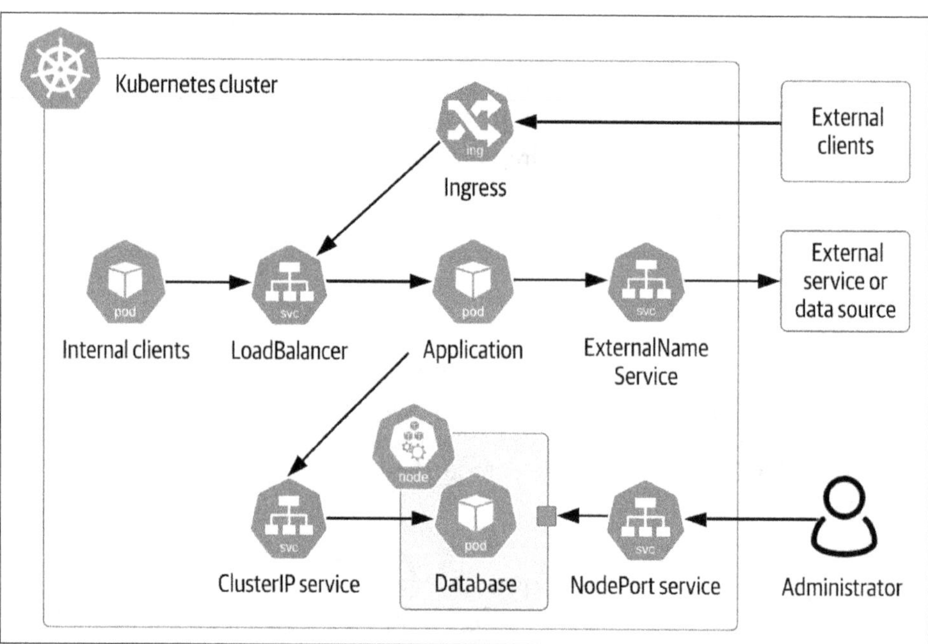

Figure 3-3. Kubernetes Service types

Note also the inclusion of *Ingress* in the figure. While Kubernetes Ingress is not a type of Service, it is related. An Ingress is used to provide access to Kubernetes services from outside the cluster, typically via HTTP. Multiple Ingress implementations are available, including Nginx, Traefik, Ambassador (based on Envoy) and others. Ingress implementations typically provide features including Secure Sockets Layer (SSL) termination and load balancing, even across multiple Kubernetes Services. As with LoadBalancer Services, Ingresses are more typically used at the application tier.

Accessing MySQL

Now that you have deployed the database, you're ready to deploy an application that uses it—the WordPress server. First, the server will need its own PVC. This helps illustrate that some applications leverage storage directly—perhaps for storing files, applications that use data infrastructure, and applications that do both. You can make a small request since this is just for demonstration purposes. The source code (*https://oreil.ly/smKtM*) is in this book's repository:

```
apiVersion: v1
kind: PersistentVolumeClaim
metadata:
  name: wp-pv-claim
  labels:
    app: wordpress
spec:
  accessModes:
    - ReadWriteOnce
  resources:
    requests:
      storage: 1Gi
```

Next, create a Deployment for a single WordPress node. The source code (*https://oreil.ly/hLPdW*) is in this book's repository:

```
apiVersion: apps/v1
kind: Deployment
metadata:
  name: wordpress
  labels:
    app: wordpress
spec:
  selector:
    matchLabels:
      app: wordpress
      tier: frontend
  strategy:
    type: Recreate
  template:
    metadata:
      labels:
        app: wordpress
        tier: frontend
    spec:
      containers:
      - image: wordpress:4.8-apache
        name: wordpress
        env:
```

```
            - name: WORDPRESS_DB_HOST
              value: wordpress-mysql
            - name: WORDPRESS_DB_PASSWORD
              valueFrom:
                secretKeyRef:
                  name: mysql-root-password
                  key: password
          ports:
          - containerPort: 80
            name: wordpress
          volumeMounts:
          - name: wordpress-persistent-storage
            mountPath: /var/www/html
        volumes:
        - name: wordpress-persistent-storage
          persistentVolumeClaim:
            claimName: wp-pv-claim
```

Notice that the database host and password for accessing MySQL are passed to WordPress as environment variables. The value of the host is the name of the Service you created for MySQL above. This is all that is needed for the database connection to be routed to your MySQL instance. The value for the password is extracted from the Secret, as with the preceding configuration of the MySQL Deployment.

You'll also notice that WordPress exposes an HTTP interface at port 80, so let's create a service to expose the WordPress server. The source code (*https://oreil.ly/tEigE*) is in this book's repository:

```
apiVersion: v1
kind: Service
metadata:
  name: wordpress
  labels:
    app: wordpress
spec:
  ports:
    - port: 80
  selector:
    app: wordpress
    tier: frontend
  type: LoadBalancer
```

Note that the service is of type LoadBalancer, which should make it fairly simple to access from your local machine. Execute the command `kubectl get services` to get the LoadBalancer's IP address; then you can open the WordPress instance in your browser with the URL `http://`*<ip>*. Try logging in and creating some pages.

Accessing Services from Kubernetes Distributions

The exact details of accessing Services will depend on the Kubernetes distribution you're using and whether you're deploying apps in production, or just testing something quickly as we're doing here. If you're using a desktop Kubernetes distribution, you may wish to use a NodePort Service instead of LoadBalancer for simplicity. You can also consult the documentation for instructions on accessing services, such as those provided for minikube (*https://oreil.ly/euQLB*) or k3d (*https://k3d.io*).

When you're done experimenting with your WordPress instance, clean up the resources specified in the configuration files you've used in the local directory using the following command, including the data stored in your PersistentVolumeClaim:

```
kubectl delete -k ./
```

At this point, you might be feeling like this was relatively easy, despite our claim to be doing things "the hard way." And in a sense, you'd be right. So far, we've deployed a single Node of a simple database with sane defaults that we didn't have to spend much time configuring. Creating a single Node is, of course, fine if your application is going to store only a small amount of data. Is that all there is to deploying databases on Kubernetes? Of course not! Now that we've introduced a few of the basic Kubernetes resources via this simple database deployment, it's time to step up the complexity a bit. Let's get down to business!

Running Apache Cassandra on Kubernetes

In this section, we'll look at running a multinode database on Kubernetes using Apache Cassandra. Cassandra is a NoSQL database first developed at Facebook that became a top-level project of the Apache Software Foundation (ASF) in 2010. Cassandra is an operational database that provides a tabular data model, and its Cassandra Query Language (CQL) is similar to SQL.

Cassandra is a database designed for the cloud, as it scales horizontally by adding nodes, where each node is a peer. This decentralized design has been proven to have near-linear scalability. Cassandra supports high availability by storing multiple copies of data or *replicas*, including logic to distribute those replicas across multiple Datacenters and cloud regions. Cassandra is built on similar principles to Kubernetes in that it is designed to detect failures and continue operating while the system can recover to its intended state in the background. All of these features make Cassandra an excellent fit for deploying on Kubernetes.

To discuss how this deployment works, it's helpful to understand Cassandra's approach to distributing data from two perspectives: physical and logical. Borrowing some of the visuals from *Cassandra: The Definitive Guide* by Jeff Carpenter and Eben Hewitt (O'Reilly), you can see these perspectives in Figure 3-4. From a physical perspective, Cassandra nodes (not to be confused with Kubernetes Worker Nodes) are organized using *racks* and *Datacenters*. While the terms betray Cassandra's origin during a time when on-premise datacenters were the dominant way software was deployed in the mid-2000s, they can be flexibly applied. In cloud deployments, racks often represent an availability zone, while Datacenters represent a cloud region. However these are represented, the important part is that they represent physically separate failure domains. Cassandra uses awareness of this topology to make sure that it stores replicas in multiple physical locations to maximize the availability of data in the event of failures, whether those failures are a single machine, a rack of servers, an availability zone, or an entire region.

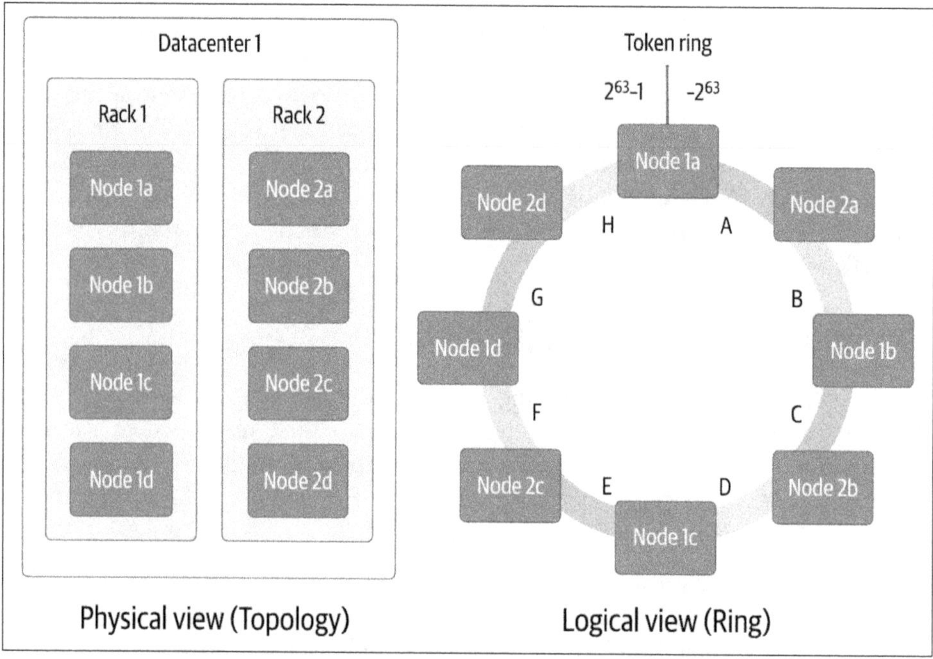

Figure 3-4. Physical and logical views of Cassandra's distributed architecture

The logical view helps us understand how Cassandra determines what data will be placed on each node. Each row of data in Cassandra is identified by a primary key, which consists of one or more partition-key columns used to allocate data across nodes, as well as optional clustering columns, which can be used to organize multiple rows of data within a partition for efficient access. Each write in Cassandra (and most reads) references a specific partition by providing the partition-key values, which Cassandra hashes together to produce a *token*, which is a value between -2^{63} and 2^{63-1}. Cassandra assigns each of its nodes responsibility for one or more token ranges (shown as a single range per node labeled with letters A–H in Figure 3-4 for simplicity). The physical topology is taken into account in the assignment of token ranges in order to ensure that copies of your data are distributed across racks and datacenters.

Now we're ready to consider how Cassandra maps onto Kubernetes. It's important to consider two implications of Cassandra's architecture:

Statefulness
: Each Cassandra node has state that it is responsible for maintaining. Cassandra has mechanisms for replacing a node by streaming data from other replicas to a new node, which means that a configuration in which nodes use local ephemeral storage is possible, at the cost of longer startup time. However, it's more common to configure each Cassandra node to use persistent storage. In either case, each Cassandra node needs to have its own unique PersistentVolumeClaim.

Identity
: Although each Cassandra node is the same in terms of its code, configuration, and functionality in a fully peer-to-peer architecture, the nodes are different in terms of their actual role. Each node has an identity in terms of where it fits in the topology of Datacenters and racks, and its assigned token ranges.

These requirements for identity and an association with a specific PersistentVolume-Claim present some challenges for Deployments and ReplicaSets that they weren't designed to handle. Starting early in Kubernetes' existence, there was an awareness that another mechanism was needed to manage stateful workloads like Cassandra.

StatefulSets

Kubernetes began providing a resource to manage stateful workloads with the alpha release of PetSets in the 1.3 release. This capability has matured over time and is now known as *StatefulSets* (see "Are Your Stateful Workloads Pets or Cattle?" on page 69). A StatefulSet has some similarities to a ReplicaSet in that it is responsible for managing the lifecycle of a set of Pods, but the way in which it goes about this management has some significant differences. To address the needs of stateful applications, like those of Cassandra that we've listed, StatefulSets demonstrate the following key properties:

Stable identity for Pods
: First, StatefulSets provide a stable name and network identity for Pods. Each Pod is assigned a name based on the name of the StatefulSet, plus an ordinal number. For example, a StatefulSet called `cassandra` would have Pods named `cassandra-0`, `cassandra-1`, `cassandra-2`, and so on, as shown in Figure 3-5.

These are stable names, so if a Pod is lost and needs replacing, the replacement will have the same name, even if it's started on a different Worker Node. A Pod's name is set as its hostname, so if you create a headless service, you can actually address individual Pods as needed—for example: `cassandra-1.cqlservice.default.svc.cluster.local`. The figure also includes a seed service, which we'll discuss in "Accessing Cassandra" on page 78.

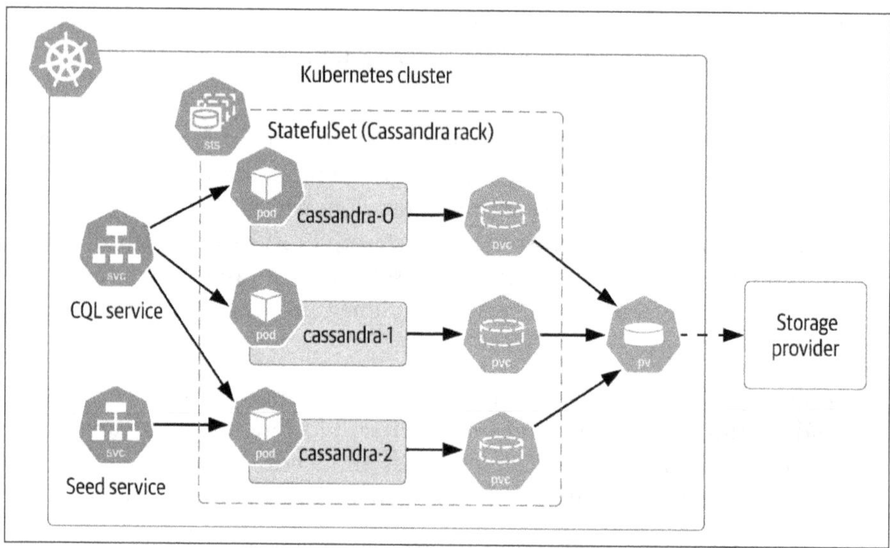

Figure 3-5. Sample Deployment of Cassandra on Kubernetes with StatefulSets

Ordered lifecycle management
: StatefulSets provide predictable behaviors for managing the lifecycle of Pods. When scaling up the number of Pods in a StatefulSet, new Pods are added according to the next available number, unlike ReplicaSets, where Pod name suffixes are based on universally unique identifiers (UUIDs). For example, expanding the StatefulSet in Figure 3-5 would cause the creation of Pods such as `cassandra-4` and `cassandra-5`. Scaling down has the reverse behavior, as the Pods with the highest ordinal numbers are deleted first. This predictability simplifies management—for example, by making it obvious which Nodes should be backed up before reducing cluster size.

Persistent disks
: Unlike ReplicaSets, which create a single PersistentVolumeClaim shared across all their Pods, StatefulSets create a PVC associated with each Pod. If a Pod in a StatefulSet is replaced, the replacement is bound to the PVC that has the state it is replacing. Replacement could occur because of a Pod failing or the scheduler choosing to run a Pod on another node in order to balance the load. For a database like Cassandra, this enables quick recovery when a Cassandra

node is lost, as the replacement node can recover its state immediately from the associated PersistentVolume rather than needing data streamed from other replicas.

Managing Data Replication

When planning your application deployment, make sure you consider whether data is being replicated at the data tier or the storage tier. A distributed database like Cassandra manages replication itself, storing copies of your data on multiple nodes according to the replication factor you request, typically three per Cassandra Datacenter. The storage provider you select may also offer replication. If the Kubernetes volume for each Cassandra Pod has three replicas, you could end up storing nine copies of your data. While this certainly promotes high data survivability, this might cost more than you intend.

Are Your Stateful Workloads Pets or Cattle?

PetSet might seem like an odd name for a Kubernetes resource, and it has since been replaced, but it provides interesting insights into the thought process of the Kubernetes community in supporting stateful workloads. The name PetSets is a reference to a discussion that has been active in the DevOps world since at least 2012. The original concept has been attributed to Bill Baker, formerly of Microsoft.

The basic idea is that there are two ways of handling servers: to treat them as pets that require care, feeding, and nurture, or to treat them as cattle, to which you don't develop an attachment or provide a lot of individual attention. If you're logging into a server regularly to perform maintenance activities, you're treating it as a pet.

The implication is that the life of an operations engineer can be greatly improved by being able to treat more elements as cattle than as pets. With the move to modern cloud native architectures, this concept has extended from servers to VMs and containers, and even to individual microservices. We now design systems to avoid single points of failure so they can survive the loss of individual components. Architectural approaches for high availability have made technologies like Kubernetes and Cassandra successful.

As you can see, naming a Kubernetes resource *PetSets* carried a lot of weight and perhaps even a bit of skepticism to running stateful workloads on Kubernetes at all. In the end, PetSets helped take the care and feeding out of managing state on Kubernetes but the name change to *StatefulSets* was appropriate. Taken together, capabilities like StatefulSets, the PersistentVolume subsystem introduced in Chapter 2, and operators (coming in Chapter 4) are bringing a level of automation that promises a day in the near future when we will manage data on Kubernetes like cattle.

Defining StatefulSets

Now that you've learned a bit about StatefulSets, let's examine how they can be used to run Cassandra. You'll configure a simple three-node cluster the "hard way" using a Kubernetes StatefulSet to represent a single Cassandra datacenter containing a single rack. The source code used in this section is located in the book's repository (*https://oreil.ly/yhg3w*). This approximates the configuration shown in Figure 3-5.

To set up a Cassandra cluster in Kubernetes, you'll first need a headless service. This service represents the CQL Service shown in Figure 3-5, providing an endpoint that clients can use to obtain addresses of all the Cassandra nodes in the StatefulSet. The source code (*https://oreil.ly/7nXxZ*) is in this book's repository:

```
apiVersion: v1
kind: Service
metadata:
  labels:
    app: cassandra
  name: cassandra
spec:
  clusterIP: None
  ports:
  - port: 9042
  selector:
    app: cassandra
```

You'll reference this service in the definition of a StatefulSet which will manage your Cassandra nodes. The source code (*https://oreil.ly/Or6Cr*) is located in this book's repository. Rather than applying this configuration immediately, you may want to wait until after we do some quick explanations. The configuration looks like this:

```
apiVersion: apps/v1
kind: StatefulSet
metadata:
  name: cassandra
  labels:
    app: cassandra
spec:
  serviceName: cassandra
  replicas: 3
  podManagementPolicy: OrderedReady
  updateStrategy:
    type: RollingUpdate
  selector:
    matchLabels:
      app: cassandra
  template:
    metadata:
      labels:
        app: cassandra
    spec:
```

```
        containers:
        - name: cassandra
          image: cassandra
          ports:
          - containerPort: 7000
            name: intra-node
          - containerPort: 7001
            name: tls-intra-node
          - containerPort: 7199
            name: jmx
          - containerPort: 9042
            name: cql
          lifecycle:
            preStop:
              exec:
                command:
                - /bin/sh
                - -c
                - nodetool drain
          env:
            - name: CASSANDRA_CLUSTER_NAME
              value: "cluster1"
            - name: CASSANDRA_DC
              value: "dc1"
            - name: CASSANDRA_RACK
              value: "rack1"
            - name: CASSANDRA_SEEDS
              value: "cassandra-0.cassandra.default.svc.cluster.local"
          volumeMounts:
          - name: cassandra-data
            mountPath: /var/lib/cassandra
  volumeClaimTemplates:
  - metadata:
      name: cassandra-data
    spec:
      accessModes: [ "ReadWriteOnce" ]
      storageClassName: standard
      resources:
        requests:
          storage: 1Gi
```

This is the most complex configuration we've looked at together so far, so let's simplify it by looking at one portion at a time:

StatefulSet metadata
: We've named and labeled this StatefulSet `cassandra`, and that same string will be used as the selector for Pods belonging to the StatefulSet.

Exposing StatefulSet Pods via a Service
: The `spec` of the StatefulSet starts with a reference to the headless service you created. While `serviceName` is not a required field according to the Kubernetes

specification, some Kubernetes distributions and tools such as Helm expect it to be populated and will generate warnings or errors if you fail to provide a value.

Number of replicas
: The `replicas` field identifies the number of Pods that should be available in this StatefulSet. The value provided (`3`) reflects the smallest Cassandra cluster that one might see in an actual production deployment, and most deployments are significantly larger, which is when Cassandra's ability to deliver high performance and availability at scale really begin to shine through.

Lifecycle management options
: The `podManagementPolicy` and `updateStrategy` describe how Kubernetes should manage the rollout of Pods when the cluster is scaling up or down, and how updates to the Pods in the StatefulSet should be managed, respectively. We'll examine the significance of these values in "StatefulSet lifecycle management" on page 74.

Pod specification
: The next section of the StatefulSet specification is the `template` used to create each Pod that is managed by the StatefulSet. The template has several subsections. First, under `metadata`, each Pod includes a label `cassandra` that identifies it as being part of the set.

This template includes a single item in the `containers` field, a specification for a Cassandra container. The `image` field selects the latest version of the official Cassandra Docker image (*https://oreil.ly/arYaE*), which at the time of writing is Cassandra 4.0. This is where we diverge with the Kubernetes StatefulSet tutorial referenced previously, which uses a custom Cassandra 3.11 image created specifically for that tutorial. Because the image we've chosen to use here is an official Docker image, you do not need to include registry or account information to reference it, and the name `cassandra` by itself is sufficient to identify the image that will be used.

Each Pod will expose `ports` for various interfaces: a `cql` port for client use, `intra-node` and `tls-intra-node` ports for communication between nodes in the Cassandra cluster, and a `jmx` port for management via the Java Management Extensions (JMX).

The Pod specification also includes instructions that help Kubernetes manage Pod lifecycles, including a `livenessProbe` and a `preStop` command. You'll learn how each of these are used next.

According to its documentation (*https://oreil.ly/WuTZo*), the image we're using has been constructed to provide two ways to customize Cassandra's configuration, which is stored in the *cassandra.yaml* file within the image. One way is to override the entire contents of the *cassandra.yaml* with a file that you provide. The second is to use environment variables that the image exposes to override a subset of Cassandra configuration options that are used most frequently. Setting these values in the `env` field causes the corresponding settings in the *cassandra.yaml* file to be updated:

`CASSANDRA_CLUSTER_NAME`
: This setting is used to distinguish which nodes belong to a cluster. Should a Cassandra node come into contact with nodes that don't match its cluster name, it will ignore them.

`CASSANDRA_DC` *and* `CASSANDRA_RACK`
: These settings identify the Datacenter and rack that each node will be a part of. This serves to highlight one interesting wrinkle in the way that StatefulSets expose a Pod specification. Since the template is applied to each Pod and container, there is no way to vary the configured Datacenter and rack names between Cassandra Pods. For this reason, it is typical to deploy Cassandra on Kubernetes using a StatefulSet per rack.

`CASSANDRA_SEEDS`
: These define well-known locations of nodes in a Cassandra cluster that new nodes can use to bootstrap themselves into the cluster. The best practice is to specify multiple seeds in case one of them happens to be down or offline when a new node is joining. However, for this initial example, it's enough to specify the initial Cassandra replica as a seed via the DNS name `cassandra-0.cassandra.default.svc.cluster.local`. We'll look at a more robust way of specifying seeds in Chapter 4 using a service, as implied by the Seed service shown in Figure 3-5.

The last item in the container specification is a `volumeMount` which requesting that a PersistentVolume be mounted at the */var/lib/cassandra* directory, which is where the Cassandra image is configured to store its datafiles. Since each Pod will need its own PersistentVolumeClaim, the name `cassandra-data` is a reference to a PersistentVolumeClaim template, which is defined next.

volumeClaimTemplates
: The final piece of the StatefulSet specification is the volumeClaimTemplates. The specification must include a template definition for each name referenced in one of the preceding container specifications. In this case, the `cassandra-data` template references the `standard` StorageClass we've been using in these examples. Kubernetes will use this template to create a PersistentVolumeClaim of the requested size of 1 GB whenever it spins up a new Pod within this StatefulSet.

StatefulSet lifecycle management

Now that we've had a chance to discuss the components of a StatefulSet specification, you can go ahead and apply the source:

```
kubectl apply -f cassandra-statefulset.yaml
```

As this gets applied, you can execute the following to watch as the StatefulSet spins up Cassandra Pods:

```
kubectl get pods -w
```

Let's describe some of the behavior you can observe from the output of this command. First, you'll see a single Pod, `cassandra-0`. Once that Pod has progressed to `Ready` status, you'll see the `cassandra-1` Pod, followed by `cassandra-2` after `cassandra-1` is ready. This behavior is specified by the selection of `podManagementPolicy` for the StatefulSet. Let's explore the available options and some of the other settings that help define how Pods in a StatefulSet are managed:

Pod management policies

The `podManagementPolicy` determines the timing for adding or removing Pods from a StatefulSet. The `OrderedReady` policy applied in our Cassandra example is the default. When this policy is in place and Pods are added, whether on initial creation or scaling up, Kubernetes expands the StatefulSet one Pod at a time. As each Pod is added, Kubernetes waits until the Pod reports a status of `Ready` before adding subsequent Pods. If the Pod specification contains a `readinessProbe`, Kubernetes executes the provided command iteratively to determine when the Pod is ready to receive traffic. When the probe completes successfully (i.e., with a zero return code), it moves on to creating the next Pod. For Cassandra, readiness is typically measured by the availability of the CQL port (9042), which means the node is able to respond to CQL queries.

Similarly, when a StatefulSet is removed or scaled down, Pods are removed one at a time. As a Pod is being removed, any provided `preStop` commands for its containers are executed to give them a chance to shut down gracefully. In our current example, the `nodetool drain` command is executed to help the Cassandra node exit the cluster cleanly, assigning responsibilities for its token range(s) to other nodes. as Kubernetes waits until a Pod has been completely terminated before removing the next Pod. The command specified in the `livenessProbe` is used to determine when the Pod is alive, and when it no longer completes without error, Kubernetes can proceed to removing the next Pod. See the Kubernetes documentation (*https://oreil.ly/SsIuO*) for more information on configuring readiness and liveness probes.

The other Pod management policy is `Parallel`. When this policy is in effect, Kubernetes launches or terminates multiple Pods at the same time in order to scale up or down. This has the effect of bringing your StatefulSet to the desired number of replicas more quickly, but it may also result in some stateful workloads taking longer to stabilize. For example, a database like Cassandra shuffles data between nodes when the cluster size changes in order to balance the load, and will tend to stabilize more quickly when nodes are added or removed one at a time.

With either policy, Kubernetes manages Pods according to the ordinal numbers, always adding Pods with the next unused ordinal numbers when scaling up, and deleting the Pods with the highest ordinal numbers when scaling down.

Update strategies

The `updateStrategy` describes how Pods in the StatefulSet will be updated if a change is made in the Pod template specification, such as changing a container image. The default strategy is `RollingUpdate`, as selected in this example. With the other option, `OnDelete`, you must manually delete Pods in order for the new Pod template to be applied.

In a rolling update, Kubernetes will delete and re-create each Pod in the StatefulSet, starting with the Pod with the largest ordinal number and working toward the smallest. Pods are updated one at a time, and you can specify a number of Pods, called a *partition*, in order to perform a phased rollout or canary. Note that if you discover a bad Pod configuration during a rollout, you'll need to update the Pod template specification to a known good state and then manually delete any Pods that were created using the bad specification. Since these Pods will not ever reach a `Ready` state, Kubernetes will not decide they are ready to replace with the good configuration.

Note that Kubernetes offers similar lifecycle management options for Deployments, ReplicaSets, and DaemonSets, including revision history.

We recommend getting more hands-on experience with managing StatefulSets in order to reinforce your knowledge. For example, you can monitor the creation of PersistentVolumeClaims as a StatefulSet scales up. Another thing to try: delete a StatefulSet and re-create it, verifying that the new Pods recover previously stored data from the original StatefulSet. For more ideas, you may find these guided tutorials helpful: "StatefulSet Basics" (*https://oreil.ly/dOovM*) from the Kubernetes documentation, and "StatefulSet: Run and Scale Stateful Applications Easily in Kubernetes" (*https://oreil.ly/TyJj2*) from the Kubernetes blog.

More Sophisticated Lifecycle Management for StatefulSets

One interesting set of opinions on additional lifecycle options for StatefulSets comes from OpenKruise, a CNCF Sandbox project, which provides an Advanced StatefulSet (*https://oreil.ly/xEqYf*). The Advanced StatefulSet adds capabilities including these:

- Parallel updates with a maximum number of unavailable Pods
- Rolling updates with an alternate order for replacement, based on a provided prioritization policy
- Updating Pods "in place" by restarting their containers according to an updated Pod template specification

This Kubernetes resource is also named `StatefulSet` to facilitate its use with minimal impact to your existing configurations. You just need to change the `apiVersion:` from `apps/v1` to `apps.kruise.io/v1beta1`.

StatefulSets are extremely useful for managing stateful workloads on Kubernetes, and that's not even counting some capabilities we didn't address, such as affinity and anti-affinity, managing resource requests for memory and CPU, and availability constraints such as PodDisruptionBudgets (PDBs). On the other hand, you might desire capabilities that StatefulSets don't provide, such as backup/restore of PersistentVolumes, or secure provisioning of access credentials. We'll discuss how to leverage or build these capabilities on top of Kubernetes in Chapter 4 and beyond.

StatefulSets: Past, Present, and Future

With Maciej Szulik, Red Hat Engineer and Kubernetes SIG Apps member

The Kubernetes Special Interest Group for Applications (SIG Apps) (*https://oreil.ly/uec9G*) is responsible for development of the controllers that help manage application workloads on Kubernetes. This includes batch workloads like Jobs and CronJobs, other stateless workloads like Deployments and ReplicaSets, and of course StatefulSets for stateful workloads.

The StatefulSet controller has a slightly different way of working from the other controllers. When you're thinking about Deployments, or Jobs, the controller just has to manage Pods. You don't have to worry about the underlying data, either because that's handled by PersistenVolumes or you're OK with just throwing each Pod's data away when you destroy and re-create it. But that behavior is not acceptable when you're trying to run a database, or any kind of workload that requires the state to be persisted between runs. This results in significant additional complexity in the StatefulSet controller. The main challenge in writing and maturing Kubernetes controllers has been handling edge cases. StatefulSets are similar in this regard, but it's even more urgent for StatefulSets to handle the failure cases correctly, so that we don't lose data.

We've encountered some interesting use cases for StatefulSets, and some users would like to change boundaries that have been set in the core implementation. For example, we've had pull requests submitted to change the way StatefulSets handle Pods during an update. In the original implementation, the StatefulSet controllers update Pods one at a time, and if something breaks during the rollout, the entire rollout is paused, and the StatefulSet requires manual intervention to make sure that data is not corrupted or lost. Some users would like the StatefulSet controller to ignore issues where a Pod is stuck in a pending state or cannot run, and just restart these Pods. However, the thing to remember with StatefulSets is that protecting the underlying data is the most important priority. We could end up making the suggested change in order to allow faster updates in parallel for development environments where data protection is less of a concern, but require opting in with a feature flag.

Another frequently requested feature is the ability to auto-delete the PersistentVolumeClaims of a StatefulSet when the StatefulSet is deleted. The original behavior is to preserve the PVCs, again as a data protection mechanism, but a Kubernetes Enhancement Proposal (KEP) for auto-deletion (*https://oreil.ly/XO0fv*) was included as an alpha feature for the Kubernetes 1.23 release.

Even though some significant differences exist in the way StatefulSets manage Pods versus other controllers, we are working to make the behaviors more similar across the controllers as much as possible. One example is the addition of a `minReadySeconds` setting (*https://oreil.ly/6Qwsz*) in the Pod template, which allows you to say, "I'd like this application to be unavailable for a little bit of extra time before sending traffic to it." This is helpful for some stateful workloads that need a bit more time to initialize themselves (e.g., to warm up caches) and brings StatefulSets in line with other controllers.

Another example is the work that is in progress to unify status reporting across all of the application controllers. Currently, if you're building any kind of higher-level orchestration or management tools, you need to have different behavior to handle the status of StatefulSets, Deployments, DaemonSets, and so on, because each was written by a different author. Each author had a different requirement for what should be in the status, how the resource should express information about whether it's available, or whether it's in a rolling update, or it's unavailable, or whatever is happening with it. DaemonSets are especially different in how they report status.

Another feature in progress allows you to set a `maxUnavailable` number of Pods (*https://oreil.ly/44jlT*) for a StatefulSet. This number would be applied during the initial rollout of a StatefulSet and allow the number of replicas to be scaled up more quickly. This is another feature that brings StatefulSets into greater alignment with the way the other controllers work. The best way to understand the work that is in progress from the SIG Apps team, is to look at Kubernetes open issues (*https://oreil.ly/Mmlp2*) that are labeled `sig/apps`.

It can be difficult to build StatefulSets as a capability that will meet the needs of all stateful workloads; we've tried to build them in such a way as to consistently handle the most common requirements. We could obviously add support for more and more edge cases, but this tends to make the functionality significantly more complicated for users to grasp. There will always be users who are dissatisfied because their use case is not covered, and there's always a balance of how much we can put in without affecting both functionality and performance.

In most cases where users need more specific behaviors (for example, to handle edge cases), it's because they're trying to manage a complex application like Postgres or Cassandra. That's where there's a great argument for creating your own controllers and even operators to deal with those specific cases. Even though it might sound super scary, it's really not that difficult to write your own controller. You can start reasonably quickly and get a basic controller up and running in a couple of days by using simple examples including the sample controller (*https://oreil.ly/NB8wk*), which is part of the Kubernetes codebase and maintained by the project. *Programming Kubernetes* by Michael Hausenblas and Stefan Schimanski (O'Reilly), also has a chapter on writing controllers. Don't assume you're stuck with the behavior that comes out of the box. Kubernetes is meant to be open and extensible; whether it's networking, controllers, CSI, plug-ins, or something else you need to customize Kubernetes, you should go for it!

Accessing Cassandra

Once you have applied the configurations we've listed, you can use Cassandra's CQL shell `cqlsh` to execute CQL commands. If you happen to be a Cassandra user and have a copy of `cqlsh` installed on your local machine, you could access Cassandra as a client application would, using the CQL Service associated with the StatefulSet. However, since each Cassandra node contains `cqlsh` as well, this gives us a chance to demonstrate a different way to interact with infrastructure in Kubernetes, by connecting directly to an individual Pod in a StatefulSet:

```
kubectl exec -it cassandra-0 -- cqlsh
```

This should bring up the `cqlsh` prompt, and you can then explore the contents of Cassandra's built-in tables using `DESCRIBE KEYSPACES` and then `USE` to select a particular keyspace and run `DESCRIBE TABLES`. Many Cassandra tutorials available online can guide you through more examples of creating your own tables, inserting and querying data, and more. When you're done experimenting with `cqlsh`, you can type `exit` to exit the shell.

Removing a StatefulSet is the same as any other Kubernetes resource—you can delete it by name, for example:

```
kubectl delete sts cassandra
```

You could also delete the StatefulSet referencing the file used to create it:

```
kubectl delete -f cassandra-statefulset.yaml
```

When you delete a StatefulSet with a policy of `Retain` as in this example, the PersistentVolumeClaims it creates are not deleted. If you re-create the StatefulSet, it will bind to the same PVCs and reuse the existing data. When you no longer need the claims, you'll need to delete them manually. The final cleanup from this exercise you'll want to perform is to delete the CQL Service:

```
kubectl delete service cassandra
```

What About DaemonSets?

If you're familiar with the resources Kubernetes offers for managing workloads, you may have noticed that we haven't yet mentioned *DaemonSets* (*https://oreil.ly/487vb*). These allow you to request that a Pod be run on each Worker Node in a Kubernetes cluster, as shown in Figure 3-6.

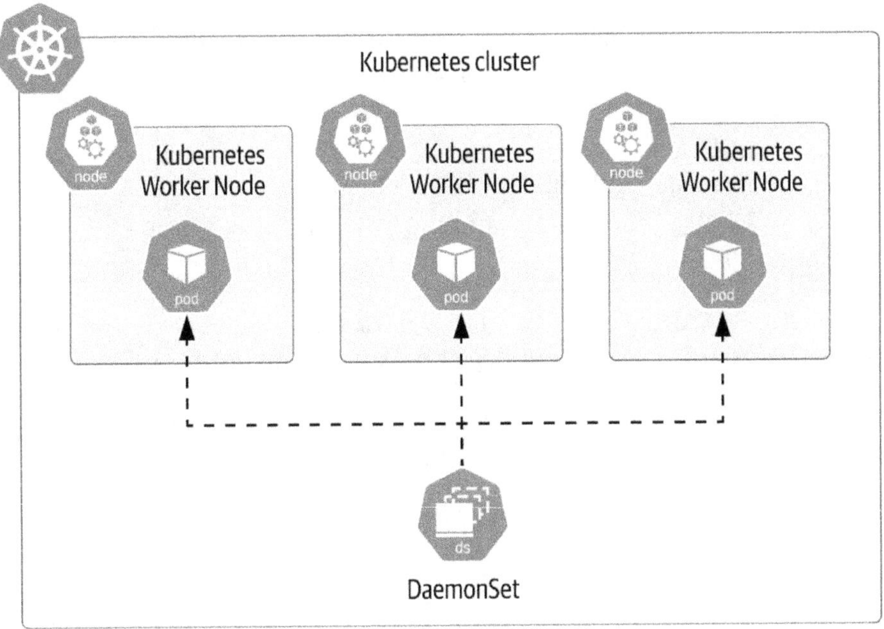

Figure 3-6. DaemonSets run a single Pod on selected Worker Nodes

Instead of specifying a number of replicas, a DaemonSet scales up or down as Worker Nodes are added or removed from the cluster. By default, a DaemonSet will run your Pod on each Worker Node, but you can use taints and tolerations (*https://*

oreil.ly/kLM6t) to override this behavior (for example, limiting some Worker Nodes). DaemonSets support rolling updates in a similar way to StatefulSets.

On the surface, DaemonSets might sound useful for running databases or other data infrastructure, but this does not seem to be a widespread practice. Instead, DaemonSets are most frequently used for functionality related to Worker Nodes and their relationship to the underlying Kubernetes provider. For example, many of the CSI implementations that we saw in Chapter 2 use DaemonSets to run a storage driver on each Worker Node. Another common usage is to run Pods that perform monitoring tasks on Worker Nodes, such as log and metrics collectors.

Summary

In this chapter, you've learned how to deploy both single-node and multinode distributed databases on Kubernetes with hands-on examples. Along the way, you've gained familiarity with Kubernetes resources such as Deployments, ReplicaSets, StatefulSets, and DaemonSets, and learned about the best use cases for each:

- Use Deployments/ReplicaSets to manage stateless workloads or simple stateful workloads like single-node databases or caches that can rely on ephemeral storage.
- Use StatefulSets to manage stateful workloads that involve multiple nodes and require association with specific storage locations.
- Use DaemonSets to manage workloads that leverage specific Worker Node functionality.

You've also learned the limits of what each of these resources can provide. Now that you've gained experience in deploying stateful workloads on Kubernetes, the next step is to learn how to automate the so-called "day two" operations involved in keeping this data infrastructure running.

CHAPTER 4

Automating Database Deployment on Kubernetes with Helm

In the previous chapter, you learned how to deploy both single-node and multinode databases on Kubernetes by hand, creating one element at a time. We did things the "hard way" on purpose to help maximize your understanding of using Kubernetes primitives to set up the compute, network, and storage resources that a database requires. Of course, this doesn't represent the experience of running databases in production on Kubernetes, for a couple of reasons.

First, teams typically don't deploy databases by hand, one YAML file at a time. That can get pretty tedious. And even combining the configurations into a single file could start to get pretty complicated, especially for more sophisticated deployments. Consider the increase in the amount of configuration required in Chapter 3 for Cassandra as a multinode database compared with the single-node MySQL deployment. This won't scale for large enterprises.

Second, while deploying a database is great, what about keeping it running over time? You need your data infrastructure to remain reliable and performant over the long haul, and data infrastructure is known for requiring a lot of care and feeding. Put another way, the task of running a system is often divided into "day one" (the joyous day when you deploy an application to production) and "day two" (every day after the first, when you need to operate and evolve your application while maintaining high availability).

These considerations around database deployment and operations mirror the larger industry trends toward DevOps, an approach in which development teams take a more active role in supporting applications in production. DevOps practices include the use of automation tools for CI/CD of applications, shortening the amount of time it takes for code to get from a developer's desktop into production.

In this chapter, we'll look at tools that help standardize the deployment of databases and other applications. These tools take an infrastructure as code (IaC) approach, allowing you to represent software installation and configuration options in a format that can be executed automatically, reducing the overall amount of configuration code you have to write. We'll also emphasize data infrastructure operations in these next two chapters and carry that theme throughout the remainder of the book.

Deploying Applications with Helm Charts

Let's start by taking a look at a tool that helps you manage the complexity of managing configurations: Helm (*https://helm.sh*). This package manager for Kubernetes is open source and a CNCF graduated project (*https://oreil.ly/cDjD3*). The concept of a package manager is a common one across multiple programming languages, such as `pip` for Python, the Node Package Manager (NPM) for JavaScript, and Ruby's Gems feature. Package managers for specific operating systems also exist, such as Apt for Linux, or Homebrew for macOS. As shown in Figure 4-1, the essential elements of a package manager system are the packages, the registries where the packages are stored, and the package manager application (or *client*), which helps the chart developers register charts and allows chart users to locate, install, and update packages on their local systems.

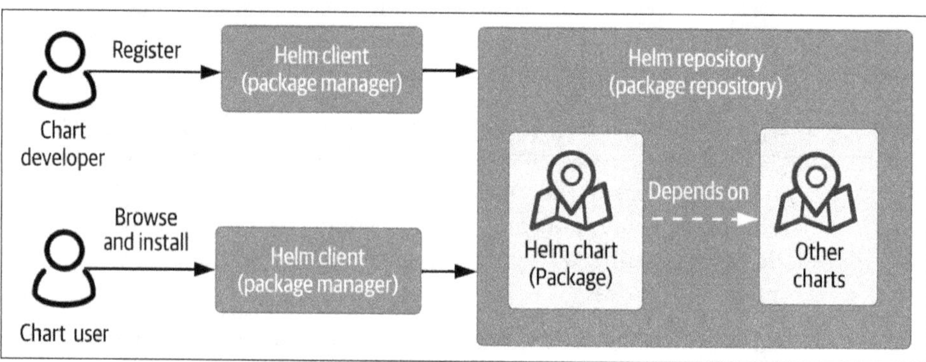

Figure 4-1. Helm, a package manager for Kubernetes

Helm extends the package management concept to Kubernetes, with some interesting differences. If you've worked with one of the package managers listed previously, you'll be familiar with the idea that a package consists of a binary (executable code) as well as metadata describing the binary, such as its functionality, API, and installation instructions. In Helm, the packages are called *charts*. Charts describe how to build a Kubernetes application piece by piece by using the Kubernetes resources for compute, networking, and storage introduced in previous chapters, such as Pods, Services, and PersistentVolumeClaims. For compute workloads, the descriptions point to container images that reside in public or private container registries.

Helm allows charts to reference other charts as dependencies, which provides a great way to compose applications by creating assemblies of charts. For example, you could define an application such as the WordPress/MySQL example from the previous chapter by defining a chart for your WordPress deployment that referenced a chart defining a MySQL deployment that you wish to reuse. Or, you might even find a Helm chart that defines an entire WordPress application including the database.

Kubernetes Environment Prerequisites

The examples in this chapter assume you have access to a Kubernetes cluster with a couple of characteristics:

- The cluster should have at least three Worker Nodes, in order to demonstrate mechanisms Kubernetes provides to allow you to request Pods to be spread across a cluster. You can create a simple cluster on your desktop by using an open source distribution called kind. See the kind quick start guide for instructions on installing kind and creating a multinode cluster (*https://oreil.ly/8nOHi*). The code for this example also contains a configuration file you may find useful to create a simple three-node kind cluster.
- You will also need a StorageClass that supports dynamic provisioning. You may wish to follow the instructions in "StorageClasses" on page 39 for installing a simple StorageClass and provisioner that expose local storage.

Using Helm to Deploy MySQL

To make things a bit more concrete, let's use Helm to deploy the databases you worked with in Chapter 3. First, if it's not already on your system, you'll need to install Helm by using the documentation (*https://oreil.ly/tUPWL*) on the Helm website. Next, add the Bitnami Helm repository:

```
helm repo add bitnami https://charts.bitnami.com/bitnami
```

The Bitnami Helm repository contains a variety of Helm charts to help you deploy infrastructure such as databases, analytics engines, and log management systems, as well as applications including ecommerce, customer relationship management (CRM), and you guessed it: WordPress. You can find the source code for the charts in the Bitnami Charts repository on GitHub (*https://oreil.ly/lmcml*). The *README* for this repo provides helpful instructions for using the charts in various Kubernetes distributions.

Now, let's use the Helm chart provided in the `bitnami` repository to deploy MySQL. In Helm's terminology, each deployment is known as a *release*. The simplest possible release that you could create using this chart would look something like this:

```
# don't execute me yet!
helm install mysql bitnami/mysql
```

If you execute this command, it will create a release called `mysql` using the Bitnami MySQL Helm chart with its default settings. As a result, you'd have a single MySQL node. Since you've already deployed a single node of MySQL manually in Chapter 3, let's do something a bit more interesting this time and create a MySQL cluster. To do this, you'll create a *values.yaml* file with contents like the following, or you can reuse the sample (*https://oreil.ly/tsnuT*) provided in the source code:

```
architecture: replication
secondary:
  replicaCount: 2
```

The settings in this *values.yaml* file let Helm know that you want to use options in the Bitnami MySQL Helm chart to deploy MySQL in a replicated architecture in which there is a primary node and two secondary nodes.

MySQL Helm Chart Configuration Options

If you examine the default *values.yaml* file (*https://oreil.ly/SGsN5*) provided with the Bitnami MySQL Helm chart, you'll see quite a few options available beyond the simple selections shown here. The configurable values include the following:

- Images to pull and their locations
- The Kubernetes StorageClass that will be used to generate PersistentVolumes
- Security credentials for user and administrator accounts
- MySQL configuration settings for primary and secondary replicas
- Number of secondary replicas to create
- Details of liveness, readiness probes
- Affinity and anti-affinity settings
- Managing high availability of the database using Pod disruption budgets

Many of these concepts you'll be familiar with already, and others like affinity and Pod disruption budgets are covered later in the book.

Once you've created the *values.yaml* file, you can start the cluster using this command:

```
helm install mysql bitnami/mysql -f values.yaml
```

After running the command, you'll see the status of the install from Helm, plus instructions that are provided with the chart under `NOTES`:

```
NAME: mysql
LAST DEPLOYED: Thu Oct 21 20:39:19 2021
NAMESPACE: default
STATUS: deployed
REVISION: 1
TEST SUITE: None
NOTES:
...
```

We've omitted the notes here since they are a bit lengthy. They describe suggested commands for monitoring the status as MySQL initializes, how clients and administrators can connect to the database, how to upgrade the database, and more.

Use Namespaces to Help Isolate Resources

Since we did not specify a Namespace, the Helm release has been installed in the default Kubernetes Namespace unless you've separately configured a Namespace in your kubeconfig (*https://oreil.ly/C2vOM*). If you want to install a Helm release in its own Namespace in order to work with its resources more effectively, you could run something like the following:

```
helm install mysql bitnami/mysql \
  --namespace mysql --create-namespace
```

This creates a Namespace called `mysql` and installs the `mysql` release inside it.

To obtain information about the Helm releases you've created, use the `helm list` command, which produces output such as this (formatted for readability):

```
helm list
NAME   NAMESPACE  REVISION  UPDATED
mysql  default    1         2021-10-21 20:39:19

STATUS    CHART        APP VERSION
deployed  mysql-8.8.8  8.0.26
```

If you haven't installed the release in its own Namespace, it's still simple to see the compute resources that Helm has created on your behalf by running `kubectl get all`, because they have all been labeled with the name of your release. It may take several minutes for all the resources to initialize, but when complete, it will look something like this:

```
kubectl get all
NAME                        READY   STATUS    RESTARTS   AGE
pod/mysql-primary-0         1/1     Running   0          3h40m
pod/mysql-secondary-0       1/1     Running   0          3h40m
pod/mysql-secondary-1       1/1     Running   0          3h38m

NAME                                TYPE        CLUSTER-IP      EXTERNAL-IP  PORT
service/mysql-primary               ClusterIP   10.96.107.156   <none>       ...
service/mysql-primary-headless      ClusterIP   None            <none>       ...
service/mysql-secondary             ClusterIP   10.96.250.52    <none>       ...
service/mysql-secondary-headless    ClusterIP   None            <none>       ...

NAME                              READY   AGE
statefulset.apps/mysql-primary     1/1     3h40m
statefulset.apps/mysql-secondary   2/2     3h40m
```

As you can see, Helm has created two StatefulSets, one for primary replicas and one for secondary replicas. The `mysql-primary` StatefulSet is managing a single MySQL Pod containing a primary replica, while the `mysql-secondary` StatefulSet is managing two MySQL Pods containing secondary replicas. See if you can determine which Kubernetes Worker Node each MySQL replica is running on by using the `kubectl describe pod` command.

From the preceding output, you'll also notice two Services created for each StatefulSet, one a headless service and another that has a dedicated IP address. Since `kubectl get all` tells you about only compute resources and services, you might also be wondering about the storage resources. To check on these, run the `kubectl get pv` command. Assuming you have a StorageClass installed that supports dynamic provisioning, you should see PersistentVolumes that are bound to PersistentVolumeClaims named `data-mysql-primary-0`, `data-mysql-secondary-0`, and `data-mysql-secondary-1`.

In addition to the resources we've discussed, installing the chart has also resulted in the creation of a few additional resources that we'll explore next.

Namespaces and Kubernetes Resource Scope

If you have chosen to install your Helm release in a Namespace, you'll need to specify the Namespace on most of your `kubectl get` commands in order to see the created resources. The exception is `kubectl get pv`, because PersistentVolumes are one of the Kubernetes resources that are not Namespaced; that is, they can be used by Pods in any Namespace. To learn more about which Kubernetes resources in your cluster are Namespaced and which are not, run the command `kubectl api-resources`.

How Helm Works

Did you wonder what happened when you executed the `helm install` command with a provided values file? To understand what's going on, let's take a look at the contents of a Helm chart, as shown in Figure 4-2. As we discuss these contents, it will also be helpful to look at the source code (*https://oreil.ly/xQbvb*) of the MySQL Helm chart you just installed.

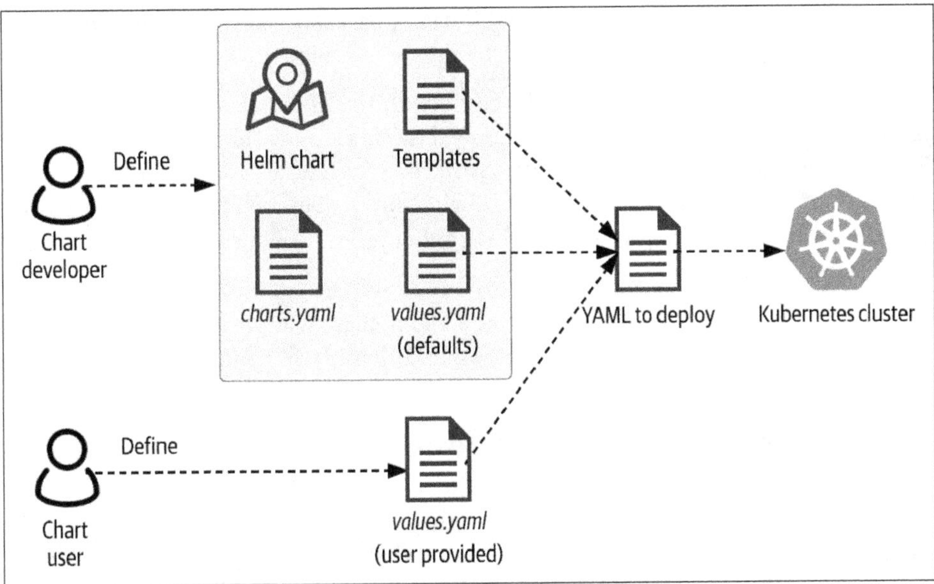

Figure 4-2. Customizing a Helm release using a values.yaml file

Looking at the contents of a Helm chart, you'll notice the following:

README file (https://oreil.ly/i7XBa)
: This explains how to use the chart. These instructions are provided along with the chart in registries.

Chart.yaml file (https://oreil.ly/zZb2Y)
: This contains metadata about the chart such as its name, publisher, version, keywords, and any dependencies on other charts. These properties are useful when searching Helm registries to find charts.

values.yaml file (https://oreil.ly/mhfhZ)
: This lists out the configurable values supported by the chart and their default values. These files typically contain a good number of comments that explain the available options. For the Bitnami MySQL Helm chart, a lot of options are available, as we've noted.

templates directory (https://oreil.ly/F21Lg)
: This contains Go templates (*https://oreil.ly/diTnu*) that define the chart. The templates include a *Notes.txt* (*https://oreil.ly/v0aky*) file used to generate the output you saw previously after executing the `helm install` command, and one or more YAML files that describe a pattern for a Kubernetes resource. These YAML files may be organized in subdirectories (for example, the template (*https://oreil.ly/iKedl*) that defines a StatefulSet for MySQL primary replicas). Finally, a *_helpers.tpl* file describes how to use the templates. Some of the templates may be used multiple times or not at all, depending on the selected configuration values.

When you execute the `helm install` command, the Helm client makes sure it has an up-to-date copy of the chart you've named by checking with the source repository. Then it uses the template to generate YAML configuration code, overriding default values from the chart's *values.yaml* file with any values you've provided. It then uses the `kubectl` command to apply this configuration to your currently configured Kubernetes cluster.

If you'd like to see the configuration that a Helm chart will produce before applying it, you can use the handy `template` command. It supports the same syntax as the `install` command:

```
helm template mysql bitnami/mysql -f values.yaml
```

Running this command will produce quite a bit of output, so you may want to redirect it to a file (append `> values-template.yaml` to the command) so you can take a longer look. Alternatively, you can look at the copy (*https://oreil.ly/DhEtc*) we have saved in the source code repository.

You'll notice that several types of resources are created, as summarized in Figure 4-3. Many of the resources shown have been discussed, including the StatefulSets for managing the primary and secondary replicas, each with its own service (the chart also creates headless services that are not shown in the figure). Each Pod has its own PersistentVolumeClaim that is mapped to a unique PersistentVolume.

Figure 4-3 also includes resource types we haven't discussed previously. Notice first that each StatefulSet has an associated ConfigMap that is used to provide a common set of configuration settings to its Pods. Next, notice the Secret named `mysql`, which stores passwords needed for accessing various interfaces exposed by the database nodes. Finally, a ServiceAccount resource is applied to every Pod created by this Helm release.

Let's focus on some interesting aspects of this deployment, including the usage of labels, ServiceAccounts, Secrets, and ConfigMaps.

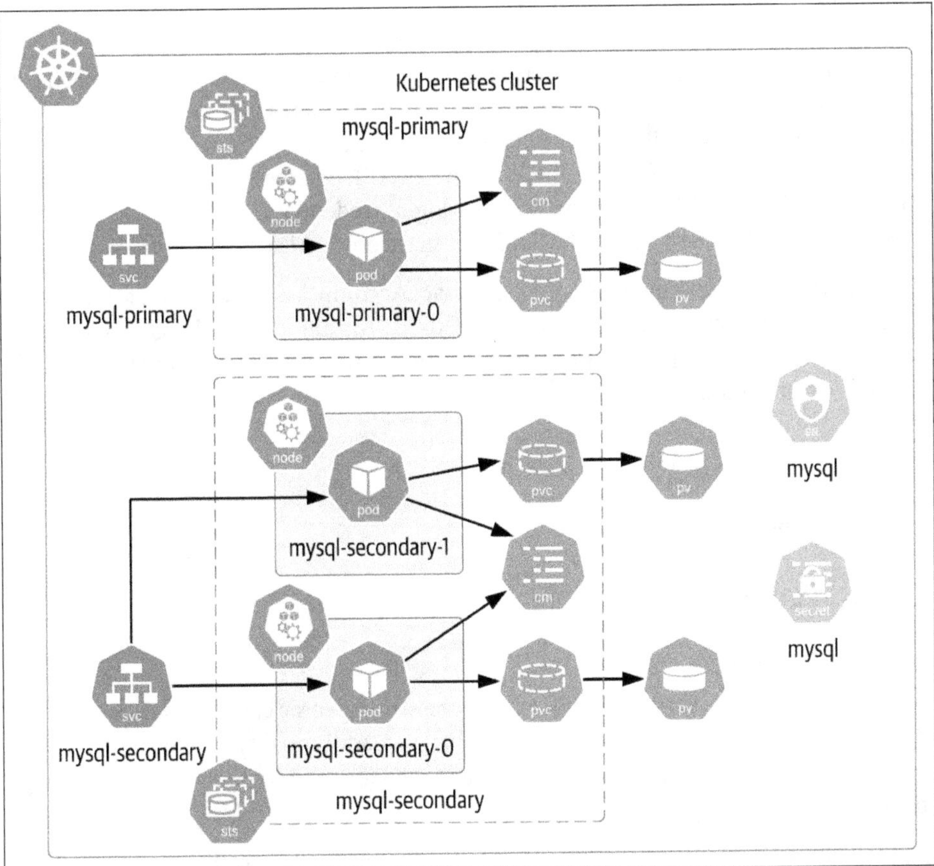

Figure 4-3. Deploying MySQL using the Bitnami Helm chart

Labels

If you look through the output from the `helm template`, you'll notice that the resources have a common set of labels:

```
labels:
  app.kubernetes.io/name: mysql
  helm.sh/chart: mysql-8.8.8
  app.kubernetes.io/instance: mysql
  app.kubernetes.io/managed-by: Helm
```

These labels help identify the resources as being part of the `mysql` application and indicate that they are managed by Helm using a specific chart version. The labels are useful for selecting resources, which is often useful in defining configurations for other resources.

ServiceAccounts

Kubernetes clusters make a distinction between human users and applications for access control purposes. A ServiceAccount is a Kubernetes resource that represents an application and what it is allowed to access. For example, a ServiceAccount may be given access to some portions of the Kubernetes API, or access to one or more secrets containing privileged information such as login credentials. This latter capability is used in your Helm installation of MySQL to share credentials between Pods.

Every Pod created in Kubernetes has a ServiceAccount assigned to it. If you do not specify one, the default ServiceAccount is used. Installing the MySQL Helm chart creates a ServiceAccount called `mysql`. You can see the specification for this resource in the generated template:

```
apiVersion: v1
kind: ServiceAccount
metadata:
  name: mysql
  namespace: default
  labels: ...
  annotations:
secrets:
  - name: mysql
```

As you can see, this ServiceAccount has access to a Secret called `mysql`, which we'll discuss shortly. A ServiceAccount can also have an additional type of Secret known as an `imagePullSecret`. These Secrets are used when an application needs to use images from a private registry.

By default, a ServiceAccount does not have any access to the Kubernetes API. To give this ServiceAccount the access it needs, the MySQL Helm chart creates a Role specifying the Kubernetes resources and operations, and a RoleBinding to associate the ServiceAccount to the Role. We'll discuss ServiceAccounts and role-based access in Chapter 5.

Secrets

As you learned in Chapter 2, a Secret provides secure access to information you need to keep private. Your `mysql` Helm release contains a Secret called `mysql` containing login credentials for the MySQL instances themselves:

```
apiVersion: v1
kind: Secret
metadata:
  name: mysql
  namespace: default
  labels: ...
type: Opaque
data:
```

```
mysql-root-password: "VzhyNEhIcmdTTQ=="
mysql-password: "R2ZtNkFHNDhpOQ=="
mysql-replication-password: "bDBiTWVzVmVORA=="
```

The three passwords represent different types of access: the `mysql-root-password` provides administrative access to the MySQL node, while the `mysql-replication-password` is used for nodes to communicate for the purposes of data replication between nodes. The `mysql-password` is used by client applications to access the database to write and read data.

ConfigMaps

The Bitnami MySQL Helm chart creates Kubernetes ConfigMap resources to represent the configuration settings used for Pods that run the MySQL primary and secondary replica nodes. ConfigMaps store configuration data as key-value pairs. For example, the ConfigMap created by the Helm chart for the primary replicas looks like this:

```
apiVersion: v1
kind: ConfigMap
metadata:
  name: mysql-primary
  namespace: default
  labels: ...
data:
  my.cnf: |-

    [mysqld]
    default_authentication_plugin=mysql_native_password
    ...
```

In this case, the key is the name `my.cnf`, which represents a filename, and the value is a multiline set of configuration settings that represent the contents of a configuration file (which we've abbreviated here). Next, look at the definition of the StatefulSet for the primary replicas. Notice that the contents of the ConfigMap are mounted as a read-only file inside each template, according to the Pod specification for the StatefulSet (again, we've omitted some detail to focus on key areas):

```
apiVersion: apps/v1
kind: StatefulSet
metadata:
  name: mysql-primary
  namespace: default
  labels: ...
spec:
  replicas: 1
  selector:
    matchLabels: ...
  serviceName: mysql-primary
  template:
```

```
metadata:
  annotations: ...
  labels: ...
spec:
  ...
  serviceAccountName: mysql
  containers:
    - name: mysql
      image: docker.io/bitnami/mysql:8.0.26-debian-10-r60
      volumeMounts:
        - name: data
          mountPath: /bitnami/mysql
        - name: config
          mountPath: /opt/bitnami/mysql/conf/my.cnf
          subPath: my.cnf
  volumes:
    - name: config
      configMap:
        name: mysql-primary
```

Mounting the ConfigMap as a volume in a container results in the creation of a read-only file in the mount directory that is named according to the key and has the value as its content. For our example, mounting the ConfigMap in the Pod's `mysql` container results in the creation of the file */opt/bitnami/mysql/conf/my.cnf*.

This is one of several ways that ConfigMaps can be used in Kubernetes applications:

- As described in the Kubernetes documentation (*https://oreil.ly/yoEYv*), you could choose to store configuration data in more granular key-value pairs, which also makes it easier to access individual values in your application.
- You can also reference individual key-value pairs as environment variables you pass to a container.
- Finally, applications can access ConfigMap contents via the Kubernetes API.

More Configuration Options

Now that you have a Helm release with a working MySQL cluster, you can point an application to it, such as WordPress. Why not try seeing if you can adapt the WordPress deployment from Chapter 3 to point to the MySQL cluster you've created here?

For further learning, you could also compare your resulting configuration with that produced by the Bitnami WordPress Helm chart, which uses MariaDB instead of MySQL but is otherwise quite similar.

Updating Helm Charts

If you're running a Helm release in a production environment, chances are you're going to need to maintain it over time. You might want to update a Helm release for various reasons:

- A new version of a chart is available.
- A new version of an image used by your application is available.
- You want to change the selected options.

To check for a new version of a chart, execute the `helm repo update` command. Running this command with no options looks for updates in all of the chart repositories you have configured for your Helm client:

```
helm repo update
Hang tight while we grab the latest from your chart repositories...
...Successfully got an update from the "bitnami" chart repository
Update Complete. ⎈Happy Helming!⎈
```

Next, you'll want to make any desired updates to your configured values. If you're upgrading to a new version of a chart, make sure to check the release notes and documentation of the configurable values. It's a good idea to test out an upgrade before applying it. The `--dry-run` option allows you to do this, producing similar values to the `helm template` command:

```
helm upgrade mysql bitnami/mysql -f values.yaml --dry-run
```

Using an Overlay Configuration File

One useful option you could use for the upgrade is to specify values you wish to override in a new configuration file, and apply both the new and old, something like this:

```
helm upgrade mysql bitnami/mysql \
  -f values.yaml -f new-values.yaml
```

Configuration files are applied in the order they appear on the command line, so if you use this approach, make sure your overridden values file appears after your original values file.

Once you've applied the upgrade, Helm sets about its work, updating only those resources in the release that are affected by your configuration changes. If you've specified changes to the Pod template for a StatefulSet, the Pods will be restarted according to the update policy specified for the StatefulSet, as we discussed in "StatefulSet lifecycle management" on page 74.

Uninstalling Helm Charts

When you are finished using your Helm release, you can uninstall it by name:

```
helm uninstall mysql
```

Note that Helm does not remove any of the PersistentVolumeClaims or PersistentVolumes that were created for this Helm chart, following the behavior of StatefulSets discussed in Chapter 3.

> ### Additional Deployment Tools: Kustomize and Skaffold
>
> In addition to Helm, other tools in the Kubernetes ecosystem are available to help you manage the configuration and deployment of applications, such as Kustomize and Skaffold.
>
> *Kustomize* is a configuration management tool for Kubernetes. Unlike a package manager, Kustomize does not provide a registry; instead, its focus is helping you manage Kubernetes configuration YAML files for different environments. Kustomize uses a template-based approach in which you create snippets of configuration code called *overlays* that are intended to override sections of a base YAML file. These overlays are typically intended for different environments such as development, test, and production, or for isolating configurations specific to different Kubernetes providers, with a similar effect to a Helm *values.yaml* file. The sections to be overridden are identified by selectors such as Kubernetes labels or annotations. You provide a *kustomization.yaml* file to describe the mapping of templates to their selectors. Kustomize works best when the YAML file you want to customize is well structured and uses labels or annotations.
>
> *Skaffold* is a tool that automates application deployment in your development environment. You can execute Skaffold imperatively from the command line, or as a daemon that watches for code changes to build artifacts such as container images. When it detects a relevant change, the daemon automatically performs actions according to the workflow you define in a *skaffold.yaml* file. The workflow can include actions such as building and tagging images, updating Helm charts or regular Kubernetes configuration files, and deploying your app using `kubectl`, Helm, or Kustomize.

Using Helm to Deploy Apache Cassandra

Now let's switch gears and look at deploying Apache Cassandra by using Helm. In this section, you'll use another chart provided by Bitnami, so there's no need to add another repository. You can find the implementation of this chart on GitHub (*https://oreil.ly/WzvXp*). Helm provides a quick way to see the metadata about this chart:

```
helm show chart bitnami/cassandra
```

After reviewing the metadata, you'll also want to learn about the configurable values. You can examine the *values.yaml* file (*https://oreil.ly/z69Z7*) in the GitHub repo, or use another option on the `show` command:

```
helm show values bitnami/cassandra
```

The list of options for this chart is shorter than the list for the MySQL chart, because Cassandra doesn't have the concept of primary and secondary replicas. However, you'll certainly see similar options for images, StorageClasses, security, liveness and readiness probes, and so on. Some configuration options are unique to Cassandra, such as those having to do with JVM settings and seed nodes (as discussed in Chapter 3).

One interesting feature of this chart is the ability to export metrics from Cassandra nodes. If you set `metrics.enabled=true`, the chart will inject a sidecar container into each Cassandra Pod that exposes a port that can be scraped by Prometheus. Other values under `metrics` configure what metrics are exported, the collection frequency, and more. While we won't use this feature here, metrics reporting is a key part of managing data infrastructure we'll cover in Chapter 6.

For a simple three-node Cassandra configuration, you could set the replica count to 3 and set other configuration values to their defaults. However, since you're overriding only a single configuration value, this is a good time to take advantage of Helm's support for setting values on the command line, instead of providing a *values.yaml* file:

```
helm install cassandra bitnami/cassandra --set replicaCount=3
```

As discussed previously, you can use the `helm template` command to check the configuration before installing it, or look at the file we've saved on GitHub. However, since you've already created the release, you can also use this command:

```
helm get manifest cassandra
```

Looking through the resources in the YAML, you'll see that a similar set of infrastructure has been established, as shown in Figure 4-4.

The configuration includes the following:

- A ServiceAccount referencing a Secret, which contains the password for the `cassandra` administrator account.
- A single StatefulSet, with a headless Service used to reference its Pods. The Pods are spread evenly across the available Kubernetes Worker Nodes, which we'll discuss in the next section. The Service exposes Cassandra ports used for intra-node communication (`7000`, with `7001` used for secure communication via TLS), administration via JMX (`7199`), and client access via CQL (`9042`).

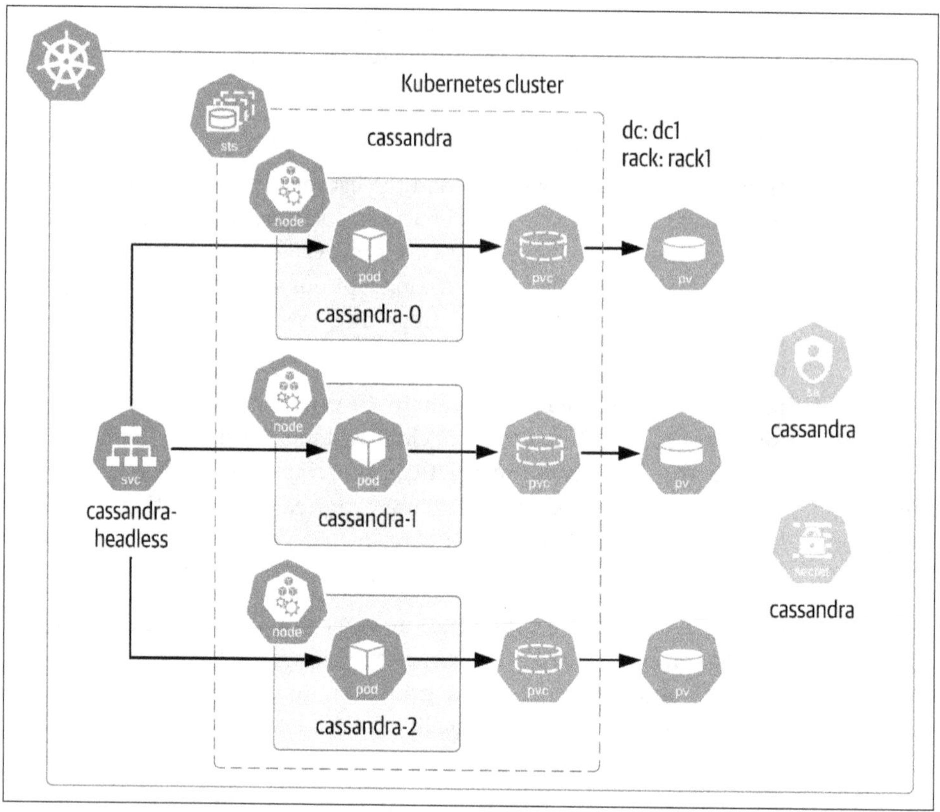

Figure 4-4. Deploying Apache Cassandra using the Bitnami Helm chart

This configuration represents a simple Cassandra topology, with all three nodes in a single Datacenter and rack. This simple topology reflects one of the limitations of this chart—it does not provide the ability to create a Cassandra cluster consisting of multiple Datacenters and racks. To create a more complex deployment, you'd have to install multiple Helm releases, using the same `clusterName` (in this case, you're using the default name `cassandra`), but a different Datacenter and rack per deployment. You'd also need to obtain the IP address of a couple of nodes in the first Datacenter to use as `additionalSeeds` when configuring the releases for the other racks.

Affinity and Anti-Affinity

As shown in Figure 4-4, the Cassandra nodes are spread evenly across the Worker Nodes in your cluster. To verify this in your own Cassandra release, you could run something like the following:

```
kubectl describe pods | grep "^Name:" -A 3
Name:          cassandra-0
Namespace:     default
Priority:      0
Node:          kind-worker/172.20.0.7
--
Name:          cassandra-1
Namespace:     default
Priority:      0
Node:          kind-worker2/172.20.0.6
--
Name:            cassandra-2
Namespace:       default
Priority:        0
Node:            kind-worker3/172.20.0.5
```

As you can see, each Cassandra node is running on a different Worker Node. If your Kubernetes cluster has at least three Worker Nodes and no other workloads, you'll likely observe similar behavior. While it is true that this even allocation could happen naturally in a cluster that has an even load across Worker Nodes, this is probably not the case in your production environment. However, to promote maximum availability of your data, we want to try to honor the intent of Cassandra's architecture to run nodes on different machines in order to promote high availability.

To help guarantee this isolation, the Bitnami Helm chart uses Kubernetes's affinity capabilities, specifically anti-affinity. If you examine the generated configuration for the Cassandra StatefulSet, you'll see the following:

```
apiVersion: apps/v1
kind: StatefulSet
metadata:
  name: cassandra
  namespace: default
  labels: ...
spec:
  ...
  template:
    metadata:
      labels: ...
    spec:
      ...
      affinity:
        podAffinity:

        podAntiAffinity:
          preferredDuringSchedulingIgnoredDuringExecution:
            - podAffinityTerm:
                labelSelector:
                  matchLabels:
                    app.kubernetes.io/name: cassandra
                    app.kubernetes.io/instance: cassandra
```

```
                namespaces:
                  - "default"
                topologyKey: kubernetes.io/hostname
              weight: 1
        nodeAffinity:
```

As shown here, the Pod template specification lists three possible types of affinity, with only the `podAntiAffinity` being defined. What do these concepts mean?

Pod affinity
: The preference that a Pod is scheduled onto a node where another specific Pod is running. For example, Pod affinity could be used to colocate a web server with its cache.

Pod anti-affinity
: The opposite of Pod affinity—that is, a preference that a Pod not be scheduled on a node where another identified Pod is running. This is the constraint used in this example, as we'll discuss shortly.

Node affinity
: A preference that a Pod be run on a node with specific characteristics.

Each type of affinity can be expressed as either hard or soft constraints. These are known as `requiredDuringSchedulingIgnoredDuringExecution` and `preferredDuringSchedulingIgnoredDuringExecution`. The first constraint specifies rules that must be met before a Pod is scheduled on a node, while the second specifies a preference that the scheduler will attempt to meet but may relax if necessary in order to schedule the Pod.

`IgnoredDuringExcecution` implies that the constraints apply only when the Pods are first scheduled. In the future, new `RequiredDuringExecution` options will be added called `requiredDuringSchedulingRequiredDuringExecution` and `requiredDuringSchedulingRequiredDuringExecution`. These will ask Kubernetes to evict Pods (that is, move them to another node) that no longer meet the criteria—for example, by a change in their labels.

Looking at the preceding example, the Pod template specification for the Cassandra StatefulSet specifies an anti-affinity rule using the labels that are applied to each Cassandra Pod. The net effect is that Kubernetes will try to spread the Pods across the available Worker Nodes.

Those are the highlights of looking at the Bitnami Helm chart for Cassandra. To clean things up, uninstall the Cassandra release:

```
helm uninstall cassandra
```

If you don't want to work with Bitnami Helm charts any longer, you can also remove the repository from your Helm client:

```
helm repo remove bitnami
```

More Kubernetes Scheduling Constraints

Kubernetes supports additional mechanisms for providing hints to its scheduler about Pod placement. One of the simplest is NodeSelectors (*https://oreil.ly/05hSU*), which is very similar to node affinity, but with a less expressive syntax that can match on one or more labels by using AND logic. Since you may or may not have the required privileges to attach labels to Worker Nodes in your cluster, Pod affinity is often a better option. Taints and tolerations (*https://oreil.ly/fbkTB*) are another mechanism that can be used to configure Worker Nodes to repel specific Pods from being scheduled on those nodes.

In general, you want to be careful to understand all of the constraints you're putting on the Kubernetes scheduler from various workloads so as not to overly constrain its ability to place Pods. See the Kubernetes documentation for more information on scheduling constraints (*https://oreil.ly/aUWsi*). We'll also look at how Kubernetes allows you to plug in different schedulers in "Alternative Schedulers for Kubernetes" on page 233.

Helm, CI/CD, and Operations

Helm is a powerful tool focused on one primary task: deploying complex applications to Kubernetes clusters. To get the most benefit from Helm, you'll want to consider how it fits into your larger CI/CD toolset:

- Automation servers such as Jenkins (*https://www.jenkins.io*) automatically build, test, and deploy software according to scripts known as *jobs*. These jobs are typically run based on predefined triggers, such as a commit to a source repository. Helm charts can be referenced in jobs to install an application under test and its supporting infrastructure in a Kubernetes cluster.
- IaC automation tools such as Terraform (*https://www.terraform.io*) allow you to define templates and scripts that describe how to create infrastructure in a variety of cloud environments. For example, you could write a Terraform script that automates the creation of a new VPC within a specific cloud provider and the creation of a new Kubernetes cluster within that VPC. The script could then use Helm to install applications within the Kubernetes cluster.

While overlaps certainly occur in the capabilities these tools provide, you'll want to consider the strengths and limitations of each as you construct your toolset. For this reason, we want to make sure to note that Helm has limitations when it comes to managing the operations of applications that it deploys. To get a good picture of the challenges involved, we spoke to a practitioner who has built assemblies of Helm charts to manage a complex database deployment. This discussion begins to introduce concepts like Kubernetes Custom Resource Definitions (CRDs) and the operator pattern, both of which we'll cover in depth in Chapter 5.

Pushing Helm to the Limit

With John Sanda, Software Engineer, DataStax

K8ssandra is a distribution of Apache Cassandra on Kubernetes built from multiple open source components, including a Cassandra operator, known as Cass Operator (*https://oreil.ly/jlAZi*); operational tools for managing anti-entropy repair, known as Reaper (*https://oreil.ly/SOXkK*); and backups, known as Medusa (*https://oreil.ly/LLjBD*). K8ssandra also includes the Prometheus-Grafana stack for metrics collection and reporting.

From the start, we used Helm to help manage the installation and configuration of these components. Helm enabled us to quickly bootstrap the project and attract developers in the Cassandra community who didn't necessarily have much Kubernetes expertise and experience. Many of these folks found it easy to grasp a package management tool and installer like Helm.

As the project grew, we began to run into some limitations with Helm. While it was pretty straightforward to get the installation of K8ssandra clusters working correctly, we encountered more issues when it came to upgrading and managing clusters:

Writing complex logic
: Helm has good support for control flow, with loops and `if` statements. However, when you start getting multiple levels deep, it's harder to read and reason through the code, and indentation becomes an issue. In particular, we found that peer-reviewing changes to Helm charts became quite difficult.

Reuse and extensibility
: Helm variables are limited to the scope of the template where you declare them, which meant we had to re-create the same variables in multiple templates. This prevented us from following the "don't repeat yourself" (DRY) principle (*https://oreil.ly/71DTv*), which we found to be a source of defects.

  Similarly, Helm has a big library of helper template functions, but that library doesn't cover every use case, and there is no interface to define your own functions. You can define your own custom templates, which allow for a lot of reuse, but those are not a replacement for functions.

Project structure and inheritance
: We also ran into difficulties as we tried to implement an umbrella chart design pattern, which is a best practice for Helm. We were able to create a top-level K8ssandra Helm chart with subcharts for Cassandra and Prometheus but ran into problems with variable scoping when attempting to create additional subcharts. Our intent was to define authentication settings in the top-level chart and push them down to subcharts, but this functionality is not supported by the Helm inheritance model.

Custom resource management
: Helm can create Kubernetes custom resources, but it doesn't manage them. This was a deliberate design choice that the Helm developers made for Helm 3. Because the definition of a custom resource is cluster-wide, it can get confusing if multiple Helm installs are trying to work off of different versions of a CRD. This presented us with some difficulties in managing updates to resources like a Cassandra Datacenter within Helm. The workaround was to implement custom Kubernetes jobs labeled as pre-upgrade hooks that Helm would execute on an upgrade. At some point, writing these jobs began to feel like we were writing an operator.

Multicluster deployments
: While we've been able to work around these Helm challenges in many cases, the next major feature on our roadmap was implementing Cassandra clusters that spanned multiple Kubernetes clusters. We realized that even without the intricacies of the network configuration, this was going to be a step beyond what we could implement effectively using Helm.

In the end, we realized that we were trying to make Helm do too much. It's easy to get into a situation where you learn how to use the hammer and everything looks like a nail, but what you really need is a screwdriver. However, we don't see Helm and operators as mutually exclusive. These are complementary approaches, and we need to use each one in terms of its strengths. We continue to use Helm to perform basic installation actions including installing operators and setting up the administrator service account used by Cassandra and other components; these are the sort of actions that package managers like Helm do best.

Note: this sidebar was adapted from the post "We Pushed Helm to the Limit, Then Built a Kubernetes Operator" (*https://oreil.ly/2xyX0*).

As John Sanda notes in his commentary, Helm is a powerful tool for scripting the deployment of applications consisting of multiple Kubernetes resources, but can be less effective at managing more complex operational tasks. As you'll see in the chapters to come, a common pattern used for data infrastructure and other complex applications is to use a Helm chart to deploy an operator, which can then in turn manage both the deployment and lifecycle of the application.

Summary

In this chapter, you've learned how a package management tool like Helm can help you manage the deployment of applications on Kubernetes, including your database infrastructure. Along the way, you've also learned how to use some additional Kubernetes resources like ServiceAccounts, Secrets, and ConfigMaps. Now it's time to round out our discussion of running databases on Kubernetes. In the next chapter, we'll take a deeper dive into managing database operations on Kubernetes by using the operator pattern.

CHAPTER 5

Automating Database Management on Kubernetes with Operators

In this chapter, we'll continue our exploration of running databases on Kubernetes, but shift our focus from installation to operations. It's not enough just to know how the elements of a database application map onto the primitives provided by Kubernetes for an initial deployment. You also need to know how to maintain that infrastructure over time in order to support your business-critical applications. In this chapter, we'll take a look at the Kubernetes approach to operations so that you can keep databases running effectively.

Operations for databases and other data infrastructure consist of a common list of "day two" tasks, including the following:

- Scaling capacity up and down, including reallocating workload across resized clusters
- Monitoring database health and replacing failed (or failing) instances
- Performing routine maintenance tasks, such as repair operations in Apache Cassandra
- Updating and patching software
- Maintaining secure access keys and other credentials that may expire over time
- Performing backups, and using them to restore data in disaster recovery

While the details of how these tasks are performed may vary among technologies, the common concern is how we can use automation to reduce the workload on human operators and enable us to operate infrastructure at larger and larger scales. How can we incorporate the knowledge that human operators have built up around these tasks? While traditional cloud operations have used scripting tools that run externally to your cloud infrastructure, a more cloud native approach is to have this database control logic running directly within your Kubernetes clusters. The question we'll explore in this chapter is: what is the Kubernetes-friendly way to represent this control logic?

Extending the Kubernetes Control Plane

The good news is that the designers of Kubernetes aren't surprised at all by this question. In fact, the Kubernetes control plane and API are designed to be extensible. Kelsey Hightower and others have referred to Kubernetes as "a platform for building platforms" (*https://oreil.ly/pFRDO*).

Kubernetes provides multiple extension points, primarily related to its control plane. Figure 5-1 includes the Kubernetes core components (*https://oreil.ly/hsxFY*) such as the API server, scheduler, Kubelet and `kubectl`, along with indications of the extension points (*https://oreil.ly/UXbo0*) they support.

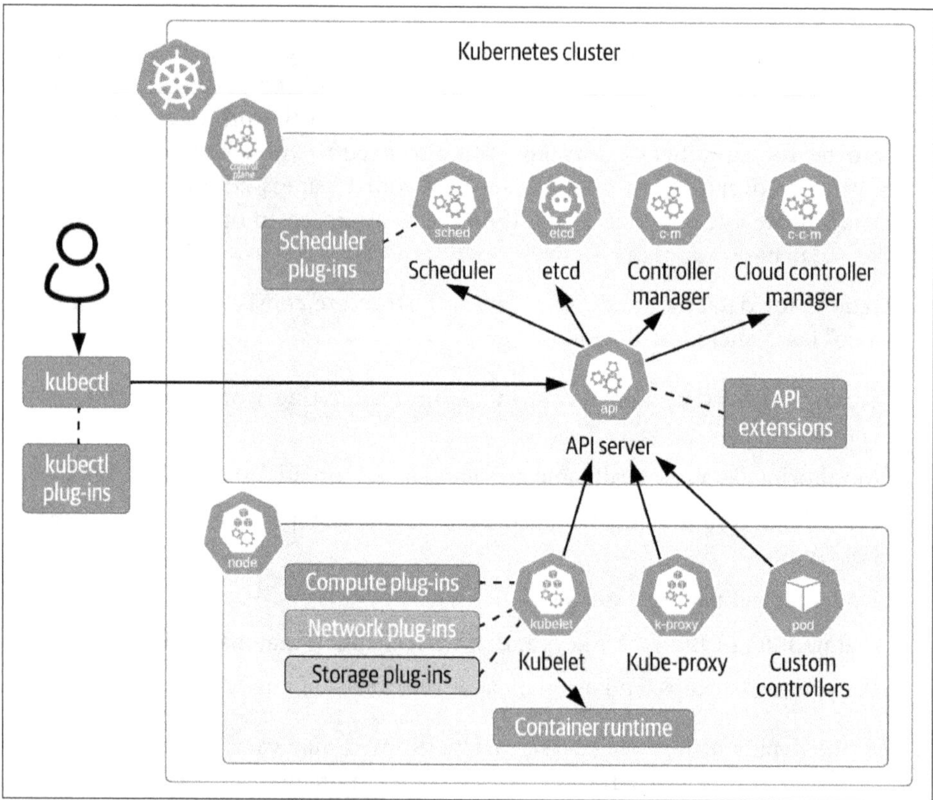

Figure 5-1. Kubernetes control plane and extension points

Now let's examine the details of extending the Kubernetes control plane, starting with components on your local client and those within the Kubernetes cluster. Many of these extension points are relevant to databases and data infrastructure.

Extending Kubernetes Clients

The `kubectl` command-line tool is the primary interface for many users for interacting with Kubernetes. You can extend `kubectl` with plug-ins (*https://oreil.ly/kbh4u*) that you download and make available on your system's `PATH`, or use Krew (*https://krew.dev*), a package manager that maintains a list of `kubectl` plug-ins (*https://oreil.ly/iw93T*). Plug-ins perform tasks such as bulk actions across multiple resources (*https://oreil.ly/AllQX*) or even multiple clusters (*https://oreil.ly/3Bsj2*), or assessing the state of a cluster and making security (*https://oreil.ly/BWbpn*) or cost (*https://oreil.ly/Exxjp*) recommendations. More particularly to our focus in this chapter, several plug-ins are available to manage operators and custom resources.

Extending Kubernetes Control Plane Components

The core of the Kubernetes control plane consists of several control plane components (*https://oreil.ly/ZnxfB*) including the API server, scheduler, controller manager, Cloud Controller Manager, and etcd. While these components can be run on any node within a Kubernetes cluster, they are typically assigned to a dedicated node which does not run any user application Pods. The components are as follows:

API server
: This is the primary interface for external and internal clients of a Kubernetes cluster. It exposes RESTful interfaces via an HTTP API. The API server performs a coordination role, routing requests from clients to other components to implement imperative and declarative instructions. The API server supports two types of extensions: custom resources and API aggregation. CRDs allow you to add new types of resources and are managed through `kubectl` without further extension. API aggregation allows you to extend the Kubernetes API with additional REST endpoints, which the API server will delegate to a separate API server provided as a plug-in. Custom resources are the more commonly used extension mechanism and will be a major focus throughout the remainder of the book.

Scheduler
: This determines the assignment of Pods to Worker Nodes, considering factors including the load on each Worker Node, as well as affinity rules, taints, and tolerations (as discussed in Chapter 4). The scheduler can be extended with plug-ins that override default behavior at multiple points in its decision-making process. For example, a *scheduling plug-in* could filter out nodes for a specific type of Pod or set the relative priority of nodes by assigning a score. *Binding plug-ins* can customize the logic that prepares a node for running a scheduled

Pod, such as mounting a network volume the Pod needs. Data infrastructure such as Apache Spark that relies on running a lot of short-lived tasks may benefit from this ability to exercise more fine-grained control over scheduling decisions, as we'll discuss in "Alternative Schedulers for Kubernetes" on page 233.

etcd
: This distributed key-value store is used by the API server to persist information about the cluster's configuration and status. As resources are added, removed and updated, the API server updates the metadata in etcd accordingly, so that if the API server crashes or needs to be restarted, it can easily recover its state. As a strongly consistent data store that supports high availability, etcd is frequently used by other data infrastructure that runs on Kubernetes, as we'll see frequently throughout the book.

Controller manager and Cloud Controller Manager
: The controller manager and Cloud Controller Manager incorporate multiple control loops called *controllers*. These managers contain multiple logically separate controllers compiled into a single executable to simplify the ability of Kubernetes to manage itself. The controller manager includes controllers which manage built-in resource types such as Pods, StatefulSets, and more. The Cloud Controller Manager includes controllers that differ among Kubernetes providers to enable the management of platform-specific resources such as load balancers or VMs.

Extending Kubernetes Worker Node Components

Some elements of the Kubernetes control plane run on every node in the cluster. These Worker Node components (*https://oreil.ly/KmmkS*) include the Kubelet, kube-proxy, and container runtime:

Kubelet
: This manages the Pods running on a node assigned by the scheduler, including the containers that run within a Pod. The Kubelet restarts containers when needed, provides access to container logs, and more.

Compute, network, and storage plug-ins
: The Kubelet can be extended with plug-ins that take advantage of unique compute, networking, and storage capabilities provided by the underlying environment on which it is running. Compute plug-ins include container runtimes, and device plug-ins (*https://oreil.ly/cdqrT*) that expose specialized hardware capabilities such as GPUs or field-programmable gate arrays (FPGA). Network plug-ins (*https://oreil.ly/aMdKH*), including those that comply with the Container Network Interface (CNI), can provide features beyond Kubernetes built-in networking, such as bandwidth management or network policy management. We've

previously discussed storage plug-ins in "Kubernetes Storage Architecture" on page 42, including those that conform to the CSI.

Kube-proxy
: This maintains network routing for the Pods running on a Worker Node so that they can communicate with other Pods running inside your Kubernetes cluster, or clients and services running outside of the cluster. Kube-proxy is part of the implementation of Kubernetes Services, providing the mapping of virtual IPs to individual Pods on a Worker Node.

Container runtime
: The Kubelet uses the container runtime to execute containers on the worker's operating system. Supported container runtimes for Linux include containerd (*https://oreil.ly/6ylhH*) and CRI-O (*https://oreil.ly/8fk2x*). Docker (*https://oreil.ly/col9R*) runtime support was deprecated in Kubernetes 1.20 and removed entirely in 1.24.

Custom controllers and operators
: These controllers are responsible for managing applications installed on a Kubernetes cluster using custom resources. Although these controllers are extensions to the Kubernetes control plane, they can run on any Worker Node.

The Operator Pattern

With this context, we're ready to examine one of the most common patterns for extending Kubernetes: the *operator pattern*. This pattern combines custom resources with controllers that operate on those resources. Let's examine each of these concepts in more detail to see how they apply to data infrastructure, and then you'll be ready to dig into an example operator for MySQL.

Controllers

The concept of a controller originates from the domain of electronics and electrical engineering, in which a controller is a device that operates in a continuous loop. On each iteration through the loop, the device receives an input signal, compares that with a set point value, and generates an output signal intended to produce a change in the environment that can be detected in future inputs. A simple example is a thermostat, which powers up your air conditioner or heater when the temperature in a space is too high or low.

A *Kubernetes controller* implements a similar control loop (*https://oreil.ly/LKefh*), consisting of the following steps:

1. Reading the current state of resources
2. Making changes to the state of resources
3. Updating the status of resources
4. Repeat

These steps are embodied both by Kubernetes built-in controllers that run in the controller manager and Cloud Controller Manager, as well as *custom controllers* that are provided to run applications on top of Kubernetes. Let's look at some examples of what these steps might entail for controllers that manage data infrastructure:

Reading the current state of resources
: A controller tracks the state of one or more resource types, including built-in resources like Pods, PersistentVolumes, and Services, as well as custom resources (which we discuss in the next section). Controllers are driven asynchronously by notification from the API server. The API server sends *watch events* (*https://oreil.ly/UvOJY*) to controllers to notify them of changes in state for resource types for which they have registered interest, such as the creation or deletion of a resource, or an event occurring on the resource.

  For data infrastructure, these changes could include a change in the number of requested replicas for a cluster, or a notification that a Pod containing a database replica has died. Because many such updates could be occurring in a large cluster, controllers frequently use caching.

Making changes to the state of resources
: This is the core business logic of a controller—comparing the state of resources to their desired state and executing actions to change the state to the desired state. In the Kubernetes API, the current state is captured in `.status` fields of resources, and the desired state is expressed in terms of the `.spec` field. The changes could include invocations of the Kubernetes API to modify other resources, administrative actions on the application being managed, or even interactions outside of the Kubernetes cluster.

  For example, consider a controller managing a distributed database with multiple replicas. When the database controller receives a notification that the desired number of replicas has increased, the controller could scale an underlying Deployment or StatefulSet that it is using to manage replicas. Later, when receiving a notification that a Pod has been created to host a new replica, the controller could initiate an action on one or more replicas in order to rebalance the workload across those replicas.

Updating the status of resources

In the final step of the control loop, the controller updates the `.status` fields of the resource using the API server, which in turn updates that state in etcd. You've viewed the status of resources like Pods and PersistentVolumes in previous chapters using the `kubectl get` and `kubectl describe` commands. For example, the status of a Pod includes its overall state (`Pending`, `Running`, `Succeeded`, `Failed`, etc.), the most recent time at which various conditions were noted (`PodScheduled`, `ContainersReady`, `Initialized`, `Ready`), as well as the state of each of its containers (`Waiting`, `Running`, `Terminated`). Custom resources can define their own status fields as well. For example, a custom resource representing a cluster might have status values reflecting the overall availability of the cluster and its current topology.

Events

A controller can also produce *events* via the Kubernetes API for consumption by human operators or other applications. These are distinct from the watcher events described previously that the Kubernetes API uses to notify controllers of changes, which are not exposed to other clients.

Writing a Custom Controller

While you may not ever need to write your own controller, being familiar with the concepts involved is helpful. *Programming Kubernetes* is a great resource for those interested in digging deeper.

The controller-runtime project (*https://oreil.ly/VjP9w*) provides a common set of libraries to help aid the process of writing controllers, including registering for notifications from the API server, caching resource status, implementing reconciliation loops, and more. Controller-runtime libraries are implemented in the Go programming language, so it's no surprise that most controllers are implemented in Go.

Go (*https://go.dev*) was first developed at Google in 2007 and used in many cloud native applications including Borg, the predecessor to Kubernetes, and then in Kubernetes itself. Go is a strongly typed, compiled language (as opposed to interpreted languages like Java and JavaScript) with a high value on usability and developer productivity (in reaction to the higher learning curve of C/C++).

If you've ever misconfigured a Pod specification and observed a `CrashLoopBackOff` status, you may have encountered events. Using the `kubectl describe pod` command, you can observe events such as a container being started and failing, followed by a backoff period, followed by the container restarting. Events expire from the API server in an hour, but common Kubernetes monitoring tools provide capabilities to track them. Controllers can also create events for custom resources.

Custom Resources

As we've discussed, controllers can operate on built-in Kubernetes resources as well as custom resources (*https://oreil.ly/62uQj*). We've briefly mentioned this concept, but let's take this opportunity to define what custom resources are and how they extend the Kubernetes API.

Fundamentally, a *custom resource* is a piece of configuration data that Kubernetes recognizes as part of its API. While a custom resource is similar to a ConfigMap, it has a structure similar to built-in resources: metadata, specification, and status. The specific attributes of a particular custom resource type are defined in a CRD. A CRD is itself a Kubernetes resource that is used to describe a custom resource.

In this book, we've been discussing how Kubernetes enables you to move beyond managing VMs and containers to managing virtual datacenters. CRDs provide the flexibility that helps make this a practical reality. Instead of being limited to the resources that Kubernetes provides off the shelf, you can create additional abstractions to extend Kubernetes for your own purposes. This is a critical component in a fast-moving ecosystem.

Let's see what you can learn about CRDs from the command line. Use `kubectl api-resources` to get a listing of all of the resources defined in your cluster:

```
kubectl api-resources
NAME                SHORTNAMES  APIVERSION  NAMESPACED  KIND
bindings                        v1          true        Binding
componentstatuses   cs          v1          false       ComponentStatus
configmaps          cm          v1          true        ConfigMap
...
```

As you look through the output, you'll see many resource types introduced in previous chapters, along with their short names: StorageClass (`sc`), PersistentVolumes (`pv`), Pods (`po`), StatefulSets (`sts`), and so on. The API versions provide some clues as to the origins of each resource type. For example, resources with version `v1` are core Kubernetes resources. Other versions such as `apps/v1`, `networking.k8s.io/v1`, or `storage.k8s.io/v1` indicate resources that are defined by various Kubernetes SIGs.

Depending on the configuration of the Kubernetes cluster you are using, you may have some CRDs defined already. If any are present, they will appear in the output of the `kubectl api-resources` command. They'll stand out by their API version, which will typically include a path other than `k8s.io`.

Since a CRD is itself a Kubernetes resource, you can also use the command `kubectl get crd` to list custom resources installed in your Kubernetes cluster. For example, after installing the Vitess Operator referenced in the following section, you would see several CRDs:

```
kubectl get crd
NAME                                   CREATED AT
etcdlockservers.planetscale.com        2021-11-21T22:06:04Z
vitessbackups.planetscale.com          2021-11-21T22:06:04Z
vitessbackupstorages.planetscale.com   2021-11-21T22:06:04Z
vitesscells.planetscale.com            2021-11-21T22:06:04Z
vitessclusters.planetscale.com         2021-11-21T22:06:04Z
vitesskeyspaces.planetscale.com        2021-11-21T22:06:04Z
vitessshards.planetscale.com           2021-11-21T22:06:04Z
```

We'll introduce the usage of these custom resources later, but for now let's focus on the mechanics of a specific CRD to see how it extends Kubernetes. You use the `kubectl describe crd` or `kubectl get crd` commands to see the definition of a CRD. For example, to get a YAML-formatted description for the `vitesskeyspace` custom resource, you could run this:

```
kubectl get crd vitesskeyspaces.planetscale.com -o yaml
...
```

Looking at the original YAML configuration (*https://oreil.ly/5ml3q*) for this CRD, you'll see something like this:

```
apiVersion: apiextensions.k8s.io/v1beta1
kind: CustomResourceDefinition
metadata:
  annotations:
    controller-gen.kubebuilder.io/version: v0.3.0
  creationTimestamp: null
  name: vitesskeyspaces.planetscale.com
spec:
  group: planetscale.com
  names:
    kind: VitessKeyspace
    listKind: VitessKeyspaceList
    plural: vitesskeyspaces
    shortNames:
    - vtk
    singular: vitesskeyspace
  scope: Namespaced
  subresources:
    status: {}
  validation:
    openAPIV3Schema:
      properties:
        ...
```

From this part of the definition, you can see the declaration of the custom resource's name or kind and `shortName`. The `scope` designation of `Namespaced` means that custom resources of this type are confined to a single Namespace.

The longest part of the definition is the `validation` section, which we've omitted due to its considerable size. Kubernetes supports the definition of attributes within custom resource types, and the ability to define legal values for these types using the OpenAPI v3 schema (*https://oreil.ly/b13qP*) (which is used to document RESTful APIs, which in turn uses JSON schema (*http://json-schema.org*) to describe rules used to validate JSON objects). Validation rules ensure that when you create or update custom resources, the definitions of the objects are valid and can be understood by the Kubernetes control plane. The validation rules are used to generate the documentation you use as you define instances of these custom resources in your application.

Once a CRD has been installed in your Kubernetes cluster, you can create and interact with the resources using `kubectl`. For example, `kubectl get vitesskeyspaces` will return a list of Vitess keyspaces. You create an instance of a Vitess keyspace by providing a compliant YAML definition to the `kubectl apply` command.

Operators

Now that you've learned about custom controllers and custom resources, let's tie these threads back together. An *operator* (*https://oreil.ly/BXc35*) is a combination of custom resources and custom controllers that maintain the state of those resources and manage an application (or *operand)* in Kubernetes.

As we'll see in examples throughout the rest of the book, this simple definition can cover a pretty wide range of implementations. The recommended pattern is to provide a custom controller for each custom resource, but beyond that, the details vary. A simple operator might consist of a single resource and controller, while a more complex operator might have multiple resources and controllers. Those multiple controllers might run in the same process space or be broken into separate Pods.

Controllers Versus Operators

While technically operators and controllers are distinct concepts in Kubernetes, the terms are frequently used interchangeably. It's common to refer to a deployed controller or collection of controllers as "the operator," and you'll see this usage reflected both in this book and the community in general.

To unpack this pattern and see how the different elements of an operator and the Kubernetes control plane work together, let's consider the interactions of a notional operator, the DBCluster operator, as shown in Figure 5-2.

After an administrator installs the DBCluster operator and `db-cluster` custom resource in the cluster, users can then create instances of the `db-cluster` resource using `kubectl` (1), which registers the resource with the API server (2), which in turns stores the state in etcd (3) to ensure high availability (other interactions with etcd are omitted from this sequence for brevity).

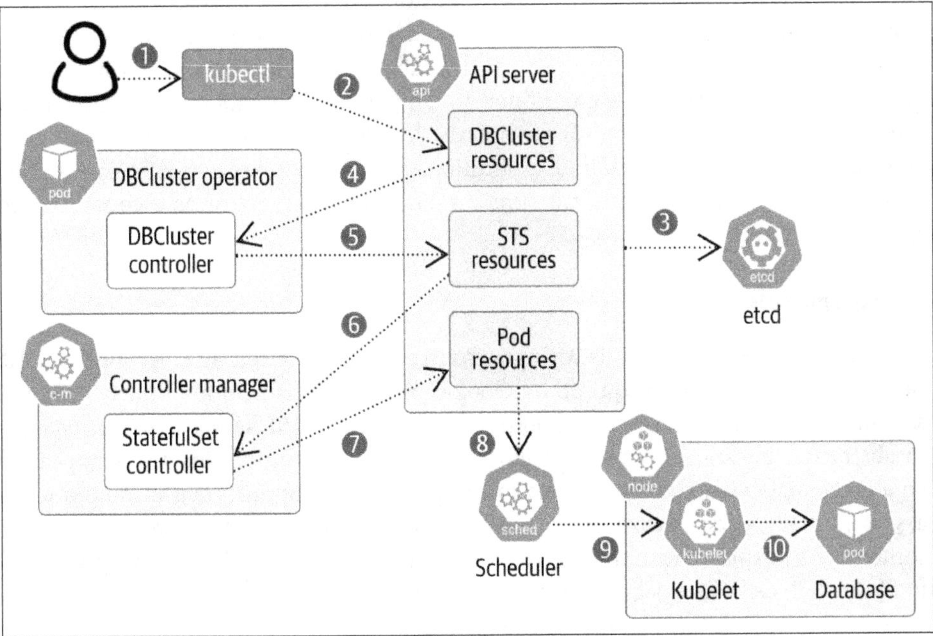

Figure 5-2. Interaction between Kubernetes controllers and operators

The DBCluster controller (part of the operator) is notified of the new `db-cluster` resource (4) and creates additional Kubernetes resources using the API server (5), which could include StatefulSets, Services, PersistentVolumes, PersistentVolume-Claims, and more, as we've seen in previous examples of deploying databases on Kubernetes.

Focusing on the StatefulSet path, the StatefulSet controller running as part of the Kubernetes controller manager is notified of a new StatefulSet (6) and creates new Pod resources (7). The API server asks the scheduler to assign each Pod to a Worker Node (8) and communicates with the Kubelet on the chosen Worker Nodes (9) to start each of the required Pods (10).

As you see, creating a `db-cluster` resource sets off a chain of interactions as various controllers are notified of changes to Kubernetes resources and initiate changes to bring the state of the cluster in line with the desired state. The sequence of interactions appears complex from a user perspective, but the design demonstrates strong encapsulation: the responsibilities of each controller are well bounded and independent of other controllers. This separation of concerns is what makes the Kubernetes control plane so extensible.

Managing MySQL in Kubernetes Using the Vitess Operator

Now that you understand how operators, custom controllers, and custom resources work, it's time to get some hands-on experience with an operator for the database we've been using as our primary relational database example: MySQL. MySQL examples in previous chapters were confined to simple deployments of a single primary replica and a couple of secondary replicas. While this could provide a sufficient amount of storage for many cloud applications, managing a larger cluster can quickly become quite complex, whether it runs on bare-metal servers or as a containerized application in Kubernetes.

Vitess Overview

Vitess (*https://oreil.ly/7I0vO*) is an open source project started at YouTube in 2010. Before the company was acquired by Google, YouTube was running on MySQL, and as YouTube scaled up, it reached a point of daily outages. Vitess was created as a layer to abstract application access to databases by making multiple instances appear to be a single database, routing application requests to the appropriate instances using a sharding approach. Before we explore deploying Vitess on Kubernetes, let's take some time to explore its architecture. We'll start with the high-level concepts shown in Figure 5-3: cells, keyspaces, shards, and primary and replica tablets.

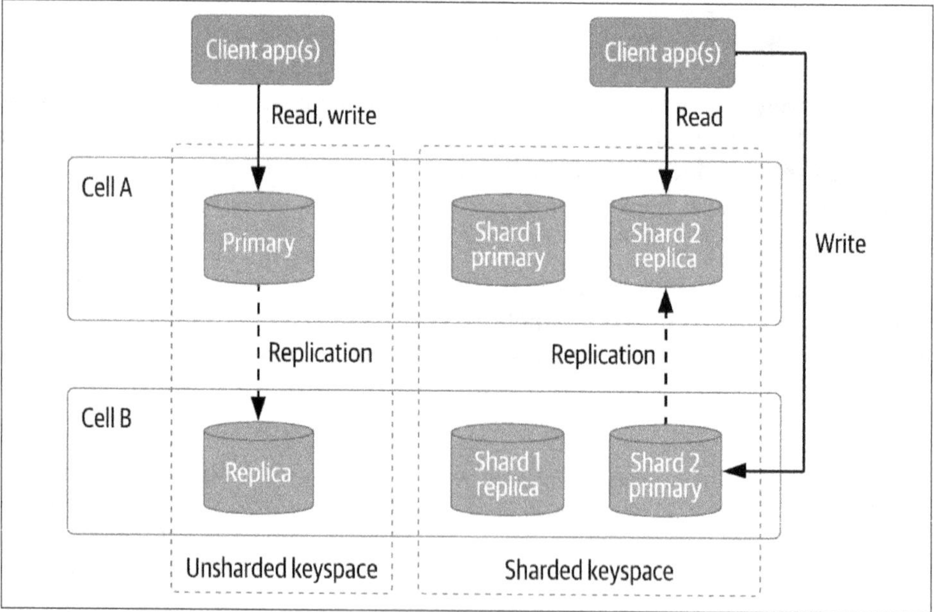

Figure 5-3. Vitess cluster topology: cells, keyspaces, and shards

At a high level, a Vitess cluster consists of multiple MySQL instances called *tablets* which may be spread across multiple datacenters, or *cells*. Each MySQL instance takes on a role as either a primary or replica, and may be dedicated to a specific slice of a database known as a *shard*. Let's consider the implications of each of these concepts for reading and writing data in Vitess:

Cell
: A typical production deployment of Vitess is spread across multiple failure domains in order to provide high availability. Vitess refers to each of these failure domains as a *cell* (*https://oreil.ly/2VDke*). The recommended topology is a cell per datacenter or cloud provider zone. While writes and replication involve communication across cell boundaries, Vitess reads are confined to the local cell to optimize performance.

Keyspace
: This is a logical database consisting of one or more tables. Each keyspace in a cluster can be *sharded* or *unsharded*. An unsharded keyspace has a primary cell where a MySQL instance designated as the *primary* will reside, while other cells will contain *replicas*. In the unsharded keyspace shown on the left side of Figure 5-3, writes from client applications are routed to the primary and replicated to the replica nodes in the background. Reads can be served from the primary or replica nodes.

Shard
: The real power of Vitess comes from its ability to scale by spreading the contents of a keyspace across multiple replicated MySQL databases known as *shards*, while providing the abstraction of a single database to client applications. The client on the right side of Figure 5-3 is not aware of how data is sharded. On writes, Vitess determines what shards are involved and then routes the data to the appropriate primary instances. On reads, Vitess gathers data from primary or replica nodes in the local cell.

  The sharding rules for a keyspace are specified in a Vitess Schema (VSchema) (*https://oreil.ly/wDmQa*), an object that contains the sharding key (known in Vitess as the *keyspace ID*) used for each table. To provide maximum flexibility over the way data is sharded, Vitess allows you to specify which columns in a table are used to calculate the keyspace ID, as well as the algorithm (or *VIndex*) used to make the calculation. Tables can also have secondary VIndexes to support more-efficient queries across multiple keyspace IDs.

To understand how Vitess manages shards and how it routes queries to the various MySQL instances, you'll want to get to know the components of a Vitess cluster shown in Figure 5-4, including VTGate, VTTablet, and the Topology Service.

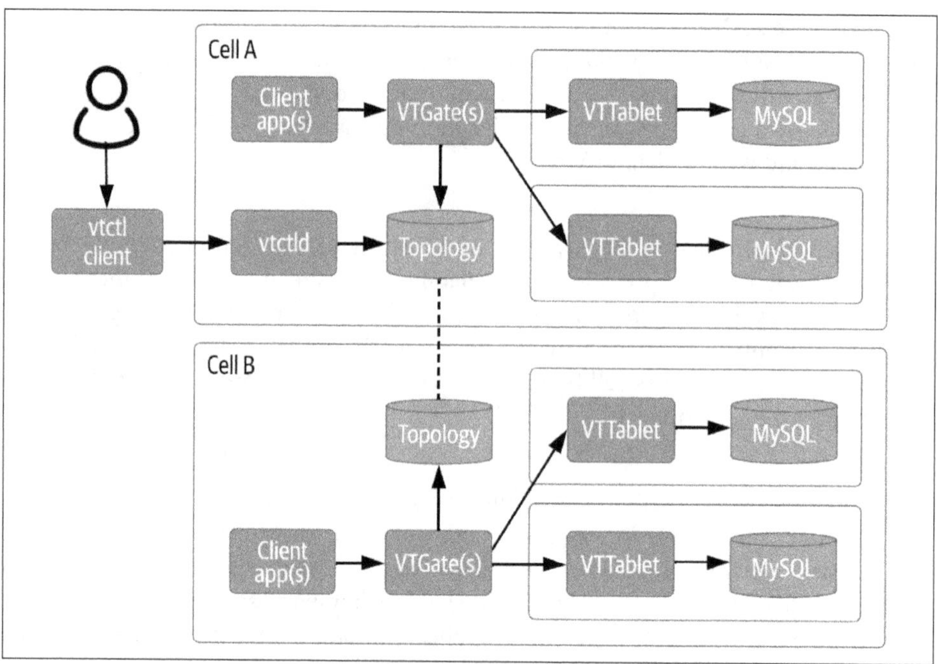

Figure 5-4. Vitess architecture including VTGate, VTTablets, and the Topology Service

Let's walk through these components to learn what they do and how they interact:

VTGate
: A Vitess gateway (VTGate) is a proxy server that provides the SQL binary endpoint used by client applications, making the Vitess cluster appear as a single database. Vitess clients generally connect to a VTGate running in the same cell (datacenter). The VTGate parses each incoming read or write query and uses its knowledge of the VSchema and cluster topology to create a query execution plan. The VTGate executes queries for each shard, assembles the result set, and returns it to the client. The VTGate can detect and limit queries that will impact memory or CPU utilization, providing high reliability and helping to ensure consistent performance. Although VTGate instances do cache cluster metadata, they are stateless, so you can increase the reliability and scalability of your cluster by running multiple VTGate instances per cell.

VTTablet
: A Vitess tablet (VTTablet) is an agent that runs on the same compute instance as a single MySQL database, managing access to it and monitoring its health. Each VTTablet takes on a specific role in the cluster, such as the primary for a shard, or one of its replicas. There are two types of replica: those that can be promoted to replace a primary and those that cannot. The latter are typically used to provide additional capacity for read-intensive use cases such as analytics.

The VTTablet exposes a gRPC interface, which the VTGate uses to send queries and control commands that the VTTablet then turns into SQL commands on the MySQL instance. VTTablets maintain a pool of long-lived connections to the MySQL node, leading to improved throughput, reduced latency, and reduced memory pressure.

Topology Service
: Vitess requires a strongly consistent data store to maintain a small amount of metadata describing the cluster topology, including the definition of keyspaces and their VSchema, what VTTablets exist for each shard, and which VTTablet is the primary. Vitess uses a pluggable interface called the Topology Service, with three implementations provided by the project: etcd (the default), ZooKeeper, and Consul. VTGates and VTTablets interface with the Topology Service in the background in order to maintain awareness of the topology, and do not interact with the Topology Service on the query path to avoid performance impact. For multicell clusters, Vitess incorporates both cell-local Topology Services and a global Topology Service with instances in multiple cells that maintains knowledge of the entire cluster. This design provides high availability of topology information across the cluster.

`vtctld` *and* `vtctlclient`
: The Vitess control daemon `vtctld` and its client, `vtctlclient`, provide the control plane used to configure and manage Vitess clusters. `vtctld` is deployed on one or more of the cells in the cluster, while `vtctlclient` is deployed on the client machine of the user administering the cluster. `vtctld` uses a declarative approach similar to Kubernetes to perform its work: it updates the cluster metadata in the Topology Service, and the VTGates and VTTablets pick up changes and respond accordingly.

Now that you understand the Vitess architecture and basic concepts, let's discuss how they are mapped into a Kubernetes environment. This is an important consideration for any application, but especially for a complex piece of data infrastructure like Vitess.

PlanetScale Vitess Operator

Over time, Vitess has evolved in a couple of key aspects. First, it can now run additional MySQL-compatible database engines such as Percona. Second, and more important for our investigations, PlanetScale has packaged Vitess as a containerized application that can be deployed to Kubernetes.

Evolving Options For Running Vitess in Kubernetes

The state of the art for running Vitess in Kubernetes has evolved over time. While Vitess once included a Helm chart, this was deprecated in the 7.0 release (*https://oreil.ly/xhUt4*) in mid-2020. The Vitess project also hosted an operator which was deprecated (*https://oreil.ly/4RPMj*) around the same time. Both of these options were retired in favor of the PlanetScale operator we examine in this section.

Let's see how easy it is to deploy a multinode MySQL cluster using the PlanetScale Vitess Operator (*https://oreil.ly/W5Dc2*). Since the Vitess project has adopted the PlanetScale Vitess Operator as its officially supported operator, you can reference the Get Started guide (*https://oreil.ly/Nl7e2*) in the Vitess project documentation. We'll walk through a portion of this guide here to get an understanding of the operator's contents and how it works.

Examples Require Kubernetes Clusters with More Resources

The examples in previous chapters have not required a large amount of compute resources, and we encouraged you to run them on local distributions such as kind or K3s. Beginning in this chapter, the examples become more complex and may require more resources than you have available on your desktop or laptop. For these cases, we will provide references to documentation or scripts for creating Kubernetes clusters with sufficient resources.

Installing the Vitess Operator

You can find the source code used in this section in this book's code repository (*https://github.com/data-on-k8s-book/examples*). The files are copied for convenience from their original source in the Vitess GitHub repo (*https://oreil.ly/Kq7dm*). First, install the operator using the provided configuration file:

```
set GH_LINK=https://raw.githubusercontent.com
kubectl apply -f \
  $GH_LINK/vitessio/vitess/main/examples/operator/operator.yaml
customresourcedefinition.apiextensions.k8s.io/
  etcdlockservers.planetscale.com created
...
```

As you'll see in the output of the `kubectl apply` command, this configuration creates several CRDs, as well as a Deployment managing a single instance of the operator. Figure 5-5 shows many of the elements you've just installed, in order to highlight a few interesting details that will not be obvious at first glance:

- The operator contains a controller corresponding to each CRD. If you're interested in seeing what this looks like in the operator source code in Go, compare the controller implementations (*https://oreil.ly/ABID9*) with the custom resource specifications (*https://oreil.ly/tUD9z*) that are used to generate the CRD configurations introduced in "Building Operators" on page 130.
- The figure depicts a hierarchy of CRDs representing their relationships and intended usage, as described in the operator's API reference (*https://oreil.ly/25qhN*). To use the Vitess Operator, you define a VitessCluster resource which contains the definitions of VitessCells and VitessKeyspaces. VitessKeyspaces, in turn, contain definitions of VitessShards. While you can view the status of each VitessCell, VitessKeyspace, and VitessShard independently, you must update them in the context of the parent VitessCluster resource.
- Currently, the Vitess Operator supports only etcd as the Topology Service implementation. The EtcdLockserver CRD is used to configure these etcd clusters.

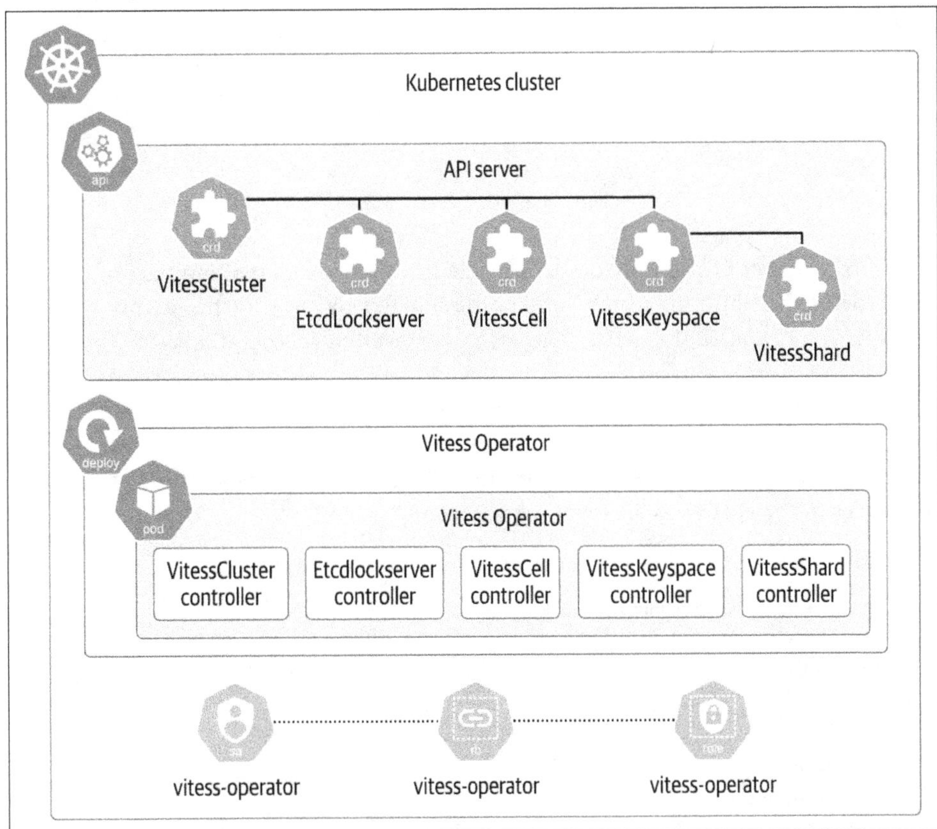

Figure 5-5. Vitess Operator and Custom Resource Definitions

Roles and RoleBindings. As shown toward the bottom of Figure 5-5, installing the operator caused the creation of a ServiceAccount, along with two new resources we have not discussed previously: a Role and a RoleBinding. These additional resources allow the ServiceAccount to access specific resources on the Kubernetes API. First, examine the configuration of the `vitess-operator` Role from the file that you used to install the operator (*https://oreil.ly/q52Iq*) (you can search for `kind: Role` to locate the pertinent code):

```
apiVersion: rbac.authorization.k8s.io/v1
kind: Role
metadata:
  name: vitess-operator
rules:
- apiGroups:
  - ""
  resources:
  - pods
  - services
  - endpoints
  - persistentvolumeclaims
  - events
  - configmaps
  - secrets
  verbs:
  - '*'
...
```

This first portion of the Role definition identifies resources that are part of the core Kubernetes distribution, which may be designated by passing the empty string as the `apiGroup` instead of `k8s.io`. The `verbs` correspond to operations the Kubernetes API provides on resources, including `get`, `list`, `watch`, `create`, `update`, `patch`, and `delete`. This Role is given access to all operations using the wildcard `*`. If you follow the URL in the example and examine more of the code, you'll also see how the Role is given access to other resources, including Deployments and ReplicaSets, and resources in the `apiGroup planetscale.com`.

The RoleBinding associates the ServiceAccount with the Role:

```
apiVersion: rbac.authorization.k8s.io/v1
kind: RoleBinding
metadata:
  name: vitess-operator
roleRef:
  apiGroup: rbac.authorization.k8s.io
  kind: Role
  name: vitess-operator
subjects:
- kind: ServiceAccount
  name: vitess-operator
```

Least Privilege for Operators

As a creator or consumer of operators, exercise care in choosing which permissions are granted to operators, and be conscious of the implications for what an operator is allowed to do.

PriorityClasses. Another detail is not depicted in Figure 5-4: installing the operator created two PriorityClass resources. PriorityClasses (*https://oreil.ly/dlkRe*) provide input to the Kubernetes scheduler to indicate the relative priority of Pods. The priority is an integer value, where higher values indicate higher priority. Whenever a Pod resource is created and is ready to be assigned to a Worker Node, the Scheduler takes the Pod's priority into account as part of its decisions. When multiple Pods are awaiting scheduling, higher-priority Pods are assigned before lower-priority Pods. When a cluster's nodes are running low on compute resources, lower-priority Pods may be stopped or *evicted* in order to make room for higher-priority Pods, a process known as *preemption*.

A PriorityClass is a convenient way to set a priority value referenced by multiple Pods or other workload resources such as Deployments and StatefulSets. The Vitess Operator creates two PriorityClasses: `vitess-operator-control-plane` defines a higher priority used for the operator and `vtctld` Deployments, while the `vitess` class is used for the data plane components such as the VTGate and VTTablet Deployments.

Kubernetes Scheduling Complexity

Kubernetes provides multiple constraints that influence Pod scheduling, including prioritization and preemption, affinity and anti-affinity, and scheduler extensions, as discussed in "Extending Kubernetes Clients" on page 105. The interaction of these constraints may not be predictable, especially in large clusters shared across multiple teams. As resources in a cluster become scarce, Pods can be preempted or fail to be scheduled in ways you don't expect. It's a best practice to maintain awareness of the various scheduling needs and constraints across the workloads in your cluster to avoid surprises.

Creating a VitessCluster

Now let's create a VitessCluster and put the operator to work. The code sample contains a configuration file defining a very simple cluster named `example`, with a VitessCell `zone1`, keyspace `commerce`, and single shard, which the operator gives the name `x-x`:

```
kubectl apply -f 101_initial_cluster.yaml
vitesscluster.planetscale.com/example created
secret/example-cluster-config created
```

The output of the command indicates a couple of items that are created directly. But more is going on behind the scenes, as the operator detects the creation of the VitessCluster and begins provisioning other resources, as summarized in Figure 5-6.

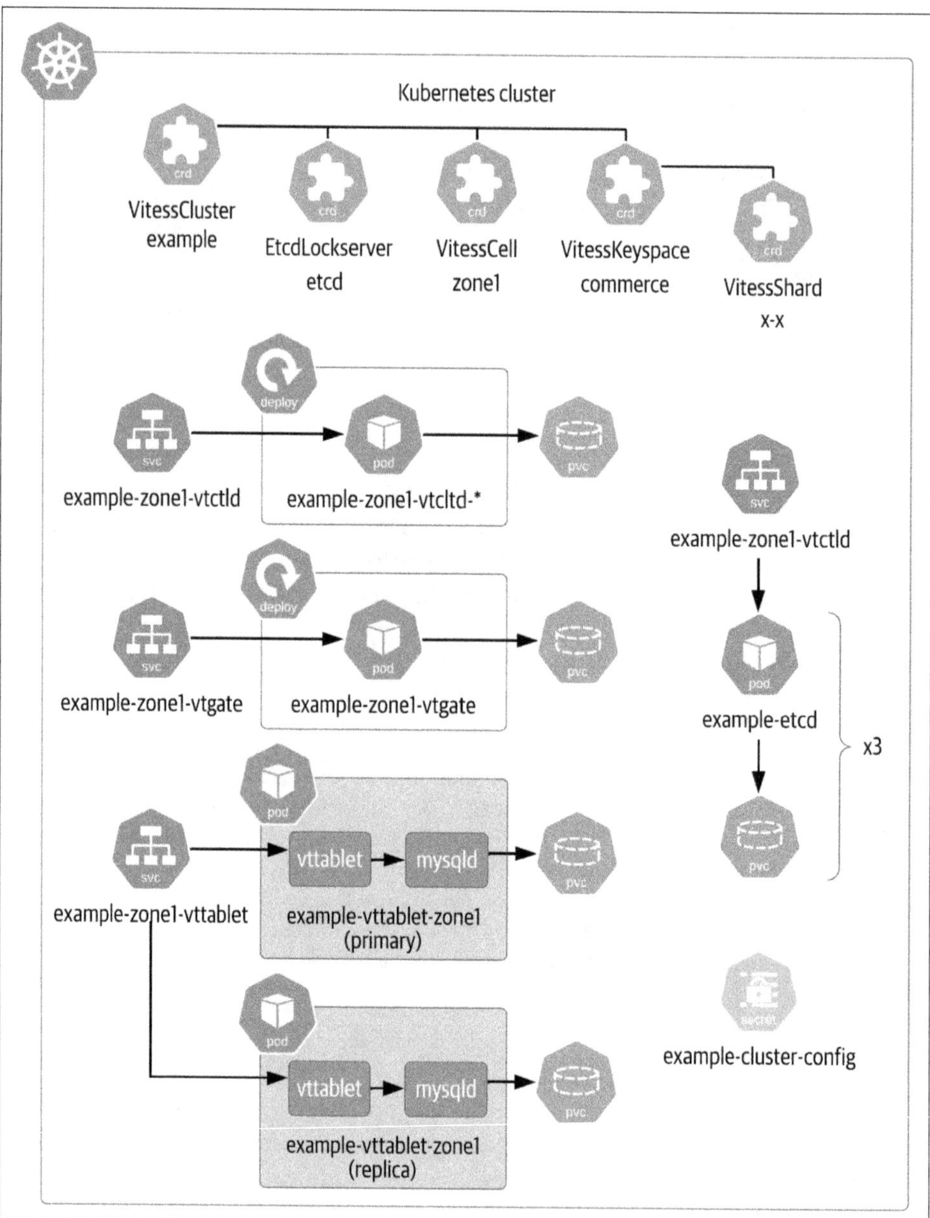

Figure 5-6. Resources managed by the VitessCluster `example`

By comparing the configuration script with Figure 5-6, you can make several observations about this simple VitessCluster. First, the top-level configuration allows you to specify the name of the cluster and the container images that will be used for the various components:

```
apiVersion: planetscale.com/v2
kind: VitessCluster
metadata:
  name: example
spec:
  images:
    vtctld: vitess/lite:v12.0.0
    ...
```

Next, the VitessCluster configuration provides a definition of the VitessCell `zone1`. The values provided for `gateway` specify a single VTGate instance to be allocated for this cell, with specific compute resource limits:

```
cells:
- name: zone1
  gateway:
    authentication:
      static:
        secret:
          name: example-cluster-config
          key: users.json
    replicas: 1
    resources:
      ...
```

The Vitess Operator uses this information to create a VTGate Deployment prefixed with `example-zone1-vtgate` containing a single replica, and a Service that provides access. The access credentials for the VTGate instance are provided in the `example-cluster-config` Secret. This Secret is used to secure other configuration values, as you'll see.

The next section of the VitessCluster configuration specifies the creation of a single `vtctld` instance (a *dashboard*) with permission to control `zone1`. The Vitess Operator uses this information to create a Deployment to manage the dashboard using the specified resource limits, and a Service to provide access to the VTGate:

```
vitessDashboard:
  cells:
  - zone1
  extraFlags:
    security_policy: read-only
  replicas: 1
  resources:
    ...
```

The VitessCluster also defines the `commerce` keyspace, which contains a single shard (essentially, an unsharded keyspace). This single shard has a pool of two VTTablets in the cell `zone1`, each of which will be allocated 10 GB of storage:

```
keyspaces:
- name: commerce
  turndownPolicy: Immediate
  partitionings:
  - equal:
      parts: 1
      shardTemplate:
        databaseInitScriptSecret:
          name: example-cluster-config
          key: init_db.sql
        replication:
          enforceSemiSync: false
        tabletPools:
        - cell: zone1
          type: replica
          replicas: 2
          vttablet:
            ...
          mysqld:
            ...
          dataVolumeClaimTemplate:
            accessModes: ["ReadWriteOnce"]
            resources:
              requests:
                storage: 10Gi
```

As shown in Figure 5-6, the Vitess Operator manages a Pod for each VTTablet and creates a Service to manage access across the tablets. The operator does not use a StatefulSet because the VTTablets have distinct roles, with one as the primary and the other as a replica. Each VTTablet Pod contains multiple containers, including the `vttablet` sidecar which configures and controls the `mysql` container. The `vttablet` sidecar initializes the `mysql` instance using a script contained in the `example-cluster-config` Secret.

While this configuration doesn't specifically include details about etcd, the Vitess Operator uses its default settings to create a three-node etcd cluster to serve as the Topology Service for the VitessCluster. Because of the shortcomings of the StatefulSets, the operator manages each Pod and PersistentVolumeClaim individually. This points to the possibility for future improvements as Kubernetes and the operator mature; perhaps the Kubernetes API server can one day serve the role of the Topology Service in the Vitess architecture.

At this point, you have a VitessCluster with all of its infrastructure provisioned in Kubernetes. The next steps are to create the database schema and configure your applications to access the cluster using the VTGate Service. You can follow the steps in Alkin Tezuysal's 2020 blog post "Vitess Operator for Kubernetes" (*https://oreil.ly/543Y8*), which also describes other use cases for managing a Vitess installation on Kubernetes, including schema migration, backup, and restore.

The backup/restore capabilities leverage VitessBackupStorage and VitessBackup CRDs, which you may have noticed during installation. VitessBackupStorage resources represent locations where backups can be stored. After you configure the backup section of a VitessCluster and point to a backup location, the operator creates VitessBackup resources as a record of each backup it performs. When you add additional replicas to a VitessCluster, the operator initializes their data by performing a restore from the most recent backup.

Visualizing Larger Kubernetes Applications

It's a good exercise to use the `kubectl get` and `kubectl describe` commands to explore all of the resources that were created when you installed the operator and created a cluster. However, you may find it easier to use a tool such as Lens (*https://github.com/lensapp/lens*), which offers a friendly graphical interface enabling you to click through the resources more quickly, or K9s (*https://k9scli.io*), which provides a command-line interface.

Resharding is another interesting use case, which you might need to perform when a cluster becomes unbalanced and one or more shards run out of capacity more quickly than others. You'll need to modify the VSchema using `vtctlclient`, and then update the VitessCluster resource (*https://oreil.ly/i0n5S*) with additional VitessShards so that the operator provisions the required infrastructure. This highlights the division of responsibility: the Vitess Operator manages Kubernetes resources, while the Vitess control daemon (`vtctld`) provides more application-specific behavior.

What We Learned Building the Vitess Operator

With Deepthi Sigireddi, Software Engineer, PlanetScale

Vitess can be described simply as a scaling infrastructure for MySQL. Vitess started at YouTube in 2010 when the team was struggling with daily outages due to MySQL. A few people got together and decided that rather than fighting fires every day, they would solve their problem from the ground up. Initially, Vitess was very customized to YouTube's environment. Applications were segmented into groups to run against one database or another, with a layer in between to route queries to the right backing database. Over time, the internal architecture became more complex—but simpler from the application's point of view. Vitess started with custom sharding, which required the application to know which database to query against. Now, the application doesn't need to know whether there are 10 MySQL databases or 100, or 1,000. As far as the application layer is concerned, it looks like a single database.

The move toward Kubernetes started when YouTube was acquired by Google. The mandate to use Google infrastructure included adapting Vitess to run on Borg, the precursor to Kubernetes. With Borg, the applications had to be tolerant to being restarted anytime, since Borg frequently reschedules components to run on different machines, but that wasn't something supported by MySQL. The team built in tolerance for this type of automation as features in Vitess, and that's how Vitess became cloud native. All this sounds familiar to us now because that's how Kubernetes operates. When the team members at YouTube decided to make Vitess run on Kubernetes, they were able to do the work without a lot of changes.

Before Vitess was donated to the CNCF in January 2018, there was a project called Metacontroller (*https://oreil.ly/5Ynco*), which predated the Operator SDK (see "Building Operators" on page 130). This was used to get Vitess working on Kubernetes, independent of Google's infrastructure. It seemed intuitive that you'd want to run Vitess using an operator, since there was already a community-contributed Helm chart and we saw the movement in the community toward operators.

There was an early community effort by an individual Vitess contributor to write a Kubernetes operator, but it was a pretty complex undertaking to take on alone, so it didn't go far. Other Vitess users such as HubSpot have built their own custom operators, which are private since they are quite specific to their own deployments. PlanetScale started building a Kubernetes operator for Vitess to run as a cloud service, and once it matured, we released 90% of that code as an open source Vitess Operator.

To write an operator for an application, you need to understand both Kubernetes and the application really well. Kubernetes moves fast, with new releases every four months. Many features that were in alpha when we first started building our operator are now a part of Kubernetes. Meanwhile, MySQL continues to evolve and add new query constructs. In MySQL 8.0, a lot of new syntax was added, and maintaining an operator requires keeping up with those changes.

To run a service in Kubernetes, you have to know the important lifecycle events and how those disrupt availability. Vitess achieves automatic failure detection and failover through a mixture of approaches. If your primary MySQL node is running with a PersistentVolume that goes down, Kubernetes will restart it with a downtime of 20 or 30 seconds. This is pretty fast—maybe more than what some applications can tolerate. We are building into Vitess the ability to detect and fail over much faster than a Kubernetes hot restart. Vitess will detect that the primary has gone down and will fail over to a replica that has kept up with the primary within 5 or 10 seconds. This will greatly improve reliability.

Another area of improvement we are focused on is speeding up startup and shutdown. Network constraints like TCP/IP timeouts limit how quickly you can detect failure, but MySQL startup and shutdown are not yet at the point of hitting that lower bound. The first operator we built at PlanetScale took 10 or 20 minutes to bring up a cluster. This was partly due to inefficiencies in the Operator SDK, and partly because we had written a single controller with a gigantic reconcile loop. We rewrote the operator to use a newer version of the Operator SDK and to have a separate controller for each resource. This made our startups and shutdowns 20 times faster, which was a hard requirement for providing a cloud service. Clients expect those operations to take 10 or 15 seconds, not 2 or 3 minutes.

We also need more primitives from Kubernetes in order to continue to mature database operators. While Kubernetes provides Deployments, ReplicaSets, and StatefulSets, it doesn't yet support the concept of primary and replicas as MySQL needs. Imagine if you could configure Kubernetes to designate a primary, and specify an action to perform if the primary is restarted. A lot of the error-handling code included in Vitess would actually not be required. While Kubernetes has a leader election module, there's no clear way to leverage this for an operator that already has the concept of primaries and replicas. This leads to more duplicated code.

One final area of improvement is data locality. Application developers are looking for more control over where their data is stored, and easy ways to ingest or load data. Every organization that provides a database solution on Kubernetes should consider providing it as a service to make it easier for developers to consume. Today if a developer is running an application in AWS and a particular data service is not available there, they have to consider using another cloud or building the capability themselves. It should be really easy to create and populate a data source for an application no matter where you run it.

Infrastructure provisioning is getting easier and easier, and long may that trend continue. Even so, there is a lot more work to do. Those of us who get paid to work on open source are fortunate because many developers aren't compensated for their open source contributions. Let's continue to champion the benefits of working on open source software in our organizations so we can continue to grow as a community.

A Growing Ecosystem of Operators

The operator pattern has become quite popular in the Kubernetes community, aided in part by the development of the Operator Framework (*https://operatorframework.io*), an ecosystem for creating and distributing operators. In this section, we'll examine the Operator Framework and related open source projects.

Choosing Operators

While we've focused in this chapter on Vitess as an example database operator, operators are clearly relevant to all of the elements of your data stack. In all aspects of cloud native data, we see a growing number of maturing, open source operators to use in your deployments, and we'll be looking at additional operators as we examine how to run different types of data infrastructure on Kubernetes in upcoming chapters.

You should consider multiple aspects in choosing an operator. What are its features? How much does it automate? How well supported is it? Is it proprietary or open source? The Operator Framework provides a great resource, the Operator Hub (*https://operatorhub.io*), which you should consider as your first stop when looking for an operator. Operator Hub is a well-organized list of various operators that cover every aspect of cloud native software. It does rely on maintainers to submit their operators for listing, which means that many existing operators may not be listed.

The Operator Framework also contains the Operator Lifecycle Manager (OLM), an operator for installing and managing other operators in your cluster. You can curate your own custom catalog of operators that are permitted in your environment, or use catalogs provided by others. For example, Operator Hub can itself be treated as a catalog (*https://oreil.ly/ble8P*).

Part of the curation the Operator Hub provides is rating the capability of each operator according to the Operator Capability Model (*https://oreil.ly/eYVEA*). The levels in this capability model are summarized in Table 5-1, with additional commentary we've added to highlight considerations for database operators. The examples are not prescriptive but indicate the type of capabilities expected at each level.

Table 5-1. Operator capability levels applied to databases

Capability level	Characteristics	Database operator examples	Tools
Level 1: Basic install	Installation and configuration of Kubernetes and workloads	The operator uses custom resources to provide a central point of configuration for a database cluster. The operator deploys the database by creating resources such as Deployments, ServiceAccounts, RoleBindings, PersistentVolumeClaims, and Secrets, and helps initialize the database schema.	Helm, Ansible, Go
Level 2: Seamless updates	Upgrade of the managed workload and operator	The operator can update an existing database to a newer version without data loss (or, hopefully, downtime). The operator can be replaced with a newer version of itself.	Helm, Ansible, Go
Level 3: Full lifecycle	Ability to create and restore from backups, ability to fail over or replace portions of a clustered application, ability to scale the application	The operator provides a way to create a consistent backup across multiple data nodes and the ability to use those backups to restore or replace failed database nodes. The operator can respond to a configuration change to add or remove database nodes or perhaps even datacenters.	Ansible, Go
Level 4: Deep insights	Providing capabilities including alerting, monitoring, events, or metering	The operator monitors metrics and logging output by the database software and uses this information to implement health and readiness checks. The operator pushes metrics and alerts to other infrastructure.	Ansible, Go

Capability level	Characteristics	Database operator examples	Tools
Level 5: Auto-pilot	Providing capabilities including auto-scaling, auto-healing, auto-tuning	The operator auto-scales the number of database nodes in the cluster up or down to meet performance requirements. The operator might also dynamically resize PVs or change the StorageClass used for various database nodes. The operator automatically performs database maintenance such as rebuilding indexes to improve slow response times. The operator detects abnormal workload patterns and takes action such as resharding to balance workloads.	Ansible, Go

These levels are useful both for evaluating operators you might want to use, and for providing targets for operator developers to aim for. They also provide an opinionated view on what Helm-based operators can accomplish, limiting them to Level 2. For full lifecycle management and automation, more direct involvement with the Kubernetes control plane is needed. For a Level 5 operator, the goal is a complete hands-off Deployment.

Let's take a quick look at a few of the available operators for popular open source databases:

Cass Operator
: In 2021, several companies in the Cassandra community that had developed their own operators came together (*https://oreil.ly/AS16G*) in support of an operator built by DataStax, known primarily by its nickname: Cass Operator (*https://oreil.ly/ueyGZ*). Cass Operator was inspired by the best features of the community operators as well as DataStax experience running Astra, a Cassandra-based database as a service (DBaaS). The operator has been donated to the K8ssandra project (*https://k8ssandra.io*), where it is part of a larger ecosystem for deploying Cassandra on Kubernetes. We'll take a deeper look at K8ssandra and Cass Operator in Chapter 7.

PostgreSQL operators
: Several operators are available for PostgreSQL, which is not surprising given that it is the second most popular open source database after MySQL. Two of the most popular operators are the Zalando Postgres Operator (*https://oreil.ly/i6Us5*), and PGO (*https://oreil.ly/A40Qf*) (which stands for Postgres Operator) from Crunchy Data. Read Nikolay Bogdanov's blog post "Comparing Kubernetes Operators for PostgreSQL" (*https://oreil.ly/AQcvB*) for a helpful comparison of these and other operators.

MongoDB Kubernetes Operator
: MongoDB is the most popular document database, beloved by developers for its ease of use. The MongoDB Community Kubernetes Operator provides basic support for creating and managing MongoDB ReplicaSets, scaling up and down, and upgrades. This operator is available on GitHub (*https://oreil.ly/dAhuV*) but

not yet listed on Operator Hub, possibly because MongoDB also offers a separate operator for its enterprise version.

Redis Operator
: Redis is an in-memory key-value store that has a broad set of use cases. Application developers typically use Redis as an adjunct to other data infrastructure when ultra-low latency is required. It excels at caching, counting, and shared data structures. The Redis Operator (*https://oreil.ly/SKLSz*) covers the basic install and upgrade but also manages harder operations such as cluster failover and recovery.

As you can see, operators are available for many popular open source databases, although it's unfortunate that some vendors have tended to think of Kubernetes operators primarily as a feature differentiator for paid enterprise versions.

Building Operators

While there is broad consensus in the Kubernetes community that you should *use* operators for distributed data infrastructure whenever possible, there are a variety of opinions about who exactly should be *building* operators. If you don't happen to work for a data infrastructure vendor, this can be a challenging question. Mary Branscombe's blog post "When to Use, and When to Avoid, the Operator Pattern" (*https://oreil.ly/hd8FE*) provides some excellent questions to consider, which we'll summarize here:

- What is the scale of the deployment? If you're deploying only a single instance of the database application, building and maintaining an operator might not be cost-effective.
- Do you have the expertise in the database? The best operators tend to be built by companies running databases at scale in production, including vendors that are providing DBaaS solutions.
- Do you need higher levels of application awareness and automation, or would deployment with a Helm chart and standard Kubernetes resources be sufficient?
- Are you trying to make the operator manage resources that are external to Kubernetes? Consider a solution that runs closer to the resources being managed with an API you can access from your Kubernetes application.
- Have you considered security implications? Since operators are extensions of the Kubernetes control plane, you'll want to carefully manage what resources your operator can access.

If you decide to write an operator, several great tools and resources are available:

Operator SDK (https://oreil.ly/HtSZt)
This software development kit, included in the Operator Framework, contains tools to build, test, and package operators. Operator SDK uses templates to autogenerate new operator projects and provides APIs and abstractions to simplify common aspects of building operators, especially interactions with the Kubernetes API. The SDK supports the creation of operators using Go, Ansible, or Helm.

Kubebuilder (https://book.kubebuilder.io)
This toolkit for building operators is managed by the Kubernetes API Machinery SIG. Similarly to Operator SDK, Kubebuilder provides tools for project generation, testing, and publishing controllers and operators. Both Kubebuilder and Operator SDK are built on the Kubernetes controller-runtime (*https://oreil.ly/XR9y4*), a set of Go libraries for building controllers. Wei Tei's blog post "Kubebuilder vs. Operator SDK" (*https://oreil.ly/NKC8d*) provides a concise summary of the differences between these toolkits.

Kubernetes Universal Declarative Operator (KUDO) (https://kudo.dev)
This operator allows you to create operators declaratively using YAML files. This is an attractive approach for some developers as it eliminates the need to write Go. Dmytro Vedetskyi's blog post "How to Deploy Your First App with Kudo Operator on K8S" (*https://oreil.ly/K71fK*) provides a helpful introduction to using KUDO and discusses some of the pros and cons of the declarative approach.

Finally, the O'Reilly books *Kubernetes Operators* (*https://oreil.ly/rWIM0*) by Jason Dobies and Joshua Wood and *Programming Kubernetes* (*https://oreil.ly/iczyv*) are great resources for understanding the operator ecosystem and getting into the details of writing operators and controllers in Go.

Can One Operator Rule Them All?

With Umair Mufti, Product Manager, Pure Storage

As discussed in this chapter, the number of Kubernetes operators for databases has been continuously growing. Database developers want their databases to run on Kubernetes, so projects like Vitess are stepping up and developing operators to make it easy for others. This initiative is great, but one potential drawback is that everyone is building operators their own way and solving similar problems with different implementations. As a result, there is no uniformity among operators for stateful workloads.

The question those who are developing operators have to reckon with is how specialized to expect end users to be. Because of the popularity of cloud native, microservice architectures, application developers now expect polyglot persistence: to run a relational database in addition to a graph database or a key-value store. This forces cluster administrators to provide different types of databases while maintaining the operational simplicity of a single platform.

No Kubernetes admin wants to maintain 10 or 15 operators on their cluster. The point of Kubernetes is the ease of operations when deploying applications, monitoring them on day two, and making lifecycle management simpler. As soon as you have the maintenance overhead of managing multiple operator lifecycles, you've already lost. Multiply that 10 or 15 times over, and you are completely at odds with the value Kubernetes provides. The only way out of this situation is to reduce the number of operators. Could there be a single operator for all our databases or stateful workloads? Let's explore.

The operator pattern is simply a design pattern for running stateful workloads in Kubernetes, just as the model–view–controller (MVC) framework is a pattern for user-facing applications. Various web frameworks such as Angular, Vue, and React use the MVC pattern, but they all implement the pattern in different ways, and your code will vary based on the implementation you use. This is a familiar experience for developers using operators today. Each operator solves the problem of running a stateful workload in Kubernetes in a unique way, and it requires specialization to become proficient with each operator. The irony is that if you're running Cassandra, Redis, or Postgres, a lot of the problems being addressed are very much the same: cluster membership, failure detection, backup and restore, and more.

Could we actually build "one operator to rule them all"? Maybe. But perhaps what we need is not literally one single operator, but a collection of higher-level interfaces that operators should adhere to, so they work with multiple data service types. This would enable administrators to choose an operator based on factors other than the vendor or project that created it. What if you could use an operator that would manage your Cassandra, Elasticsearch, and Kafka clusters? This is what we need to reduce the burden on operations teams and fully realize the benefits of managing stateful workloads on Kubernetes.

We need to build another layer of abstraction on top of the operator pattern. As a community, we can develop a common set of custom resources, and each controller can manage them in their own way. For example, we might define a `TopologyAwareStatefulSet` as a new CRD, or a `ClusterMembership` CRD that describes how a node joins a cluster. Instead of Elasticsearch developers and Cassandra developers creating separate definitions of a server group or topology, we could all agree that a distributed database has a concept of topology, agree on a CRD, and controllers can implement the specified behavior as needed.

The ideal end-state is a world with multiple implementations that adhere to a common standard. Kubernetes itself has a specification, and each Kubernetes distribution has to provide certain APIs to be considered a valid distribution. Users can choose which operators to use in the same way, knowing that they can expect a baseline standard while applying other criteria.

Kubernetes still shows signs that it was born of a stateless world, but there's an exciting future for stateful workloads on Kubernetes. We are very much in that "Crossing the Chasm" moment and still just hitting the inflection point with stateful workloads. With more advanced operators, we'll no longer be working in silos, solving the same problems over and over again. Then we can use our collective talents and skills to solve bigger and higher-level problems.

As you can see, the state of the art in Kubernetes operators is continuing to mature. Whether the goal is to build a unified operator or just to make it easier to build database-specific operators, it's clear that great progress can be made as multiple communities begin to collaborate on common CRDs to address problems like cluster membership, topology awareness, and leader election.

Summary

In this chapter, you've learned about several ways of extending the Kubernetes control plane, especially operators and custom resources. The operator pattern provides the critical breakthrough that enables us to simplify database operations in Kubernetes through automation. While you should definitely be using operators to run distributed databases in Kubernetes, think carefully before starting to write your own operator. If building an operator is the right course for you, there are plenty of resources and frameworks to help you along the way. There are certainly ways in which Kubernetes itself could improve to make writing operators easier, as you've learned from the experts we spoke to in this chapter.

While we've spent the past couple of chapters focusing primarily on running databases on Kubernetes, let's expand our focus to consider how those databases interact with other infrastructure.

CHAPTER 6

Integrating Data Infrastructure in a Kubernetes Stack

In this book, we are illuminating a future of modern, cloud native applications that run on Kubernetes. Up until this point, we've noted that historically, data has been one of the hardest parts of making this a reality. In previous chapters, we've introduced the primitives Kubernetes provides for managing compute, network, and storage (Chapter 2) resources, and considered how databases (Chapter 3) can be deployed on Kubernetes using these resources. We've also examined the automation of infrastructure using controllers and the operator pattern (Chapter 4).

Now let's expand our focus to consider how data infrastructure fits into your overall application architecture in Kubernetes. In this chapter, we'll explore how to assemble the building blocks discussed in previous chapters into integrated data infrastructure stacks that are easy to deploy and tailor to the unique needs of each application. These stacks represent a step toward the vision of the virtual datacenter we introduced in Chapter 1. To learn the considerations involved in building and using these larger assemblies, let's take an in-depth look at K8ssandra (*https://k8ssandra.io*). This open source project provides an integrated data stack based on Apache Cassandra, a database we first discussed in "Running Apache Cassandra on Kubernetes" on page 65.

K8ssandra: Production-Ready Cassandra on Kubernetes

To set the context, let's consider some of the practical challenges of moving application workloads into Kubernetes. As organizations have begun to migrate existing applications to Kubernetes and create new cloud native applications in Kubernetes, modernizing the data tier is a step that is often deferred. Whatever the causes of these delays—the belief that Kubernetes is not ready for stateful workloads, a lack of development resources, or other factors—the result has been mismatched architectures in which applications are running in Kubernetes with databases and other data infrastructure running externally. This leads to a division of focus for developers and SREs that can limit productivity. It's also common to see distinct toolsets for monitoring applications and database infrastructure, which increases cloud computing costs.

This adoption challenge became evident in the Cassandra community. Despite the growing collaboration and consensus around building a single Cassandra operator as discussed in Chapter 5, developers were still confronted with key questions about how the database and operator would fit in the larger application context:

- How can you have an integrated view of the health of your entire stack, including both applications and data?
- How can you tailor the automation of installation, upgrades, and other operational tasks in a Kubernetes native way that fits the way we manage your Datacenters?

To help address these questions, John Sanda and a team of engineers at DataStax launched an open source project called K8ssandra with the goal of providing a production-ready deployment of Cassandra that embodies best practices for running Cassandra in Kubernetes. K8ssandra provides custom resources that help manage tasks including cluster deployment, upgrades, scaling up and down, data backup and restore, and more. You can read more about the motivations for the project in Jeff Carpenter's blog post "Why K8ssandra?" (*https://oreil.ly/dB6mJ*).

K8ssandra Architecture

K8ssandra is deployed in units known as *clusters*, which is similar terminology to that used by Kubernetes and Cassandra. A K8ssandra cluster includes a Cassandra cluster along with additional components depicted in Figure 6-1 to provide a full data management ecosystem. Let's consider these in roughly clockwise order starting from the top center:

Cass Operator
: A Kubernetes operator first introduced in Chapter 5. It manages the lifecycle of Cassandra nodes on Kubernetes, including provisioning new nodes and storage, and scaling up and down.

Cassandra Reaper
: This manages the details of repairing Cassandra nodes in order to maintain high data consistency.

Cassandra Medusa
: Provides backup and restore for data stored in Cassandra.

Prometheus and Grafana
: Used for the collection and visualization of metrics.

Stargate
: A data gateway that provides API access to client applications as an alternative to CQL.

K8ssandra Operator
: Orchestrates all of the other components, including multicluster support for managing Cassandra clusters that span multiple Kubernetes clusters.

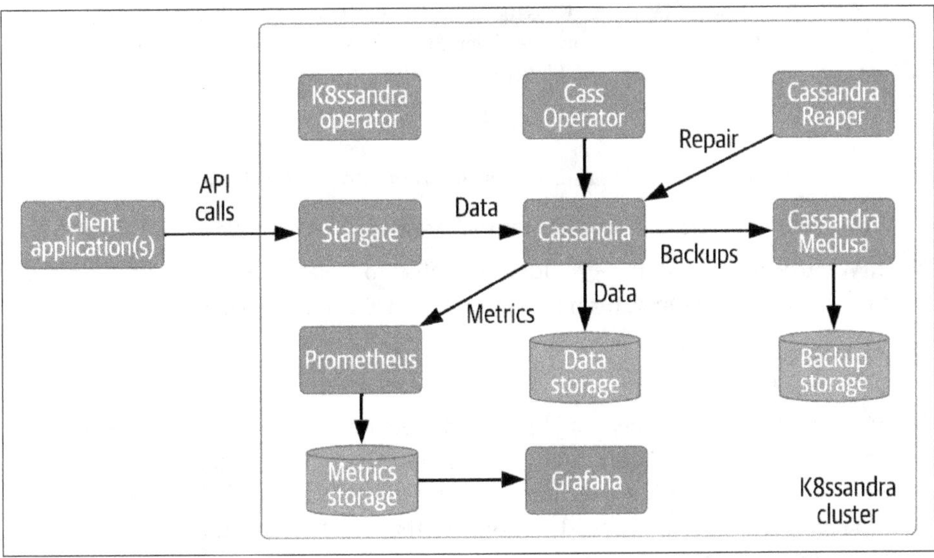

Figure 6-1. K8ssandra architecture

In the following sections, we'll take a look at each component of the K8ssandra project to understand the role that it plays within the architecture and its relationship to other components.

Installing the K8ssandra Operator

Let's dive in with some hands-on experience of installing K8ssandra. To get a basic installation of K8ssandra running that fully demonstrates the power of the operator, you'll need a Kubernetes cluster with several Worker Nodes.

To make the deployment simpler, the K8ssandra team has provided scripts to automate the process of creating Kubernetes clusters and then deploying the operator to these clusters. These scripts use kind clusters (*https://kind.sigs.k8s.io*) for simplicity, so you'll want to make sure you have this installed before starting.

Instructions for installing on various clouds are also available on the K8ssandra website. The instructions we provide here are based on an installation guide (*https://oreil.ly/4z2oH*) in the K8ssandra Operator repository (*https://oreil.ly/kgeWY*).

K8ssandra 2.0 Release Status

This chapter focuses on the K8ssandra 2.0 release, including the K8ssandra Operator. At the time of writing, K8ssandra 2.0 is still in beta status. As K8ssandra 2.0 moves toward a full GA release, the instructions on the "Get Started" section of the K8ssandra website (*https://oreil.ly/nT1n5*) will be updated to reference the new version.

First, start by cloning the K8ssandra operator repository from GitHub:

```
git clone https://github.com/k8ssandra/k8ssandra-operator.git
```

Next, you'll want to use the provided Makefile to create a Kubernetes cluster and deploy the K8ssandra Operator into it (this assumes you have `make` installed):

```
cd k8ssandra-operator
make single-up
```

If you examine the Makefile, you'll notice the operator is installed using Kustomize, which we discussed in "Additional Deployment Tools: Kustomize and Skaffold" on page 94. The target you just executed creates a kind cluster with four Worker Nodes and changes your current context to point to that cluster, as you can see by running the following:

```
% kubectl config current-context
kind-k8ssandra-0
% kubectl get nodes
NAME                         STATUS   ROLES                  AGE     VERSION
k8ssandra-0-control-plane    Ready    control-plane,master   6m45s   v1.22.4
k8ssandra-0-worker           Ready    <none>                 6m13s   v1.22.4
k8ssandra-0-worker2          Ready    <none>                 6m13s   v1.22.4
k8ssandra-0-worker3          Ready    <none>                 6m13s   v1.22.4
k8ssandra-0-worker4          Ready    <none>                 6m13s   v1.22.4
```

Now examine the list of CRDs that have been created:

```
% kubectl get crd
NAME                                             CREATED AT
cassandrabackups.medusa.k8ssandra.io             2022-02-05T17:31:35Z
cassandradatacenters.cassandra.datastax.com      2022-02-05T17:31:35Z
cassandrarestores.medusa.k8ssandra.io            2022-02-05T17:31:35Z
cassandratasks.control.k8ssandra.io              2022-02-05T17:31:36Z
certificaterequests.cert-manager.io              2022-02-05T17:31:16Z
certificates.cert-manager.io                     2022-02-05T17:31:16Z
challenges.acme.cert-manager.io                  2022-02-05T17:31:16Z
clientconfigs.config.k8ssandra.io                2022-02-05T17:31:36Z
clusterissuers.cert-manager.io                   2022-02-05T17:31:17Z
issuers.cert-manager.io                          2022-02-05T17:31:17Z
k8ssandraclusters.k8ssandra.io                   2022-02-05T17:31:36Z
orders.acme.cert-manager.io                      2022-02-05T17:31:17Z
reapers.reaper.k8ssandra.io                      2022-02-05T17:31:36Z
replicatedsecrets.replication.k8ssandra.io       2022-02-05T17:31:36Z
stargates.stargate.k8ssandra.io                  2022-02-05T17:31:36Z
```

As you can see, several CRDs are associated with the cert-manager and K8ssandra. There is also the CassandraDatacenter CRD used by Cass Operator. The K8ssandra and Cass Operator CRDs are all Namespaced, which you can verify using the `kubectl api-resources` command, meaning that resources created according to these definitions are assigned to a specific Namespace. That command will also show you the acceptable abbreviations for each resource type (for example, `k8c` for `k8ssandracluster`).

Next, you can examine the contents that have been installed within the kind cluster. If you list the Namespaces using `kubectl get ns`, you'll note two new Namespaces: `cert-manager` and `k8ssandra-operator`. As you may suspect, K8ssandra is using the same cert-manager project as Pulsar, as described in "Securing Communications by Default with cert-manager" on page 207. Let's examine the contents of the `k8ssandra-operator` Namespace, which are summarized in Figure 6-2 along with related K8ssandra CRDs.

Examine the workloads and you'll notice that two Deployments have been created: one for the K8ssandra Operator and one for Cass Operator. Take a look at the K8ssandra Operator source code, and you'll see that it contains multiple controllers, while the Cass Operator consists of a single controller. This packaging reflects the fact that Cass Operator is an independent project which can be used by itself without having to adopt the entire K8ssandra framework—otherwise, it could have been included as a controller within the K8ssandra Operator.

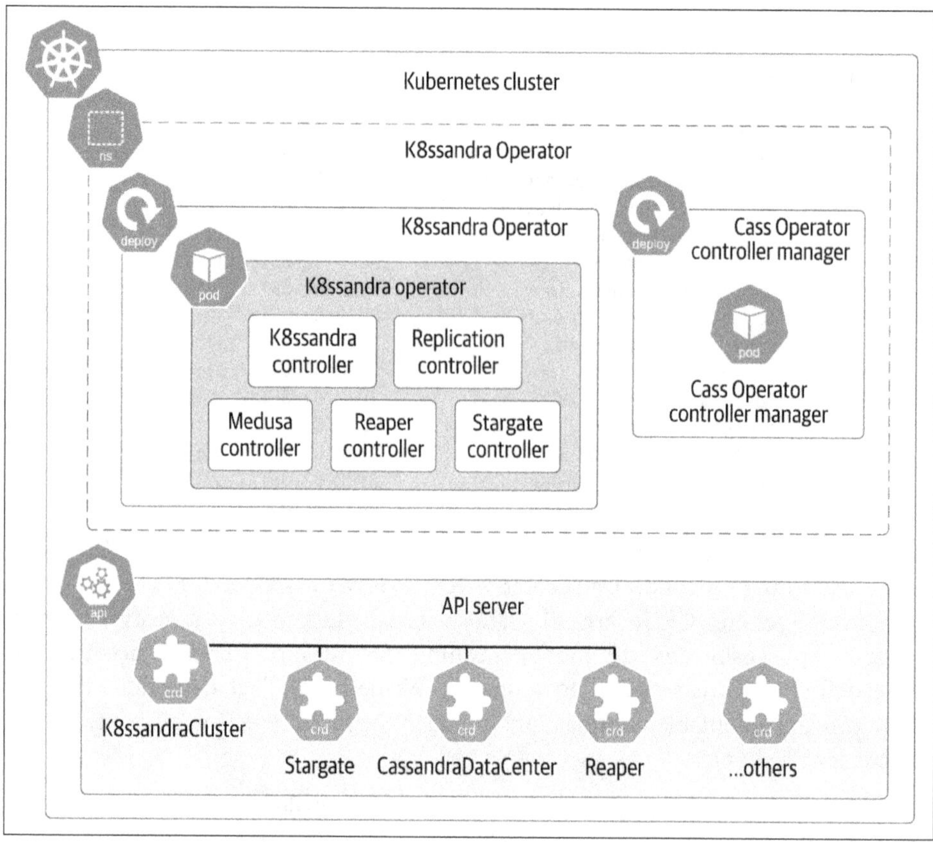

Figure 6-2. K8ssandra Operator architecture

Table 6-1 describes the mapping of these various controllers to the key resources with which they interact.

Table 6-1. Mapping K8ssandra CRDs to controllers

Operator	Controller	Key custom resources
K8ssandra Operator	K8ssandra controller	`K8ssandraCluster`, `CassandraDatacenter`
	Medusa controller	`CassandraBackup`, `CassandraRestore`
	Reaper controller	`Reaper`
	Replication controller	`ClientConfig`, `ReplicatedSecret`
	Stargate controller	`Stargate`
Cass Operator	Cass Operator controller manager	`CassandraDatacenter`

We'll introduce each K8ssandra and Cass Operator CRD in more detail in the following sections:

Creating a K8ssandraCluster

Once you've installed the K8ssandra Operator, the next step is to create a K8ssandraCluster. The source code used in this section is available in the "Vitess Operator Example" section of the book's repository (*https://oreil.ly/1n3k7*), based on samples available in the K8ssandra Operator GitHub repo (*https://oreil.ly/5WxRO*). First, have a look at the *k8ssandra-cluster.yaml* file:

```
apiVersion: k8ssandra.io/v1alpha1
kind: K8ssandraCluster
metadata:
  name: demo
spec:
  cassandra:
    cluster: demo
    serverVersion: "4.0.1"
    datacenters:
      - metadata:
          name: dc1
        size: 3
        storageConfig:
          cassandraDataVolumeClaimSpec:
            storageClassName: standard
            accessModes:
              - ReadWriteOnce
            resources:
              requests:
                storage: 1Gi
        config:
          jvmOptions:
            heapSize: 512M
        stargate:
          size: 1
          heapSize: 256M
```

This code specifies a K8ssandraCluster resource consisting of a single Datacenter `dc1` running three nodes of Cassandra 4.0.1, where the Pod specification for each Cassandra node requests 1 GB of storage using a PersistentVolumeClaim that references the `standard` StorageClass. This configuration also includes a single Stargate node to provide API access to the Cassandra cluster. This is a minimal configuration that accepts the chart defaults for most of the other components. Create the `demo` K8ssandraCluster in the `k8ssandra-operator` Namespace with this command:

```
% kubectl apply -f k8ssandra-cluster.yaml -n k8ssandra-operator
k8ssandracluster.k8ssandra.io/demo created
```

Once the command completes, you can check on the installation of the K8ssandraCluster using commands such as `kubectl get k8ssandraclusters` (or `kubectl get k8c` for short). Figure 6-3 depicts some of the key compute, network, and storage resources that the operator built on your behalf when you created the `demo` K8ssandraCluster.

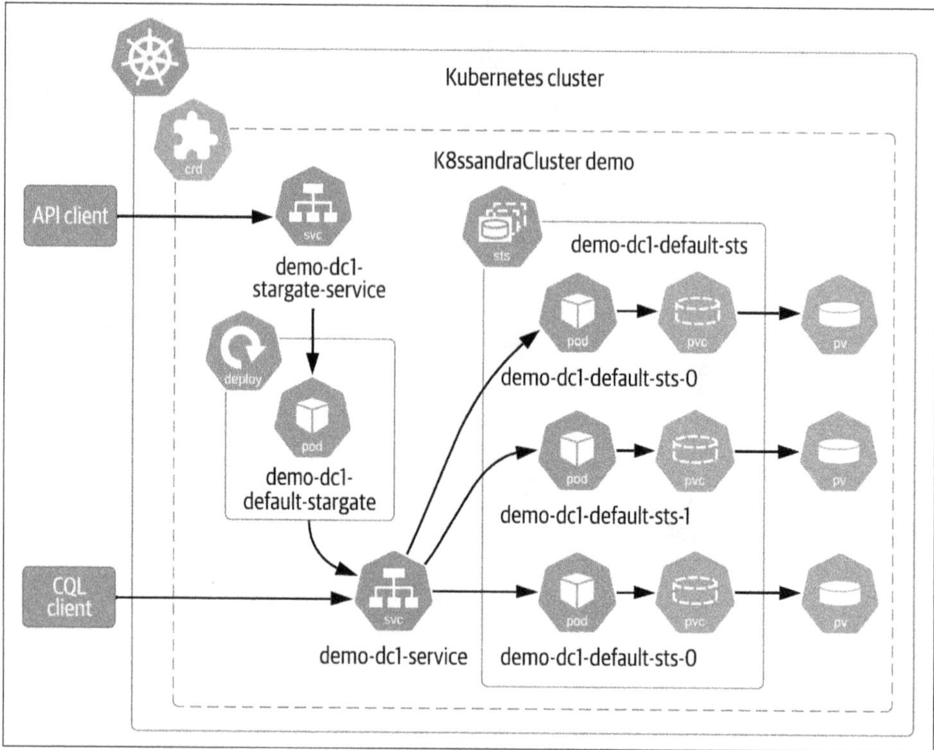

Figure 6-3. A simple K8ssandraCluster

Here are some key items to note:

- A single StatefulSet has been created to represent the Cassandra Datacenter `dc1`, with three Pods containing the replicas you specified. As you'll learn in the next section, K8ssandra uses a CassandraDatacenter CRD to manage this StatefulSet via the Cass Operator.
- While the figure shows a single Service `demo-dc1-service` exposing access to the Cassandra cluster as a single endpoint, this is a simplification. You will find multiple Services configured to provide access for various clients.
- There is a Deployment managing a single Stargate Pod, as well as Services that provide client endpoints to the various API services provided by Stargate. This is another simplification, and we'll explore this part of configuration in more detail in "Enabling Developer Productivity with Stargate APIs" on page 147.

- Similar to examples of infrastructure we've shown in previous chapters, the K8ssandra Operator also creates additional supporting security resources such as ServiceAccounts, Roles, and RoleBindings.

Once you have a K8ssandraCluster created, you can point client applications at the Cassandra interfaces and Stargate APIs, and perform cluster maintenance operations. You can remove a K8ssandraCluster just by deleting its resource, but you won't want to do that yet as we have a lot more to explore! We'll describe several of these interactions as we examine each of the K8ssandra components in more detail. Along the way, we'll make sure to note some of the interesting design choices made by contributors to K8ssandra and related projects in terms of how they use Kubernetes resources and how they adapt data infrastructure that predates Kubernetes into the Kubernetes way of doing things.

StackGres: An Integrated Kubernetes Stack for Postgres

The K8ssandra project is not the only instance of an integrated data stack that runs on Kubernetes. Another example can be found in StackGres (*https://stackgres.io*), a project managed by OnGres. StackGres uses Patroni (*https://github.com/zalando/patroni*) to support clustered, highly available Postgres deployments and adds automated backup functionality. StackGres supports integration with Prometheus and Grafana for metrics aggregation and visualization, along with an optional Envoy proxy for getting more fine-grained metrics at the protocol level. StackGres is composed of open source components and uses the AGPLv3 License (*https://www.gnu.org/licenses/agpl-3.0.en.html*) for its community edition.

Managing Cassandra in Kubernetes with Cass Operator

Cass Operator is the shorthand name for the DataStax Kubernetes Operator for Apache Cassandra. This open source project available on GitHub (*https://oreil.ly/xWjZr*) was brought under the umbrella of the K8ssandra project in 2021, replacing its previous home under the DataStax GitHub organization (*https://oreil.ly/JAF3Y*).

Cass Operator is a key part of K8ssandra, since a Cassandra cluster is the basic data infrastructure around which all the other infrastructure elements and tools are added. However, Cass Operator was developed before K8ssandra and will continue to exist as a separately deployable project. This is helpful since not every capability of Cass Operator is exposed via K8ssandra, especially more advanced Cassandra configuration options. Cass Operator is listed as its own project in Operator Hub (*https://oreil.ly/gPtl3*) and can be installed via Kustomize.

Cass Operator provides a mapping of Cassandra's topology concepts including clusters, Datacenters, racks, and nodes onto Kubernetes resources. The key construct is the CassandraDatacenter CRD, which represents a Datacenter within the topology of a Cassandra cluster. (Reference Chapter 3 if you need a refresher on Cassandra topology.)

When you created a K8ssandraCluster resource in the previous section, the K8ssandra Operator created a single CassandraDatacenter resource, which would have looked something like this:

```
apiVersion: cassandra.datastax.com/v1beta1
kind: CassandraDatacenter
metadata:
  name: dc1
spec:
  clusterName: demo
  serverType: cassandra
  serverVersion: 4.0.1
  size: 3
  racks:
  - name: default
```

Since you didn't specify a rack in the K8ssandraCluster definition, K8ssandra interprets this as a single rack named `default`. By creating the CassandraDatacenter, K8ssandra Operator is delegating the operation of the Cassandra nodes in this Datacenter to Cass Operator.

Cass Operator and Multiple Datacenters

You may be wondering why Cass Operator does not define a CRD representing a Cassandra cluster. From the perspective of the Cass Operator, the Cassandra cluster is basically just a piece of metadata—the CassandraDatacenter's `clusterName`—rather than an actual resource. This reflects the convention that Cassandra clusters used in production systems are typically deployed across multiple physical datacenters, which is beyond the scope of a Kubernetes cluster.

While you can certainly create multiple CassandraDatacenters and link them together using the same `clusterName`, they must be in the same Kuberneters cluster for Cass Operator to be able to manage them. It's also recommended to use a separate Namespace to install a dedicated instance of Cass Operator to manage each cluster. You'll see how K8ssandra supports the ability to create Cassandra clusters that span multiple physical datacenters (and Kubernetes clusters) in multicluster topologies.

When Cass Operator is notified by the API server of the creation of the CassandraDatacenter resource, it creates resources used to implement the datacenter, including a StatefulSet to manage the nodes in each rack, as well as various Services and security-related resources. The StatefulSet will start the requested number of Pods in parallel. This brings up a situation in which Cass Operator provides logic to adapt between how Cassandra and Kubernetes operate.

If you have worked with Cassandra previously, you may be aware that the best practice for adding nodes to a cluster is to do so one one at a time, to simplify the process of a node joining the cluster. This process, called *bootstrapping*, includes the step of negotiating which data the node will be responsible for, and may include streaming data from other nodes to the new node. However, since the StatefulSet is not aware of these constraints, how can adding multiple nodes to a new or existing cluster one at a time be accomplished?

The answer lies in the composition of the Pod specification that Cass Operator passes to the StatefulSet, which is then used to create each Cassandra node, as shown in Figure 6-4.

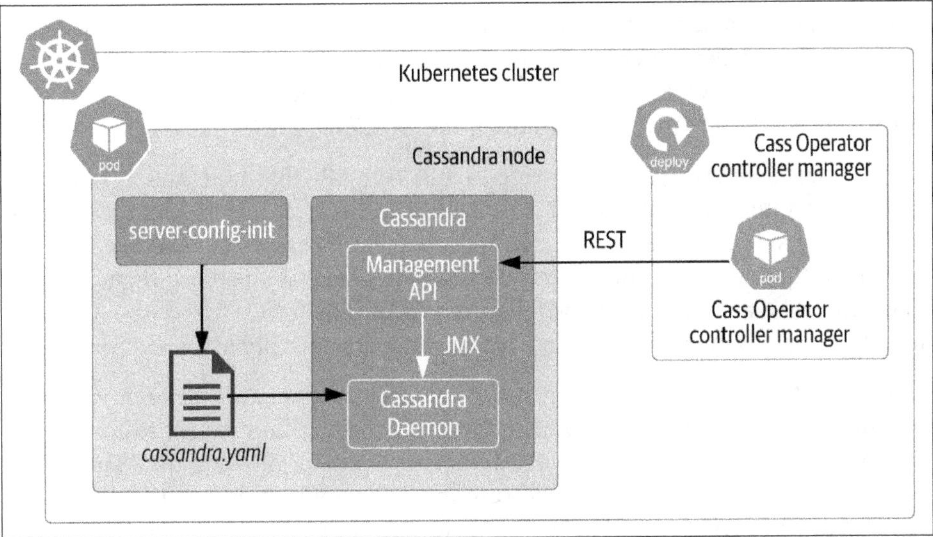

Figure 6-4. Cass Operator interactions with Cassandra Pods

Cass Operator deploys a custom image of Cassandra in each Cassandra Pod that it manages. The Pod specification includes at least two containers: an init container called `server-config-init` and a Cassandra container called `cassandra`.

As an init container, `server-config-init` is started before the Cassandra container. It's responsible for generating the *cassandra.yaml* configuration file based on the selected configuration options for the CassandraDatacenter. You can specify additional configuration values using the `config` section of the CassandraDatacenter resource, as described in the K8ssandra documentation (*https://oreil.ly/SlN0F*).

Additional Sidecar Containers in Cassandra Pods

As you'll learn in the following sections, the Cassandra Pod may have additional sidecar containers when deployed in a K8ssandraCluster, depending on which of the additional K8ssandra components you have enabled. For right now, though, we are focusing on the most basic installation.

The `cassandra` container actually contains two separate processes: the daemon that runs the Cassandra instance and a Management API. This goes somewhat against the traditional best practice of running a single process per container, but there is a good reason for this exception.

Cassandra's management interface is exposed via the Java Management Extensions (JMX). While this was a legitimate design choice for a Java-based application like Cassandra when the project was just starting out, JMX has fallen out of favor because of its complexity and security issues. While there has been some progress toward an alternate management interface for Cassandra, the work is not yet complete, so the developers of Cass Operator decided to integrate another open source project, the Management API for Apache Cassandra (*https://oreil.ly/1XIPi*).

The Management API project provides a RESTful API that translates HTTP-based invocations into calls on Cassandra's legacy JMX interface. By running the Management API inside the Cassandra container, we avoid having to expose the JMX port outside of the Cassandra containers. This is an instance of a pattern frequently used in cloud native architectures to adapt custom protocols into HTTP-based interfaces, for which there is much better support for routing and security in ingress controllers.

Cass Operator discovers and connects to the Management API on each Cassandra Pod in order to perform management operations that are not related to Kubernetes. When adding new nodes, this involves the simple action of using the Management API to verify that the node is up and running successfully and updating the CassandraDatacenter's status accordingly. This sequence is described in more detail in the K8ssandra documentation (*https://oreil.ly/T7io1*).

Customizing the Cassandra Image Used by Cass Operator

The Management API project provides images for recent Cassandra versions in the 3.*x* and 4.*x* series, which are available on Docker Hub (*https://oreil.ly/FQa3q*). While it is possible to override the Cassandra image that Cass Operator uses with one of your own, Cass Operator does require that the Management API is available on each Cassandra Pod. If you need to build your own custom image including the Management API, you could use the Dockerfiles and supporting scripts from the GitHub repository (*https://oreil.ly/GKRP1*) as a starting point.

While this section focused largely on the startup and scaling of Cassandra clusters just described, Cass Operator provides several features for deploying and managing Cassandra clusters:

Topology management
: Cass Operator uses Kubernetes affinity principles to manage the placement of Cassandra nodes (Pods) across Kubernetes Worker Nodes to maximize availability of your data.

Scaling down
: Just as nodes are added one at a time to scale up, Cass Operator manages scaling down one node at a time.

Replacing nodes
: If a Cassandra node is lost because it crashes or the Worker Node on which it is running goes down, Cass Operator relies on the StatefulSet to replace the node and bind the new node to the appropriate PersistentVolumeClaim.

Upgrading images
: Cass Operator also leverages the capabilities of StatefulSet to perform rolling upgrades of the images used by the Cassandra Pods.

Managing seed nodes
: Cass Operator creates Kubernetes Services to expose the seed nodes in each Datacenter according to Cassandra's recommended conventions of one seed node per rack, for a minimum of three per Datacenter.

You can read about these and other features in the Cass Operator documentation (*https://oreil.ly/UafkF*).

Enabling Developer Productivity with Stargate APIs

Our focus so far in this book has been primarily on deployment of data infrastructure such as databases in Kubernetes, more than on the way that infrastructure is used in cloud native applications. The usage of Stargate (*https://stargate.io*) in K8ssandra gives us a good opportunity to have that discussion.

In many organizations, there is an ongoing conversation about the pros and cons of direct application access to databases versus abstracting the details of database interactions. This debate occurs especially frequently in larger organizations that divide responsibilities between application development teams and teams that manage platforms including data infrastructure. However, it can also be observed in organizations that employ modern practices including DevOps and microservice architectures, where each microservice may have a different data store behind it.

The idea of providing abstractions over direct database access has taken many forms over the years. Even in the days of monolithic client-server applications, it was common to use stored procedures or isolate data access and complex query logic behind object-relational mapping tools such as Hibernate, or to use patterns like data access objects (DAOs).

More recently, as the software industry has moved toward service oriented architecture (SOA) and microservices, similar patterns for abstracting data access have appeared. As described in Jeff's article "Data Services for the Masses" (*https://oreil.ly/u6K58*), many teams have found themselves creating a layer of microservices in their architecture dedicated to data access, providing create, read, update, and delete (CRUD) operations on specific data types or entities. These services abstract the details of interacting with a specific database backend, and if well executed and maintained, can help increase developer productivity and facilitate migration to a different database when needed.

The Stargate project was born out of the realization that multiple teams were building very similar abstraction layers to provide data access via APIs. The goal of the Stargate project is to provide an open source *data API gateway*—a common set of APIs for data access to help eliminate the need for teams to develop and maintain their own custom API layers. While the initial implementation of Stargate is based on Cassandra, the goal of the project is to support multiple database backends, and even other types of data infrastructure such as caches and streaming.

With Cassandra used as the backend data store, the Stargate architecture can be described as having three layers, as shown in Figure 6-5.

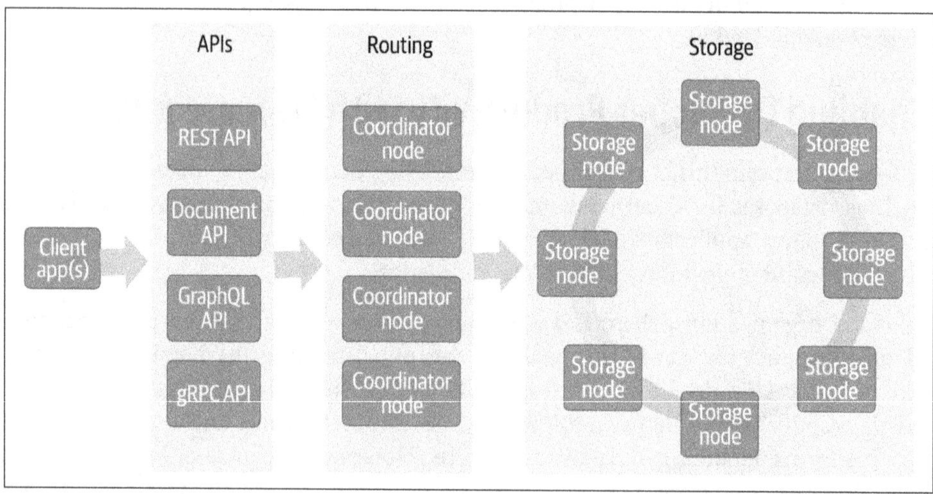

Figure 6-5. Stargate conceptual architecture with Cassandra

The *API layer* is the outermost layer, consisting of services that implement various APIs on top of the underlying Cassandra cluster. Available APIs include a REST API (*https://oreil.ly/qTEY6*), a Document API (*https://oreil.ly/ekhlV*) that provides access to JSON documents over HTTP, a GraphQL API (*https://oreil.ly/BescX*), and a gRPC API (*https://oreil.ly/k2fNY*). The *routing layer* (or *coordination layer*) consists of a set of nodes that act as Cassandra nodes, but perform only routing of queries, not data storage. The *storage layer* consists of a traditional Cassandra cluster, which can currently be Cassandra 3.11, Cassandra 4.0, or DataStax Enterprise 6.8.

One of the key benefits of this architecture is that it recognizes the separation of concerns for managing usage of compute and storage resources and provides the ability to scale this usage independently based on the needs of client applications:

- The number of storage nodes can be scaled up or down to provide the storage capacity required by the application.
- The number of coordinator nodes and API instances can be scaled up or down to match the application's read and write load and optimize throughput.
- APIs that are not used by the application can be scaled to zero (disabled) to reduce resource consumption.

K8ssandra supports the provision of Stargate on top of an underlying Cassandra cluster via the Stargate CRD. The CassandraDatacenter deployed by Cass Operator serves as the storage layer, and the Stargate CRD specifies the configuration of the routing and API layers. An example configuration is shown in Figure 6-6.

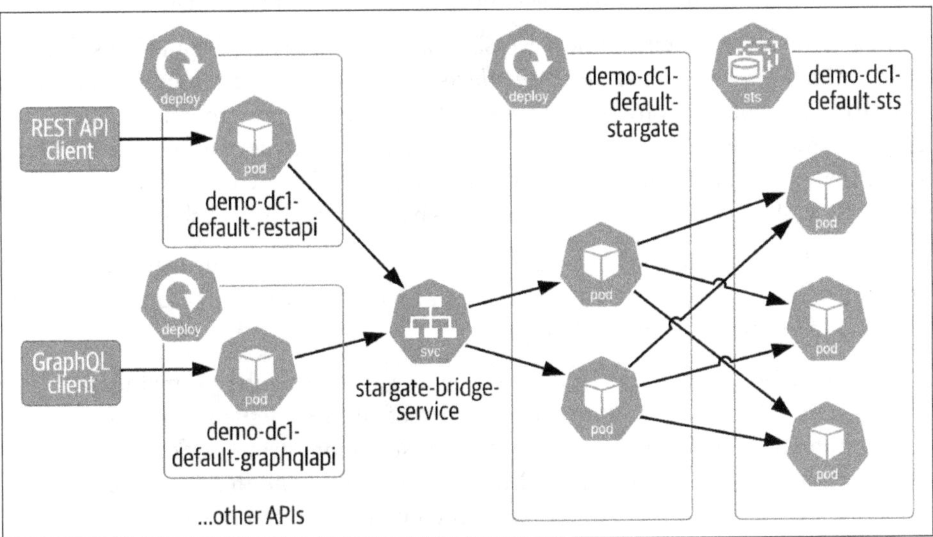

Figure 6-6. Stargate deployment on Kubernetes

The installation includes a Deployment to manage the coordinator nodes, and a Service to provide access to the Bridge API, a private gRPC interface exposed on the coordinator nodes that can be used to create new API implementations. See the Stargate v2 design (*https://oreil.ly/6ct5m*) for more details on the Bridge API. There is also a Deployment for each of the APIs that is enabled in the installation, along with a Service to provide access to client applications.

As you can see, the Stargate project provides a promising framework for extending your data infrastructure with developer-friendly APIs that can scale along with the underlying database.

Unified Monitoring Infrastructure with Prometheus and Grafana

Now that we've considered the addition of infrastructure that makes life easier for application developers, let's look at some of the more operations-focused aspects of integrating data infrastructure in a Kubernetes stack. We'll start with monitoring.

Observability is a key attribute of any application deployed on Kubernetes, since it has implications for your awareness of its availability, performance, and cost. Your goal should be to have an integrated view across both your application and the infrastructure it depends on. Observability is often described as consisting of three types of data: metrics, logs, and tracing. Kubernetes itself provides capabilities for logging as well as associating events with resources, and you've already learned how the Cass Operator facilitates the collection of logs from Cassandra nodes.

In this section, we'll focus on how K8ssandra incorporates the Prometheus/Grafana stack, which provides metrics. *Prometheus* is a popular open source monitoring platform. It supports a variety of interfaces for collecting data from applications and services and stores them in a time series database which can be queried efficiently using the Prometheus Query Language (PromQL). It also includes an Alertmanager which generates alerts and other notifications based on metric thresholds.

While previous releases of K8ssandra in the 1.*x* series incorporated the Prometheus stack as part of a K8ssandra, K8ssandra 2.*x* provides the capability to integrate with an existing Prometheus installation.

One easy way to install the Prometheus Operator is to use kube-prometheus (*https://oreil.ly/tzDmJ*), a repository provided as part of the Prometheus Operator project. Kube-prometheus is intended as a comprehensive monitoring stack for Kubernetes including the control plane and applications. You can clone this repository and use the library of manifests (YAML files) that it contains to install the integrated stack of components shown in Figure 6-7.

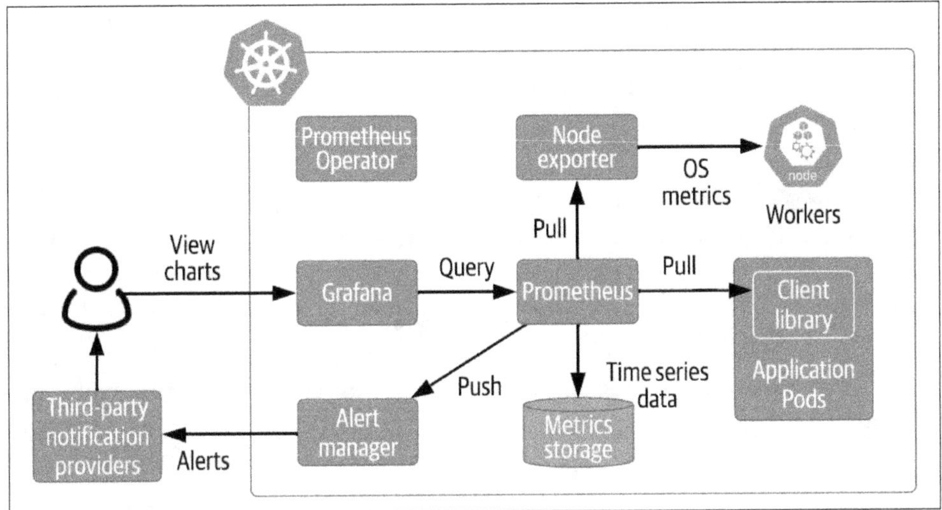

Figure 6-7. Components of the kube-prometheus stack

These components include the following:

Prometheus Operator
: The operator, which is set apart in the figure, manages the other components.

Prometheus
: The metrics database is run in a high-availability configuration managed via a StatefulSet. Prometheus stores data using a time series database with a backing PersistentVolume.

Node exporter
: The node exporter (*https://oreil.ly/Yt0YO*) runs on each Kubernetes Worker Node, allowing Prometheus to pull operating system metrics via HTTP.

Client library
: Applications can embed a Prometheus client library, which allows Prometheus to pull metrics via HTTP.

Alert manager
: This can be configured to generate alerts based on thresholds for specific metrics for delivery via email or third-party tools such as PagerDuty. The kube-prometheus stack comes with built-in alerts for the Kubernetes cluster; application-specific alerts can also be added.

Grafana
: This is deployed to provide charts that are used to display metrics to human operators. Grafana uses PromQL to access metrics from Prometheus, and this interface is available to other clients as well.

While not shown in the figure, the stack also includes the Prometheus Adapter for Kubernetes Metrics APIs (*https://oreil.ly/g033n*), an optional component that exposes metrics collected by Prometheus to the Kubernetes control plane so that they can be used to auto-scale applications.

Connecting K8ssandra with Prometheus can be accomplished in a few quick steps. The instructions (*https://oreil.ly/UOt4t*) in the K8ssandra documentation walk you through installing the Prometheus Operator using kube-prometheus if you do not have it already. Since kube-prometheus installs Prometheus Operator in its own Namespace, you'll want to make sure the operator has permissions to manage resources in other Namespaces.

To integrate K8ssandra with Prometheus, you set attributes on your K8ssandraCluster resource to enable monitoring on Cassandra and Stargate nodes. For example, you could do something like the following to enable monitoring for nodes in all Datacenters in the cluster:

```
apiVersion: k8ssandra.io/v1alpha1
kind: K8ssandraCluster
metadata:
  name: demo
spec:
  cassandra:
    datacenters:
      ...
    telemetry:
      prometheus:
        enabled: true
  stargate:
    telemetry:
      prometheus:
        enabled: true
```

It's also possible to selectively enable monitoring on individual datacenters.

Let's take a look at how the integration works. First, let's consider how the Cassandra nodes expose metrics. As discussed in "Managing Cassandra in Kubernetes with Cass Operator" on page 143, Cassandra exposes management capabilities via JMX, and this includes metrics reporting. The Metric Collector for Apache Cassandra (MCAC) (*https://oreil.ly/CHNMQ*) is an open source project that exposes metrics so that they can be accessed by Prometheus or other backends that use the Prometheus protocol via HTTP. K8ssandra and Cass Operator use a Cassandra Docker image that includes MCAC as well as the Management API as additional processes that run in the Cassandra container. This configuration is shown on the left side of Figure 6-8.

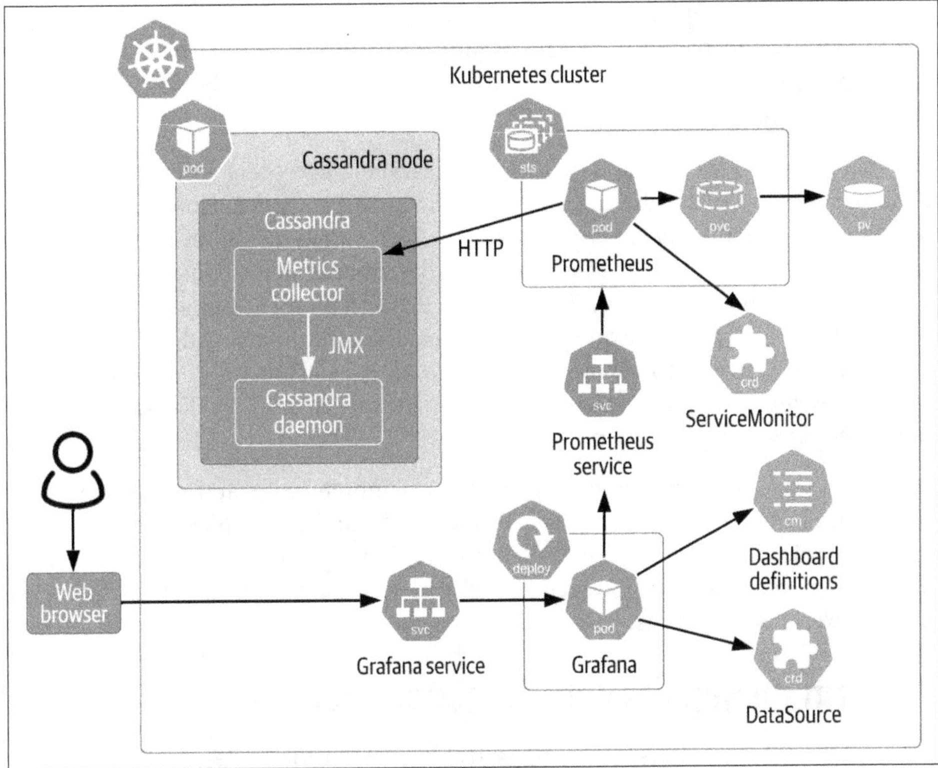

Figure 6-8. Monitoring Cassandra with the kube-prometheus stack

The right side of Figure 6-8 shows how Prometheus and Grafana are configured to consume and expose the Cassandra metrics. The K8ssandra Operator creates ServiceMonitor resources for each CassandraDatacenter for which monitoring has been enabled. The ServiceMonitor, a CRD defined by the Prometheus Operator, contains configuration details describing how to collect metrics from a set of Pods, including the following:

- A `selector` referencing the name of a label which identifies the Pods
- Connection information such as the `scheme` (protocol), `port`, and `path` to use to gather metrics from each Pod
- The `interval` at which metrics should be pulled
- Optional `metricRelabelings`, which are instructions that indicate any desired renaming of metrics, or even indicate metrics that should be dropped and not ingested by Prometheus

K8ssandra creates separate ServiceMonitor instances for Cassandra and Stargate nodes, since the metrics exposed are slightly different. To observe the ServiceMonitors deployed in your cluster, you can execute a command such as `kubectl get servicemonitors -n monitoring`.

Prometheus provides access to its metrics to Grafana and other tools via a PromQL endpoint exposed as a Kubernetes service. The kube-prometheus installation configures an instance of Grafana to connect to Prometheus using an instance of the Grafana Datasource CRD. Grafana accepts dashboards defined using YAML files, which you can provide as ConfigMaps. See the K8ssandra documentation (*https://oreil.ly/vCfmR*) for guidance on loading dashboard definitions that display Cassandra and Stargate metrics. You may also wish to create dashboards that display your application metrics alongside the data tier metrics provided by K8ssandra for an integrated view of application performance.

As you can see, kube-prometheus provides a comprehensive and extensible monitoring stack for Kubernetes clusters, much as K8ssandra provides a stack for data management. The integration of K8ssandra with kube-prometheus is a great example of how you can assemble integrated stacks of Kubernetes resources to form even more powerful applications.

Performing Repairs with Cassandra Reaper

As a NoSQL database, Cassandra emphasizes high performance (especially for writes) and high availability by default. If you're familiar with the CAP theorem, you'll understand that this means that sometimes Cassandra will temporarily sacrifice consistency of data across nodes in order to deliver this high performance and high availability at scale, an approach known as *eventual consistency*. Cassandra does provide the ability to tune the amount of consistency to your needs via options for specifying replication strategies and the consistency level required per query. Users and administrators should be aware of these options and their behavior in order to use Cassandra effectively.

Cassandra has multiple built-in "anti-entropy" mechanisms such as hinted handoff and repair that help maintain consistency of data between nodes over time. Repair is a background process by which a node compares a portion of the data it owns with the latest contents of other nodes that are also responsible for that data. While these checks can be somewhat optimized through the use of checksums, repair can still be a performance-intensive process and is best performed when a cluster is under reduced or off-peak load. Combined with the fact that multiple options are available, including full and incremental repairs, executing repairs has traditionally required some tailoring for each cluster. It also has tended to be a manual process that was unfortunately frequently neglected by some Cassandra cluster administrators.

More Detail on Repairs in Cassandra

For a deeper treatment of repair, see *Cassandra: The Definitive Guide*, where repair concepts and the available options are described in Chapters 6 and 12, respectively.

Cassandra Reaper (*http://cassandra-reaper.io*) was created to take the difficulty out of executing repairs on Cassandra clusters and optimize repair performance to minimize the impact of running repairs on heavily used clusters. Reaper was created by Spotify and enhanced by The Last Pickle, which currently manages the project on GitHub (*https://oreil.ly/2MttB*). Reaper exposes a RESTful API for configuring repair schedules for one or more Cassandra clusters, and also provides a command-line tool and web interface which guides administrators through the process of creating schedules.

K8ssandra provides the option to incorporate an instance of Cassandra Reaper as part of a K8ssandraCluster. The K8ssandra Operator includes a Reaper controller that is responsible for managing the local Cassandra Reaper manager process through its associated Reaper CRD. By default, enabling Reaper in a K8ssandraCluster will cause an instance of Reaper to be installed in each Kubernetes cluster represented in the installation, but you can also use a single instance of Reaper to manage repairs across multiple Datacenters, or even across multiple Cassandra clusters, provided they are accessible via the network.

How Important Is It to Be Kubernetes Native?

K8ssandra's usage of Reaper is an example of the trade-offs involved in building more complex stacks of data infrastructure. For example, a more Kubernetes native design for the Reaper manager might involve factoring out each repair task into a Kubernetes CronJob that could be scheduled alongside the associated CassandraDatacenter, thus making more use of Kubernetes built-in resources. For now, the K8ssandra project has made the choice to integrate Reaper as is.

We saw another example of this "wrap versus rewrite" type of decision in Chapter 5, where the Vitess Operator reuses the Vitess control daemon `vtctld` and its `vtctlclient` as is. In both of these examples, the project developers have made pragmatic choices to do initial deployments that do "just enough" to port existing infrastructure to run in Kubernetes, while leaving room for more Kubernetes native approaches in the future. In Chapter 7, we'll examine what it looks like to start with a Kubernetes native approach from scratch on new infrastructure projects.

Backing Up and Restoring Data with Cassandra Medusa

Managing backups is an important part of maintaining high availability and disaster recovery planning for any system that stores data. Cassandra supports both full and differential backups by creating hard links to the SSTable files it uses for data persistence. Cassandra itself does not take responsibility for copying the SSTable files to backup storage. Instead, this is left to the user. Similarly, recovering from backup involves copying the SSTable files to the Cassandra node where the data is to be reloaded; then Cassandra can be pointed to the local files to restore their contents.

Cassandra's backup and restore operations are traditionally executed on individual nodes using nodetool, a command-line tool that leverages Cassandra's JMX interface. Cassandra Medusa (*https://oreil.ly/tmP91*) is an open source command-line tool created by Spotify and The Last Pickle that executes nodetool commands to perform backups, including synchronization of backups across multiple nodes. Medusa supports Amazon S3, Google Cloud Storage (GCS), Azure Storage, and S3-compatible storage such as MinIO and Ceph Object Gateway, and can be extended to support other storage providers via the Apache Libcloud project.

Medusa can restore either individual nodes to support fast replacement of a downed node, or entire clusters in a disaster recovery scenario. Restoring to a cluster can either be to the original cluster or to a new cluster. Medusa is able to restore data to a cluster with a different size or topology than the original cluster, which has traditionally been a challenge to figure out manually.

K8ssandra has incorporated Medusa in order to provide backup and restore capabilities for Cassandra clusters running in Kubernetes. To configure the use of Medusa in a K8ssandraCluster, you'll want to configure the `medusa` properties:

```
apiVersion: k8ssandra.io/v1alpha1
kind: K8ssandraCluster
metadata:
  name: demo
spec:
  cassandra:
    ...
  medusa:
    storageProperties:
      storageProvider: google_storage
      storageSecretRef:
        name: medusa-bucket-key
      bucketName: k8ssandra-medusa
      prefix: test
      ...
```

The options shown here include the storage provider, the bucket to use for backups, an optional prefix to add to directory names used to organize backup files, and the name of a Kubernetes Secret containing login credentials for the bucket. See the documentation (*https://oreil.ly/ujZYw*) for details on the contents of the Secret. Other available options include enabling SSL on the bucket connection, and setting the policies for purging old backups such as a maximum age or number of backups.

Creating a Backup

Once the K8ssandraCluster has been started, you can create backups using the CassandraBackup CRD. For example, you could initiate a backup of the CassandraDatacenter `dc1` using a command like this:

```
cat <<EOF | kubectl apply -f -n k8ssandra-operator -
apiVersion: medusa.k8ssandra.io/v1alpha1
kind: CassandraBackup
metadata:
  name: medusa-backup1
spec:
  cassandraDatacenter: dc1
  name: medusa-backup1
EOF
```

The steps in processing of this resource are shown in Figure 6-9.

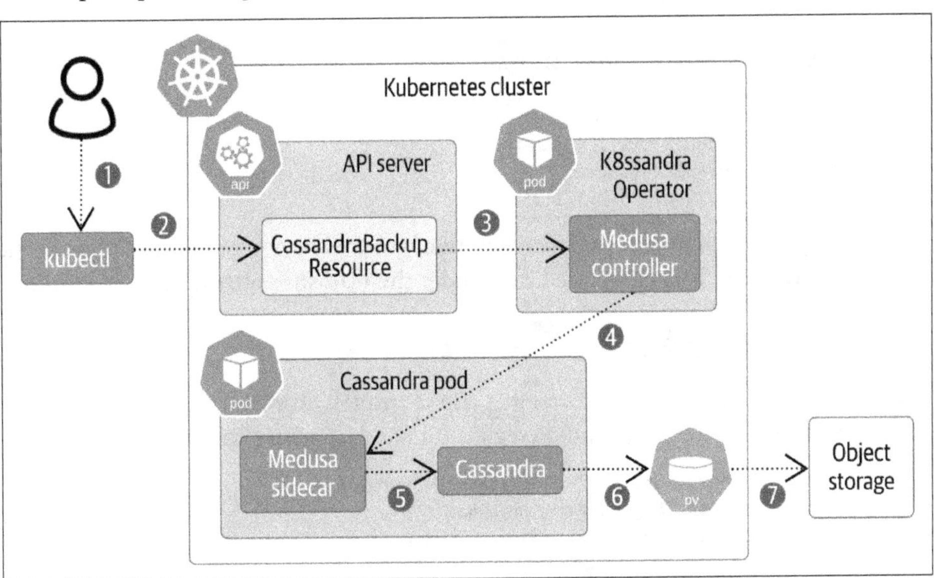

Figure 6-9. Performing a Datacenter backup using Medusa

When you apply the resource definition (1), `kubectl` registers the resource with the API Server (2). The API server notifies the Medusa Controller running as part of the K8ssandra Operator (3).

The Medusa Controller contacts a sidecar container (4), which K8ssandra has injected into the Cassandra Pod because you chose to enable Medusa on the K8ssandraCluster. The Medusa sidecar container uses nodetool commands to a backup on the Cassandra node via JMX (5) (the JMX interface is exposed only within the Pod).

Cassandra performs a backup (6), marking the SSTable files on the PersistentVolume that mark the current snapshot. The Medusa sidecar copies the snapshot files from the PV to the bucket (7). Steps 4–7 are repeated for each Cassandra Pod in the CassandraDatacenter.

You can monitor the progress of the backup by checking the status of the resource:

```
kubectl get cassandrabackup/medusa-backup1 -n k8ssandra-operator -o yaml
kind: CassandraBackup
metadata:
    name: medusa-backup1
spec:
  backupType: differential
  cassandraDatacenter: dc1
  name: medusa-backup1
status:
  ...
  ...
  finishTime: "2022-02-26T09:21:38Z"
  finished:
  - demo-dc1-default-sts-0
  - demo-dc1-default-sts-1
  - demo-dc1-default-sts-2
  startTime: "2022-02-26T09:21:35Z"
```

You'll know the backup is complete when the `finishTime` attribute is populated. The Pods that have been backed up are listed under the `finished` attribute.

Restoring from Backup

The process of restoring data from a backup is similar. To restore an entire Datacenter from backed-up data, you could create a CassandraRestore resource like this:

```
cat <<EOF | kubectl apply -f -n k8ssandra-operator -
apiVersion: medusa.k8ssandra.io/v1alpha1
kind: CassandraRestore
metadata:
  name: restore-backup1
spec:
  cassandraDatacenter:
    name: dc1
    clusterName: demo
  backup: medusa-backup1
  inPlace: true
  shutdown: true
EOF
```

When the Medusa Controller is notified of the new resource, it locates the CassandraDatacenter and updates the Pod spec template within the StatefulSet that is managing the Cassandra Pods. The updates consist of adding a new init container called `medusa-restore` and setting environment variables that `medusa-restore` will use to locate the datafiles that are to be restored. The update to the Pod spec template causes the StatefulSet controller to perform a rolling update of the Cassandra Pods in the StatefulSet. As each Pod restarts, `medusa-restore` copies the files from object storage onto the PersistentVolume for the node, and then the Cassandra container starts as usual. You can monitor the progress of the restore by checking the status of the CassandraRestore resource.

A Common Language for Data Recovery?

It is interesting to note the similarities and differences between the ways backup and restore operations are supported by the K8ssandra Operator we've discussed in this chapter and the Vitess Operator discussed in Chapter 5.

In K8ssandra, the CassandraBackup and CassandraRestore resources function in a manner similar to Kubernetes Jobs—they represent a task that you would like to have performed as well as the results of the task. In contrast, the VitessBackup resource represents a record of a backup that the Vitess Operator has performed based on the configuration of a VitessCluster resource. There is no equivalent resource to the CassandraRestore operator in Vitess.

Although K8ssandra and Vitess differ significantly in their approach to managing backups, both represent each backup task as a resource. Perhaps this common ground could be the starting point toward the development of common resource definitions for backup and restore operations, helping fulfill the vision introduced in Chapter 5.

Similar to the behavior of Cassandra Reaper, a single instance of Medusa can be configured to manage backup and restore operations across multiple Datacenters or Cassandra clusters. See the K8ssandra documentation (*https://oreil.ly/Y2EkE*) for more details on performing backup and restore operations with Medusa.

Deploying Multicluster Applications in Kubernetes

One of the main selling points of a distributed database like Cassandra is its ability to support deployments across multiple Datacenters. Many users take advantage of this in order to promote high availability across geographically distributed Datacenters, to provide lower-latency reads and writes for applications and their users.

However, Kubernetes itself was not originally designed to support applications that span multiple Kubernetes clusters. This has traditionally meant that creating such multiregion applications leaves a lot of work to development teams.

This work takes two main forms: creating the network infrastructure to connect the Kubernetes clusters, and coordinating interactions between resources in those clusters. Let's examine these requirements and the implications for an application like Cassandra:

Multicluster networking requirements
: From a networking perspective, the key is to have secure, reliable networking between Datacenters. If you're using a single cloud provider for your application, this may be relatively simple to achieve using VPC capabilities offered by the major cloud vendors.

  If you're using multiple clouds, you'll need a third-party solution. For the most part, Cassandra requires routable IPs between its nodes and does not rely on name resolution, but it is helpful to have DNS in place as well to simplify the process of managing Cassandra's seed nodes.

  Jeff's blog post "Deploy a Multi-Data Center Cassandra Cluster in Kubernetes" (*https://oreil.ly/HpCYX*) describes an example configuration in Google Cloud Platform (GCP) using the CloudDNS service, while Raghavan Srinivas's blog post "Multi-Region Cassandra on EKS with K8ssandra and Kubefed" (*https://oreil.ly/9byYo*) describes a similar configuration on Amazon EKS.

Multicluster resource coordination requirements
: Managing an application that spans multiple Kubernetes clusters means that there are distinct resources in each cluster which have no relationship to resources in other clusters that the Kubernetes control plane is aware of. To manage the lifecycle of an application including deployment, upgrade, scaling up and down, and teardown, you need to coordinate resources across multiple Datacenters.

  The Kubernetes Cluster Federation project (KubeFed (*https://oreil.ly/yvUCm*) for short) provides one approach to providing a set of APIs for managing resources across clusters that can be leveraged to build multicluster applications. This includes mechanisms that represent Kubernetes clusters themselves as resources. While KubeFed is still in beta, the K8ssandra Operator uses a similar design approach for managing resources across clusters. We'll examine this in more detail in "Kubernetes Cluster Federation" on page 163.

To achieve a multicluster Kubernetes deployment of Cassandra, you'll need to establish networking between Datacenters according to your specific situation. Given that foundation, the K8ssandra Operator provides the facilities to manage the lifecycle of resources across the Kubernetes clusters. For a simple example of deploying a multiregion K8ssandraCluster, use the instructions (*https://oreil.ly/bmcil*) found in the K8ssandra documentation, again using the Makefile:

```
make multi-up
```

This builds two kind clusters, deploys the K8ssandra Operator in each of them, and creates a multicluster K8ssandraCluster. One advantage of using kind for a simple demonstration is that Docker provides the networking between clusters. We'll walk through some of the key steps in this process in order to describe how the K8ssandra Operator accomplishes this work.

The K8ssandra Operator supports two modes of installation: control plane (the default) and data plane. For a multicluster deployment, one Kubernetes cluster must be designated as the control plane cluster, and the others as data plane clusters. The control plane cluster can optionally include a CassandraDatacenter, as in the configuration shown in Figure 6-10.

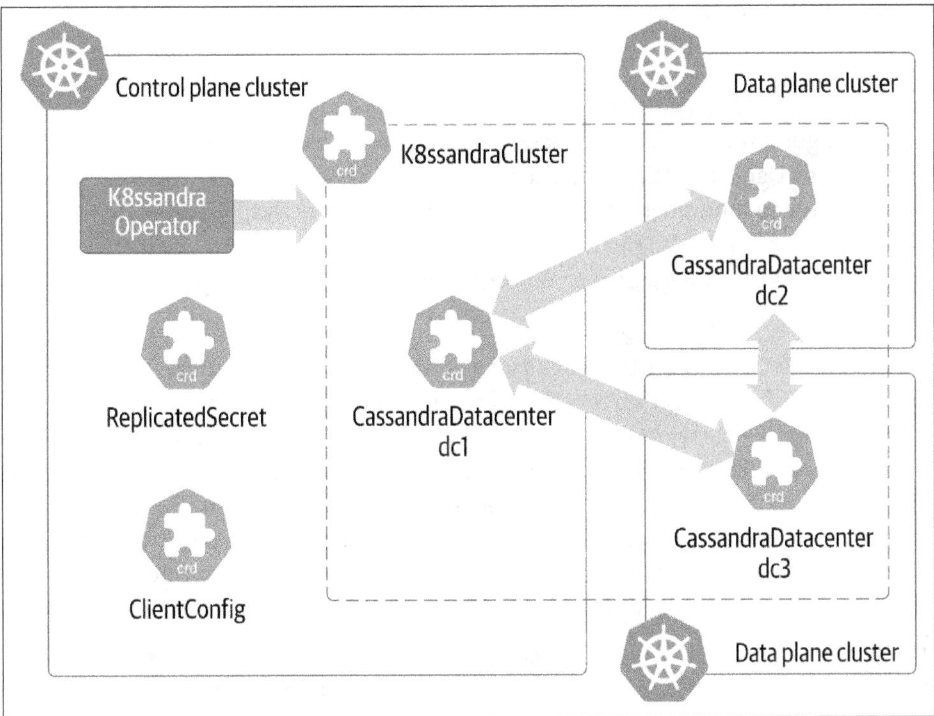

Figure 6-10. K8ssandra multicluster architecture

When installed in control plane mode, the K8ssandra Operator uses two additional CRDs to manage multicluster deployments: ReplicatedSecret and ClientConfig. You can see evidence of the ClientConfig in the K8ssandraCluster configuration that was used, which looks something like the following:

```
apiVersion: k8ssandra.io/v1alpha1
kind: K8ssandraCluster
metadata:
  name: demo
spec:
  cassandra:
    serverVersion: "4.0.1"
    ...
    networking:
      hostNetwork: true
    datacenters:
      - metadata:
          name: dc1
        size: 3
        stargate:
          size: 1
      - metadata:
          name: dc2
        k8sContext: kind-k8ssandra-1
        size: 3
        stargate:
          size: 1
```

This configuration specifies a K8ssandraCluster `demo` consisting of two CassandraDatacenters, `dc1` and `dc2`. Each Datacenter has its own configuration so that you can select a different number of Cassandra and Stargate nodes, or different resource allocations for the Pods. In the `demo` configuration, `dc1` is running in the control plane cluster `kind-k8ssandra-0`, and `dc2` is running in the data plane cluster `kind-k8ssandra-1`.

Notice the `k8sContext: kind-k8ssandra-1` line in the configuration. This is a reference to a ClientConfig resource that was created by the `make` command. A ClientConfig is a resource that represents the information needed to connect to the API server of another cluster, similar to the way `kubectl` stores information about different clusters on your local machine. The ClientConfig resource references a Secret that is used to store access credentials securely. The K8ssandra Operator repo includes a convenience script (*https://oreil.ly/wPINU*) that can be used to create ClientConfig resources for Kubernetes clusters.

When you create a K8ssandraCluster in the control plane cluster, it uses the ClientConfigs to connect to each remote Kubernetes cluster in order to create the specified resources. For the preceding configuration, this includes CassandraDatacenter and Stargate resources, but can also include other resources such as Medusa and Prometheus ServiceMonitor.

The ReplicatedSecret is another resource involved in sharing access credentials. The control plane K8ssandra Operator uses this resource to keep track of Secrets that it creates in each remote cluster. These Secrets are used by the various K8ssandra components to securely communicate information such as the default Cassandra administrator credentials with each other. The K8ssandra Operator creates and manages ReplicatedSecret resources itself; you don't need to interact with them.

The K8ssandraCluster, ClientConfig, and ReplicatedSecret resources exist only in the control plane cluster, and when the K8ssandra Operator is deployed in data plane mode, it does not even run the controllers associated with those resource types.

More Detail on the K8ssandra Operator

This is a quick summary of a complex design for a multicluster operator. For more details on the approach, see the K8ssandra Operator architecture overview (*https://oreil.ly/ACAD2*) and John Sanda's presentation (*https://oreil.ly/RMK3E*) at the Data on Kubernetes Community (DoKC) meetup.

Now let's consider a more general approach to building multicluster applications that we can compare and contrast with K8ssandra's approach.

Kubernetes Cluster Federation

With Irfan Ur Rehman, Senior Engineer, Turbonomic (an IBM company)

KubeFed is a project for building multicluster applications, managed by the Kubernetes Multicluster SIG (*https://oreil.ly/lfWvB*). The project was initially called *Federation*, but was renamed *Kubernetes Cluster Federation (KubeFed)*, to distinguish it from the term *federation* being used in projects outside of Kubernetes.

KubeFed defines *federation* as joining a set of clusters into a pool, which then provides a unified API to the user to distribute applications into those clusters. To use KubeFed, you create federated resources in a base cluster. A federated resource contains templates for Kubernetes built-in or custom resources. KubeFed acts as a resource reconciler, using the templates you provide to push resources to the member clusters.

You might want the templates to be applied in slightly different ways in each member cluster, so KubeFed supports concepts called placements and overrides. A *placement* defines where applications and their resources are deployed. For example, you could use a placement to push resources in cluster 1 but not cluster 2 or to indicate you want more replicas in one cluster than another cluster. *Overrides* allow you to provide different values for resource attributes for a specific cluster.

KubeFed also provides resources to support higher-order things you might want to do. The ReplicaScheduler is a resource that manages Deployments and ReplicaSets. This allows you to deploy your application by specifying the total number of replicas desired across clusters, without worrying about which clusters they go to. You can do something similar for StatefulSets.

Cluster federation, placements, and overrides are three key concepts defined by KubeFed, along with others defined on the concepts page (*https://oreil.ly/xByUc*). These terms have gained wide popularity and are used across other projects as well. For example, Argo CD is a GitOps toolset for Kubernetes which employs similar concepts such as placement rules and overrides.

Other multicluster projects in the Kubernetes ecosystem have similar goals but differ in implementation and scope:

Kubernetes Armada (Karmada) (https://oreil.ly/yLA6g)
: This project, sponsored by Huawei, is similar to KubeFed but takes a different API approach. Karmada reuses existing Kubernetes resources but extends them with additional attributes in order to provide the appearance of a single Kubernetes cluster.

Crossplane (https://crossplane.io)
: This CNCF incubating project aims to provide a single API surface for you to distribute resources and consume services from multiple clouds. Crossplane uses the same declarative approach as Kubernetes but goes beyond just Kubernetes resources, allowing you to incorporate offerings from the major cloud providers such as database as a service (DBaaS) or network as a service (NaaS).

Open Cluster Management (OCM) (https://oreil.ly/v6nV5)
: This project, sponsored by Red Hat, provides an ecosystem of components for working across multiple Kubernetes clusters.

Each of these projects takes a similar approach at a high level but has its own opinionated APIs and nuances which might be more suitable to different users.

KubeFed and these similar projects are primarily concerned with resource replication. To have multicluster applications, you also need networking solutions, which can get a little more complex. One approach is to create cross-cluster network overlays using open source projects like Submariner (*https://oreil.ly/ZalRQ*) or Cilium (*https://oreil.ly/hy7ck*).

Even with the network in place, you still have the problem of discovering applications and resources across clusters and connecting them securely. The Multi-Cluster Services API (*https://oreil.ly/lMVf4*) is a proposal in the Kubernetes Multicluster SIG for providing this discovery. It is based on *endpoint slices*, which allow a cluster to discover services from another cluster. An alpha implementation (*https://oreil.ly/kDReX*) is available.

Although KubeFed is still in Beta status, it is in a mature state, and some organizations are already using it in production. The core functionality of reconciling resources across clusters is something that just works. The main item in the KubeFed roadmap is a GA release, which should lead to further adoption.

Adoption can be a chicken-and-egg problem, because organizations often prefer to back established projects. Throughout its history, KubeFed has had support from RedHat/IBM, Huawei, D2iQ, and others, and backing by larger organizations is important for driving adoption by the larger community.

Coming up with a single standard is challenging. Major cloud providers have a lack of incentive (*https://oreil.ly/1Hc43*) to contribute to these efforts as opposed to supporting tooling centered on their own platforms, so it is up to us in the open source community to invest in this area.

As you can see, there is a lot of potential for growth in the area of Kubernetes federation and the ability to manage resources across Kubernetes cluster boundaries. For example, as a database whose primary superpower is running across multiple Datacenters, Cassandra seems like a great match for a multicluster solution like KubeFed.

The K8ssandra Operator and KubeFed have taken similar architectural approaches, where custom "federated" resources provide templates used to define resources in other clusters. This commonality points to the possibility for future collaboration across these projects and others based on similar design principles. Perhaps in the future, CRDs like K8ssandra's ClientConfig and ReplicatedSecret can be replaced by equivalent functionality provided by KubeFed.

Summary

In this chapter, you've learned how data infrastructure can be composed with other infrastructure to build reusable stacks on Kubernetes. Using the K8ssandra project as an example, you've learned about aspects including integrating data infrastructure with API gateways and monitoring solutions to provide more full-featured solutions.

You've also learned some of the opportunities and challenges with adapting existing technologies onto Kubernetes and creating multicluster data infrastructure deployments. In the next chapter, we'll explore how to design new cloud native data infrastructure that takes advantage of everything that Kubernetes provides without requiring adaptation and discover what new possibilities that opens up.

CHAPTER 7

The Kubernetes Native Database

The software industry is flush with terms that define major trends in a single word or short phrase. You can see one of them in the title of this book: *cloud native*. Another example is *microservice*, a major architectural paradigm that touches much of the technology we're discussing here. More recently, terms like *Kubernetes native* and *serverless* have emerged.

While succinct and catchy, distilling a complex topic or trend down to a single sound bite leaves room for ambiguity, or at least for reasonable questions such as "What does this *actually* mean?" To further muddy the waters, terms such as these are frequently used in the context of marketing products as a way to gain leverage or differentiate against other competitive offerings. Whether the content you're consuming makes an overt statement or it's just the subtext, you may have wondered whether a given technology must be better to run on Kubernetes than other offerings because it's labeled *Kubernetes native*.

Of course, for these terms to be useful to us in evaluating and picking the right technologies for our applications, the real task is to unpack what they really mean, as we did with the term *cloud native data* in Chapter 1. In this chapter, we'll look at what it means for data technology to be Kubernetes native and see if we can arrive at a definition that we can agree on. To do this, we'll examine a couple of projects that claim these terms and derive the common principles: TiDB and Astra DB. Are you ready? Let's dive in!

Why a Kubernetes Native Approach Is Needed

First, let's discuss why the idea of a Kubernetes native database came up in the first place. Up to this point in the book, we've focused on deployment of existing databases on Kubernetes including MySQL and Cassandra. These are mature databases that were around before Kubernetes existed and have proven themselves over time. They have large install bases and user communities, and because of this investment, you can see why there's a large incentive to run these databases in Kubernetes environments, and why there has been such interest in creating operators to automate them.

At the same time, you've probably noticed some of the awkwardness in adapting these databases to run on Kubernetes. While it is pretty straightforward to point a database to Kubernetes-based storage just by changing a mount path, tighter integration with Kubernetes to manage databases that consist of multiple nodes can be a bit more involved. This can range from relatively simple tasks like deploying a legacy management UI in a Pod and exposing access to the HTTP port, to the more complex deployment of sidecars that we saw in Chapter 6 to provide APIs for management and metrics collection.

The recognition of this complexity has led some innovators to develop new databases that are designed to be Kubernetes native from day one. It's a well-known axiom in the database industry that it takes 5–10 years for a new database engine to reach a point of maturity. Because of this, these Kubernetes native databases tend not to be completely new implementations, but rather refactoring of existing databases into microservices that can be scaled independently, while maintaining compatibility with existing APIs that developers are accustomed to. Thus, the trend of decomposing the monolith has arrived at the data tier. The emerging generation of databases will be based on new architectures to truly leverage the benefits of Kubernetes.

To help us assess what might qualify these new databases as Kubernetes native, let's use the cloud native data principles introduced in "Principles of Cloud Native Data Infrastructure" on page 14 as a guide to formulate some questions to ask how a database interacts with Kubernetes:

Principle 1: Leverage compute, network, and storage as commodity APIs
: How does the database use Kubernetes compute resources (Pods, Deployments, StatefulSets), network resources (Services and Ingress), and storage resources (PersistentVolumes, PersistentVolumeClaims, StorageClasses)?

Principle 2: Separate the control and data planes
: Is the database deployed and managed by an operator? What custom resources does it define? Are other workloads in the control plane besides the operator?

Principle 3: Make observability easy
: How do the various services in the architecture expose metrics and logs to support collection by the Kubernetes control plane and third-party extensions?

Principle 4: Make the default configuration secure
: Do the database and associated operator use Kubernetes Secrets to share credentials, and use Roles and RoleBindings to manage access by Role? Do services minimize the number of exposed points and require secure access to them?

Principle 5: Prefer declarative configuration
: Extending Principle 2, can the database be managed entirely by creating, updating, or deleting Helm charts and Kubernetes resources (whether built-in or custom resources), or are other tools required?

In the sections that follow, we'll explore the answers to these questions for two databases and see what else we can learn about what it means to be Kubernetes native. That will help us to build a checklist at the end of this chapter that will help solidify our definition. (See "What to Look for in a Kubernetes Native Database" on page 189 for what we come up with.)

Hybrid Data Access at Scale with TiDB

The databases that have received most of our focus in this book so far represent two major trends in database architecture that trace their lineage back for decades or more. MySQL is a relational database that provides its own flavor of the Standard Query Language (SQL), based on rules developed by Edgar Codd in the 1970s.

In the early 2000s, companies building web-scale applications began to push the limits of what could be accomplished with the relational databases of the day. As database sizes began growing beyond what could feasibly be managed on a single instance, techniques like sharding were used to scale across multiple instances. These were frequently expensive, difficult to operate, and not always reliable.

In response to this need, Cassandra and other so-called *NoSQL* databases emerged in a period of intense innovation and experimentation. These databases provide linear scalability through adding additional nodes. They offer different data models, or ways of representing data: for example, key-value stores such as Redis, document databases such as MongoDB, graph databases such as Neo4j, and others. NoSQL databases tended to provide weaker consistency guarantees and omit support for more complex behaviors like transactions and joins to achieve high performance and availability at scale, a trade-off documented by Eric Brewer in his CAP theorem (*https://oreil.ly/aJq6M*).

Because of the continued developer demand for traditional relational semantics such as strong consistency, transactions, and joins, multiple teams began to revive the idea of supporting these capabilities in distributed databases starting around 2012. These so-called *NewSQL* databases were based on more efficient and performant consensus algorithms. Two key papers helped drive the emergence of the NewSQL movement. First, the Calvin paper (*https://oreil.ly/HLw2M*) introduced a global consensus protocol which represented a more reliable and performant approach for guaranteeing strong consistency, later adopted by FaunaDB and other databases. Second, Google's Spanner paper (*https://oreil.ly/zDl5z*) introduced a design for a distributed relational database using sharding and a new consensus algorithm that leveraged the improved ability of cloud infrastructure to provide time synchronization across datacenters. Besides Google Spanner, this approach was implemented by databases including CockroachDB and YugabyteDB.

More on Consistency and Consensus

While we don't have space in this book to dive deeply into the trade-offs between various consensus algorithms and how they are used to provide various data consistency guarantees, an understanding of these concepts is helpful in choosing the right data infrastructure for your cloud applications. If you're interested in learning more in this area, Martin Kleppmann's *Designing Data-Intensive Applications* (O'Reilly) is a great source, especially Chapter 9, "Consistency and Consensus".

TiDB (*https://oreil.ly/jZNAI*) (where *Ti* stands for *Titanium*) represents a continuation of the NewSQL trend in the cloud native space. TiDB is an open source, MySQL-compatible database that supports both transactional and analytic workloads. It was initially developed and is primarily supported by PingCAP. While TiDB is a database designed to embody cloud native principles of scalability and elasticity, what makes it especially interesting for our discussion is that it has been explicitly designed to run on Kubernetes and to rely on capabilities provided by the Kubernetes control plane. In this way, one could argue that TiDB is not merely a Kubernetes native database, but also a Kubernetes *only* database. Let's dig into the details.

TiDB Architecture

A key characteristic of TiDB which distinguishes it from other databases we've examined so far in this book is its ability to support transactional and analytic workloads. This approach, known as *hybrid transactional/analytical processing (HTAP)*, supports both types of queries without a separate extract, transform, and load (ETL) process. As shown in Figure 7-1, TiDB does this by providing two database engines under the hood: TiKV and TiFlash. This approach was inspired by Google's F1 project (*https://oreil.ly/lakAf*), a layer built on top of Spanner.

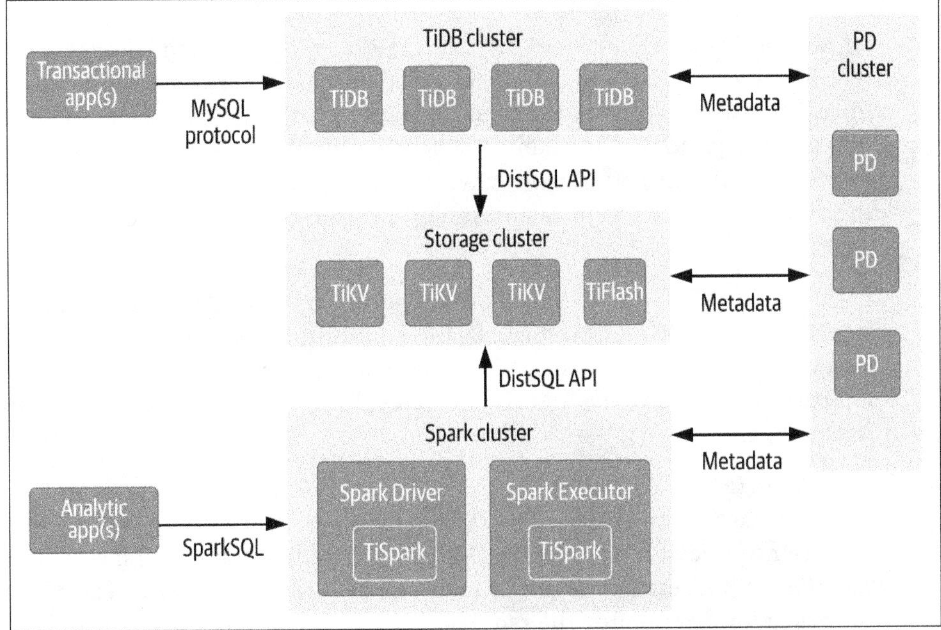

Figure 7-1. TiDB architecture

One key aspect that gives TiDB a cloud native architecture is the packaging of compute and storage operations into separate components, each of which is composed of independently scalable services organized in clusters. Let's examine the roles of each of these components:

TiDB
: Each TiDB instance is a stateless service that exposes a MySQL endpoint to client applications. TiDB parses incoming SQL requests and uses metadata from the Placement Driver (PD) to create an execution plan containing queries to make on specific TiKV and TiFlash nodes in the storage cluster. TiDB executes these queries, assembles the results, and returns to the client application. The TiDB cluster is typically deployed with a proxy in front of it to provide load balancing.

TiKV
: The storage cluster consists of a mixture of TiKV and TiFlash nodes. First, let's examine *TiKV* (*https://tikv.org*), an open source, distributed key-value database that uses RocksDB (*http://rocksdb.org*) as its backing storage engine. TiKV exposes a custom distributed SQL API that the TiDB nodes use to execute queries to store and retrieve data and manage distributed transactions. TiKV stores multiple replicas of your data, typically at least three, to support high availability and automatic failover. TiKV is a CNCF graduated project (*https://oreil.ly/ypLlC*) which can be used independently from TiDB, as we'll discuss later.

TiFlash
: The storage cluster also includes TiFlash nodes, to which data is replicated from TiKV nodes as it is written. TiFlash is a columnar database based on the open source ClickHouse analytic database (*https://oreil.ly/PCVlg*), which means that it organizes data storage in columns rather than rows. Columnar databases can provide a significant performance advantage for analytic queries requiring the extraction of the same column across multiple rows.

TiSpark
: This library is built for Apache Spark to support complex OLAP queries. TiSpark integrates with the Spark Driver and Spark Executors, providing the capability to ingest data from TiFlash instances using the distributed SQL API. We'll examine the Spark architecture and the details of deploying Spark on Kubernetes in Chapter 9.

Placement Driver (PD)
: The PD manages the metadata for a TiDB installation. PD instances are deployed in a cluster of at least three nodes. TiDB uses a range-based sharding mechanism where the keys in each table are divided into ranges called *regions*. The PD is responsible for determining the ranges of data assigned to each region, and the TiKV nodes that will store the data for each region. It monitors the amount of data in each region and splits regions that become too large, to facilitate scaling up, and merging smaller regions to scale down.

Because the TiDB architecture consists of well-defined interfaces between the components, it is an extensible architecture in which different pieces can be plugged in. For example, TiKV provides a distributed key-value storage solution that can be reused in other applications. The TiPrometheus project (*https://oreil.ly/PkmqK*) is an example, providing a Prometheus-compliant compute layer on top of TiKV. For another example, you could provide an alternate implementation of TiKV that implements the distributed SQL API on top of a different storage engine.

Pluggable Storage Engines

In this chapter so far, we've made several mentions of "storage engines" or "database engines." This term refers to the part of the database that manages the storage and retrieval of data on persistent media. In distributed databases, a distinction is often made between the storage engine and the proxy layer which sits on top of it to manage data replication between nodes. Chapter 3, "Storage and Retrieval," from *Designing Data-Intensive Applications* includes discussion of storage engine types such as the B-trees used in most relational databases and the log-structured merge tree (LSM tree) used in Apache Cassandra and other NoSQL databases.

One interesting aspect of TiDB is the way in which it reuses existing technology. We've seen examples of this in the usage of components including RocksDB and Spark. TiDB also uses algorithms developed by other organizations. Here are a couple of examples:

Raft consensus protocol
: At the TiDB layer, the Raft consensus protocol (*https://oreil.ly/Oi6Dk*) is used to manage consistency between replicas. Raft is similar to the Paxos algorithm used by Cassandra in terms of its behavior, but it's designed to be much simpler to learn and use. TiDB uses a separate Raft group for each region, where a group typically consists of a leader and two or more replicas. If a leader node is lost, an election is run to select a new leader, and a new replica can be added to ensure the desired number of replicas. In addition, the TiFlash nodes are configured as a special type of replica called *learner replicas*. Data is replicated to learner replicas from the TiDB nodes, but they cannot be selected as a leader. You can read more about how TiDB uses Raft for high availability (*https://oreil.ly/BddzV*) and other related topics on the PingCAP blog (*https://oreil.ly/Y2YuS*).

Percolator transaction management
: At the TiDB layer, distributed transactions are supported using an implementation of the Percolator algorithm (*https://oreil.ly/heMho*) with optimizations specific to the TiDB project. Percolator was originally developed at Google for supporting incremental updates to search indexes.

One of the arguments we're making in this chapter is that part of what it means for data infrastructure to be cloud native is to compose existing APIs, services, and algorithms wherever possible, and TiDB is a great example of this.

Deploying TiDB in Kubernetes

While TiDB can be deployed in a variety of ways including bare metal and VMs, the TiDB team has invested a large effort in tooling and documentation to make TiDB a truly Kubernetes native database. The TiDB Operator (*https://oreil.ly/xZtGq*) manages TiDB clusters in Kubernetes, including deployment, upgrade, scaling, backup and restore, and more.

The operator documentation (*https://oreil.ly/iIZc0*) provides quick start guides (*https://oreil.ly/5heDA*) for desktop Kubernetes distributions such as kind, minikube, and Google Kubernetes Engine (GKE). These instructions guide you through steps including installing CRDs and the TiDB operator using Helm, and a simple TiDB cluster including monitoring services. We'll use the quick start instructions as a vehicle to talk about what makes TiDB a Kubernetes native database.

Installing the TiDB CRDs

After making sure you have a Kubernetes cluster that meets the defined prerequisites such as having a default StorageClass (*https://oreil.ly/7myfI*), the first step in deploying TiDB using the operator is installing the CRDs used by the operator. This is done using an instruction such as the following (note the actual operator version number `v1.3.2` may vary):

```
set GH_LINK=https://raw.githubusercontent.com
kubectl create -f \
  $GH_LINK/pingcap/tidb-operator/v1.3.2/manifests/crd.yaml
```

This results in the creation of several CRDs, which you can observe by running the command `kubectl get crd` as we have done in previous chapters. We'll quickly discuss the purpose of each resource since several of them hint at additional features of interest:

- The TidbCluster is the primary resource that describes the desired configuration of a TiDB cluster. We'll look at an example later.
- The TidbMonitor resource is used to deploy a Prometheus-based monitoring stack to observe one or more TidbClusters. As we have seen with other projects, Prometheus (or at least its API) has become a de facto standard for metrics collection for databases and other infrastructure deployed on Kubernetes.
- The Backup and Restore resources represent the actions of performing a backup or restoring from a backup. This is similar to other operators we've examined previously from the Vitess (see "PlanetScale Vitess Operator" on page 117) and K8ssandra (Chapter 6) projects. The TiDB Operator also provides a BackupSchedule resource that can be used to configure regular backups.
- The TidbInitializer is an optional resource that you can create to perform initialization tasks (*https://oreil.ly/qFsmu*) on a TidbCluster, including setting administrator credentials and executing SQL statements for schema creation or initial data loading.
- The TidbClusterAutoScaler is another optional resource which can be used to configure auto-scaling (*https://oreil.ly/wVbf2*) behavior of a TidbCluster. The number of TiKV or TiDB nodes in a TidbCluster can be configured to scale up or down between minimum and maximum limits based on CPU utilization. The addition of scaling rules based on other metrics is on the project roadmap. As we discussed in "Choosing Operators" on page 127, auto-scaling is considered a feature of an operator at Level 5 or Autopilot, the highest maturity level.
- The TidbNGMonitoring is an optional resource that configures a TidbCluster to enable continuous profiling (*https://oreil.ly/2n8k5*) down to the system call level. The resulting profiling data and flame graph visualizations can be observed using the TiDB Dashboard (*https://oreil.ly/23pLs*), which is deployed separately.

This is typically used by project engineers looking to optimize the database, but application and platform developers may find this useful as well.

- The DMCluster resource is used to deploy an instance of the TiDB Data Migration (*https://oreil.ly/C5NG0*) (DM) platform that supports migration of MySQL and MariaDB database instances into a TidbCluster. It can also be configured to migrate from an existing TiDB installation outside of Kubernetes to a TidbCluster. The ability to deploy data migration services alongside a destination TidbCluster in Kubernetes managed by the same operator is a great example of what it means to develop data ecosystems in Kubernetes, a pattern that we hope to see more of in the future.

For the remainder of this section, we'll focus on the TidbCluster and TidbMonitoring resources.

Installing the TiDB Operator

After installing the CRDs, the next step is to install the TiDB Operator using Helm. You'll need to add the Helm repository first before installing the TiDB Operator in its own Namespace:

```
helm repo add pingcap https://charts.pingcap.org
helm install -create-namespace --namespace tidb-admin tidb-operator \
  pingcap/tidb-operator --version v1.3.2
```

You can watch the resulting Pods come online using `kubectl get pods` and referencing the `tidb-admin` Namespace. Figure 7-2 provides a summary of the elements that you've installed up to this point. This includes Deployments to manage the TiDB Operator (labeled as `tidb-controller-manager`) and the TiDB Scheduler.

The TiDB Scheduler is an optional extension to the Kubernetes built-in scheduler. While it is deployed by default as part of the TiDB Operator, it can be disabled. Assuming the TiDB Scheduler is not disabled, using it for a specific TidbCluster still requires opting in by setting the `schedulerName` property to `tidb-scheduler`. If this property is set, the TiDB Operator will assign the TiDB Scheduler as the scheduler that Kubernetes will use when creating TiKV, and PD Pods.

The TiDB Scheduler extends the Kubernetes built-in scheduler to add custom scheduling rules for Pods that are part of a TidbCluster, helping to achieve high availability of the database while spreading the load evenly across the available Worker Nodes in the Kubernetes cluster. While for many types of infrastructure, the existing mechanisms Kubernetes offers for influencing the default scheduler such as affinity rules, taints, and tolerations are sufficient, TiDB provides a useful example of when and how to implement custom scheduling logic. We'll look at Kubernetes scheduler extensions in more detail in Chapter 9.

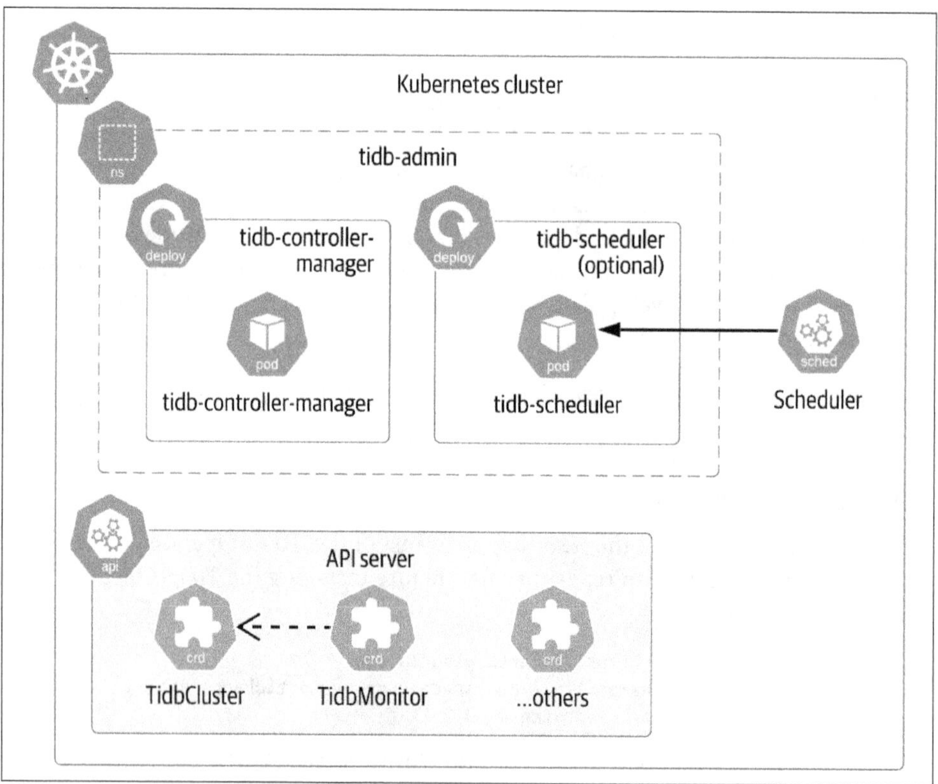

Figure 7-2. Installing the TiDB Operator and CRDs

TiDB Operator Helm Chart Options

This installation omits usage of a *values.yaml* file, but you can see the available options by running following command:

```
helm show values pingcap/tidb-operator
```

This includes the option to disable the TiDB Scheduler.

Creating a TidbCluster

Once the TiDB Operator has been installed, you're ready to create a TidbCluster resource. While many example configurations (*https://oreil.ly/66uf7*) are available in the TiDB Operator GitHub repository, let's use the one referenced in the quick start guide:

```
set GH_LINK=https://raw.githubusercontent.com
kubectl create namespace tidb-cluster
kubectl -n tidb-cluster apply -f \
  $GH_LINK/pingcap/tidb-operator/master/examples/basic/tidb-cluster.yaml
```

While the TidbCluster is being created, you can reference the contents of this file, which look something like this (with comments and some details removed):

```
apiVersion: pingcap.com/v1alpha1
kind: TidbCluster
metadata:
  name: basic
spec:
  version: v5.4.0
  ...
  pd:
    baseImage: pingcap/pd
    maxFailoverCount: 0
    replicas: 1
    requests:
      storage: "1Gi"
    config: {}
  tikv:
    baseImage: pingcap/tikv
    maxFailoverCount: 0
    evictLeaderTimeout: 1m
    replicas: 1
    requests:
      storage: "1Gi"
    config:
      ...
  tidb:
    baseImage: pingcap/tidb
    maxFailoverCount: 0
    replicas: 1
    service:
      type: ClusterIP
    config: {}
```

Notice that this results in the creation of a TidbCluster named `basic` in the `tidb-cluster` Namespace, with one replica each of TiDB, TiKV, and PD, using the standard PingCAP images for each. Additional options are used to specify the minimum amount of compute and storage resources required to achieve a functioning cluster. No TiFlash nodes are included in this simple configuration.

TidbCluster API

The full list of options for a TidbCluster can be found as part of the API (*https://oreil.ly/XoC02*) available in the GitHub repository. This same page includes options for the other CRDs used by the TiDB Operator. As you explore the options for these CRDs, you'll see evidence of the common practice of allowing many of the options that will be used to specify underlying resources to be overridden (for example, the Pod specification that will be set on a Deployment).

We encourage you to take the opportunity to use `kubectl` or your favorite visualization tool to explore the resources created as part of the TidbCluster, a summary of which is provided in Figure 7-3.

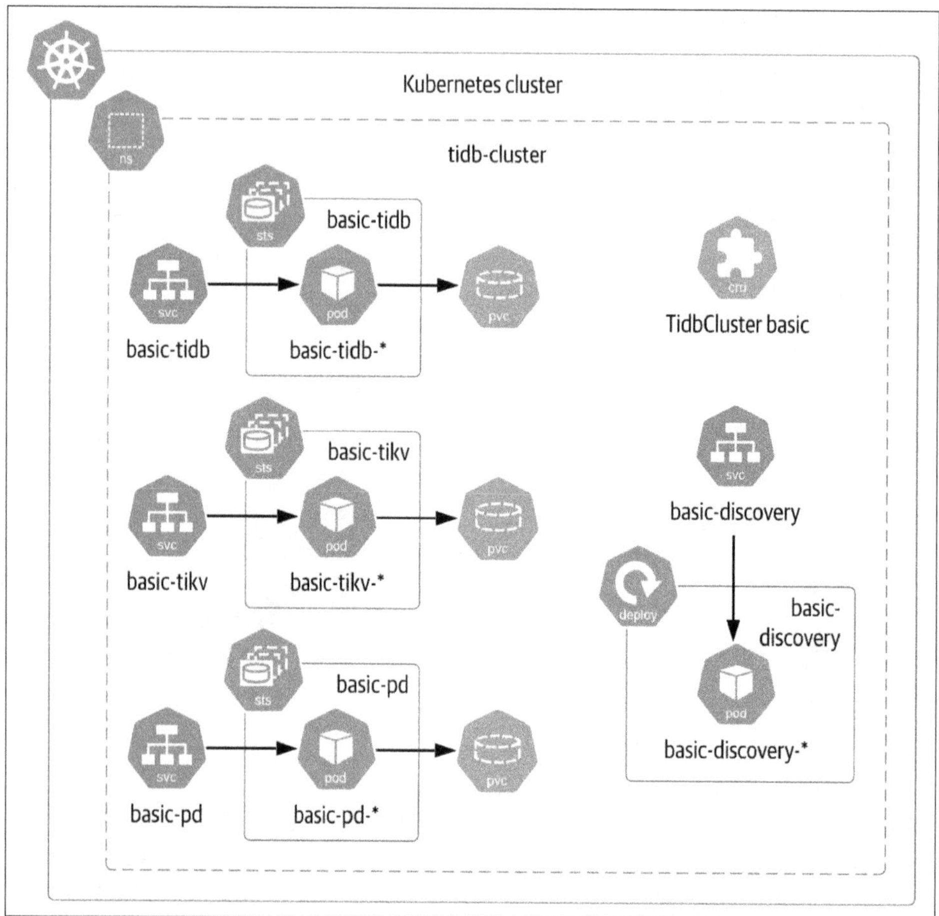

Figure 7-3. A basic TidbCluster

As you can see, the TiDB Operator creates StatefulSets to manage the TiDB, TiKV, and Placement Driver instances, allocating a PVC for each instance. As an I/O-intensive application, the default configuration is to use local PersistentVolumes as the backing store.

In addition, a Deployment is created to run a Discovery Service which the various components use to learn of each other's location. The Discovery Service performs a similar role to that of etcd in other data technologies we've examined in the book. The TiDB Operator also configures services for each StatefulSet and Deployment that facilitate communication within the TiDB cluster as well as exposing capabilities to external clients.

The TiDB Operator supports the deployment of a Prometheus monitoring stack that can manage one or more TiDB clusters. You can add monitoring to the cluster created previously using the following command:

```
set GH_LINK=https://raw.githubusercontent.com
kubectl -n tidb-cluster apply -f \
  $GH_LINK/pingcap/tidb-operator/master/examples/basic/tidb-monitor.yaml
```

While this is deploying, let's examine the contents of the *tidb-monitor.yaml* configuration file:

```
apiVersion: pingcap.com/v1alpha1
kind: TidbMonitor
metadata:
  name: basic
spec:
  replicas: 1
  clusters:
  - name: basic
  prometheus:
    baseImage: prom/prometheus
    version: v2.27.1
  grafana:
    baseImage: grafana/grafana
    version: 7.5.11
  initializer:
    baseImage: pingcap/tidb-monitor-initializer
    version: v5.4.0
  reloader:
    baseImage: pingcap/tidb-monitor-reloader
    version: v1.0.1
  prometheusReloader:
    baseImage: quay.io/prometheus-operator/prometheus-config-reloader
    version: v0.49.0
  imagePullPolicy: IfNotPresent
```

As you can see, the TidbMonitor resource can point to one or more TidbClusters. This TidbMonitor is configured to manage the `basic` cluster you created previously. The TidbMonitor resource also allows you to specify the versions of Prometheus, Grafana, and additional tools that are used to initialize and update the monitoring stack. If you examine the contents of the `tidb-cluster` Namespace, you'll see additional workloads that have been created to manage these elements.

TiDB uses the Prometheus stack in a similar way to the K8ssandra project, as we discussed in "Unified Monitoring Infrastructure with Prometheus and Grafana" on page 150. In both of these projects, the Prometheus stack is supported as an optional extension to provide a monitoring capability you can use with very little customization. The configurations and provided visualizations focus on the key metrics that drive awareness of database health. Even if you are already managing your own monitoring infrastructure or using a third-party software-as-a-service (SaaS) solution, the configurations and charts can give you a head start on incorporating database monitoring into the rest of your observability approach.

A Roadmap for Cloud Native Databases on Kubernetes

With Dongxu (Ed) Huang, Cofounder and CTO, PingCAP

TiDB was created out of the experience of maintaining a storage system for a large internet company who ran an Android app store. The distributed MySQL sharding cluster we were using was innovative at the time but also too hard to maintain. With manual sharding, you cannot do cross-shard joins or transactions. It's painful for the application developer. The Google Spanner and F1 papers provided the inspiration for future databases like TiDB with scalability and high availability, consistency, full-featured SQL, and global transaction support. From the application developers' perspective, it should feel like going back to the old days of single-node development, but now with horizontal scalability.

The problem statement was straightforward. We wanted to provide scalable online transaction processing (OLTP) queries with reduced migration cost and an easy-to-use MySQL interface. At that time, there was no open source implementation of Spanner, so we started to build TiKV and donated it to the CNCF. As more and more users started running OLAP queries on top of their real-time data in TiDB, we expanded our OLAP capability to create HTAP—a hybrid approach. The TiFlash engine that supports OLAP queries has recently been made open source as well.

The TiDB architecture does have some cloud native aspects from its original design, especially since it has a shared-nothing architecture. However, being called a cloud native database requires a higher standard. A cloud native database should make maximum use of the infrastructure your cloud vendor provides (for example, a storage engine that leverages S3 or uses a cloud's serverless features). By this standard, the most cloud native database is Snowflake. The approach that customers need is this: pay for only what you use. If you have to buy it by the node, it's not serverless.

We like to refer to TiDB as a Kubernetes native database. When we saw the first etcd operator released in 2016, we were inspired to create our own operator. At that time, Kubernetes was not as mature as it is today. We didn't have CRDs, just third-party resources. We had to build our own scheduler to make sure we could handle failover correctly. The hardest part was handling local storage. Kubernetes was not designed from the database engineer's point of view. At Google, the team didn't focus on providing access to local disk for databases, since most of the systems were built on top of columnar stores. The team didn't care about local state, but as a database engineer, you have to be very careful with your use of local disk. Since there was no local storage API in Kubernetes when we started, we wrote our own controller to manage local disks. We put a lot of resources into this effort. It was very complicated and might have been the wrong decision.

Today things are a lot better. Kubernetes networking, StatefulSets, and CRDs are mature and frequently utilized by application developers and database engineers. At PingCAP, we use Kubernetes to run our managed service on public clouds. We have a lot of users, and yet it's very stable. We can work with it.

In the future of cloud native architectures, storage and compute will be separated more and more clearly over time. In the past, you would never have built a database on top of remote storage. But now it might be time to give up doing persistence on local disks. We're working on a new storage engine for TiDB built on top of shared storage.

One area where Kubernetes needs to improve is support for multitenancy. Today, building a multitenant application in Kubernetes is hard. Namespaces are not enough of an abstraction to support multitenancy. Similar to control groups (cgroups) for Linux, Kubernetes needs a virtualized cluster or some other multitenancy mechanism within the cluster. A Kubernetes SIG (*https://oreil.ly/RY0bJ*) is looking into multitenancy, and the work on virtual clusters, or *vclusters* (*https://www.vcluster.com*), is promising.

A second area where Kubernetes could improve is better support for hypervisors. When you have large clusters, you don't want to have virtualization on top of hardware and then run Kubernetes on top of that. The Kubernetes community could be more ambitious and put more resources toward embracing hypervisors such as Cloud Hypervisor (*https://oreil.ly/18jj8*).

For its part, the database world needs to be more focused on Kubernetes. DevOps and application engineers are the mainstream Kubernetes community, but the database folks are outside of that. Most database operators are not written by experienced DBAs. Once you get beyond deploying the database, tuning a database is a hard job; you have a lot of maintenance to do. Once you put a database in Kubernetes Pods, tuning it requires going inside the Pods. For the DBA or DevOps engineer, that's the trickiest part. As a user, you should always prefer an operator provided by the database vendor. If you're a database vendor, you need to help the user by making it easier to tune in the Kubernetes environment, not just deployment or upgrades. The real world is not like running a demo.

As you can see, TiDB is a database with a flexible, extensible architecture that has been designed with cloud native principles in mind. It also has a strong bias toward being able to deploy and manage a database effectively in Kubernetes and has provided us with some valuable insights on what it means to be Kubernetes native. Consult the TiDB documentation for more information on features such as deploying to multiple Kubernetes clusters (*https://oreil.ly/NPHxy*).

Serverless Cassandra with DataStax Astra DB

Since the advent of cloud computing in the early 2000s, public cloud providers and infrastructure vendors have made continual advances in commoditizing various layers of our architectural stacks as service offerings. This trend began with offering compute, network, and storage as *infrastructure as a service* (IaaS) and proceeded into other trends including *platform as a service* (PaaS), *software as a service* (SaaS), and *functions as a service* (FaaS), sometimes conflated with the term *serverless*.

Most pertinent to our investigation here is the emergence of managed data infrastructure offerings known as *database as a service* (DBaaS). This category includes the following:

- Traditional databases offered as a managed cloud service, such as Amazon Relational Database Service (RDS) and PlanetScale
- Cloud databases like Google BigTable, Amazon Dynamo, and Snowflake that are available only as cloud offerings
- Managed NoSQL or NewSQL databases that can also be run on premises under an open source or source available license—for example, MongoDB Atlas, DataStax Astra DB, TiDB, and Cockroach DB

Over the past several years, many of the vendors behind these DBaaS services have begun migrating onto Kubernetes to automate operations, manage compute resources more efficiently, and make their solutions portable across clouds. DataStax was one of several vendors that began offering Cassandra as a service. These vendors typically used an architecture based on running traditional Cassandra clusters in a cloud environment, with various "glue code" to integrate aspects like networking, monitoring, and management that didn't quite fit target deployment environments like Kubernetes and public cloud IaaS. These include techniques like using sidecars to collect metrics and logs, or deploying Cassandra nodes using StatefulSets to manage scaling up and down in an orderly fashion.

Even with these workarounds for running in Kubernetes, Cassandra's monolithic architecture doesn't readily promote the separation of compute and storage, which can lead to some awkwardness when scaling. You scale up a Cassandra cluster by adding additional nodes, where each node has the following capabilities:

Coordination
: Receiving read and write requests and forwarding them to other nodes as needed to achieve the requested number of replicas (also known as *consistency level*)

Writing and reading
: Writing data to in-memory cache (memtables) and persistent storage (SSTables), and reading it back as needed

Compaction and repair
: Since Cassandra is an LSM-tree database, it does not update datafiles once they are written to persistent storage. Compaction and repair are tasks that run in the background as separate threads. Compaction helps Cassandra stay performant by consolidating SSTables written at different times, ignoring obsolete and deleted values. Repair is the process of comparing stored values across nodes to ensure consistency.

Each node in a Cassandra cluster implements all of these capabilities and consumes equivalent compute and storage resources. This makes it difficult to scale compute and storage independently and can lead to situations where a cluster is overprovisioned in compute or storage resources.

In 2021, DataStax published a paper entitled "DataStax Astra DB: Designing a Serverless Cloud-Native Database-as-a-Service" (*https://oreil.ly/yHSxz*) that describes a different approach. *Astra DB* is a version of Cassandra that has been refactored into microservices to allow more fine-grained scalability and to take advantage of the benefits of Kubernetes. In fact, Astra DB is not only Kubernetes native; it is essentially a Kubernetes-only database. Figure 7-4 shows the Astra DB architecture at a high level, broken into a control plane, data plane, and supporting infrastructure.

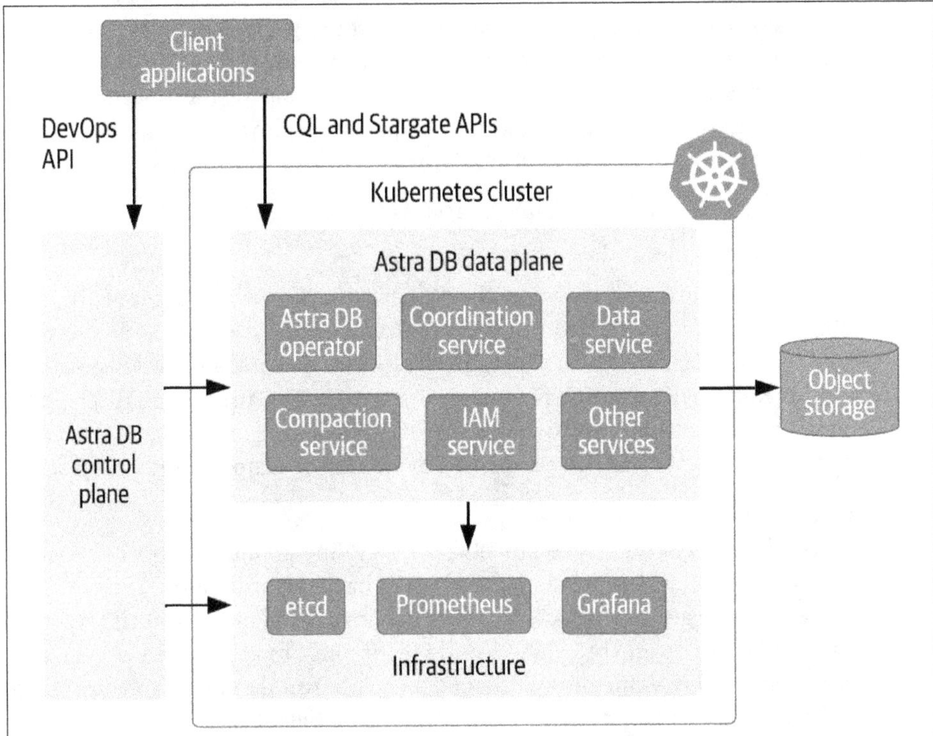

Figure 7-4. Astra DB architecture

Let's do a quick overview of the layers in this architecture:

Astra DB control plane
: The control plane is responsible for provisioning Kubernetes clusters in various cloud provider regions. It also provisions Astra DB clusters within those Kubernetes clusters and provides the APIs that allow clients to create and manage databases, either through the Astra DB web application, or programmatically through the DevOps API. Jim Dickinson's blog post "How We Built the DataStax Astra DB Control Plane" (*https://oreil.ly/jhU2Q*) describes the architecture of the control plane and how it was migrated to be Kubernetes native.

Astra DB data plane
: The data plane is where the actual Astra DB databases run. The data plane consists of multiple microservices which together provide the capabilities that would have been a part of a single monolithic Cassandra node. Each database is deployed in a Kubernetes cluster in a dedicated Namespace and may be shared across multiple tenants, as described in more detail later on.

Astra DB infrastructure
: Each Kubernetes cluster also contains a set of infrastructure components that are shared across the Astra DB databases in that cluster, including etcd, Prometheus, and Grafana. etcd is used to store metadata, including the assignment of tenants to databases and database schema for each tenant. It also stores information about the cluster topology, replacing the role of gossip in the traditional Cassandra architecture. Prometheus and Grafana are deployed in a similar way as described in other architectures in this book.

Now let's dig more into a few of the microservices in the data plane:

Astra DB Operator
: The Astra DB Operator manages the Kubernetes resources required for each database instance as described by a DBInstallation custom resource, as shown in Figure 7-5. Similar to the Cass Operator project we discussed in "Managing Cassandra in Kubernetes with Cass Operator" on page 143, the Astra DB Operator automates many of the operational tasks associated with managing a Cassandra cluster that would typically be performed by human operators using *nodetool*.

Coordination Service
: The Coordination Service is responsible for handling application queries including reads, writes, and schema management. Each Coordination Service is an instance of Stargate (as discussed in "Enabling Developer Productivity with Stargate APIs" on page 147 that exposes endpoints for CQL and other APIs, with an Astra DB–specific plug-in that enables it to route requests intelligently to Data Service instances to actually store and retrieve data. Factoring this compute-intensive routing functionality into its own microservice enables it to be scaled

up or down based on query traffic, independent of the volume of data being managed.

Data Service
: Each Data Service instance is responsible for managing a subset of the data for each assigned tenant based on its position in the Cassandra token ring. The Data Service takes a tiered approach to data storage, maintaining in-memory data structures such as memtables, using local disk for caching, commit logs and indexes, and object storage for longer-term persistence of SSTables. The usage of object storage is one of the key differentiators of Astra DB from other databases we've examined so far, and we'll examine other benefits of this approach throughout this section.

Compaction Service
: The Compaction Service is responsible for performing maintenance tasks including compaction and repair on SSTables in object storage. Compaction and repair are compute-intensive tasks that experienced Cassandra operators have historically scheduled for off-peak hours to limit their impact on cluster performance. In Astra DB, these tasks can be performed at any time the need arises without impacting query performance. The work is handled by a pool of Compaction Service instances which can scale up or down independently to generate repaired, compacted SSTables which are immediately accessible to Data Services.

IAM Service
: All incoming application requests are routed through the Identity and Access Management (IAM) Service, which uses a standard set of roles and permissions defined in the control plane. While Cassandra has long had a pluggable architecture for authentication and authorization, factoring this out into its own microservice allows for more flexibility and support for additional providers such as Okta.

The data plane includes additional services which have been omitted from Figure 7-4 for simplicity, including a Commitlog Replayer Service for recovery of failed Data Service instances, and an Autoscaling Service which uses analytics and machine learning to recommend to the operator when to scale the number of instances of each service up or down.

Figure 7-5 shows what a typical DBInstallation looks like in terms of Kubernetes resources. Let's walk through a few typical interactions focusing on individual instances of key services to demonstrate how each resource plays its part.

A Kubernetes Ingress is configured for each cluster to manage incoming requests from client applications (1) and route requests to Coordinator Services by the tenant using a Kubernetes Service (2).

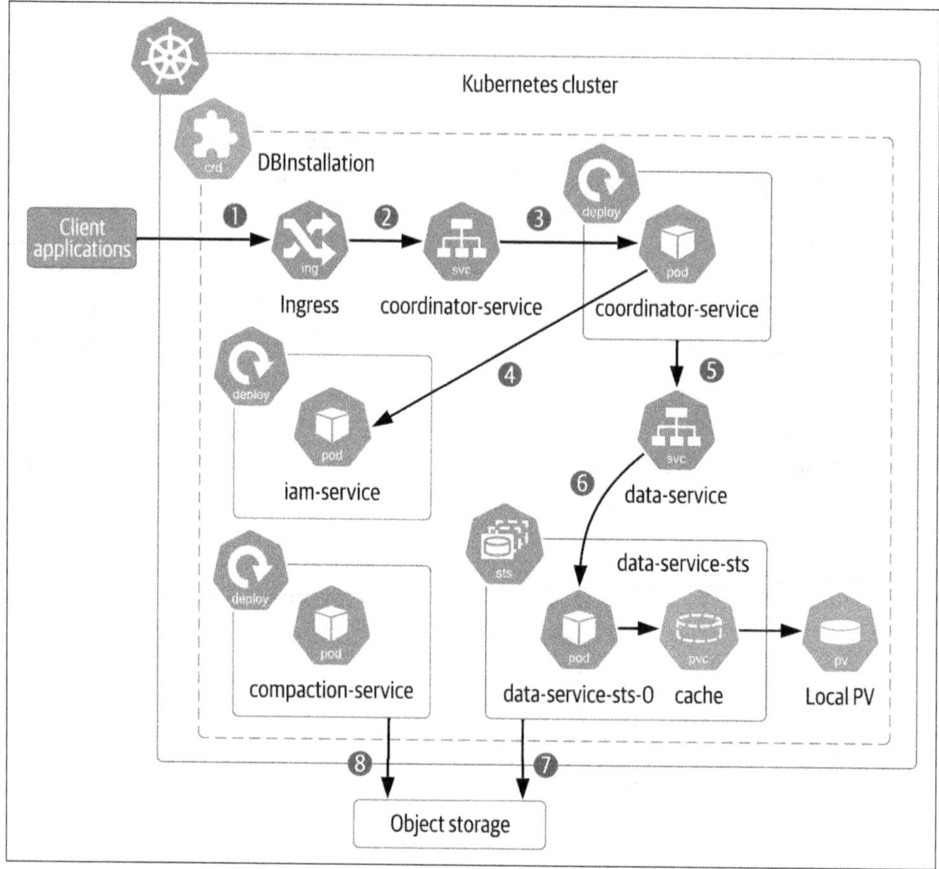

Figure 7-5. Astra DB cluster in Kubernetes

The Coordinator Service is a stateless service managed by a Deployment (3) which delegates authentication and authorization checks on each call to the IAM Service (4).

Authorized requests are then routed to one or more Data Services based on the tenant, again using a Kubernetes Service (5).

Data Services are managed using StatefulSets (6), which are used to assign each instance to a local PersistentVolume used for managing intermediate datafiles such as the commit log, which is populated immediately on writes. When possible, reads are served directly from in-memory data structures.

As is typical for Cassandra and other LSM tree storage engines, the Data Service occasionally writes SSTable files out to a persistent store (7). For Astra DB, that persistent store is an external object store managed by the cloud provider for high availability. A separate object storage bucket is used per tenant to ensure data privacy.

The Compaction Service can perform compaction and repair on SSTables in the object store asynchronously (8), with no impact to write and read queries.

Astra DB also supports multiregion database clusters, which by definition span multiple Kubernetes clusters. Coordinator and Data Services are deployed across Datacenters (cloud regions) and racks (availability zones) using an approach similar to that described for K8ssandra in "Deploying Multicluster Applications in Kubernetes" on page 159.

Astra DB's microservice architecture allows it to make more optimal use of compute and storage resources and isolate compute-intensive operations, leading to overall cost savings to operate Cassandra clusters in the cloud. These cost savings are extended by the addition of multitenant features that allow each cluster to be shared across multiple tenants. The Astra DB whitepaper (*https://oreil.ly/Zq0yc*) describes a technique called *shuffle sharding* which is used to match each tenant to a subset of the available Coordinator and Data Services, effectively creating a separate Cassandra token ring per tenant. As the population of tenants in an Astra DB instance changes, this topology can be easily updated to rebalance load without downtime, and larger tenants can be configured to use their own dedicated databases (DBInstallations). This approach minimizes cost while meeting SLAs for performance and availability.

Building a Serverless Cassandra

With Jake Luciani, Engineering Leader, DataStax

Cassandra has always been considered a cloud native database, but it's not Kubernetes native. The K8ssandra project represents a first step in the direction of making Cassandra more Kubernetes native. It's a systematic way to run Cassandra on Kubernetes in a more traditional cloud native way, but it represents more of a "lift and shift" approach. The Astra DB approach is more like throwing all of our bags on the Kubernetes bus. It's a version of Cassandra that you can't run without Kubernetes.

We realized early on in the process of building Astra DB that we had to make some modifications to Cassandra's architecture to make it work in an even more cloud native way. The cost of running stateful systems in the cloud can get very expensive if you do it the wrong way. If you focus on optimizing for cost, you'll actually end up with the most cloud native solution, because the services that are cheap in the clouds are the ones that have become the most commoditized. They're also the most hardened parts of the system. By standing on the shoulders of proven cloud technologies like object storage and etcd, you'll end up with a more reliable solution.

We often refer to Astra DB as a *serverless database*, which came from the original inspiration for the project: "How do we make Cassandra more serverless?" *Serverless* is a term for techniques engineers use in the cloud to make applications more scalable and stateless. The first breakthrough was separating compute from storage. Storing SSTables as immutable data on the object store allows us to scale our IOPS the same way we scale our processing engine. You can remove any component, and it doesn't matter to the system. Just as you can scale up lambda serverless functions, you can scale up your database.

The topology is completely ephemeral, just like Cassandra; it can change on the fly. Cassandra has traditionally used a gossip-type protocol to coordinate topology and replicate state across nodes in an eventually consistent way. But since Cassandra was first built, systems like etcd have come along that do a great job of maintaining metadata about schema and topology in a transactional way. etcd is a stateful service in its own right, but we use it only as a way to transition from one state to the next. The object store is ultimately the source of truth for the entire system. You can lose an entire Kubernetes cluster with all of the databases running on it, rebuild the cluster, wipe the disks, and bring the whole system back. This is a great feeling when you go to sleep at night. Currently, we have to run our own etcd inside Kubernetes, even though Kubernetes runs its own etcd cluster. It would be great if we could utilize that infrastructure that's already running. Instead, we've had to build up our own etcd expertise to make sure we know how to run it.

We use StatefulSets to manage the Cassandra nodes in each availability zone. StatefulSets provide the exact behavior we need in terms of scaling up and down in a fixed order. Although we usually use only local ephemeral disks and the local path provisioner, we're not precluded from using a PVC with persistent storage if we needed to; it would just be more expensive. To perform upgrades, we create an entire StatefulSet with new Cassandra nodes. Once all of the nodes have joined, we can delete the old StatefulSet. We treat the StatefulSets as immutable infrastructure, throwing them away and starting over.

One big problem with data on Kubernetes is the rough edges in working with attached disks. Many databases need to stripe disks before using them. On Kubernetes, this means mounting volumes as raw disks and then striping them during Pod startup. To scale the available IOPS, you have to attach more raw disks and stripe them as well. We avoided this problem in Astra DB by going all in on object storage and local ephemeral disks. The ephemeral disks are just a cache of what's in the object storage, but they give us the IOPS we need. Cassandra uses ann LSM-tree style of storage engine, similar to RocksDB. This provides a great opportunity for a cloud native separation of disk and storage, because the datafiles are immutable. We never need to perform in-place updates of data on disk, which works out well because object storage doesn't allow that anyway. Compaction can run as a separate process and scale on its own right, which keeps the reads fast.

Another challenge with Kubernetes is choosing the right VM types and figuring out how to map Pods to them efficiently. Unfortunately, the Kubernetes APIs are decoupled from the underlying cloud provider capabilities. You have to do a lot of math in your head to set up quotas and node groups, and we haven't even gotten to disks. There's a massive market opportunity out there for someone who can solve this problem.

When you're running a SaaS, the way you lower prices and keep margins is by being as efficient as possible. For us, this means multitenancy and the ability to shift resources between tenants based on usage. We use a giant, shared pool of Pods and resources, which enables us to move users and their data to different parts of the fleet. This allows us to provide a usage-based pricing model for developers who just want to use it and go, and it empowers them to build cool applications.

Zooming back out, Kubernetes did a great job with stateless services from the beginning, but stateful workloads are harder. People in Kubernetes want to solve this with changes to Kubernetes, and people who build infrastructure want to solve this in the infrastructure. We'll get there eventually through a combination of the two. In the meantime, we're circumventing the issue by using the immutable systems that work well on Kubernetes and moving the state out into object storage. This is the way open source technology works. People try things and make progress. Adopting a new architecture can be a big risk, but once you do, the payoff can be huge.

In this section, we've focused on the architecture Astra DB uses to provide a multi-tenant, serverless Cassandra that embodies both cloud native and Kubernetes native principles using a completely different style of deployment. This continues the tradition of the Amazon Dynamo and Google BigTable papers in generating public discussion around novel database architectures. In addition, several open source projects mentioned in this book including Cass Operator, K8ssandra, and Stargate trace their origins to Astra DB. A lot of innovation is going on in areas such as the core database, control plane, change data capture, streaming integration, data migration, and more, so look for more open source contributions and architecture proposals from this team in the future.

What to Look for in a Kubernetes Native Database

After everything you've learned in the past few chapters about what it takes to deploy and manage various databases on Kubernetes, we are in a great position to define what you should look for in a Kubernetes native database.

Basic Requirements

Following our cloud native data principles, the following are a few areas that should be considered basic requirements:

Maximum leverage of Kubernetes APIs
: The database should be as tightly integrated with Kubernetes APIs as possible (for example, using PersistentVolumes for both local and remote storage, using Services for routing rather than maintaining lists of IPs of other nodes, and so on). Kubernetes extension points described in Chapter 5 should be used to supplement built-in Kubernetes functionality.

In some areas, the existing Kubernetes APIs may not provide the exact behavior required for a given database or other application, as demonstrated by the creation of alternate StatefulSet implementations by the Vitess and TiDB projects. In these cases, every effort should be made to donate improvements back to the Kubernetes project.

Automated, declarative management via operators
: Databases should be deployed and managed on Kubernetes using operators and custom resources. Operators should serve as the primary control plane elements for managing databases. While it's arguably helpful to have command-line tools or `kubectl` extensions that allow DBAs to intervene manually to optimize database performance and fix issues, these are ultimately functions that should be performed by an operator as it achieves the higher levels of maturity discussed in Chapter 5.

The goal should be that all required changes to a database can be accomplished by updating the desired state in a custom resource and letting the operator handle the rest. We'll be in a great place when we can configure a database in terms of service-level objectives such as latency, throughput, availability, and cost per unit. Operators can determine how many database nodes are needed, what compute and storage tiers to use, when to perform backups, and so on.

Observable through standard APIs
: We're beginning to see common expectations for observability for data infrastructure on Kubernetes in terms of the familiar triad of metrics, logs, and tracing. The Prometheus-Grafana stack is somewhat of a de facto standard for metrics collection and visualization, with exposure of metrics from database services using the Prometheus format as a minimum criteria. Projects providing Prometheus integration should be flexible enough to provide their own dedicated stack, or push metrics to an existing installation shared with other applications.

Logs from all database application containers should be pushed to standard output (stdout) using sidecars if necessary—so they can be collected by log aggregation services. While it may take longer to see adoption for tracing, the ability to follow individual client requests through application calls down into the database tier through APIs such as OpenTracing will be an extremely powerful debugging tool for future cloud native applications.

Secure by default
: The Kubernetes project itself provides a great example of what it means to be secure by default—for example, by exposing access to ports on Pods and containers only when specifically enabled, and by providing primitives like Secrets that we can use to protect access to login credentials or sensitive configuration data.

Databases and other infrastructure need to make use of these tools and adopt industry standards and best practices for zero trust (including changing default administrator credentials), limiting exposure of application and management APIs. Exposed APIs should prefer encrypted protocols such as HTTPS. Data stored in PersistentVolumes should be encrypted, whether this encryption is performed by the application, the database, or the StorageClass provider. Audit logs should be provided as part of application logging, especially with respect to actions that configure user access.

To summarize, a Kubernetes native database is sympathetic to the way that Kubernetes works. It maximizes reuse of Kubernetes built-in capabilities instead of bringing along its own set of duplicative supporting infrastructure. The experience of using a Kubernetes native database is therefore very much like using Kubernetes itself.

The Future of Kubernetes Native

As these basic requirements and more advanced expectations for what it means to be Kubernetes native solidify, what comes next? We're starting to see common patterns within projects deploying databases on Kubernetes that could point to where things are headed in the future. These are admittedly a bit fuzzier, but let's try to bring a couple of them into focus.

Scalability through multidimensional architectures

You may have noticed the repetition of several terms throughout the past few chapters such as *multicluster*, *multitenancy*, *microservices*, and *serverless*. A common thread uniting these terms is that they represent architectural approaches to scalability, as shown in Figure 7-6.

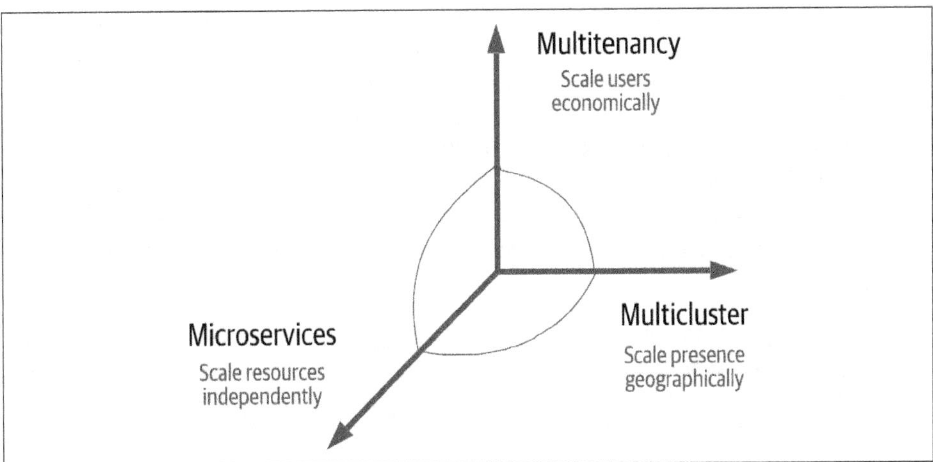

Figure 7-6. Architectural approaches for scaling in multiple dimensions

Consider how each of these approaches provides an independent axis for scalability. The visualization in Figure 7-6 depicts the impact of your application as a three-dimensional surface that grows as you scale along each axis:

Microservice architectures
: Microservice architectures break the various functions of a database into independently scalable services. The serverless approach builds on this, encouraging the isolation of persistent state to a limited number of stateful services or even external services as much as possible. Kubernetes storage APIs in the Persistent-Volume subsystem make it possible to leverage both local and networked storage options. These trends allow a true separation of compute and storage, and scale these resources independently.

Multicluster
: *Multicluster* refers to the ability to scale an application across multiple Kubernetes clusters. Along with related terms like *multiregion*, *multi-datacenter*, and *multicloud*, this implies expanding the geographic footprint of the capabilities provided across potentially heterogeneous environments. This distribution of capability has positive implications for meeting users where they are with minimum latency, cloud provider cost optimization, and disaster recovery. As we discussed in Chapter 6, Kubernetes has historically not been as strong in its support for cross-cluster networking and service discovery. It will be interesting to track how databases and other applications take advantage of expected advances in Kubernetes federation in the coming years.

Multitenancy
: This is the ability to share infrastructure between multiple users to achieve the most efficient use of resources. As the public cloud providers have demonstrated in their IaaS offerings, a multitenant approach can be very effective at providing users a low-cost, low-risk access to infrastructure for innovative new projects, and then providing additional resources as these applications grow. Adopting a multitenant approach for data infrastructure has great potentiial value as well, so long as security guarantees are properly met and there is a seamless transition path to dedicated infrastructure for high-volume users before they become "noisy neighbors." At this point in time, Kubernetes does not provide explicit support for multitenancy, although Namespaces can be a useful tool for providing dedicated resources for specific users.

While you may not have immediate need for all three of these axes of scalability for applications or data infrastructure you're building, consider how growing in each of them can enhance the overall value you're offering the world.

Community-focused innovation through open source and cloud services

Another pattern you may have noticed in our narrative is the continual innovation loop between open source database projects and DBaaS offerings. PingCAP took the open source MySQL and ClickHouse databases, created a database service leveraging Kubernetes to help it manage the databases at scale, and then released open source projects including TiDB and TiFlash. DataStax took open source Cassandra, factored it into microservices, added an API layer, and deployed it on Kubernetes for its Astra DB, and has created multiple open source projects including Cass Operator, K8ssandra, and Stargate. In the spirit of Dynamo, BigTable, Calvin and other papers, these companies have open source architectures as well.

This innovation loop mirrors that of the larger Kubernetes community, in which the major cloud providers and storage vendors have helped drive the maturation of the core Kubernetes control plane and PersistentVolume subsystem, respectively. It's interesting to observe that the highest momentum and fastest cycle time occurs within innovation loops that center around cloud services, rather than around the classic open core model focused on enterprise versions of open source projects.

As a software vendor, providing a cloud service allows you to iterate and evaluate new architectures and features more quickly. Flowing these innovations back to open source allows you to grow adoption by supporting a flexible consumption model. Both "run it yourself" and "rent it from us" become legitimate deployment options for your customers, with the ability to flex between approaches for different use cases. Customers gain confidence in the overall maturity and security of your technology, knowing that the open source version they can inspect and contribute to is largely the same as what you are running in your DBaaS.

A final side effect of these innovation trends is an implicit pull toward proven architectures and components. Consider these examples:

- etcd is used as a metadata store across multiple projects we've examined in this book, including Vitess and Astra DB.
- TiDB leverages the architecture of F1, implemented the Raft consensus protocol, and extended the ClickHouse columnar store.
- Astra DB leverages both the PersistentVolume subsystem and S3-compliant object storage.

Instead of inventing new technologies to solve problems like metadata management and distributed transactions, these projects are investing their innovation in new features, developer experience, and the scalability axes we've examined in this chapter.

Summary

In this chapter, we've taken a deep look at TiDB and Astra DB to search out what makes them Kubernetes native. What was the point of this exercise? Our hope is that this analysis provides a deeper understanding to help consumers ask more insightful questions about the data infrastructure they are consuming, and to help those building data infrastructure and ecosystems to create technology that meets those expectations. We believe that data infrastructure that is not only cloud native but also Kubernetes native will lead to the best outcomes for everyone in terms of performance, availability, and cost.

CHAPTER 8

Streaming Data on Kubernetes

When you think about data infrastructure, persistence is the first thing that comes to mind for many—storing the state of running applications. Accordingly, our focus up to this point has been on databases and storage. It's now time to consider the other aspects of the cloud native data stack.

For those of you managing data pipelines, streaming may be your starting point, with other parts of your data infrastructure being of secondary concern. Regardless of your starting place, data movement is a vitally important part of the overall data stack. In this chapter, we'll examine how to use streaming technologies in Kubernetes to share data securely and reliably in your cloud native applications.

Introduction to Streaming

In Chapter 1, we defined *streaming* as the function of moving data from one point to another and, in some cases, processing data in transit. The history of streaming is almost as long as that of persistence. As data was pooling in various isolated stores, it became evident that moving data reliably was just as important as storing data reliably. In those days, it was called *messaging*. Data was transferred slowly but deliberately, which resembled something closer to postal mail. Messaging infrastructure put data in a place where it could be read asynchronously, in order, with delivery guarantees. This met a critical need when using more than one computer and is one of the foundations of distributed computing.

Modern application requirements have evolved from what was known as messaging into today's definition of streaming. Typically, this means managing large volumes of data that require more immediate processing, which we call *near real-time*. Ordering and delivery guarantees become a critically important feature in the distributed applications deployed in Kubernetes and in many cases are a key enabler of the scale required. How can adding more infrastructure complexity help scale? By providing an orderly way to manage the flow from the creation of data to where it can be used and stored. Rarely are streams used as the source of truth, but more importantly, they are used as the *conduit* of truth.

There is a lot of software and terminology around streaming that can confuse first-time users. As with any complex topic, decomposing the parts can be helpful as we build understanding. There are three areas to evaluate when choosing a streaming system for your use case:

- Types of delivery
- Delivery guarantees
- Feature scope for streaming

Let's take a closer look at each of these areas.

Types of Delivery

To use streaming in your application, you will need to understand the delivery methods available to you from the long choice list of streaming systems. You will need to understand your application requirements to efficiently plan how data flows from producer to consumer. For example, "Does my consumer need exclusive access?" The answer will drive which system fits the requirements. Figure 8-1 shows two of the most common choices in streaming systems: point to point and publish/subscribe:

Point to point
: In this data flow, data created by the producer is passed through the broker and then to a single consumer in a one-to-one relationship. This is primarily used as a way to decouple direct connections from producer to consumer. It serves as an excellent feature for resilience as consumers can be removed and added with no data loss. At the same time, the broker maintains the order and last message read, addressable by the consumer using an offset.

Publish/subscribe (pub/sub)
: In this delivery method, the broker serves as a distribution hub for a single producer and one or more consumers in a one-to-many relationship. Consumers subscribe to a topic and receive notifications for any new messages created by the producer—a critical component for reactive or event-driven architectures.

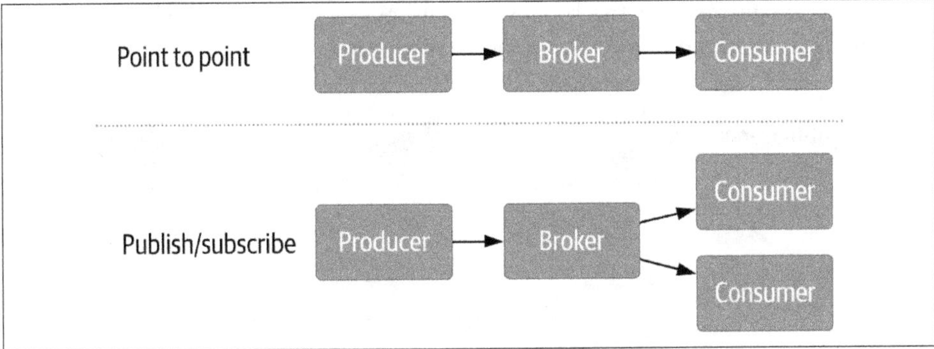

Figure 8-1. Delivery types

Delivery Guarantees

In conjunction with the delivery types, the broker maintains delivery guarantees from producer to consumer per message type in an agreement called a *contract*. The typical delivery types are shown in Figure 8-2: at-most-once, at-least-once, and exactly once. The diagram shows the important relationship between when the producer sends a message and the expectation of how the consumer receives the message:

At-most-once
: The lowest guarantee is used to avoid any potential data duplication due to transient errors that can happen in distributed systems. For example, the producer could get a timeout on send. However, the message may have just gone through without acknowledgment. In this gray area, the safest choice to avoid duplicate data will be for the producer to not attempt a resend and proceed. The critical downside to understand is that data loss is possible by design.

At-least-once
: This guarantee is the opposite side of at-most-once. Data created by the producer is guaranteed to be picked up by a consumer. The added aspect allows for redelivery any number of times after the first. For example, this might be used with a unique key such as a date stamp or ID number that is considered idempotent on the consumer side that multiple processing won't impact. The consumer will always see data delivered by the producer but could see it numerous times. Your application will need to account for this possibility.

Exactly once
: The strictest of the three guarantees, this means that data created by a producer will be delivered only one time to a producer—for example, in exact transactions such as money movement, which require subtractions or additions to be delivered and processed one time to avoid problems. This guarantee puts a more

significant burden on the broker to maintain, so you will need to adjust the resources allocated to the broker and your expected throughput.

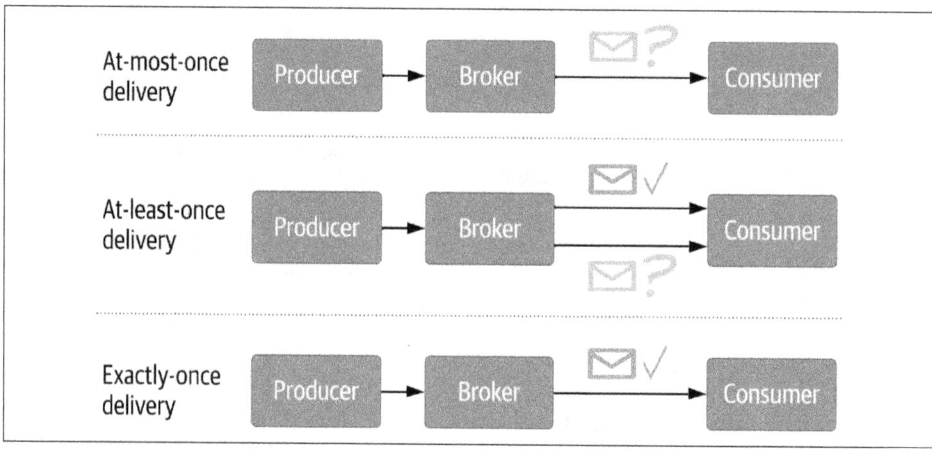

Figure 8-2. Delivery guarantees

Exercise care in selecting delivery guarantees for each type of message. Delivery guarantees are ones to carefully evaluate as they can have unexpected downstream effects on the consumer if not wholly understood. Questions like "Can my application handle duplicate messages?" need a good answer. "Maybe" is not good enough.

Feature Scope

Many streaming technologies are available, some of which have been around for quite a few years. On the surface, these technologies may appear similar, but each solves a different problem because of new requirements. The majority are open source projects, so each has a community of like-minded individuals who join in and advance the project. Just as many different persistent data stores fit under the large umbrella of "database," features under the heading of data streaming can vary significantly.

Feature scope is likely the most important selection criterion when evaluating which streaming technology to use. Still, you should also challenge yourself to add suitability for Kubernetes as a criterion and consider whether more complex features are worth the added resource cost. Fortunately, the price for getting your decision wrong the first time is relatively low. Streaming data systems tend to be some of the easiest to migrate because of their ephemeral nature. The deeper into your feature stack the streaming technology goes, the harder it is to move. The scope of streaming features can be broken into the two large buckets shown in Figure 8-3:

Message broker

This is the simplest form of streaming technology that facilitates the moving of data from one point to another with one or more of the delivery methods and guarantees listed previously. It's easy to discount this feature's simplistic appearance, but it's the backbone of modern cloud native applications. It's like saying FedEx is just a package delivery company, but imagine what would happen to the world economy if it stopped for even one day? Example OSS message brokers include Apache Kafka, Apache Pulsar, RabbitMQ, and Apache ActiveMQ.

Stream analytics

In some cases, the best or only time to analyze data is while it is moving. Waiting for data to persist and then begin the analysis could be far too late, and the insight's value is almost useless. Consider fraud detection. The only opportunity to stop the fraudulent activity is when it's happening; waiting for a report to run the next day just doesn't work. Example OSS stream analytics systems include the Apache prooducts Spark, Flink, Storm, Kafka Streams, and Pulsar.

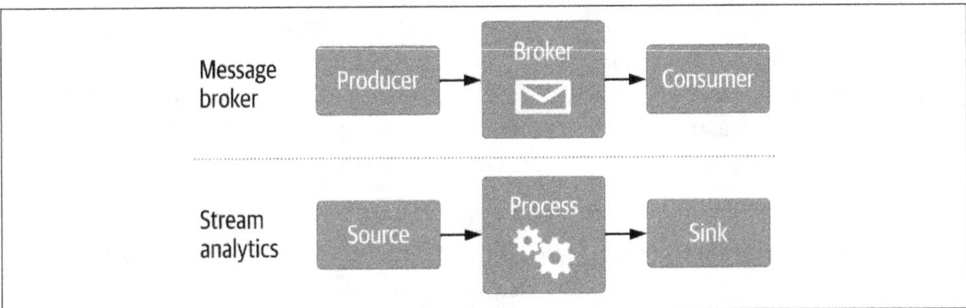

Figure 8-3. Streaming types

The Role of Streaming in Kubernetes

Now that we have covered the basic terminology, how does streaming fit into a cloud native application running on Kubernetes? Database applications follow the pattern of create, read, update and delete (CRUD). For a developer, the database provides a single location for data. The addition of streaming assumes some sort of motion in the data from one place to another. Data may be short-lived if used to create new data. Some data may be transformed in transit, and some may eventually be persisted. Streaming assumes a distributed architecture, and the way to scale a streaming system is to manage its resource allocation of compute, network, and storage. This is landing right into the sweet spot of cloud native architecture. In the case of stream-driven applications in Kubernetes, you're managing the reliable flow of data in an environment that can change over time. Allocate what you need when you need it.

Streaming and Data Engineering

Data engineering is a relatively new and fast-growing discipline, so we want to be sure to define it. This is especially applicable to the practice of data streaming. Data engineers are concerned with the efficient movement of data in complex environments. The two T's are important in this case: transport and transformation. The role of the data scientist is to derive meaning and insights from data. In contrast, the data engineer is building the pipeline that collects data from various locations, organizes it, and in most cases, persists to something like a data lake. Data engineers work with application developers and data scientists to make sure application requirements are met in the increasingly distributed nature of data.

The most critical aspect of your speed and agility is how well your tools work together. When developers dream up new applications, how fast can that idea turn into a production deployment? Deploying and managing separate infrastructure (streaming, persistence, microservices) for one application is burdensome and prone to error. When asking why you would want to add streaming into your cloud native stack, you should consider the cost of not integrating your entire stack in terms of technical debt. Creating custom ways of moving data puts a huge burden on application and infrastructure teams. Data streaming tools are built for a specific purpose, with large communities of users and vendors to aid in your success.

Cloud Native Streaming Is Game-Changing, but Remember the Fundamentals

With Jesse Anderson, Managing Director, Big Data Institute

What makes streaming a good fit for Kubernetes? If you think about which component in your system is the most dynamic, it's probably streaming. Your database won't have as much need to scale up and down in the course of a day. The typical demand curve in a 24-hour period is going to require more scaling for streaming, especially the processing. If you're moving to Kubernetes from VMs, you will be tempted to copy your exact environment into Pods and forget about it. By doing this, you are missing the primary value of cloud native for streaming workloads. In my experience, teams pre-provisioning for expected loads typically end up wasting over 50% of resources by over-provisioning. The best way to manage cost is to add resources when needed and release them when you are finished. The real measurement of success is when end users have no idea that infrastructure is coming and going. They get a smooth experience and a consistent service level. On the other hand, artificially constraining your streaming capacity because of costs can reduce response times and degrade service levels. In the worst case, the real-time processing window falls behind without any way to catch up.

The challenge in deploying streaming workloads in Kubernetes is one of matching system architectures to balance provisioning and service levels. If the technology wasn't designed with the idea of dynamic workload matching, it could take a lot of effort to force it to do something it wasn't designed to accomplish. Kafka is a highly scalable distributed system, but the idea of scaling down wasn't part of the initial design. A Kafka cluster is designed to maintain the declared operational state. If ten brokers have been deployed and one is lost, Kafka tries to return to the state of ten brokers. While this is a critically important feature for resiliency, it takes a different approach to achieve elasticity. Pulsar is an example of a streaming system that has been designed with cloud native thinking to handle dynamic workloads from day one. Flink is a stream-processing system designed with the same considerations. Used in combination, a deployment will consume compute and storage at different times and in different volumes. That is a closer match to the Kubernetes architecture.

Storage has been an area of rapid change for the Kubernetes project but one that you should avoid making assumptions about in your streaming deployments. When the data you are streaming needs to be persisted, where is it going? A great resilience question to ask is "What happens if I mistakenly delete my Kubernetes cluster?" I have worked with teams deploying streaming on Kubernetes that were unknowingly using ephemeral storage by mistake. You have to make sure you are thinking about the durability of your storage from the earliest stages of your move to Kubernetes. Streaming requires a higher level of operational excellence. Having five nines of uptime or better isn't optional. In contrast to a batch system where downtime isn't a high impact, you can just rerun the job if there is a failure. With streaming, if you are down, you've potentially lost data. Having an operational outage due to losing a StatefulSet can be a big deal.

The final thing to consider is your disaster recovery plan. Do not assume that cloud native deployments eliminate potentially devastating failures. You can mitigate many of them, but in my experience, some amount of failure is inevitable, which is why planning is so important. At a minimum, be ready for the various failures that can happen with infrastructure, such as loss of a Pod, a StatefulSet, or an entire Kubernetes cluster. The most common and impactful failures are due to human error, like purposefully deleting data thinking you are working in a QA environment, or getting a configuration wrong. It happens to everyone, and we just need to plan for it.

For data engineers and site reliability engineers (SREs), your planning and implementation of streaming in Kubernetes can greatly impact your organization. Cloud native data should allow for more agility and speed while squeezing out all the efficiency you can get. As a reader of this book, you are already on your way to thinking differently about your infrastructure. Taking some advice from Jesse Anderson, there are two areas you should be focusing on as you begin your journey into streaming data on Kubernetes:

Resource allocation
: Are you planning for peaks as well as the valleys? As you'll recall from Chapter 1, elasticity is one of the more challenging aspects of cloud native data to get right. Scaling up is a commonly solved problem in large-scale systems, but scaling down can potentially result in data loss, especially with streaming systems. Traffic to resources needs to be redirected before they are decommissioned, and any data they are managing locally will need to be accounted for in other parts of the system. The risk involved with elasticity is what keeps it from being widely used, and the result is a lot of unused capacity. Commit yourself to the idea that resources should never be idle and build streaming systems that use what they need and no more.

Disaster recovery planning
: Moving data efficiently is an important problem to solve, but just as important is how to manage inevitable failure. Without understanding your data flows and durability requirements, you can't just rely on Kubernetes to handle recovery. Disaster recovery is about more than backing up data. How are Pods scheduled so that physical server failure has a reduced impact? Can you benefit from geographic redundancy? Are you clear on where data is persisted and understand the durability of those storage systems? And finally, do you have a clear plan to restore systems after a failure? In all cases, writing down the procedure is the first step, but testing those procedures is the difference between success and failure.

We've covered the what and why of streaming data on Kubernetes, and it's time we start looking at the how with a particular focus on cloud native deployments. We'll give a quick overview of how to install these technologies on Kubernetes and highlight some important details to aid your planning. You've already learned in previous chapters how to use many of the Kubernetes resources we'll need, so we'll speed up the pace a bit. Let's get started on the first cloud native streaming technology.

Streaming on Kubernetes with Apache Pulsar

Apache Pulsar is an exciting project to watch for cloud native streaming applications. Streaming software was mostly built in an era before Kubernetes and cloud native architectures. Pulsar was originally developed at Yahoo!, which is no stranger to high-scale cloud native workloads. Donated to the Apache Software Foundation, it was accepted as a top-level project in 2018. Additional projects, like Apache Kafka or RabbitMQ, may suit your application's needs, but they will require more planning and well-written operators to function at the level of efficiency of Pulsar. In terms of the streaming definitions we covered previously, Pulsar supports the following characteristics:

- Types of delivery: one-to-one and pub/sub
- Delivery guarantees: at-least-once, at-most-once, exactly once
- Feature scope for streaming: message broker, analytics (through functions)

So what makes Pulsar a good fit for Kubernetes?

We use Kubernetes to create virtual datacenters to efficiently use compute, network, and storage. Pulsar was designed from the beginning with a separation of compute and storage resource types linked by the network, similar to a microservices architecture.

These resources can even span multiple Kubernetes clusters or physical datacenters, as shown in Figure 8-4. Deployment options give operators the flexibility to install and scale a running Pulsar cluster based on use case and workload. Pulsar was also designed with multitenancy in mind, making a big efficiency difference in large deployments. Instead of installing a separate Pulsar instance per application, many applications (tenants) can use one Pulsar instance with guardrails to prevent resource contention. Finally, built-in storage tiering creates automated alternatives for storage persistence as data ages, and lower-cost storage can be utilized.

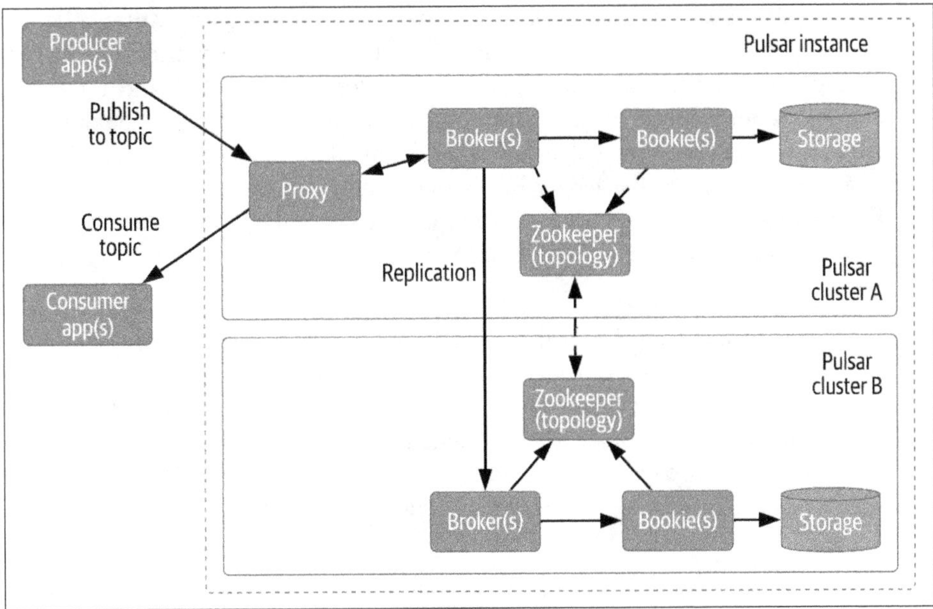

Figure 8-4. Apache Pulsar architecture

Pulsar's highest level of abstraction is an instance that consists of one or more clusters. We call the local logical administration domain a *cluster* and deploy in a Kubernetes cluster, where we'll concentrate our attention. Clusters can share metadata and configuration, allowing producers and consumers to see a single system regardless of location. Each cluster is made of several parts acting in concert that primarily consume either compute or storage. They are:

Broker (compute)
: Producers and consumers pass messages via the broker, a stateless cluster component. This means it is purely a compute scaling unit and can be dynamically allocated based on the number of tenants and connections. Brokers maintain an HTTP endpoint used for client communication, which presents a few options for network traffic in a Kubernetes deployment. When multiple clusters are used, the brokers support replication between clusters in the instance. Brokers can run in a memory-only configuration, or with Apache BookKeeper (labeled as *bookies*) when message durability is required.

Apache BookKeeper (storage)
: The BookKeeper project provides infrastructure for managing distributed write-ahead logs. In Pulsar, the individual instances used are called *bookies*. The storage unit is called a *ledger*; each topic can have one or more ledgers. Multiple bookie instances provide load-balancing and failure protection. They also offer storage tiering functionality, allowing operators to offer a mix of fast and long-term storage options based on use case. When brokers interact with bookies, they read and write to a topic ledger, an append-only data structure. Bookies provide a single reference to the ledger but manage the replication and load balancing behind the primary interface. In a Kubernetes environment, knowing where data is stored is critical for maintaining resilience.

Apache ZooKeeper (compute)
: ZooKeeper is a standalone project used in many distributed systems for coordination, leader election, and metadata management. Pulsar uses ZooKeeper for service coordination, similar to the way etcd is used in a Kubernetes cluster, storing important metadata such as tenants, topics, and cluster configuration state so that the brokers can remain stateless. Bookies use ZooKeeper for ledger metadata and coordination between multiple storage nodes.

Proxy (network)
: The proxy is a solution for dynamic environments like Kubernetes. Instead of exposing every broker to HTTP traffic, the proxy serves as a gateway and creates an Ingress route to the Pulsar cluster. As brokers are added and removed, the proxy uses service discovery to keep the connections flowing to and from the cluster. When using Pulsar in Kubernetes, the proxy service IP should be the single access for your applications to a running Pulsar cluster.

Functions (compute)

Since Pulsar Functions operate independently and consume their own compute resources, we chose not to include them in Figure 8-4. However, they're worth mentioning in this context because Pulsar Functions work in conjunction with the message broker. When deployed, they take data from a topic, alter it with user code, and return it to a different topic. The component added to a Pulsar cluster is the worker, which accepts function runtimes on an ad hoc basis. Operators can deploy Functions as a part of a larger cluster or standalone for more fine-grained resource management.

Preparing Your Environment

When preparing to do your first installation, you need to make some choices. Since every user will have unique needs, we recommend you check the official documentation (*https://oreil.ly/KCqT2*) for the most complete and up-to-date information on installing Pulsar in Kubernetes before reading this section. The examples within this section will take a closer look at the choices available and how they pertain to different cloud native application use cases to help inform your decision making.

To begin, create a local clone directory of the Pulsar Helm chart repository:

```
git clone https://github.com/apache/pulsar-helm-chart
```

This subproject of Pulsar is well documented, with several helpful examples to follow. When using Helm to deploy Pulsar, you will need a *values.yaml* file that contains all of the options to customize your deployment. You can include as many parameters as you want to change. The Pulsar Helm chart has a complete set of defaults for a typical cluster that might work for you, but you will want to tune the values for your specific environment. The *examples* directory has various deployment scenarios. If you choose the default installation as described in the *values-local-cluster.yaml* file, you'll have a set of resources like that shown in Figure 8-5. As you can see, the installation wraps the proxy and brokers in Deployments and presents a unified service endpoint for applications.

Affinity is a mechanism built into Kubernetes to create rules for which Pods can and cannot be colocated on the same physical node (if needed, refer to the more in-depth discussion in Chapter 4). Pulsar, being a distributed system, has deployment requirements for maximum resilience. An example is brokers. When multiple brokers are deployed, each Pod should run on a different physical node in case of failure. If all broker Pods were grouped on the same node and the node went down, the Pulsar cluster would be unavailable. Kubernetes would still recover the runtime state and restart the Pods. However, there would be downtime as they came back online.

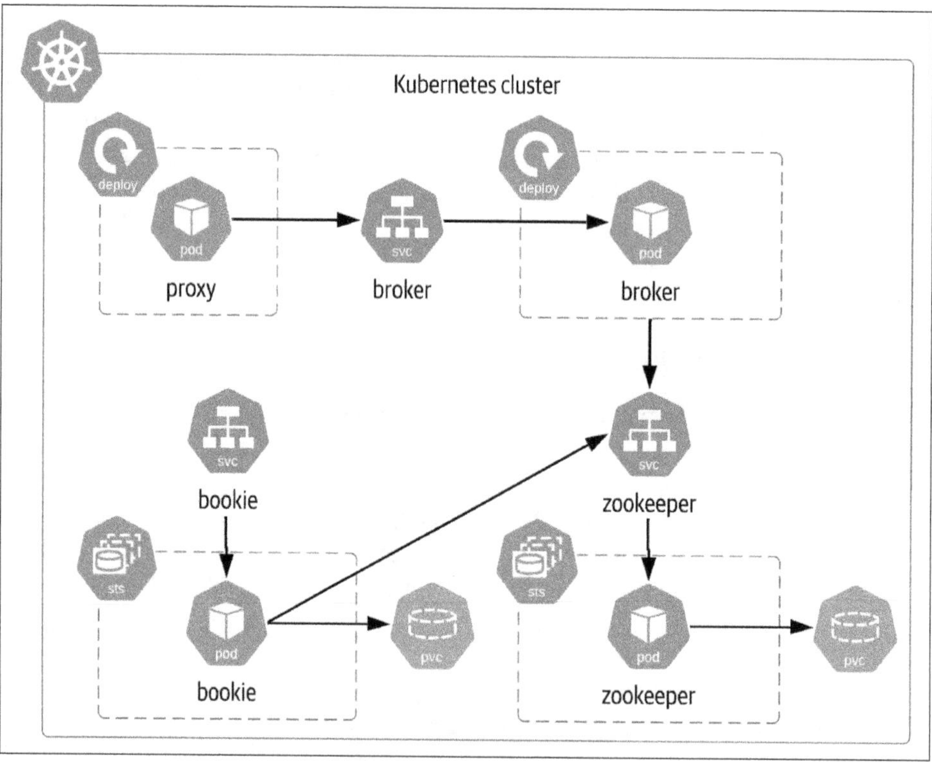

Figure 8-5. A Simple Pulsar installation on Kubernetes

The easiest thing is not allowing Pods of the same type to group together onto the same nodes. When enabled, anti-affinity will keep this from happening. If you are running on a single-node system such as a desktop, disabling it will allow your cluster to start without blocking based on affinity:

```
affinity:
  anti_affinity: true
```

Fine-grained control over Pulsar component replica counts lets you tailor your deployment based on the use case. Each replica Pod consumes resources and should be considered in the application's lifecycle. For example, starting with a low number of brokers and BookKeeper Pods can manage some level of traffic. Still, more replicas can be added and configuration updated via Helm as traffic increases:

```
zookeeper:
  replicaCount: 1

bookkeeper:
  replicaCount: 1

broker:
```

```
    replicaCount: 1

  proxy:
    replicaCount: 1
```

You now have a foundational understanding of how to reliably move data to and from applications and outside of your Kubernetes cluster. Pulsar is a great fit for cloud native application deployments because it can scale compute and storage independently. The declarative nature of deployments makes it easy for data engineers and SREs to deploy easily with consistency. Now that we have the means for data communication, let's take it a step further with the right kind of network security.

Securing Communications by Default with cert-manager

An unfortunate reality we face at the end of product development is what gets left to complete: security or documentation. Unfortunately, Kubernetes doesn't have much in the way of building documentation, but when it comes to security, there has been some great progress on starting earlier without compromise!

As you can see, installing Pulsar has created a lot of infrastructure and communication between the elements. High traffic volume is a typical situation. When we build out virtual datacenters in Kubernetes, it will create a lot of internode (*https://oreil.ly/YySn7*) and external network traffic. All traffic should be encrypted with Transport Layer Security (TLS) and Secure Socket Layer (SSL) using X.509 certificates (*https://oreil.ly/JG794*). The most important part of this system is the certificate authority (CA). In a public key infrastructure (PKI) arrangement acts as a trusted third party that digitally signs certificates used to create a chain of trust between two entities. Going through the procedure to have a certificate issued by a CA historically has been a manual and arduous process, which unfortunately has led to a lack of secure communications in cloud-based applications.

cert-manager is a tool that uses the Automated Certificate Management Environment (ACME) protocol to add certificate management seamlessly to your Kubernetes infrastructure. We should always use TLS to secure the data moving from one service to another for our streaming application. The cert-manager project is arguably one of the most critical pieces of your Kubernetes infrastructure that you will eventually forget about. That's the hallmark of a project that fits the moniker of "it just works."

Adding TLS to your Pulsar deployment has been made incredibly easy with just a few configuration steps. Before installing Pulsar, you'll need to set up the cert-manager service inside the target Kubernetes cluster. First, add the cert-manager repo to your local Helm installation:

```
helm repo add jetstack https://charts.jetstack.io
```

What Is ACME?

When working with X.509 certificates, you'll frequently see references to the Automated Certificate Management Environment (ACME). ACME allows for automated deployment of certificates between user infrastructure and certificate authorities. It was designed by the Internet Security Research Group when it was building its free certificate authority, Let's Encrypt. It would be putting it lightly to say this fantastic free service has been a game-changer for cloud native infrastructure.

The installation process takes a few parameters, which you should make sure to use. First is declaring a separate Namespace to keep the cert-manager neatly organized in your virtual datacenter. The second is installing the CRD assets. This combination allows you to create services that automate your certificate management:

```
helm install \
  cert-manager jetstack/cert-manager \
  --namespace cert-manager \
  --create-namespace \
  --set installCRDs=true
```

After the cert-manager is installed, you'll then need to configure the certificate issuer that will be called when new certificates are needed. You have many options based on the environment you are operating in, and these are covered quite extensively in the documentation. One of the custom resources created when installing cert-manager is `Issuer`. The most basic `Issuer` is the `selfsigned-issuer` that can create a certificate with a user-supplied private key. You can create a basic `Issuer` by applying the following YAML configuration:

```
apiVersion: cert-manager.io/v1
kind: Issuer
metadata:
  name: selfsigned-issuer
  namespace: cert-manager
spec:
  selfSigned: {}
---
apiVersion: cert-manager.io/v1
kind: ClusterIssuer
metadata:
  name: selfsigned-cluster-issuer
spec:
  selfSigned: {}
```

When installing Pulsar with Helm, you can secure inter-service communication with a few lines of YAML configuration. You can pick which services are secured by setting the TLS `enabled` to `true` or `false` for each service in the YAML that defines your

Pulsar cluster. The examples provided by the project are quite large, so for brevity, we'll look at some key areas:

```
tls:
  # settings for generating certs for proxy
  proxy:
    enabled: true
    cert_name: tls-proxy
  # settings for generating certs for broker
  broker:
    enabled: true
    cert_name: tls-broker
  # settings for generating certs for bookies
  bookie:
    enabled: false
    cert_name: tls-bookie
  # settings for generating certs for zookeeper
  zookeeper:
    enabled: false
    cert_name: tls-zookeeper
```

Alternatively, you can secure the entire cluster with just one command:

```
tls:
  enabled: true
```

Later in your configuration file, you can use self-signing certificates to create TLS connections between components:

```
# issue selfsigning certs
certs:
  internal_issuer:
    enabled: true
    type: selfsigning
```

If you have been involved in securing infrastructure communication any time in the past, you know the toil in working through all the steps and applying TLS. Inside a Kubernetes virtual datacenter, you no longer have an excuse to leave network communication unencrypted. With a few lines of configuration, everything is secured and maintained.

cert-manager: Making Security Easy (So You'll Just Use It)

With Josh van Leeuwen, Software Engineer, Jetstack

The cert-manager is a project born of necessity as our cloud native world grows. Previously, you might have a bunch of VMs or bare metal running somewhere in a ringed fence. You could get away with sticking an SSL certificate in the front gateway and moving on. All of that has now changed, with the thousands or even hundreds of thousands of machines that need to be secured in our cloud native systems. With all of these small containers running microservices continually coming and going, automation is the only way to manage the volume of changes. There is no way a human can do that alone. Of course, this opens a new challenge of reliable automation—one that Kubernetes has taken head-on.

Soon after the ACME protocol was created, custom resources and CRDs became a feature in Kubernetes. cert-manager is a project that joins those two concepts, providing a declarative way to represent what an X.509 certificate should look like inside a Kubernetes Deployment. ACME happened at just the right time for the Kubernetes Ingress use case, and the first use case for cert-manager was for ACME SSL certificates. However, it quickly became apparent that this would not be the only secure networking problem that needed solving in Kubernetes. Those growing numbers of machines all need to talk to each other, and they all need some kind of security in place, which is generally done with TLS. TLS certificates require the concept of an issuer, and cert-manager was expanded to allow for different types of issuers to automate the complete lifecycle further of those certificates.

Because it emerged so early in the project, cert-manager has become the de facto X.509 provider and certificate manager for Kubernetes. With this comes a responsibility to make securing communications in Kubernetes easy. Security is only as good as it is easy. If security is challenging to implement, it's practically useless. Many people don't like GNU Privacy Guard (GPG), for these reasons—not because it's necessarily flawed security-wise, but because it's challenging to use. cert-manager should continue to see wide adoption in cloud native applications. It makes everything secure by default, with little intervention or minimal knowledge of how Rivest–Shamir–Adleman (RSA) or TLS works. It's a project that is easy to use and solves people's problems by default.

One thing that has made cert-manager easy for end users is having a well-defined API to describe their application requirements in a simple way. It is a way of abstracting the more complicated questions, such as "What does it mean to have a certificate signed?" or "What is an issuer?" These APIs provide the guardrails to make sure you do the right thing as much as possible. Some things still require planning and thoughtfulness, such as not reusing private key passwords, which is allowed but discouraged.

Guardrails and standardization are topics that need to become more prevalent in other parts of Kubernetes. The declarative nature and extensibility of Kubernetes are powerful tools, but with great power comes great responsibility. Different people within an organization can make extension points in a Kubernetes cluster. With a single command, you can have an endpoint exposed on the internet without even realizing it. No single pane of glass is available to security professionals for those extensions. Nor are there guardrails to prevent unexpected behaviors. Without proper guardrails in place, it's too easy to self-own quite badly. As Kubernetes matures, we'll need more ways to avoid unhappy accidents.

The cert-manager project is in an excellent state, being vendor-neutral and mature in its current form. If you search the project changelog for the word "feature," you'll see a decrease in occurrence in each successive release. This means we have a core API that is useful and stable, which is an excellent place to be for a core security-based project. The bulk of changes happening in the project are focused on taking advantage of this stable core API to add new issuers. This stability ensures that the project stays up-to-date with the latest requirements without a disruptive breaking change.

As for the future, the cert-manager project will continue to work with the Kubernetes community to continue the path of "default secure" and make security so easy that it's used universally. There are still some challenges to overcome, like how secrets are stored and how to manage trust chains, and the momentum of Kubernetes practically ensures that those are problems that will be solved shortly. If these are interesting problems, I urge you to get involved in one of the many ways security professionals can impact the future of Kubernetes.

cert-manager should be one of the first things you install in a new Kubernetes cluster. The combination of project maturity and simplicity makes security the easy first thing to add to your project instead of the last. This is true not only for Pulsar but for every service you deploy in Kubernetes that requires network communication.

Using Helm to Deploy Apache Pulsar

Now that we have covered how to design a Pulsar cluster to maximize resources, you can use Helm to carry out the deployment into Kubernetes. First, add the Pulsar Helm repository:

```
helm repo add apache https://pulsar.apache.org/charts
```

One of the special requirements for a Helm install of Pulsar is preparing Kubernetes. The Git repository you cloned earlier has a script that will run through all the preparations, such as creating the destination Namespace. The more complicated setup is the roles with associated keys and tokens. These are important for inter-service communication inside the Pulsar cluster. From the docs, you can invoke the prep script by using this example:

```
./scripts/pulsar/prepare_helm_release.sh -n <k8s-namespace> -k <release-name>
```

Once the Kubernetes cluster has been prepared for Pulsar, the final installation can be run. At this point, you should have a YAML configuration file with the settings you need for your Pulsar use case as we described earlier. The `helm install` command will take that config file and direct Kubernetes to meet the desired state you have specified. When creating a new cluster, use `initalize=true` to create the base metadata configuration in ZooKeeper:

```
helm install \
    --values <config yaml file> \
    --set initialize=true \
```

```
    --namespace <namespace from prepare script> \
    <pulsar cluster name> apache/pulsar
```

In a typical production deployment, you should expect the setup time to take 10 minutes or more. There are a lot of dependencies to walk through as ZooKeeper, bookies, brokers, and finally, proxies are brought online and in order.

Stream Analytics with Apache Flink

Now, let's look at a different type of streaming project that is quickly gaining popularity in cloud native deployments: Apache Flink. Flink is a system primarily designed to focus on stream analytics at an incredible scale. As we discussed at the beginning of the chapter, streaming systems come in many flavors, and this is a perfect example. Flink has its competencies that overlap very little with other systems; in fact, it's widespread to see Pulsar and Flink deployed together to complement each other's strengths in a cloud native application.

As a streaming system, the following are available in Flink:

- Type of delivery: one-to-one
- Delivery guarantee: exactly once
- Feature scope for streaming: analytics

The two main components of the Flink architecture are shown in Figure 8-6—the JobManager and TaskManager:

JobManager
: This is the control plane for any running Flink application code deployed. A JobManager consumes CPU resources but only to maintain Job control; no actual processing is done on the JobManager. In high availability (HA) mode, which is exclusive to Flink running on Kubernetes, multiple standby JobManagers will be provisioned but remain idle until the primary is no longer available.

TaskManager
: This is where the work gets done on a running Flink job. The JobManger uses TaskManagers to satisfy the chain of tasks needed in the application. A chain is the order of operation. In some cases, these operations can be run in parallel, and some need to be run in series. The TaskManger will run only one discrete task and pass it on. Resource management can be controlled through the number of TaskManagers in a cluster and execution slots per TaskManager. The current guidance says that you should allocate one CPU to each TaskManager or slot.

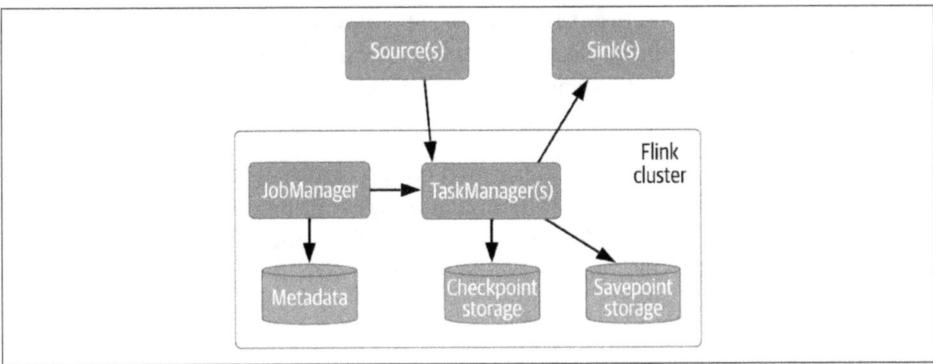

Figure 8-6. Apache Flink architecture

The Flink project is designed for managing stateful computations, which should cause you to immediately think of storage requirements. Every transaction in Flink is guaranteed to be strongly consistent with no single point of failure. These are the features you need when you are trying to build the kind of highly scalable systems that Flink was designed to accomplish. There are two types of streaming, bounded and unbounded:

Unbounded streaming
: These streaming systems react to new data whenever the data arrives—there is no endpoint where you can stop and analyze the data gathered. Every piece of data received is independent. The use cases for this can be alerting on values or counting when exactness is essential. Reactive processing can be very resource-efficient.

Bounded streaming
: This is also known as *batch processing* in other systems but is a specific case within Flink. Bounded windows can be marked by time or specific values. In the case of time windows, they can also slide forward, giving the ability to do rolling updates on values. Resource considerations should be given based on the data window size to be processed. The limit of the boundary size is constrained mainly by memory.

One of the foundational tenets of Flink is a strong focus on operations. At the scale required for cloud native applications, easy to use and deploy can be the difference between using it or not. This includes core support for continuous deployment workloads in Kubernetes and feature parity with cloud native applications in the areas of reliability and observability:

Continuous deployment
: The core unit of work for Flink is called a *job*. Jobs are Java or Scala programs that define how the data is read, analyzed, and output. Jobs are chained together

and compiled into a JAR file to create a Flink application. Flink provides a Docker image that encapsulates the application in a form that makes deployment on Kubernetes an easy task and facilitates continuous deployment.

Reliability
: Flink also has built-in support for savepoints, which makes updates easier by pausing and resuming jobs before and after system updates. Savepoints can also be used for fast recovery if a processing Pod fails mid-job. Tighter integration with Kubernetes allows Flink to self-heal on failure by restoring Pods and restarting Jobs with savepoints.

Observability
: Cluster metrics are instrumented to output in Prometheus format. Operations teams can keep track of lifecycle events inside the Flink cluster with time-based details. Application developers can expose custom metrics using the Flink metric system (*https://oreil.ly/0x0IS*) for further integrated observability.

Flink provides a way for data teams to participate in the overall cloud native stack while giving operators everything needed to manage the entire deployment. Application developers building microservices can share a CI/CD pipeline with developers building the stream analytics of data generated from the application. As changes occur in any part of the stack, they can be integration tested entirely and deployed as a single unit. Teams can move faster with more confidence knowing there aren't disconnected requirements that may show up in production. This sort of outcome is a solid argument to employ cloud native methodologies in your entire stack, so it's time to see how this is done.

Deploying Apache Flink on Kubernetes

When deploying a Flink cluster into a running Kubernetes cluster, there are a few things to consider. The Flink project has gone the route of offering what it calls "Kubernetes Native," which programmatically installs the required Flink components without `kubectl` or Helm. These choices may change in the future. Side projects in the Flink ecosystem already bring a more typical experience that Kubernetes operators might expect, including operators and Helm charts. For now, we will discuss the official method endorsed by the project.

As shown in Figure 8-7, a running Flink cluster has two main components we'll deploy in Pods: the *JobManager* and *TaskManager*. These are the basic units, but choosing which deployment mode is the critical consideration for your use case. They dictate how compute and network resources are utilized. Another thing of note is how to deploy on Kubernetes. As mentioned before, there are no official project operators or Helm charts. The Flink distribution (*https://flink.apache.org/downloads.html*) contains command-line tools that will deploy into a running Kubernetes cluster based on the mode for your application.

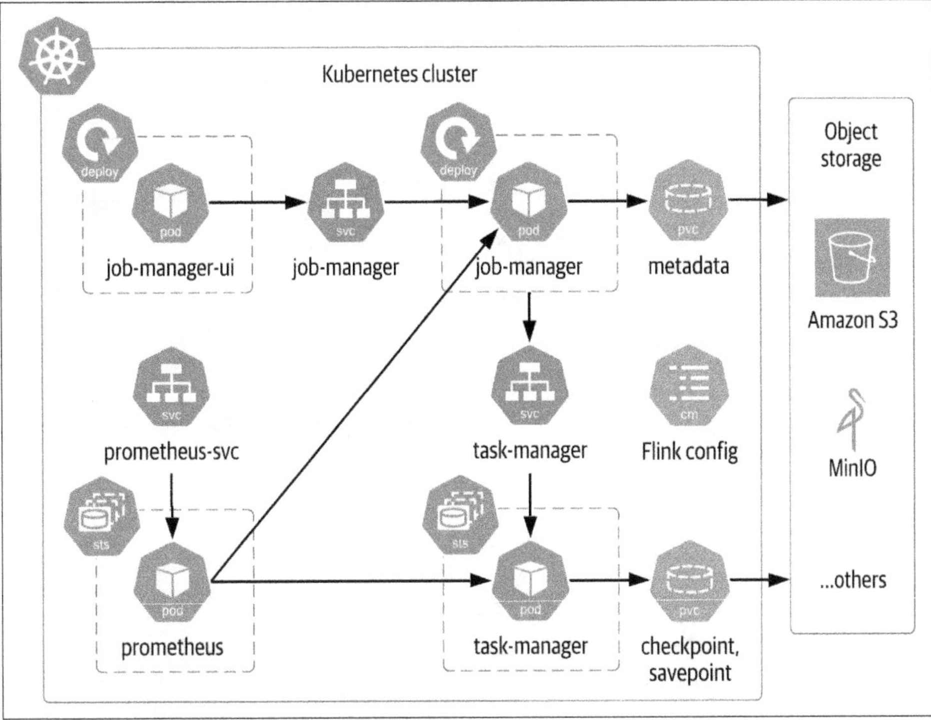

Figure 8-7. Deploying Flink on Kubernetes

Figure 8-8 shows the modes available for deploying Flink clusters in Kubernetes: Application Mode and Session Mode. Flink also supports a third mode called Per-Job Mode, but this is not available for Kubernetes deployments, which leaves us with Application Mode and Session Mode.

The selection of either Application Mode or Session Mode comes down to resource management inside your Kubernetes cluster, so let's look at both to make an informed decision.

Application Mode isolates each Flink application into its own cluster. As a reminder, a Flink application JAR can consist of multiple jobs chained together. The startup cost of the cluster can be minimized with a single application initialization and Job graph. Once deployed, resources are consumed for client traffic and execution of the jobs in the application. Network traffic is much more efficient since there is only one JobManager and client traffic can be multiplexed.

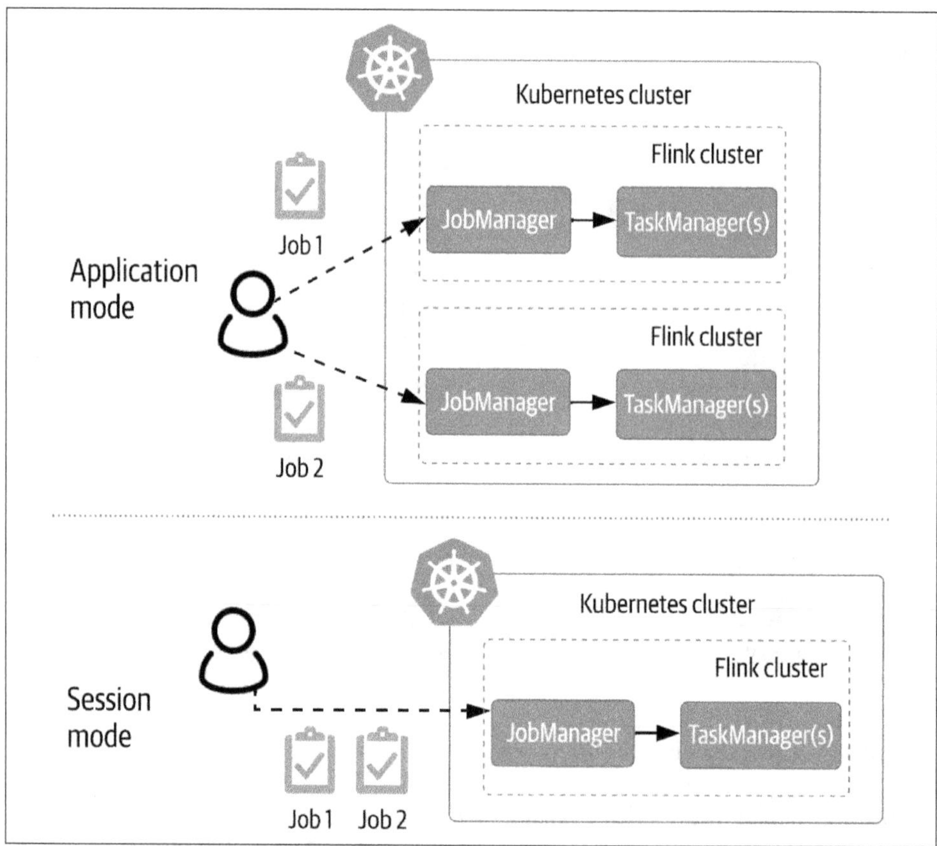

Figure 8-8. Apache Flink modes

To start in Application Mode, you invoke the `flink` command with the target of `kubernetes-application`. You will need the name of the running Kubernetes cluster accessible via `kubectl`. The application to be run is contained in a Docker image, and the path to the JAR file supplied in the command line. Once started, the Flink cluster is created, application code is initialized, and will then be ready for client connections:

```
./bin/flink run-application \
    --target kubernetes-application \
    -Dkubernetes.cluster-id=<kubernetes cluster name> \
    -Dkubernetes.container.image=<custom docker image name> \
    local:///opt/flink/usrlib/my-flink-job.jar
```

Session Mode changes resource management by creating a single Flink cluster that can accept any number of applications on an ad hoc basis. Instead of having multiple independent clusters running and consuming resources, you may find it more efficient to have a single cluster that can grow and shrink when new applications are submitted. The downside for operators is that you now have a single cluster that will take several applications with it if it fails. Kubernetes will restart the downed Pods, but you will have a recovery time to manage as resources are reallocated. To start in Session Mode, use the `kubernetes-session` shell file and give it the name of your running Kubernetes cluster. The default is for the command to execute and detach from the cluster. To reattach or remain in an interactive mode with the running cluster, use the `execution.attached=true` switch:

```
./bin/kubernetes-session.sh \
    -Dkubernetes.cluster-id=<kubernetes cluster name> \
    -Dexecution.attached=true
```

This was a quick fly-by of a massive topic, but hopefully, it inspires you to look further. One resource we recommend is *Stream Processing with Apache Flink* (*https://oreil.ly/Iocv6*) by Fabian Hueske and Vasiliki Kalavri (O'Reilly). Adding Flink to your application isn't just about choosing a platform to perform stream processing. In cloud native applications, we should be thinking holistically about the entire application stack we are attempting to deploy in Kubernetes. Flink uses containers, as encapsulation lends itself to working with other development workflows.

Summary

In this chapter, we have branched out from persistence-oriented data infrastructure into the world of streaming. We defined what streaming is, how to navigate all the terminology, and how it fits into Kubernetes. From there, we took a deeper look into Apache Pulsar and learned how to deploy it into your Kubernetes cluster according to your environment and application needs. As a part of deploying streaming, we took a side trip into default secure communications with cert-manager to see how it works and how to create self-managed encrypted communication. Finally, we looked at Kubernetes deployments of Apache Flink, which is used primarily for high-scale stream analytics.

As you saw in this chapter with Pulsar and cert-manager, running cloud native data infrastructure on Kubernetes frequently involves the composition of multiple components as part of an integrated stack. We'll discuss more examples of this in the next chapter and beyond.

CHAPTER 9

Data Analytics on Kubernetes

> *Progress in technology is when we have the ability to be more lazy.*
>
> —Dr. Laurian Chirica

In the early 2000s, Google captivated the internet with a declared public goal: "to organize the world's information and make it universally accessible and useful." This was an ambitious goal and accomplishing it would, to paraphrase, take "computer sciencing" the bits out of it. Given the increasing rate of data creation, Google needed to invent (and reinvent) ways of managing data volumes no one had ever considered. An entirely new community, culture, and industry were born around analyzing data called *analytics*, tackling what was eventually labeled "big data." Today, analytics is a full-fledged member of almost every application stack and not just relegated to a Google problem. Now it's everyone's problem; instead of an art form restricted to a small club of experts, we all need to know how to make analytics work. Organizations need reliable and fast ways to deploy applications with analytics so that they can do more with less.

The laziness Dr. Chirica was talking about in a tongue-in-cheek way in the quote that opens this chapter describes an ideal future. Instead of having a hundred-person team working night and day to analyze a petabyte of data, what if you could reduce that to one person and a few minutes? The cloud native way of running data infrastructure is a path we should all work toward to achieve that kind of glorious laziness.

We've already looked at several aspects of moving stateful workloads onto Kubernetes, including storage, databases, and streaming. In this chapter, it's time to look at analytics to complete the picture. As a bit of a preview, Figure 9-1 shows how data analytics fits as the final part of our roadmap of managing the complete data stack using Kubernetes.

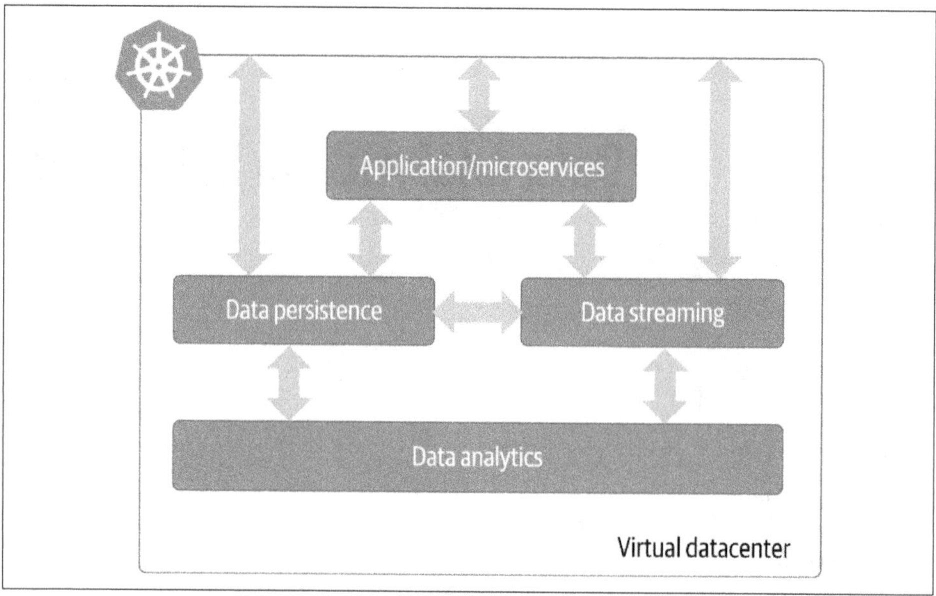

Figure 9-1. The cloud native virtual datacenter

In this architecture, there are no more external network requirements bridging to resources in or out of the Kubernetes cluster, just a single, virtual datacenter that serves our bespoke needs for cloud native applications. The large blocks represent the macro components of data infrastructure we discussed in Chapter 1, with the addition of user application code, deployed in microservices.

Introduction to Analytics

Analytic workloads and the accompanying infrastructure operations are much different from other workloads. Analytics isn't just another containerized system to orchestrate. The typical stateful applications like databases we examined in previous chapters have many similar characteristics but tend to stay static or predictably slow-growing once deployed.

However, one aspect of analytic workloads strikes fear in many administrators: volume. While persistent data stores like databases can consume gigabytes to terabytes of storage, analytic volumes can easily soar into petabytes, creating an entirely new class of problems to solve. They don't call it "big data" for nothing.

The *Oxford English Dictionary* defines analytics as "the systematic computational analysis of data or statistics." Wikipedia (*https://oreil.ly/Hc1Pp*) adds, "It is used for the discovery, interpretation, and communication of meaningful patterns in data." Combine those definitions with large volumes of data and what sort of outcome should we expect for cloud native applications? Let's break down the different types of analytics workflows and methodologies:

Batch analytics
: In computer science, a *batch* is a series of instructions applied to data with little or no user interaction. The idea of running batch Jobs is as old as general-purpose computing. In distributed systems such as Apache Hadoop or Apache Spark, each individual Job consists of a program that can operate on smaller bits of data in parallel and in stages or pipelines. The smaller results are combined into a single, final result at the end of a Job. An example of this is MapReduce, discussed later in this chapter. In most cases, statistical analysis such as count, average, and percentile measurement is done. Batch analytics is the focus of this chapter.

Stream analytics
: As discussed in Chapter 8, stream analytics is about what is *happening*, whereas batch analytics is about what *happened*. Many of the same APIs and developer methodologies are used in both stream analytics and batch analytics. This can be confusing and lead people to believe that they are the same thing when, in fact, they have very different use cases and implementations. A good example is fraud detection. The time frames for detecting and stopping fraud can be measured in milliseconds to seconds, which fits the stream analytics use case. Batch analytics would be used to find fraud patterns over larger time periods.

Artificial intelligence/machine learning (AI/ML)
: While AI and ML can be considered a subset of batch analytics, they are such specialized fields that they deserve a special callout. AI and ML are often mentioned together; however, they have two different output goals. AI attempts to emulate human cognition in decision making. ML uses algorithms to derive meaning from pools of data, sometimes in ways that aren't readily obvious. Both approaches require the application of computing resources across volumes of data. This topic is discussed in greater detail in Chapter 10.

Deploying Analytic Workloads in Kubernetes

The original focus of Kubernetes was on scaling and orchestrating stateless applications. As you're learning in this book, Kubernetes is evolving to support stateful applications. The promise of operational efficiency by moving more and more workloads into virtual datacenters has been highly motivating. The world of analytics can take advantage of the progress made in reducing the operational burden for stateless and stateful workloads. However, Kubernetes has some unique challenges in managing analytic workloads; many are still a work in progress. What features of Kubernetes are required to complete the data picture and put analytic workloads on par with other parts of the stack like microservices and databases? Here are a few of the key considerations we'll examine in this chapter:

Orderly execution
: An essential aspect of analytic workloads is the order of operations required to analyze large volumes of data. This involves far more than just making sure Pods are started with the proper storage and networking resources. It also includes a mapping of the application with the orderly execution run in each Pod. The Kubernetes component primarily responsible for this task is `kube-scheduler` (see Chapter 5), but the controllers for Jobs and CronJobs are involved as well. This is a particular area of attention for the Kubernetes communities focusing on analytics, which we will further cover in the chapter.

Storage management
: Analytic workloads use ephemeral and persistent storage in different Jobs that process data. The real trouble occurs when it comes to identifying and selecting the right storage per Job. Many analytic workloads require ephemeral storage for short periods and more-efficient (cheaper) persistent storage for long terms. As you learned in Chapter 2, Kubernetes storage has greatly increased maturity. Analytics projects that run on Kubernetes need to take advantage of the work already done with stateful workloads and continue to partner with the Kubernetes community for future enhancements in areas like StorageClasses and different access patterns.

Efficient use of resources
: There is an old saying that "everything counts in large amounts," and nothing makes that more evident than analytics. A Job may require 1,000 Pods for 10 minutes, but what if it needs 10,000? That's a challenging problem for the Kubernetes control plane. Another Job might require terabytes of swap disk space that is needed only for the duration of a Job. In a cloud native world, Jobs should be able to quickly allocate the resources they need and release the resources when finished. Making these operations as efficient as possible saves time and, more importantly, money. The fast and bursty nature of analytics has created some challenges for the Kubernetes API server and scheduler to keep up with all the Jobs that need to be run. Several of those challenges are already being addressed, as discussed later in the chapter, and some are still a work in progress.

Those are the challenges, but none of them are showstoppers that will get in the way of our dream of a complete cloud native stack deployed as a single virtual datacenter in Kubernetes.

Analytics on Kubernetes Is the Next Frontier

With Holden Karau, Open Source Engineer, Apache Spark PMC

Running analytic workloads has been the boss-level challenge for infrastructure engineers from day one. There is the challenge of massive volumes of needed resources, which in many cases are the most significant part of your infrastructure. Then, coordination is required to use all those resources efficiently, and this is where frameworks like Spark come into play. Projects like YARN from Hadoop and then Mesos were developed to help with the container management game. Today, infrastructure engineers everywhere are very happy with migrating the best aspects of those systems to Kubernetes.

Let's consider a few examples. Running multiple Spark tenants in Kubernetes provides better isolation between your workloads, which is really important if you don't trust each workload to the same degree. Historically, the support for Python dependencies inside Spark Jobs has been poor, but deploying on Kubernetes makes it possible to use leading-edge Python libraries for ML and GPU usage. SREs can spend more time optimizing resources rather than chasing down obscure errors typical with large, distributed systems.

Ultimately, we are still in the early days of learning how to run our analytic workloads in Kubernetes most effectively. The difficulty curve starts getting much steeper as data volumes increase. Once you start going over the tens or hundreds of terabytes, you will find yourself on the leading edge of Spark operations in Kubernetes. This is probably not a big surprise, because that tends to be how infrastructure engineering works. The upper-limit scale problems with Kubernetes are rooted in the early use cases it was designed for. The dynamic and elastic nature of Kubernetes works well for the use cases for which it was first designed, but it gets overwhelmed at the levels required to run Spark applications. This is not impossible to solve, and the Spark and Kubernetes communities are working to improve a few critical areas.

Kubernetes SREs love the idea of elastic workloads, but in Spark, that's been much more painful than it needs to be. Regular execution of a Spark Job can cause a rapid increase in Pods while the Job is processing, and then those resources are released when the Job is complete. Scaling up is, unfortunately, much easier than scaling down. Spark can now make use of externalized resource allocation that opens the possibility for better solutions. Open source projects such as Volcano and Apache YuniKorn are already working on resource allocation solutions inside Kubernetes, which the execution allocator and shuffle service can leverage to align more closely to the way Kubernetes works. Taken together, these efforts provide a significant path forward for more efficient resource usage in a dynamic Spark environment.

Resource-intensive applications like Spark can benefit from having more insight from the underlying systems to balance Jobs as they are run. Today, Kubernetes and Spark do not share as much information as they need for the best outcomes, and you should adjust your expectations accordingly. A specific example is the way Kubernetes approaches storage quota enforcement, which can work against Spark in some cases. Ephemeral storage is a key part of Spark execution, but Kubernetes provides no system-level APIs that Spark could use to check the utilization against the storage quota, which can cause Job failures. Previous applications that have been deployed on Kubernetes haven't needed this level of insight. Spark creates a compelling case for significant changes to expose additional system-level APIs in Kubernetes, which will make it possible to build much more reliable analytic workloads.

If you are interested in solving these problems, these solutions will happen in open source projects. You can get involved today and help us move forward by participating in the larger community (*https://spark.apache.org/community.html*). Apache Spark has room for improvement and so does Kubernetes, but the future direction is clear. Kubernetes is where cloud native analytics will happen, and Spark will continue to evolve. There will be a lot of interesting work in this area for the next several years at least, and it's a pretty exciting community to be a part of.

Engineers can be their own worst enemies. Often when we go to solve one problem, it creates a few more that need to be solved. We can count this as progress, however, when it comes to managing data. Every step up we take, despite the challenges, allows for new solutions that were never available before. It's a staggering thought—today, a small number of people can perform analytics tasks that massive teams would not have been able to accomplish just a few years ago. See the quote about laziness at the beginning of the chapter. There is still work to be done, and next we will look at the tools available for analyzing data in Kubernetes.

Introduction to Apache Spark

Google changed the world of data analytics with the MapReduce algorithm simply by describing it to the world in an academic paper. Not long after the MapReduce paper (*https://oreil.ly/mryO0*) got engineers talking, an open source implementation was created: the now-famous Apache Hadoop. A massive ecosystem was built up around Hadoop with tooling and complementary projects such as Hadoop Distributed File System (HDFS).

Growing pains from this fast-moving project opened the door for the next generation of tools that built on the lessons learned with Hadoop. One project that grew in popularity as an alternative to Hadoop was Apache Spark (*https://oreil.ly/BlT4i*). Spark addressed reliability and processing efficiency problems by introducing the Resilient Distributed Dataset (RDD) API and Directed Acyclic Graph (DAG).

The RDD was a significant improvement over the forced linear processing patterns of MapReduce, which involved a lot of reading from disk, processing, and then writing back to disk only to be redone over and over. This put the burden on developers to reason through how data was processed. RDDs shifted the responsibility away from developers as an API that created a unified view of all data while abstracting the actual processing details. Those details were created in a workflow to perform each task expressed in a DAG. The DAG is nothing more than an optimized path that describes data and operations to be completed in an orderly fashion until the final result is produced. RDDs were eventually replaced with the Dataset and DataFrame APIs, further enhancing developer productivity over large volumes of data.

Spark's operational complexity is greatly reduced compared to Hadoop, which notoriously tipped the scale with the infrastructure required even for basic Jobs. Spark is an excellent example of one of the benefits of being a next-generation implementation with great hindsight. Much effort was put into simplifying Spark's architecture, leveraging distributed systems concepts. The result is the three familiar components you should be familiar with in a Spark cluster, shown in Figure 9-2.

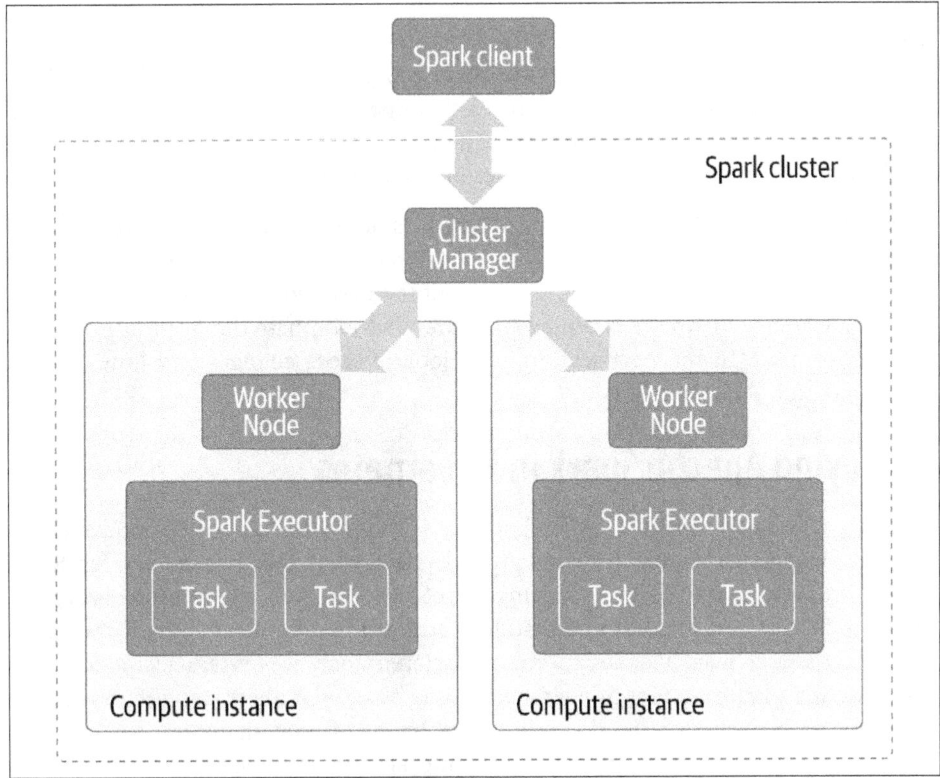

Figure 9-2. Components of a Spark cluster

Let's review the responsibilities of each of these components:

Cluster Manager
: The Cluster Manager is the central hub for activity in the Spark cluster where new Jobs are submitted for processing. The Cluster Manager also acquires the resources needed to complete the task submitted. Different versions of the Cluster Manager are primarily based on how resources are managed (standalone, YARN, Mesos, and Kubernetes). The Cluster Manager is critical for deploying your Spark application using Kubernetes.

Worker Node
: When Spark Jobs run, they are broken into manageable pieces by the Cluster Manager and handed to the Worker Nodes to perform the processing. They serve as the local manager for hardware resources as a single point of contact. Worker Nodes invoke and manage Spark Executors.

Spark Executor
: Each application sent to a Worker Node will get its own Spark Executor. Each Executor is a standalone JVM process that operates independently and communicates back with the Worker Node. The tasks for the application are broken into threads that consume the compute resources allocated.

These are the traditional components of Spark as designed early in the project. We'll see that the need to deploy a cloud native version of Spark forced some architectural evolution. The fundamentals are the same, but the execution framework has adapted to take advantage of what Kubernetes provides and eliminate duplication in orchestration overhead. In the next section, we'll look at those changes and how to work with Spark in Kubernetes.

Deploying Apache Spark in Kubernetes

As of Apache Spark version 2.3, Kubernetes is one of the supported modes in the Cluster Manager. It would be easy to understate what that has meant for Spark as a cloud native analytics tool. Starting with Spark 3.1, Kubernetes mode is considered production-ready, continually adding steady improvements. When the Spark project looked at what it takes to run a clustered analytics system inside a cluster orchestration platform, a lot of overlaps became obvious. Kubernetes already had the mechanisms in place for the lifecycle management of containers and the dynamic provisioning and deprovisioning of compute elements, so Spark lets Kubernetes take care of this work. The redundant parts were removed, and Spark is closer to the way Kubernetes works as a result. The `spark-submit` command-line tool was extended to interface with Kubernetes clusters using the Kubernetes API, maintaining a familiar toolchain for developers and data engineers. These unique aspects of a Spark deployment in Kubernetes are shown in Figure 9-3.

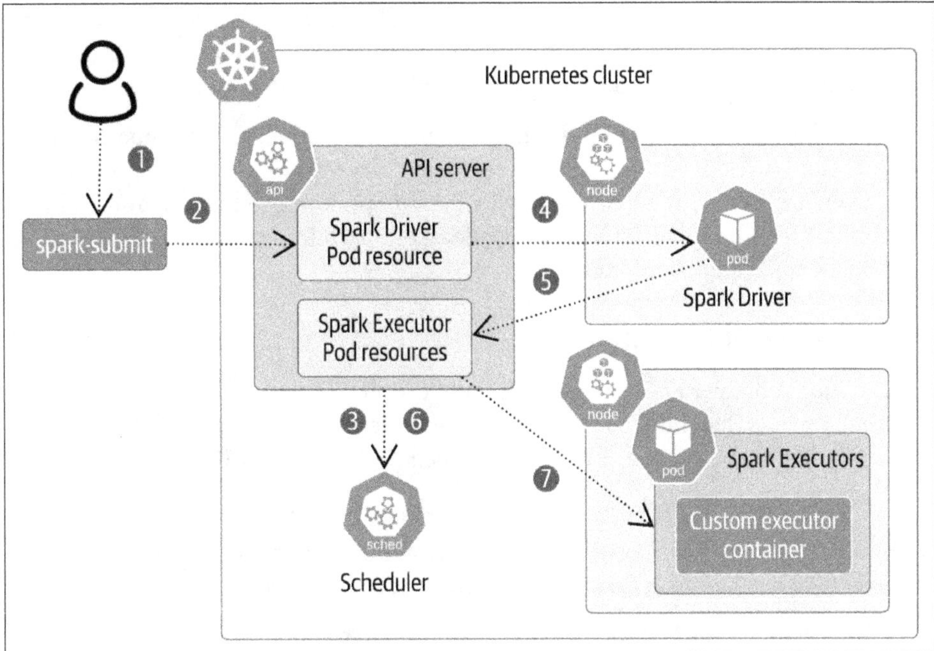

Figure 9-3. Spark on Kubernetes

Let's highlight a few of the differences:

Spark Driver
: The dedicated Cluster Manager of a standalone Spark cluster is replaced with native Kubernetes cluster management and the Spark Driver for Spark-specific management. The Spark Driver Pod is created when the Kubernetes API server receives a Job from the `spark-submit` tool. It invokes the Spark Executor Pods to satisfy the Job requirements. It is also responsible for cleaning up Executor Pods after the Job, making it a crucial part of elastic workloads.

Spark Executor
: Like a standalone Spark cluster, Executors are where the work gets done and where the most compute resources are consumed. Invoked from the Spark Driver, they take Job instructions passed by `spark-submit` with details such as CPU and memory limits, storage information, and security credentials. The containers used in Executor Pods are pre-created by the user.

Custom Executor container
: Before a Job is sent for processing using `spark-submit`, users must build a custom container image tailored to meet the application requirements. The Spark distribution download contains a Dockerfile that can be customized and used in conjunction with the *docker-image-tool.sh* script to build and upload the

container required when submitting a Spark Job in Kubernetes. The custom container has everything it needs to work within a Kubernetes environment, like a Spark Executor based on the Spark distribution version required.

The workflow for preparing and running Spark Jobs when using Kubernetes and defaults can be relatively simple, requiring only a couple of steps. This is especially true if you are already familiar with and running Spark in production. You will need a running Kubernetes cluster and a download of Spark in a local filepath along with your Spark application source code.

Build Your Custom Container

An executor container encapsulates your application and the runtime needed to act as an executor Pod. The build script takes an argument for the source code repository and a tag assignment for the output image when pushed to your Docker registry:

```
./bin/docker-image-tool.sh -r <repo> -t <tag> build
```

The output will be a Docker image with a JAR file containing your application code. You will then need to push this image to your Docker registry:

```
./bin/docker-image-tool.sh -r <repo> -t <tag> push
```

Docker Image Tags

Be mindful that your tag name is labeled and versioned correctly. Reusing the same tag name in production could have unintended consequences, as some of us have learned from experience.

Submit and Run Your Application

Once the Docker image is pushed to the repo, use **`spark-submit`** to start the process of running the Spark application inside Kubernetes. This is the same `spark-submit` used for other modes, so many of the same arguments are used. This corresponds to (1) in Figure 9-3:

```
./bin/spark-submit \
    --master k8s://https://<k8s-apiserver-host>:<k8s-apiserver-port> \
    --deploy-mode cluster \
    --name <application-name> \
    --class <fully-qualified-class-name> \
    --conf spark.executor.instances=<instance-number> \
    --conf spark.kubernetes.container.image=<spark-image> \
    local:///path/to/application.jar
```

Quite a few things are happening here, but the *most important* is in the `--master` parameter. To indicate this is for Kubernetes, the URL in the argument must start with `k8s://` and point to the API server in the default Kubernetes cluster specified in your local *.kubeconfig* file. The *`<spark-image>`* is the Docker image you created in (1), and the application path refers to your application stored inside the image.

Next is (2), where `spark-submit` interacts with the Kubernetes cluster to schedule the Spark Driver Pod (3) and (4). The Spark Driver parses the Job parameters and works with the Kubernetes scheduler to set up Spark Executor Pods (5), (6), and (7) to run the application code contained in the customer container image. The application will run to completion, and eventually the Pod used will be terminated and resources returned to the Kubernetes cluster in a process called *garbage collection*.

This is just an overview of how Spark natively works with Kubernetes. Please refer to the official documentation (*https://oreil.ly/upJeL*) to go into much greater detail. There are many ways to customize the arguments and parameters to best fit your specific needs.

Security Considerations when Running Spark in Kubernetes

Security is not enabled by default when using Spark in Kubernetes. The first line of defense is authentication. Production Spark applications should use the built-in authentication in Spark to ensure that the users and processes accessing your application are the ones you intended.

When creating a container for your application, the Spark documentation highly recommends changing the `USER` directive to an unprivileged unique identifier (UID) and group identifier (GID) to mitigate against privilege escalation attacks. This can also be accomplished with a SecurityContext inside the Pod template file provided as a parameter to `spark-submit`.

Storage access should also be restricted with the Spark Driver and Spark Executor. Specifically, you should limit the paths that can be accessed by the running application to eliminate any accidental access in the event of a vulnerability. These can be set inside a PodSecurityAdmission, which the Spark documentation recommends (*https://oreil.ly/xQcom*).

For optimal security of your Spark applications, use the security primitives Kubernetes provides and customize the defaults for your environment. The best security is the one you don't have to think about. If you are an SRE, this is one of the best things you can do for your developers and data engineers. Default secure!

Kubernetes Operator for Apache Spark

If Spark can run in Kubernetes via `spark-submit`, why do we need an operator? As you learned in previous chapters, Kubernetes operators give you more flexibility in managing applications and a more cloud native experience overall. Using `spark-submit` to run your Spark applications requires your production systems to be set up with a local installation of Spark, including all dependencies. The Spark on Kubernetes Operator allows SREs and developers to manage park applications declaratively using Kubernetes tools such as Helm and `kubectl`. It also allows better observability on running Jobs and exporting metrics to external systems like Prometheus. Finally, using the operator provides an experience much closer to running other applications in Kubernetes.

The first step is to install the operator into your Kubernetes cluster using Helm:

```
helm repo add spark-operator \
  https://googlecloudplatform.github.io/spark-on-k8s-operator

helm install my-release spark-operator/spark-operator \
  --namespace spark-operator --create-namespace
```

Once completed, you will have a SparkApplication controller running and looking for SparkApplication objects. This is the first big departure from `spark-submit`. Instead of a long list of command-line arguments, you use the SparkApplication CRD to define the Spark Job in a YAML file. Let's look at a config file from the Spark on Kubernetes Operator documentation (*https://oreil.ly/quNfG*):

```
apiVersion: "sparkoperator.k8s.io/v1beta2"
kind: SparkApplication
metadata:
  name: spark-pi
  namespace: default
spec:
  type: Scala
  mode: cluster
  image: "gcr.io/spark-operator/spark:v3.1.1"
  imagePullPolicy: Always
  mainClass: org.apache.spark.examples.SparkPi
  mainApplicationFile:
    "local:///opt/spark/examples/jars/spark-examples_2.12-3.1.1.jar"
  sparkVersion: "3.1.1"
  restartPolicy:
    type: Never
  volumes:
    - name: "test-volume"
      hostPath:
        path: "/tmp"
        type: Directory
  driver:
```

```
    cores: 1
    coreLimit: "1200m"
    memory: "512m"
    labels:
      version: 3.1.1
    serviceAccount: spark
    volumeMounts:
      - name: "test-volume"
        mountPath: "/tmp"
  executor:
    cores: 1
    instances: 1
    memory: "512m"
    labels:
      version: 3.1.1
    volumeMounts:
      - name: "test-volume"
        mountPath: "/tmp"
```

The `spec:` section is similar to the parameters you passed in `spark-submit` with details about your application. The most important is the location of the container image. This example uses a default Spark container with the `spark-examples` JAR file preinstalled. You will need to use *docker-image-tool.sh* to build the image for your application as described in "Build Your Custom Container" on page 228, and modify the `mainClass` and `mainApplicationFile` as appropriate for your application.

Two other notable fields under `spec` are `driver` and `executor`. These provide the specifications for the Spark Driver Pods and Spark Executor Pods that the Spark Operator will deploy. For `driver`, only one core is required, but CPU and memory allocations need to be enough to maintain the number of executors you require. The number is set in the `executor` section under `instances`.

Minding Your Resources

For resource management, the requests you make under `driver` and `spec` need to be carefully considered for resource management. The number of instances plus their allocated CPU and memory could use up resources quickly. Jobs can hang indefinitely while waiting for resources to free up, which may never happen.

Now that your configuration YAML is ready, it's time to put it into action. For a walk-through, refer to Figure 9-4.

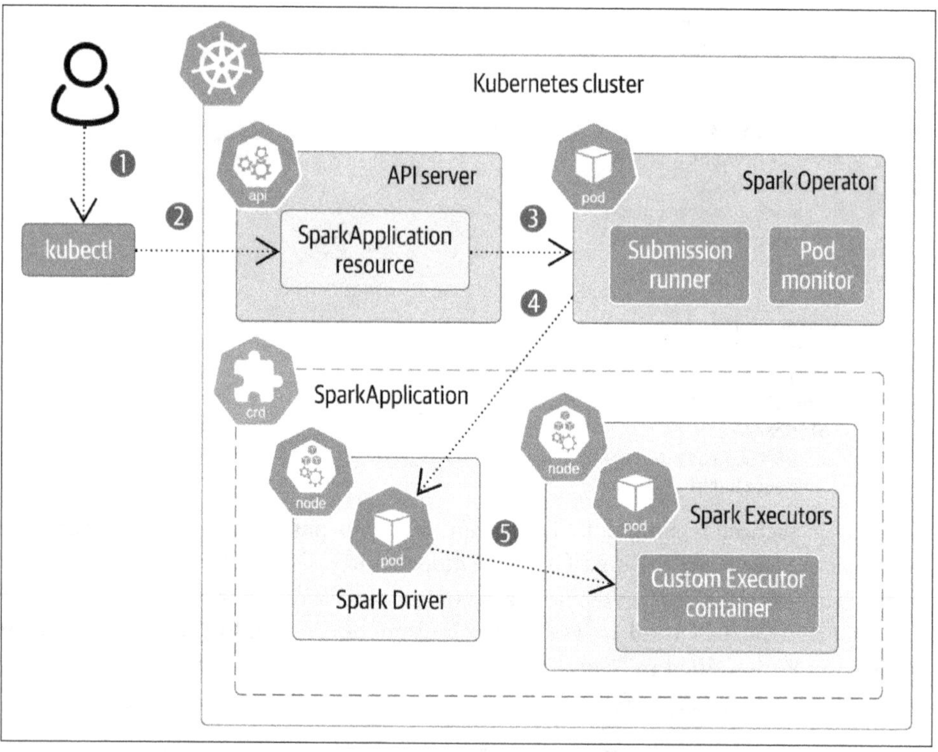

Figure 9-4. Spark on Kubernetes Operator

First, use `kubectl apply -f <filename>` (1) to apply the SparkApplication into your running Kubernetes cluster (2). The Spark Operator listens for new applications (3), and when a new config object is applied, the submission runner controller begins the tasks of building out the required Pods. From here the actions taken in the Kubernetes cluster are the same as if you used `spark-submit`, with all of the parameters being supplied in this case via the SparkApplication YAML. The submission runner starts the Spark Driver Pod (4) which in turn directs the Spark Executor Pods (5), which runs the application code to completion. The Pod monitor included in the Spark Operator exports Spark metrics to observability tools such as Prometheus.

The Spark Operator fills in the gaps between the way `spark-submit` works and the way SREs and developers typically deploy applications into Kubernetes. This was a long answer to the question posed at the beginning of this section. We need an operator to make using Spark more cloud native and thus more manageable in the long run. The cloud native way of doing things includes taking a declarative approach to managing resources and making those resources observable.

Alternative Schedulers for Kubernetes

As you learned in Chapter 5, the Kubernetes scheduler has a basic but essential job: take requests for resources and assign the compute, network, and storage to satisfy the requirements. Let's look at the default approach for this action, as shown in Figure 9-5.

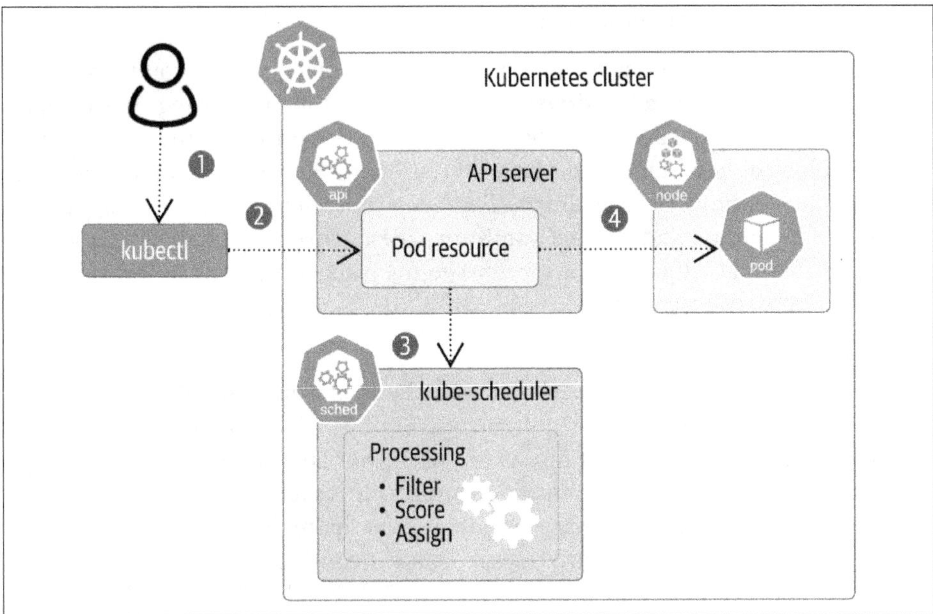

Figure 9-5. Typical Kubernetes scheduling

A typical scheduling effort begins when you create a *deployment.yaml* file describing the resources required (1), including which Pod resources are needed and how many. When the YAML file is submitted (2) to the Kubernetes cluster API server using `kubectl apply`, the Pod resources are created with the supplied parameters and are ready for assignment to a node. Nodes have the needed pool of resources, and it's the job of `kube-scheduler` to be the matchmaker between nodes and Pods. The scheduler performs state matching whenever a new Pod resource is created (3), and checks whether the Pod has an assigned node. If not, the scheduler makes the calculations needed to find an available node. It examines the requirements for the Pod, scores the available nodes using an internal set of rules, and selects a node to run the Pod (4). This is where the real work of container orchestration in Kubernetes gets done.

However, we have a problem with analytic workloads: the default Kubernetes scheduler was not designed for batch workloads. The design is just too basic to work the way that's needed for analytics. As mentioned in "Analytics on Kubernetes Is the Next

Frontier" on page 223, Kubernetes was built for the needs of stateless workloads. These are long-running processes that may expand or contract over time but tend to remain relatively static. Analytic applications such as Spark are different, requiring the scheduling of potentially thousands of short-lived jobs.

Thankfully, the developers of Kubernetes anticipated expanded requirements for future scheduling needs and made it possible for users to specify their scheduler in a configuration, bypassing the default scheduling approach.

The strong desire to manage the entire application stack with a common control plane has been an innovation driver. As demonstrated in "Deploying Apache Spark in Kubernetes" on page 226, Spark has been moving closer to Kubernetes. In this section, we'll look at how some teams have been bringing Kubernetes closer to Spark by building more appropriate schedulers. Two open source projects are leading the way in this effort: Volcano and Apache YuniKorn. These schedulers share similar guiding principles that make them more appropriate for batch workloads by providing the following alternative features:

Multitenant resource management
: The default Kubernetes scheduler allocates Pods as requested until no more available resources match Pod requirements. Both YuniKorn and Volcano provide a wide variety of resourcing modes to match your application needs better, especially in multitenant environments. Fairness in resource management prevents one analytic Job from starving out other Jobs for required resources. As these Jobs are scheduled, the entire resource pool is considered to balance utilization based on priority and throughput.

: *Gang scheduling* adds another layer of intelligence. If a submitted Job needs a certain amount of resources, it doesn't make sense to start the Job if every Pod can't be started. The default scheduler will start Pods until the cluster runs out of resources, potentially stranding Jobs as they wait for more Pods to come online. Gang scheduling implements an all-or-nothing approach, as Jobs will start only when all resources needed are available for the complete Job.

Job queue management
: Smarter queue management can also lead to better resource management. If one Job needs few resources and can be run while larger Jobs are being run, the scheduler can fit the Job in and therefore increase the Kubernetes cluster's overall throughput. In some cases, users need control over what Jobs have priority and which can preempt or pause other running Jobs as they are submitted. Queues can be reordered or reprioritized after Jobs are submitted. Observability tooling provides queue insights that help determine total cluster health and resource usage.

If you are considering a production deployment of analytic workloads, you should avoid using the default scheduler, `kube-scheduler`. It wasn't designed for your needs in this case. Starting with a better scheduler lets you future-proof your Kubernetes experience. Let's examine some highlights of each scheduler.

Apache YuniKorn

The *YuniKorn project* was built by engineers from Cloudera out of the operational frustration of working with analytic workloads in Spark. In the spirit of using open source to solve problems as a community, YuniKorn was donated to the Apache Software Foundation and accepted as an incubating project in 2020. The name comes directly from the two systems it supports, YARN and Kubernetes. (Y unified K. YuniKorn. Get it?) It addresses the specific resource management and user control needs of analytic workloads from a Spark cluster administration point of view. YuniKorn also added support for TensorFlow and Flink jobs with the same level of resource control. No doubt, this support was born of the same operation frustrations found in Spark.

YuniKorn is installed (*https://yunikorn.apache.org/docs*) in Kubernetes using Helm. The goal of YuniKorn is to transform your Kubernetes cluster into a place that is friendly to the resource requirements of batch Jobs. A key part of that transformation is replacing the default `kube-scheduler`. To demonstrate how, let's use Figure 9-6 to walk through the components.

YuniKorn is meant to be a drop-in scheduler replacement with minimal changes to your existing Spark workflow, so we will start there. When new resource requests (1) are sent to the Kubernetes API server via `spark-submit` (2), the default `kube-scheduler` (3) is typically used to match Pods and nodes. When YuniKorn is deployed in your cluster, an `admissions-controller` Pod is created. The function of the `admissions-controller` is to listen for new resource requests (4) and make a small change, adding `schedulerName: yunikorn` to the resource request. If you need more fine-grained control, you can disable the `admissions-controller` and enable YuniKorn on a per Job basis by manually adding the following line to the SparkApplication YAML:

```
spec:
schedulerName: yunikorn
```

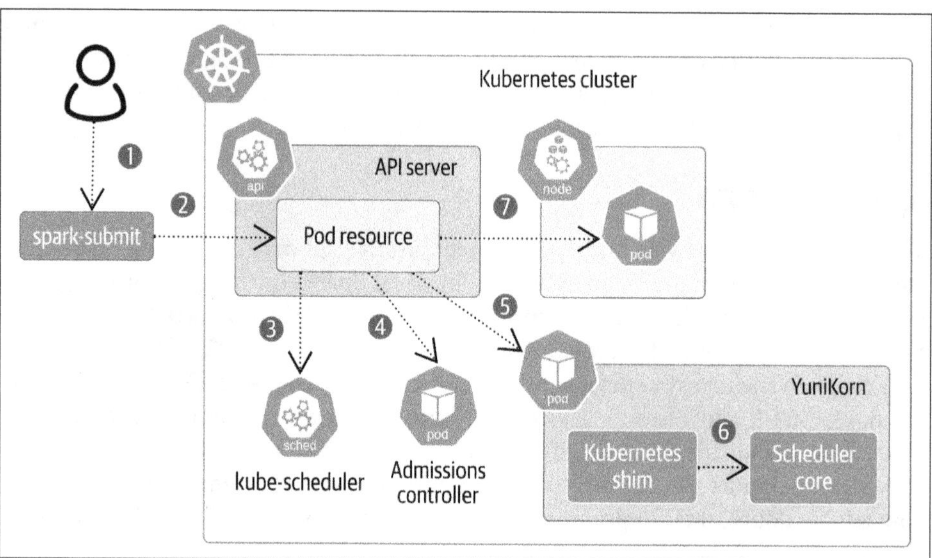

Figure 9-6. YuniKorn architecture

All scheduling needs will now be handled by the YuniKorn Scheduler (5). YuniKorn is built to run with multiple orchestration engines and provides an API translation layer called *Kubernetes shim* to manage communication between Kubernetes and the YuniKorn core (6). yunikorn-core extends the basic filter and score algorithm available in the default `kube-scheduler` by adding options appropriate for batch workloads such as Spark. These options range from simple resource-based queues to more advanced hierarchical queue management that allows for queues and resource pools to map to organizational structures. Hierarchical pooling can be helpful for those with a massive analytics footprint across many parts of a large enterprise and is critical for multitenant environments when running in a single Kubernetes cluster.

YuniKorn core is configured (*https://oreil.ly/2Tp19*) using the *queues.yaml* file, which contains all the details of how YuniKorn will schedule Pods to nodes, including the following:

Partitions
: One or more named configuration sections (*https://oreil.ly/kxtHf*) for different application requirements.

Queues
: Fine-grained control (*https://oreil.ly/M5W1A*) over resources in a hierarchical arrangement to provide resource guarantees in a multitenant environment.

Node sort policy
How Nodes are selected by available resources. Choices are FairnessPolicy (*https://oreil.ly/RUI7q*) and BinPackingPolicy (*https://oreil.ly/sED2J*).

Placement Rules
Description and filters (*https://oreil.ly/sHvMP*) for Pod placement based on user or group membership.

Limits
Definitions (*https://oreil.ly/ytYU9*) for fine-grained resource limits on partitions or queues.

New Jobs are processed by YuniKorn core by matching details and assigning the right queue. At this point, the scheduler can make a decision to assign Pods to nodes, which are then brought online (7).

YuniKorn also ships with an observability web-based tool called *scheduler UI* that provides insights into Job and queue status. It can be used to monitor scheduler health and provide better insights to troubleshoot any Job issues.

Volcano

Volcano was developed as a general-purpose scheduler for running high performance computing (HPC) workloads in Kubernetes. Volcano supports a variety of workloads, including Spark, Flink, PyTorch, TensorFlow, and specialized systems such as Kube-Gene for genome sequencing. Engineers built Volcano at Huawei, Tencent, and Baidu, to name a few of the long list of contributors. Donated to the CNCF, it was accepted as a Sandbox project in 2020.

Volcano is installed using Helm and creates CRDs for Jobs and queues, making the configuration a core part of your Kubernetes cluster as compared with YuniKorn, which is more of a bypass. This is a reflection of the general-purpose nature of Volcano. When installed, the Volcano scheduler is available for any process needing advanced scheduling and queuing. Let's use Figure 9-7 to walk through how it works.

To use Volcano with your batch Jobs, you will need to explicitly add the scheduler configuration to your Job YAML file (1). If you are using Volcano for Spark, it is recommended (*https://volcano.sh/en/docs/spark_on_volcano*) by the Volcano project to use the Spark Operator for Kubernetes and add one field to your SparkApplication YAML:

```
spec:
batchScheduler: "volcano"
```

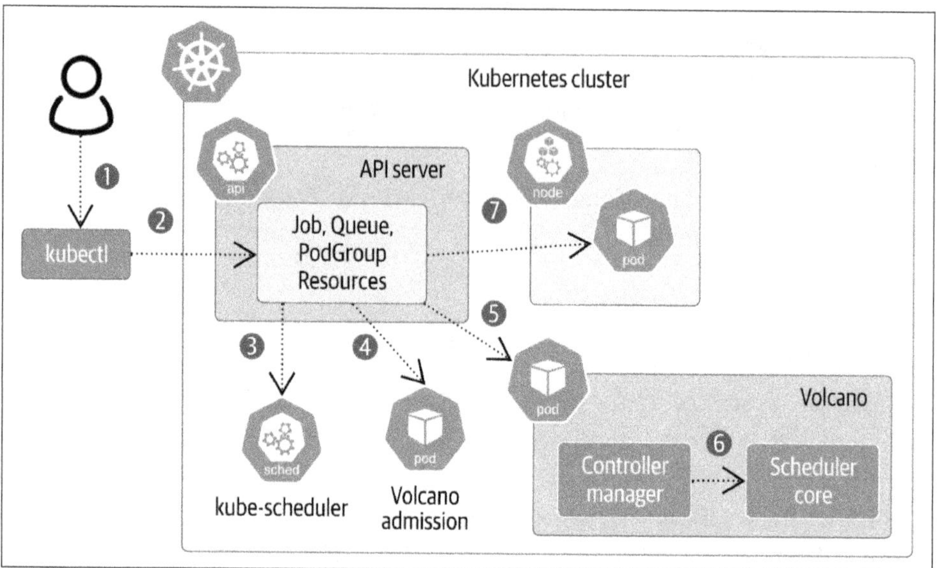

Figure 9-7. Volcano architecture

You can then use `kubectl apply` as you normally would to submit your Job (2). Without specifying the Volcano scheduler, Kubernetes will match Pods and nodes with the default `kube-scheduler` (3).

A Helm installation of Volcano will install the CRDs for Job, queue, and PodGroup and create a new Pod called Volcano Admission. Volcano Admission (4) attaches to the API server and validates Volcano-specific CRD entries and Jobs asking for the Volcano scheduler:

Job
: A Volcano-specific Job with extended configuration (*https://oreil.ly/CknE0*) for HPC.

Queue
: A collection of PodGroups to be managed as a first in, first out (FIFO) resource group. Configuration (*https://oreil.ly/MW2xq*) dictates the behavior of the queue for different situations.

PodGroup
: A collection of Pods related to their purpose. Examples would be groups for Spark and TensorFlow with different properties (*https://oreil.ly/LzeBj*) for each.

When selected as the scheduler for a Job (5), the Volcano scheduler will take the CRDs and start to work (6). Incoming Jobs marked to use Volcano as the scheduler are matched with a PodGroup and queue. Based on this assignment, a final node placement is made for each Pod (7).

The cluster-specific configuration for the Volcano scheduler core is stored in a ConfigMap named `volcano-scheduler-configmap`. This config file contains two main sections: `actions` and `plugins`. Actions (*https://oreil.ly/frTKk*) are an ordered list of each step in the node selection for each Job: enqueue, allocate, preempt, reclaim, and backfill. Each step is optional and can be reordered to match the type of work that needs to be performed.

Plug-ins are the algorithms used to match Pods with nodes. Each has a different use case and purpose and can be combined as an ensemble:

Gang
: This plug-in looks for higher-priority tasks in the queue and performs preemption and eviction if needed to free up resources for them.

BinPack
: This is a classic algorithm for finding the best fit for using every resource available by mixing different-size resource requests in the most efficient manner.

Conformance
: This ignores any task in the Namespace `kube-system` for eviction decisions.

Dominant Resource Fairness (DRF)
: This is an algorithm to address issues of fairness across multiple resource types to ensure that all Jobs have equal throughput.

Proportion
: This is a multitenant algorithm to allocate dedicated portions of cluster allocation for running Jobs.

Task-topology
: This algorithm uses affinity to put network-intensive Jobs physically closer together for more efficient network use.

NodeOrder
: This plug-in takes multiple user-defined dimensions to score every available node before selection.

Predicate
: This looks for certain predicates in nodes for selection (but currently supports only the GPU sharing predicate).

Priority
: This plug-in chooses task priority based on the user-supplied configuration in `priorityClassName`, `createTime`, and `id`.

Service level agreement (SLA)
: This uses the parameter `JobWaitingTime` to allow individual Jobs the control over priority based on when they are needed.

Time-division multiplexing (TDM)
: When nodes are used for both Kubernetes and YARN, TDM will schedule Pods that share resources in this arrangement.

NUMA-aware
: This provides scheduling for Pods with an awareness of CPU resource topology.

Outside of the Kubernetes installation, Volcano also ships with a command-line tool called `vcctl`. Managing Volcano can be done solely through the use of `kubectl`. However, `vcctl` presents an interface for operators more familiar with Job control systems.

As you can see from the list of features offered by YuniKorn and Volcano, having choices is a beautiful thing. Regardless of which project you choose, you'll have a better experience running analytic workloads in Kubernetes with one of these alternate schedulers.

Analytic Engines for Kubernetes

Spark is a powerful tool that solves many use cases in analytics. However, having just a single choice can be restrictive once that tool no longer works the way you do. Google developed MapReduce in 2004 to fill a need for data transformation, such as taking a pool of data and creating a count of the things in it, and this is still a relevant problem today given the volumes of data we create. Even before MapReduce, massively parallel processing (MPP) was a popular approach for data analysis. These "supercomputers" consisted of rows and rows of individual computers presented as a single processing grid for researchers in fields such as physics and meteorology to run massive calculations that would take far too long on a single computer.

A similar computing need arises when tackling the ML and AI tasks in analytics: many processes need to analyze a large volume of data. Libraries such as TensorFlow require analytic tools beyond data transformation. With Kubernetes, data scientists and engineers can now create virtual datacenters quickly with commodity compute, network, and storage to rival some of the supercomputers of the past. This combination of technologies brings a completely new and exciting future for developers: building ML-based and AI-based applications based on a self-service usage model without having to wait for time on a very expensive supercomputer (yes, this was a thing).

The Evolution of Analytics for Developers in a Cloud Native World

With Dean Wampler, Product Engineering Director for Accelerated Discovery, IBM Research

There has been speculation that streaming and batch analytics will somehow converge into a single, universal approach for every project or product. I believe with Kubernetes that vision becomes less ideal as developers determine what they need to be successful, and it's all about choosing the best tool for the job. In fact, more choices will likely become available for analyzing data that fit different use cases inside and outside of Kubernetes. Developers and data engineers will need a variety of tools to overcome limitations and trade-offs.

Let's suppose you have bought into the idea that you could do everything with streams. What does that actually mean in practice and where are the limitations? Suppose I wanted to know exactly how many of each SKU I sold in every store, segmented into hourly buckets. The challenge with that calculation is some uncertainty in knowing when all the data is delivered for each hour bucket. You can't start the Job exactly on the hour because data might still be in flight. In the worst case, some data may be significantly delayed because of network partitions or other outages. Now it's up to the developers to build in the sophistication for provisional results, which might be calculated as quickly as possible, and then integrate corrections when late data arrives. With more diversity in data tooling, they can better solve the problem. For this example, maybe they would use Apache Flink for dashboards with some percentage of accuracy about what's happening immediately. Data that is captured later would be used in an overnight Apache Spark Job to do the final accounting and produce the canonical results per hourly bucket. You could argue this is a much more reasonable level of sophistication based on using the simplest, correct tool for each Job, composable using Kubernetes.

At larger data scales, organizations still like using Spark for big analytics tasks. However, in a growing trend, data scientists and data engineers are starting to recognize it's reasonable to have data in a database, rather than a data lake, as a matter of choosing the right tool for the job. Some teams will use something like Cassandra because they don't want the complexity of keeping track of HDFS and Apache Parquet files, and they want the benefits of indexing and queries. They accept a performance hit from scanning tables versus a file. These are teams experienced in making trade-off decisions for convenience or reliability, and sometimes even for less performance. Kubernetes can encourage a more extensive choice of alternatives by reducing the up-front costs of trying new things. It's still early days for cloud native analytics, but the leaders in this space make it work by being more agile with underlying data infrastructure.

A new generation of analytic tools is expanding the choices that can be made. With all its dominance, Spark is still very dependent on the Java Virtual Machine (JVM), and that feature is becoming a trade-off consideration. Some data engineering shops don't want to deal with the JVM anymore: they just want to run Python, sometimes with C-based library kernels for high performance. This has created an opportunity for projects like Ray and Dask to cater directly to teams that want to use Python first. Developers gravitate to tools that help them go faster with fewer trade-offs. However, while the JVM might be a liability in some cases, Spark has enormous mindshare and years of continuous improvement. Keeping with the theme of choice, it's easy to see how Kubernetes can help create a place where Spark and Ray could be used in the same application. Cloud native analytics could eliminate the zero-sum game of all-in-one tools.

The analytics convergence that people have talked about will likely happen at the interface level, giving developers a single interface with access to the appropriate tooling underneath—the right mix of services for a cloud native world. Batch offline analytics with data warehouses augmented with online databases. Streaming analytics that provide real-time updates to the same data used for the batch Jobs. All are provided as services deployed in Kubernetes. The most important factor is the easy access it provides. Citizen data scientists can use Microsoft Excel to explore data. Visualization tools can connect to any underlying service with low or no code. Python is increasingly the language of choice for data engineers and scientists building pipelines. Support for SQL across streaming and batch analytics has remained universally popular, leveraging a data language that has been the standard for decades. Kubernetes will have to support this by enabling the fine-grained concurrency within a single process that some data processing systems require while leveraging Pod boundaries for big chunks of resources. It's a balance of trade-offs. The winner will be the developers and data scientists who no longer have to worry about making bad tool choices, allowing them to spend more time writing code that creates value.

Access via the right APIs and ability via the right infrastructure built on Kubernetes is a powerful combination that the data science and Python community has been working to make a reality. Two new projects are already making a mark: Dask and Ray. As pointed out by Dean, Python is the preferred language for data science. Both Ray and Dask provide a native Python interface for massively parallel processing both inside and outside of Kubernetes.

Dask

Dask (*https://www.dask.org*) is a Python-based clustering tool for large-scale processing that abstracts away the complicated setup steps. It can be used for anything that you can express in a Python program but has found a real home in data science with the countless libraries available. scikit-learn, NumPy, TensorFlow, and Pandas are all mature data science libraries that can be used on a laptop and then scaled to a massive cluster of computers thanks to Dask.

Dask integrates nicely with Kubernetes to provide the easy user experience that operators and developers have come to expect with Python. The Dask storage primitives Array, DataFrame, and Bag map to many cloud native storage choices. For example, you could map a DataFrame to a file stored in a PersistentVolume or an object bucket such as S3. Your storage scale is limited only by the underlying resources and your budget. As the Python code is working with your data, Dask manages the chunking across multiple workers seamlessly.

Deployment options include the manual Helm install we are now familiar with from Chapter 4, as you can see in this example:

```
helm repo add dask https://helm.dask.org/
helm repo update
helm install my-dask dask/dask
```

Or as an alternative, you can install a Dask cluster in Kubernetes with a Jupyter Notebook instance for working inside the cluster:

```
helm install my-dask dask/daskhub
```

Once your Dask cluster is running inside Kubernetes, you can connect as a client and run your Python code across the compute nodes using the `HelmCluster` object. Connect using the name you gave your cluster given at the time of installation:

```
from dask_kubernetes import HelmCluster
from dask.distributed import Client

# Connect to the name of the helm installation
cluster = HelmCluster(release_name="my-dask")

# specify the number of workers(pods) explicitly
cluster.scale(10)

# or dynamically scale based on current workload
cluster.adapt(minimum=1, maximum=100)

# Your Python code here
```

If that wasn't easy enough, you can completely skip the Helm installation and just let Dask do that part for you. The `KubeCluster` object takes an argument specifying the Pod configuration either using a `make_pod_spec` method or specifying a YAML configuration file. It will connect to the default Kubernetes cluster accessible via `kubectl` and invoke the cluster creation inside your Kubernetes cluster as a part of the running Python program:

```
from dask.distributed import Client
from dask_kubernetes import KubeCluster, make_pod_spec

pod_spec = make_pod_spec(image='daskdev/dask:latest',
                         memory_limit='4G', memory_request='4G',
                         cpu_limit=1, cpu_request=1)
```

```
cluster = KubeCluster(pod_spec)

# specify the number of workers(pods) explicitly
cluster.scale(10)

# or dynamically scale based on current workload
cluster.adapt(minimum=1, maximum=100)

# Connect Dask to the cluster
client = Client(cluster)

# Your Python code here
```

Developer access to Kubernetes clusters for parallel computing couldn't get much easier, and this is the appeal new tools like Dask can provide.

Ray

In a significant difference from the arbitrary Python code in Dask, *Ray* takes a different approach to Python clustering by operating as a parallel task manager that includes a distributed computing framework with a large ecosystem of integrations (*https://oreil.ly/XY5rC*). For the end user, Ray provides low-level C++ libraries to run distributed code purpose-built for compute-intensive workloads typical in data science. The base is Ray Core, which does all the work of distributing workloads using the concept of a task. When developers write Python code using Ray, each task is expressed as a remote function, as shown in this example from the Ray documentation (*https://oreil.ly/gCmBs*):

```
# By adding the `@ray.remote` decorator, a regular Python function
# becomes a Ray remote function.
@ray.remote
def my_function():
    return 1
```

In this basic example, you can see the difference in the approach Ray takes for distributing work. Developers have to be explicit in what work is distributed with Ray Core handling the compute management with the Cluster Manager.

A Ray deployment in Kubernetes is designed to leverage compute and network resource management within dynamic workloads. The Ray Operator includes a custom controller and CRD to deploy everything needed to attach code to a Ray cluster. A Helm chart is provided for easy installation. However, since the chart is unavailable in a public repository, you must first download the entire Ray distribution to your local filesystem. An extensive configuration YAML file can be modified, but to get a simple Ray cluster working, the defaults are fine, as you can see in this example from the documentation (*https://oreil.ly/XjXJo*):

```
cd ray/deploy/charts
helm -n ray install example-cluster --create-namespace ./ray
```

This results in the creation of two types of Pods being installed. The head node handles the communication and orchestration of running tasks in the cluster, and the Worker Node handles where tasks execute their code. With a Ray cluster running inside a Kubernetes cluster, there are two ways to run a Ray Job: interactively with the Ray client or as a Job submitted via `kubectl`.

The Ray client is embedded into a Python program file and initializes the connection to the Ray cluster. This requires the head service IP to be exposed through either Ingress or local port forwarding. Along with the remote function code, an initializer will establish the connection to the externalized Ray cluster host IP and port:

```
import ray

ray.init("ray://<host>:<port>")

@ray.remote
def my_function():
    return 1
```

Another option is to run your code inside the Kubernetes cluster and attach it to an internal service and port. You use `kubectl` to submit the Job to run and pass a Job description YAML file that outlines the Python program to use and Pod resource information. Here is an example Job file from the Ray documentation (*https://oreil.ly/gCmBs*):

```
apiVersion: batch/v1
kind: Job
metadata:
  name: ray-test-job
spec:
  template:
    spec:
      restartPolicy: Never
      containers:
        - name: ray
          image: rayproject/ray:latest
          imagePullPolicy: Always
          command: [ "/bin/bash", "-c", "--" ]
          args:
            - "wget <URL>/job_example.py &&
              python job_example.py"
          resources:
            requests:
              cpu: 100m
              memory: 512Mi
```

This file can then be submitted to the cluster using `kubectl`:

```
kubectl -n ray create -f job-example.yaml
```

Inside the Python file submitted, we can use the DNS name of the Ray service head and let Kubernetes ensure that the network path is routed:

```
ray.init("ray://example-cluster-ray-head:10001")
```

For both external and internal modes of running Ray programs, the head node utilizes the Kubernetes scheduler to manage the Worker Node Pod lifecycle to complete the submitted Job. Ray provides a simple programming API for developers to utilize large-scale cluster computing without learning Kubernetes administration. SREs can create and manage Kubernetes clusters that can be easily used by data scientists using their preferred Python programming language.

Summary

This wraps up the tour of data components in your cloud native application stack. Adding analytics completes the total data picture by enabling you to find insights in larger volumes of data that can complement other parts of your application.

Analytics is at the frontier of cloud native data innovation, and for this reason big data isn't something you should assume fits into Kubernetes in the same way as other data infrastructure. Two primary differences are the volumes of data involved and the bursty nature of the workloads. Further improvements are needed to make Apache Spark run more effectively on Kubernetes, especially in the areas of Job management and storage APIs However, the knowledge is available to help you deploy with confidence today. Projects such as Apache YuniKorn and Volcano are already leading the way in open source to give Kubernetes a better foundation for analytic workloads. Emerging analytic engines such as Dask and Ray may be a better choice for your use case, and they can be used in combination with other tools.

While analytic workloads may not have been in your original plans for deployment in Kubernetes, they can't be skipped if your goal is to build the complete picture of a virtual datacenter, purpose-designed to run your application.

CHAPTER 10

Machine Learning and Other Emerging Use Cases

In previous chapters, we covered traditional data infrastructure including databases, streaming platforms, and analytic engines with a focus on Kubernetes. Now it's time to start looking beyond, exploring the projects and communities that are beginning to make cloud native their destination, especially concerning AI and ML.

Any time multiple arrows start pointing in the same direction, it's worth paying attention. The directional arrows in data infrastructure all point to an overall macro trend of convergence on Kubernetes, supported by several interrelated trends:

- Common stacks are emerging for managing compute-intensive AI/ML workloads, including those that leverage specific hardware such as GPUs.
- Common data formats are helping to promote the efficient movement of data across compute, network, and storage resources.
- Object storage is becoming a common persistence layer for data infrastructure.

In this chapter, we will look at several emerging technologies that embody these trends, the use cases they enable, and how they contribute to helping you further manage the precious resources of compute, network, and storage. We have chosen a few projects that touch on different aspects of ML and using data—this is by no means an exhaustive survey of every technology in use today. We hear directly from the engineers working on each project and provide some details on how they fit into a cloud native data stack. You are highly encouraged to continue your journey into your interests beyond what is presented here. Follow your curiosity and contribute to the communities supporting new use cases in Kubernetes.

The Cloud Native AI/ML Stack

As discussed in Chapter 9, analytics, AI, and ML on Kubernetes is a topic worthy of more detailed examination. If you aren't familiar with this specialty in the world of data, it's an exciting domain that enhances our ability to produce real-time, data-driven decisions at scale. While many of the core algorithms have existed for decades, the nature of this work has been changing rapidly over the past few years. Data science as a profession has traditionally been relegated to the back office, where volumes of historical data were gleaned for insight to find meaning and predict the future. Data scientists rarely had any direct involvement with end-user applications, and their work was disconnected from user-facing applications.

This began to change with the emergence of the data engineer role. Data engineers build the processing engines and pipelines to productionalize data science and break down silos between disciplines. As is typical for emerging fields in data infrastructure, the largest, most vocal organizations set the tempo for data engineering, and their tools and methods have become the mainstream.

The real-time nature of data in applications can't be left just to databases and streaming platforms. Products built by data scientists must be closer to the end user to maximize their effectiveness in applications. Many organizations have recognized this as both a problem and an opportunity: how can we make data science another near-real-time component of application deployments? True to form, when faced with a challenge, the community has risen to the occasion to build new projects and create new disciplines. As a result, a new category of data infrastructure on Kubernetes is emerging alongside the traditional categories of persistence, streaming, and analytics. This new stack consists of tools that support the real-time serving of data specific to AI and ML.

AI/ML Definitions

If you are new to the field of AI/ML, it's easy to become overwhelmed by the terminology. Before we look at a few cloud native technologies that solve problems in the AI stack, let's spend some time understanding the new terms and concepts that are critical to understanding this specialty. If you are familiar with AI/ML, you can safely skip to the next section.

First, let's briefly review some common terms used in AI/ML. These frequently appear in descriptions of projects and features, and you'll need to understand them to select the right tools and apply them effectively:

Algorithm
: The basic computational building block of ML is the algorithm. Algorithms are expressed in code as a set of instructions to analyze data. Common algorithms include linear regression, decision trees, k-means, and random forest. Data

scientists spend their time working with algorithms to gain insights from data. When the procedures and parameters are right, the final, repeatable form is output into models.

Model
: ML aims to build systems that mimic the way humans learn so that they can answer questions based on provided data without explicit programming. Example questions include identifying whether two objects are similar, the likelihood of occurrence of a particular event, or choosing the best option given multiple candidates. The answering system for these questions is described in a mathematical model (or simply *model* for short). A model acts as a function machine: data that describes a question goes in, and new data that represents an answer comes out.

Feature
: Features are the portions of a more extensive data set relevant to a specific use case. Features are used both to train models and to provide input to models in production. For example, if you wanted to predict the weather, you might select time, location, and temperature from a much larger data set, ignoring other data such as air quality. *Feature selection* is the process of determining what data you'll use, which can be an iterative process. When you hear the word *feature*, you can easily translate that to *data*.

Training
: A model consists of an algorithm plus data (features) that apply that algorithm to a particular domain. To train a model, training data is passed through the algorithm to help refine the output to match the expected answer based on the data presented. This training data contains the same features that will be used in production, with the key difference that the expected answer is known. For example, given historical temperatures, do the parameters used in the model predict what actually happened? Training is the most resource-intensive phase of ML.

Flow
: Flow is a shorthand term for *workflow*. An ML workflow describes the steps required to build a working model. The flow generally includes data collection, preprocessing and cleaning, feature engineering, model training, validation, and performance testing. These are typically fully automated processes.

Vector
: The classic mathematical definition of a vector is a quantity that indicates direction and magnitude. ML models are mathematical formulas that use numerical data. Since not all source data is represented as numbers, normalizing input data into vector representations is the key to using general-purpose algorithms

in ML. Images and text are examples of data that can be vector encoded in the preprocessing step of the flow.

Prediction
: Prediction is the step of using the created model to produce a likely answer based on input data. For example, we might ask the expected temperature for a given location, date, and time by using a weather model. The question being answered takes the form "What will happen?"

Inference
: Inference models look for reasons by reversing the relationship of input and output data. Given an answer, what features contributed to arriving at this answer? Here's another weather example: based on rainfall, what are the most associated temperatures and barometric pressures? The question being answered is "How did this happen?"

Drift
: Models are trained with snapshots of data from a point in time. Drift is a condition that occurs as the model loses accuracy due to conditions that have changed over time or are no longer relevant based on the original training data. When drift happens in a model, the solution is to refine the model with updated training data.

Bias
: Models are only as good as the algorithms used and how those algorithms are trained. Bias can be introduced at several points: in the algorithm itself, sample data that contains user prejudice or faulty measurement, or exclusion of data. In any case, the goal of ML is to be as accurate as possible, and bias is an accuracy measurement. Detecting bias in data is a complex problem and is easier to address early through good data governance and process rigor.

These are some of the key concepts that will help you understand the rest of this section. For a more complete introduction, consider *Introduction to Machine Learning with Python* (O'Reilly) by Andreas C. Müller and Sarah Guido, or one of the many quality online courses available from your favorite learning platform.

Defining an AI/ML Stack

Given these definitions, we can describe the elements of a cloud native AI stack and the purposes such a stack can serve. Emerging disciplines and communities have similar implementations with minor variations as various teams innovate to solve their own specific needs. We can identify some common patterns by looking at organizations that use AI/ML in production at scale and the trends around Kubernetes adoption. Figure 10-1 shows some of the typical elements found in architectures currently in production. Without being prescriptive, we'll use this as an example of the types of tools in the stack and how they might fit together to serve the real-time components of AI/ML.

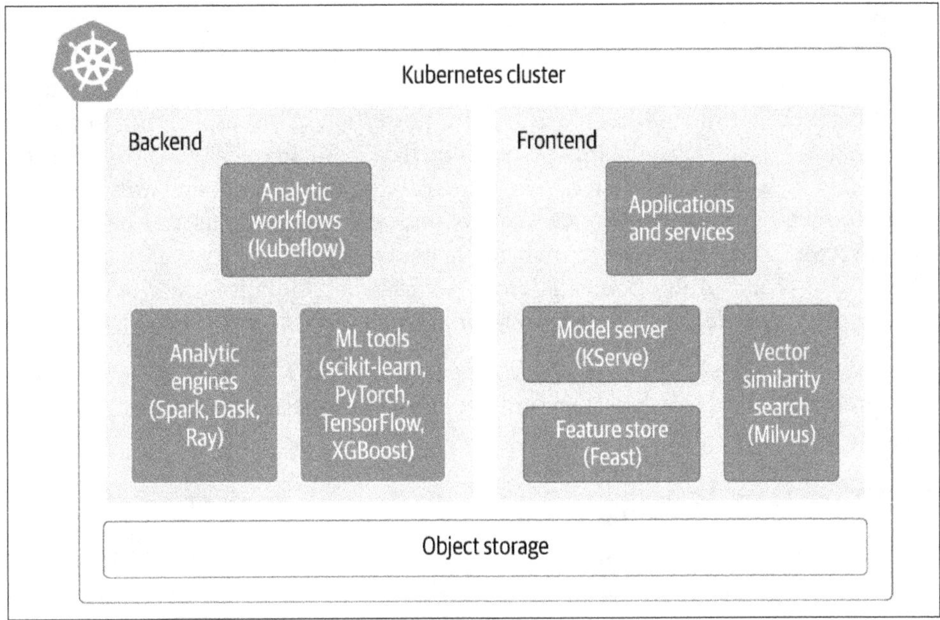

Figure 10-1. Common elements of a cloud native AI/ML stack

The goal of a cloud native AI/ML stack should be to get the insights produced by AI/ML as close to your users as possible, which means shortening the distance between backend analytic processes and using their output in frontend production systems. Data exploration happens using algorithms provided in libraries such as scikit-learn (*https://scikit-learn.org*), PyTorch (*https://pytorch.org*), TensorFlow (*https://www.tensorflow.org*), and XGBoost (*https://xgboost.readthedocs.io*) using data stored in databases or static files. Python is the most commonly used language with ML libraries. The systems we discussed in Chapter 9, including Apache Spark, Dask, and Ray, are used to scale up the processing required to use Python libraries to build models. Kubeflow (*https://www.kubeflow.org*) and similar tools allow data engineers to create ML workflows for model generation. The workflows output a model file to object storage, providing the bridge between the backend processes and frontend production use.

Models are meant to be used, and this is the role of real-time model serving tools such as KServe (*https://github.com/kserve/kserve*), Seldon (*https://www.seldon.io*), and BentoML (*https://www.bentoml.com*). These tools perform predictions on behalf of applications using existing models from object storage and feature stores such as Feast (*https://feast.dev*). Feature stores perform full lifecycle management of feature data, storing new feature data in an online database such as Cassandra, training, and serving features to models.

Vector similarity search engines are a new but familiar addition to the real-time serving stack for applications. While traditional search engines such as Apache Solr (*https://solr.apache.org*) provide convenient APIs for text searching, including fuzzy matching, vector similarity search is a more powerful algorithm, helping to answer the question "What is like the thing I currently have?" To do this, it uses relationships in the data instead of just the terms in your search query. Vector similarity supports many formats, including text, video, audio, and anything else that can be analyzed into a vector. Many open source tools implement vector similarity search, including Milvus (*https://milvus.io*), Weaviate (*https://weaviate.io*), Qdrant (*https://qdrant.tech*), Vald (*https://vald.vdaas.org*), and Vearch (*https://github.com/vearch/vearch*).

Let's examine a few of the tools that support frontend ML usage by applications in more detail and learn how they are deployed in Kubernetes: KServe, Feast, and Milvus.

Real-Time Model Serving with KServe

The "last mile" problem of real-time access to analytic products in AI/ML is one that Kubernetes is well poised to solve. Consider the architecture of modern web applications: HTTP servers that seem to simply serve a web page often have much more complexity behind them. The reality is that application logic and data infrastructure are combined to hide the complexity. Much like the HTTP server that listens for requests and serves a web page, a model server hides the complexity of loading and executing models. It focuses on the developer experience after the data science is done.

KServe is a Kubernetes native model server that makes it easy to provide prediction capabilities to applications in production environments. Let's learn more about the origins and functionality of KServe from one of the project founders.

Operationalizing ML Models with KServe

With Theofilos Papapanagiotou, Data Science Architect at Prosus

Google is well known for its contributions to the ML community with projects such as TensorFlow. Based on the framework it used to run TensorFlow internally, Google also created Kubeflow, an open source project to help data scientists and engineers use TensorFlow in production. Kubeflow contains multiple subprojects for different aspects of deploying ML workflows. One subproject that addressed the externalization (making available for use by other systems) of models was called Kubeflow serving (KFServing). Initially, it was built only for TensorFlow, but new contributors joined in and added support for other models such as PyTorch, scikit-learn, and

XGBoost. In 2021, KFServing became an independent project from KubeFlow and was renamed KServe.

The core function of KServe is to provide an API endpoint for deploying previously built ML models in Kubernetes. Deploying each model involves multiple steps. KServe handles the fetching of the model from an object store, loading it into memory, and determining whether the model needs to use CPU or GPU. When GPU is required, KServe manages the copying of the model from CPU memory to GPU memory. This behavior can be specified with just a few lines of YAML, which eliminates a lot of the toil when working with ML in production environments. For SREs, there is additional integration with Knative Eventing (*https://oreil.ly/IGDcM*) to manage the scale-out, and observability features like metrics and logging. These are expected behaviors of an HTTP API and important aspects of putting ML models in production.

KServe has many contributors, and all are driven by a similar mission: operationalizing ML to be used by as many people as possible. Data is significant intellectual property to your organization, and data scientists are tasked to build models that make efficient use of that data. The real treasure for an organization is the ability to take those models and apply them to data to make predictions that can be used in your products, which in turn creates added value for your customers. KServe emphasizes using data in real time over pushing it to a data lake where it might be forgotten. For this reason, KServe does not provide a general-purpose data store; it's simply a hosting system for models. It functions as a microservice in your cloud native application, accepting inference requests containing a list of features. The data returned is a prediction based on the input, and it has to happen quickly, efficiently, and securely.

Bloomberg is one of the top contributors to KServe, and its use case is an excellent example of how KServe adds value. Bloomberg News is a real-time news feed that has a diminishing time value for its users, so articles it provides must be timely and relevant. Bloomberg uses a massive collection of natural language processing (NLP) models to score incoming news articles from a variety of sources. Each article is labeled, classified, and provided to users through a service it calls the Terminal. This processing isn't a back-office problem that can be done later, and the inferencing must be updated dynamically. Fortunately, KServe allows the models to be updated on the fly. This sort of problem is common in many mobile applications and SaaS products, and the ease of integration is key.

Beyond just serving models, KServe also helps manage the lifecycle of ML models. One feature, called an *explainer*, provides further information about each prediction. For example, it can offer insight into why a decision was made to approve or reject a loan application. KServe does this by providing feature importance and highlighting features in the model that led to the loan decision outcome, such as income level or credit history. Knowing more than just a binary yes or no decision helps build trust in the application. For ML operations (MLOps) you can use feature importance to detect model drift by integrating KServe with other services to compare results with training data to see if the production model is diverging. You can even include bias detection with AI Fairness (*https://lfaidata.foundation/projects/ai-fairness-360*), which is now a Linux Foundation incubating project. These features help KServe reduce the effort involved in MLOps.

ML affects all our lives, from food delivery to entertainment. Serving models dynamically in a Kubernetes environment is a crucial step toward integrating ML and AI in more and more applications, and KServe will play a large role in making that happen.

Figure 10-2 shows how KServe is deployed on Kubernetes. The control plane consists of the KServe controller, which manages custom resources known as InferenceServices. Each InferenceService instance contains two microservices, a `Transformer` Service and a `Predictor` Service, each consisting of a Deployment and a Service. The Knative framework is used for request processing, treating these as serverless microservices that can scale to zero when they are not being used for maximum efficiency.

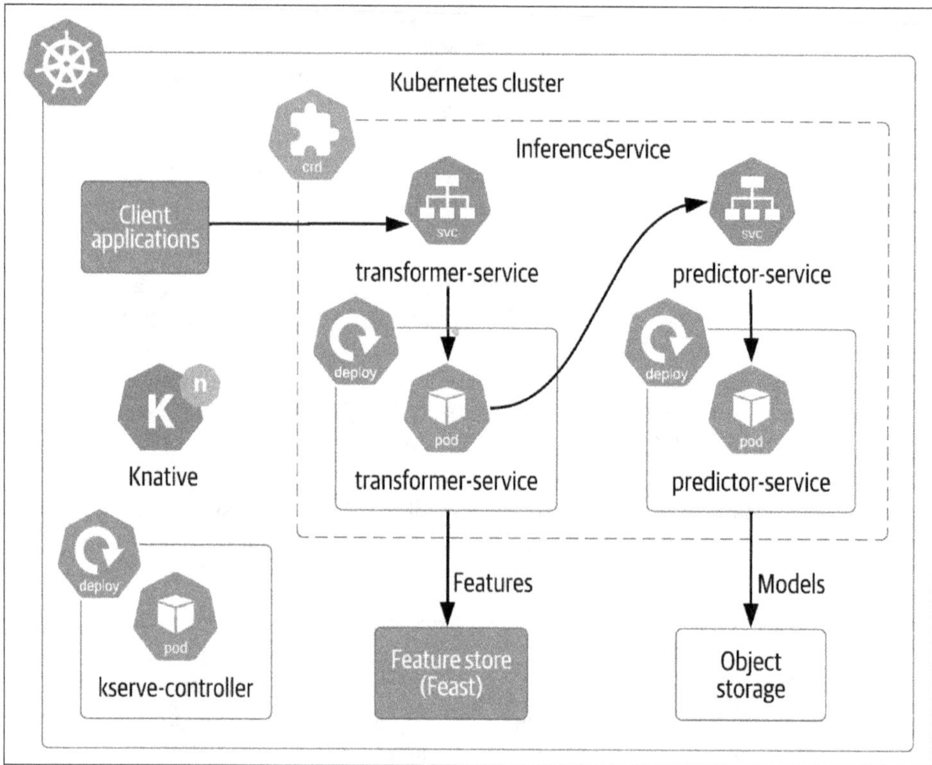

Figure 10-2. Deploying KServe in Kubernetes

The `Transformer` Service provides the endpoint for prediction requests from client applications. It also implements a three-stage process of preprocessing, prediction, and post-processing:

Preprocessing
: The `Transformer` Service converts the incoming data into a usable form for the model. For example, you may have a model that predicts whether a hot dog is in a picture. The `Transformer` Service will convert an incoming picture to a vector before passing it to the inference service. During preprocessing, the `Transformer` Service also loads feature data from a feature store such as Feast.

Prediction
: The `Transformer` Service delegates the work of prediction to the `Predictor` Service, which is responsible for loading the model from object storage and executing it using the provided feature data.

Post-processing
: The `Transformer` Service receives the prediction result and performs any needed post-processing to prepare the response to the client application.

If you are familiar with traditional web serving, you can see the helpful analog that model serving creates. Instead of serving HTML pages, KServe covers the modern application needs for serving AI/ML workloads. As a Kuberentes native project, it fits seamlessly into your cloud native datacenter and application stack.

Full Lifecycle Feature Management with Feast

Lifecycle management is a common theme in any data architecture, encompassing how data is added, updated, and deleted over time. Feature stores serve a helpful coordination role by managing the lifecycle of features used by ML models from discovery to their use in production systems, eliminating the versioning and coordination issues that can arise when different teams are involved. How did Feast come to exist?

Bridging ML Models and Data with Feast

With Willem Pienaar, Principal Engineer, Tecton

The Feast project was born from the experiences of the ML platform team at GoJek. After building out the core ML tooling, we realized our data scientists were struggling to get models into production. We needed a different kind of tooling to enable the data scientists to help themselves.

The same operational rigor we applied to the deployment of traditional data infrastructure was also needed for ML infrastructure. These realizations led to the creation of what we now know as the Feast project. After observing emerging tools from other teams, especially what the Uber team had been doing with Michaelangelo, the idea of a feature store became a first-class priority for us.

To help understand what a feature store does, consider the problem space. GoJek had hundreds of millions of users using a variety of services including ride-hailing, food delivery, and digital payments. Each service had an element of ML, requiring many steps to go from the back-office data science team to production. We used tools like Flink to help with the large-scale SQL batch transformation and stream processing required for model creation, and systems like Redis and Cassandra to serve data, but there were remaining problems to operationalize our ML models. We needed a framework on top of those data systems unifying offline and online access, and so the concept of the feature store emerged.

Feature stores serve as a layer to give models a consistent way to access data, effectively providing a bridge between ML models and data within your organization. In production ML models there are two stages: the training and the online phases. Whether the data is coming from a stream, request data, or a data warehouse, your model can't have different copies of data in different environments in each stage. During the training phase, a feature store manages scale requirements for data processing when computing data for model export, similar to other big data tools like Spark. In the online phase, the feature store provides low-latency, real-time access to models and, in some cases, derives features in real time, also known as *on-demand features*. Feast ensures the consistency of data for both phases, and it meets both online and offline requirements. Traditional database systems can provide only a subset of those features. For example, Cassandra supports many of the online features, but not offline scalability or specialized features like point-in-time correctness.

Feast began as a place to store computed features, but as we got further into the problem, we also needed to serve those features in production against our models in a consistent way, as an integrated part of our Job flow. As the Feast project grew, Google became a key collaborator, and within a few months, we had the first working parts of the project. The Kubeflow team at Google suggested we open source the project to make it available to a larger community. With the support of our management, we released a minimum viable product very quickly. So fast, in fact, we released Feast without a lot of things needed to help new users get started, like documentation!

Despite the minimal state, it became clear that Feast met a huge need as a community quickly formed around the project. Teams having similar issues with ML flows were coming to the same realization that they needed an assistant or data platform for operationalizing ML.

In the early days of the project, deploying Feast in Kubernetes included a big stack of components. Today, Feast has evolved to be more lightweight; many of the extra components have been stripped away, making it more efficient and easier to manage. The best approach to building ML platforms on Kubernetes is to make your processing components as stateless as possible and store state externally. The registry doesn't even have to be in Kubernetes since it can just be a file in an object store. Feast is frequently deployed alongside Redis or Cassandra inside Kubernetes and connected externally to data warehouses like BigQuery and Redshift. Providing external access to Feast is an important aspect. This is typically done using an Ingress to access the API server directly. In other cases, KServe is used as an intermediate serving layer to provide a scalable solution when a popular ML model is used by external services.

The future for Feast is to be more cloud native and fully integrated with Kubernetes. Quite a few challenges remain to be solved in deploying ML in Kubernetes, with the biggest being operational maturity. It still takes quite a bit of work for engineers to install many of the components, and the day two maintenance is more demanding than it should be. More community involvement will help grow the maturity of ML as an emerging part of the Kubernetes data stack.

As Willem noted, the deployment of Feast on Kubernetes is at a basic state of maturity. As no operator or custom resources are defined, you install Feast using a Helm chart. Figure 10-3 shows a sample installation using the example documented on the Feast website (*https://oreil.ly/GYNjR*), which consists of the feature server and other supporting services.

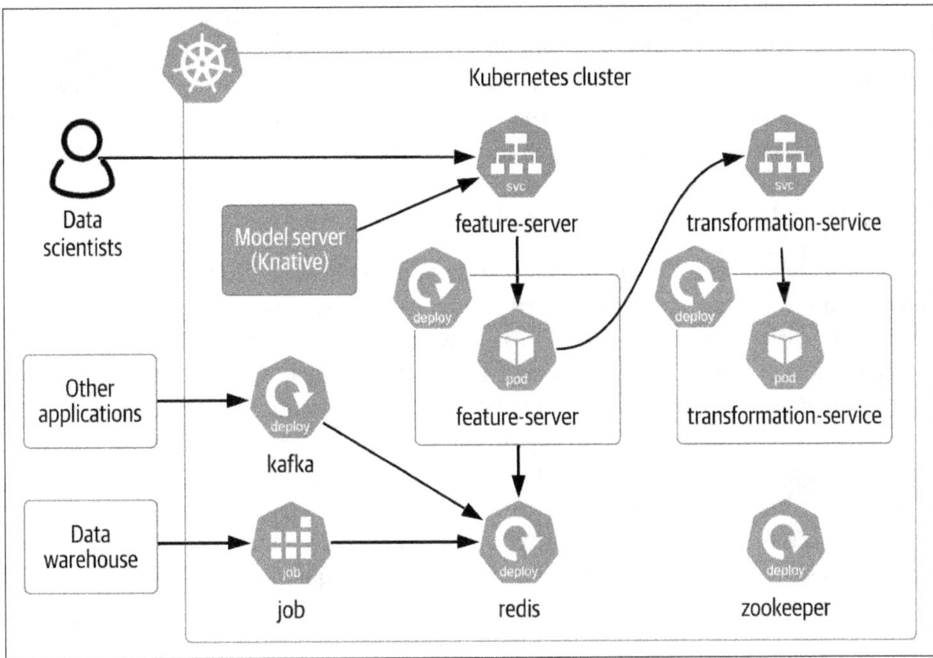

Figure 10-3. Deploying Feast in Kubernetes

Let's examine these components and how they interact. Data scientists identify features from existing data sources in a process called *feature engineering* and create features using an interface exposed by the feature server (as defined in "Bridging ML

Models and Data with Feast" on page 255). The user can either provide feature data at the time of creating the feature or can connect to various backend services so that the data can be updated continuously. Feast can consume data published to Kafka topics, or through Kubernetes Jobs that pull data from an external source such as a data warehouse. The feature data is stored in an online database such as Redis or Cassandra so that it can be easily served to production applications. ZooKeeper is used to coordinate metadata and service discovery. The Helm chart also supports the ability to deploy Grafana for visualization of metrics. This may sound familiar to you, because the reuse of common building blocks like Redis, ZooKeeper, and Grafana is a pattern we've seen used in several other examples in this book.

When model serving tools like KServe are asked to make predictions, they use the features stored in Feast as a record of truth. Any updated training by data scientists is done using the same feature store, eliminating the need for multiple sources of data. The `Transformation` Service provides an optional capability to generate new features on demand by performing transformations on existing feature data.

KServe and Feast are often used together to create a complete real-time model serving stack. Feast performs the dynamic part of feature management, working with online and offline data storage as new features arrive through streaming and data warehouses. KServe handles the dynamic provisioning for the model serving by using the serverless capabilities of Knative. This means that when not in use, KServe can scale to zero and react when new requests arrive, saving valuable resources in your Kubernetes-based AI/ML stack by using only what you need.

Vector Similarity Search with Milvus

Now that we've looked at tools that enable you to use ML models and features in production systems, let's switch gears and look at a different type of AI/ML tool: vector similarity search (VSS). As discussed in "AI/ML Definitions" on page 248, a vector is a number object representing direction and magnitude from an origin in vector space. VSS is an application of vector mathematics in ML. The k-nearest neighbors (KNN) algorithm is a way to find how "close" two things are next to each other. This algorithm has many variations, but all rely on expressing data as a vector. The data to be searched is vectorized using a CPU-intensive KNN-type algorithm; typically, this is more of a backend process. VSS servers can then index the vector data for less CPU-intensive searching and provide a query mechanism that allows end users to provide a vector and find things that are close to it.

Milvus is one of many servers designed around the emerging field of VSS. Let's learn how Milvus came to exist and why it's a great fit for Kubernetes.

A New Era of Search for Kubernetes Applications

With Xiaofan Luan, Director of Engineering, Zilliz, and Milvus Maintainer

There is a growing community around the newly emerging field of VSS, most notably in the use of libraries such as Facebook AI Similarity Search (FAISS) and Hierarchical Navigable Small World (HNSW). These libraries are used to take the output of computationally expensive ML algorithms and create end-user applications. Algorithms like convolutional neural networks (CNN) can take data including images and generate vectors that are simply a list of numbers. The real value of the analysis comes from what you do with that list of numbers.

Structured data searching has been a standard feature of traditional relational database management systems (RDBMSs) in which all the values in columns are indexed for fast lookup. Projects like Apache Lucene built on this, making text search a new kind of competency for unstructured data. Users can provide all or part of the text they are searching for and get back multiple results with varying confidence values. Lucene is the engine for higher-level systems such as Apache Solr and Elasticsearch. Combined, they create a data server that is used in almost every kind of application now.

Milvus was designed to fulfill a similar purpose as Solr and Elasticsearch. However, instead of working with only text, Milvus exposes a general-purpose VSS capability. It provides a top-level operational server for users who want more than just a library and need a system that can handle important details like durability, failure, and recovery. Milvus is a system that can be deployed and managed in Kubernetes to manage storage and helper features like computation disaggregation. Most importantly, it provides the Milvus API interface for application developers to use VSS in their code to do things that aren't possible with previous databases.

To give an example of how this works, imagine a library containing photos of meals. Using an image analysis tool such as you only look once (YOLO), the objects in the images are separated into main dishes such as a sandwich and various side dishes like french fries. The next step is to process each object by using ResNet to extract its dimensions. The output of ResNet is a 256-dimensional vector for each item, which is then loaded into Milvus and assigned a unique ID. Milvus indexes the different objects so they can be accessed via its search interface. User-facing applications can provide a picture of a hamburger and fries and ask for similar meals based on the indexed images and the similarities.

Let's compare this example to the experience of using a text search engine like Elasticsearch. To start, you would need a text description of each meal, which you would index using Lucene, and then you would be able to search for the words "french fries." Similarly to the way Elasticsearch makes searching text easier, Milvus enables the searching of vectorized video, audio, and even natural language text.

Milvus 1.0 was deployed as a single node for storing, indexing, and serving data. This worked for anyone needing a simple package, but it wasn't cloud native or Kubernetes friendly. For the 2.0 release, we decided that Milvus needed to change into a distributed architecture and become more cloud native, separating the compute elements from storage. Our goal was to make Milvus scale horizontally by independent function with an additional benefit of disaster recovery. Four layers are deployed in a Milvus cluster: the access layer, coordinator service, Worker Node, and storage nodes. Breaking Milvus into something similar to microservices reduces the reliance on state to only the storage nodes. The access layer, coordinator service, and Worker Nodes are stateless, making the system much easier to scale up and down and eliminating single points of failure. One of the essential features for the Milvus operator in the 2.0 release was the change to object storage and away from StatefulSets. With these updates, Kubernetes is now the preferred way to deploy Milvus.

Milvus is now a graduated project under the governance of the LF AI & Data Foundation (*https://oreil.ly/BqwqQ*). The projects in this foundation are all looking toward a cloud native future for data and the emergence of AI and ML as a core part of every application. The focus for Milvus post 2.0 is performance. Applications based on AI/ML require fast responses, and search is a speed-dependent operation. Code improvements are a more traditional way of gaining performance, but in the AI/ML world, hardware plays a big part as well. Taking advantage of GPUs or custom field-programmable gate array (FPGA) applications will again help developers take advantage of AI/ML performance advances using a simple API. Overall, we want to provide an easy path for people building cloud native applications to go from the leading edge to mainstream with a great experience.

As Xiaofan mentions, Milvus supports both standalone and clustered deployments, using the four layers described. Both models are supported in Kubernetes via Helm, with the clustered deployment shown in Figure 10-4.

The access layer contains the proxy Service, which uses a Kubernetes LoadBalancer to route requests from client applications. The services in the coordination layer handle incoming search and index queries, routing them to the core server components in the worker layer that handle queries and manage data storage and indexing. The data nodes manage persistence via files in object storage. The message storage uses Apache Pulsar or Apache Kafka to store the stream of incoming data that is then passed to data nodes.

As you can see, Milvus is designed to be Kubernetes native, with a horizontally scalable architecture that makes it well poised to scale up to massive data sets including billions or even trillions of vectors.

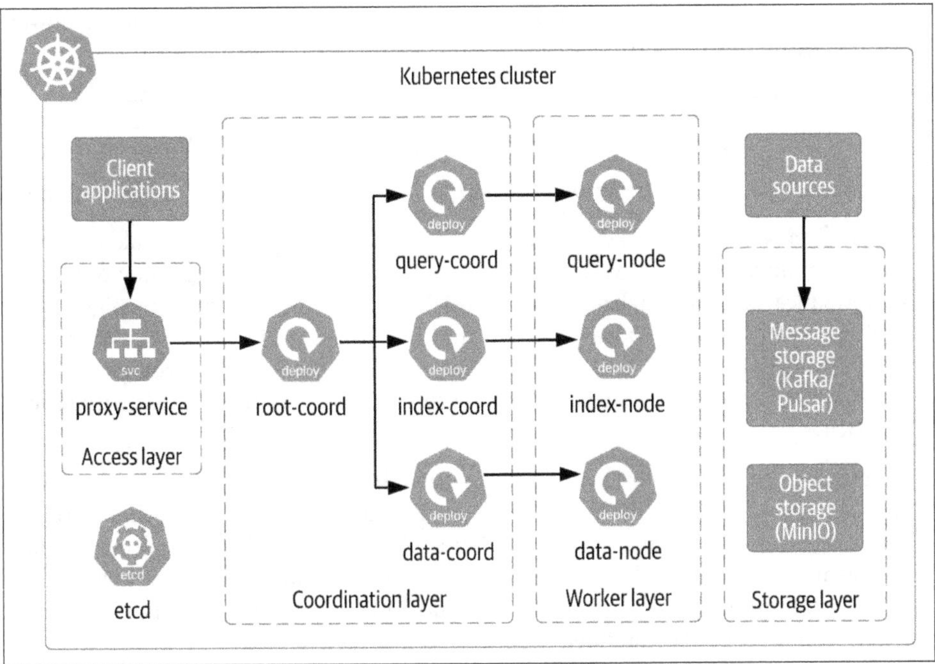

Figure 10-4. Deploying Milvus in Kubernetes

Efficient Data Movement with Apache Arrow

Now that we have explored an AI/ML Kubernetes stack that helps you manage compute resources more efficiently, you might be wondering what can be done with network resources. The "fallacies of distributed computing" we discussed in "Embrace Distributed Computing" on page 14 include two important points: the fallacies of believing that bandwidth is infinite and that transport cost is zero. Even when compute and storage resources seem much more finite, it's easy to forget how easily you can run out of bandwidth. The deeper you get into deploying your data infrastructure into Kubernetes, the more likely it is you will find out. Early adopters of Apache Hadoop often shared that as their clusters grew, their network switches needed to be replaced with the best that could be purchased at the time. Just consider what it takes to sort 10 terabytes of data. How about 1 petabyte? You get the idea.

Apache Arrow is a project that addresses the problem of bandwidth utilization by providing a more efficient format. This actually isn't an unknown approach in the history of computer science. IBM introduced Extended Binary Coded Decimal Interchange Code (EBCDIC) (*https://oreil.ly/MI488*) character encoding to create efficiency for the preferred transport of the time: the punch card. Arrow attacks the problem of efficiency from the ground up in order to avoid the endless upgrading to add more resources, proving that the solution to a control problem is never "add more power." Let's hear from some experts to learn how this works.

Efficient Data Movement with Apache Arrow

With Josh Patterson, CEO, Voltron Data, and Keith Kraus, VP of Product, Voltron Data

As big data technologies like Spark, Kudu, and Cassandra made it possible to move larger amounts of data between systems, it became clear that the computational and performance cost of serializing and deserializing data was getting too high. Wes McKinney and Jacques Nadeau, along with others, made a bid to address this problem with a project called Apache Arrow (*https://arrow.apache.org*). Arrow provides a standard way to represent the layout of data so systems can share that data with fewer headaches.

Arrow uses an in-memory columnar format—that is, data arranged in a tabular format of rows and columns. In traditional relational databases, each record is represented as a row with multiple columns. Arrow pivots this arrangement: data is organized in sequentially ordered columns. This provides significant advantages when searching and processing large amounts of data, especially because of how it aligns with modern CPU architectures.

Arrow Flight is a subproject to bring the same efficiency we see in processing to network communications. Highly connected distributed systems consume network resources quickly, and any efficiency gains quickly make a big difference at high volumes. Flight is a remote procedure call (RPC) layer that drastically reduces resource utilization for communications between data services by eliminating serialization costs. Flight uses gRPC for network efficiency, which enables it to send data in parallel using multiple channels. Using Arrow in all of your Kubernetes native analytics stack reduces resource usage and therefore cost.

Arrow doesn't just provide benefits for network utilization; it also has promise for more efficient compute processing for AI/ML workloads. Arrow provides a fast access pattern for data analytics and tabular data that Kubernetes applications can take advantage of. Arrow was one of the first projects in the data analytics space to encourage users to think carefully about the usage of memory and processing hardware, and this timing has coincided nicely with the rise of deep learning. Kubernetes native analytics workloads powered by Arrow will help keep costs low while allowing higher processing volumes.

In fact, Kubernetes was a key driver that moved the Arrow project forward. As the GPU-accelerated stack was being defined around 2018, Kubernetes was emerging as an industry standard, replacing Hadoop YARN as the leading resource management tool for big data processing. The Kubernetes community was developing key features more rapidly, like support for the remote direct memory access (RDMA) protocol and topology awareness of nodes containing GPUs. Kubernetes also supported faster SLAs for cluster operations. With modern GPUs offering 50 times faster processing times, the Job of analyzing dozens of terabytes might take 5 minutes, while scheduling and provisioning the machines with YARN to perform that Job could take 10 minutes. The auto-scaling abilities in Kubernetes offered the right reaction time to match these cyclical workloads. New advanced schedulers such as YuniKorn and Volcano now make those operations even faster and more efficient.

Finding ways to take advantage of new hardware technology is a critical part of our battle to keep up with the ever-increasing volumes of data created. The trend toward using GPUs for big data processing is already increasing, and adopting Arrow will only make this easier. In fact, the effect on the community has already reached a tipping point. With the momentum of GPUs adopting the Arrow format, data tools have started adopting Arrow for compatibility, helping to cement Arrow as a data interoperability standard. Arrow could be more than just a language-agnostic connector; it could be a hardware connector. We've come to believe that an increasing number of systems will become Arrow native in the near future.

The data and analytics ecosystem will continue to drive the future of Kubernetes and Arrow. Frameworks like Dask and Ray use Python as their underlying compute library, with Arrow used as the format within Pandas DataFrames sent over the wire between workers. Getting your tabular data efficiently over the wire is a huge benefit, and Arrow provides an easy-to-implement standard that is completely interchangeable, open, and widely adopted. It allows future tool developers to focus on the special thing they are building and less on optimizing interconnect.

The Arrow community has become a center of gravity attracting large and innovative projects. The data and analytics community has a pattern of rebuilding new infrastructure about every 10 years. This time the revolution is defined not by starting over, but by refining the things that we have, biased toward optimizing the primitives. Arrow provides a modular building block that can be used, optimized, extended, and composed with multiple other systems. The groundwork for the next 10 years of data infrastructure can start on a sound foundation learned from the mistakes of the past decade. Then we can focus on problems like improving Parquet, using single instruction, multiple data (SIMD) vectorization, or building storage that could be compacted tightly and quickly. Arrow can be a big part of these solutions because it touches so many systems. Even though its focus on the way we represent data is simple, minor improvements here can have massive ripple effects on our cloud native future.

Using Arrow-enabled projects enables you to share data efficiently, reducing your resource usage across compute, network, and storage. Example usage of Arrow with Spark is shown in Figure 10-5.

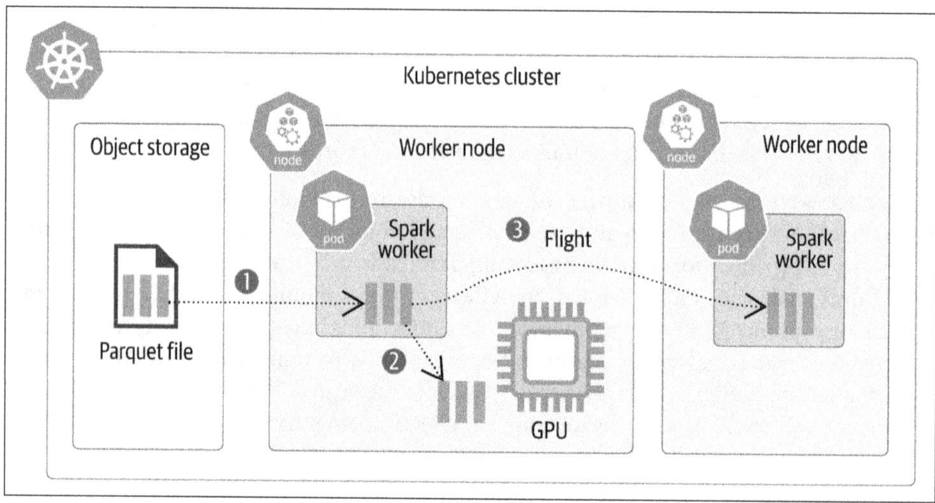

Figure 10-5. Moving data with Apache Arrow

Parquet datafiles containing Arrow-formatted data persisted to object storage can be easily loaded without a deserialization step (1). The data can then be analyzed by a Spark application (2), including loading directly into a GPU for processing where available. The same efficiency level is maintained when passing data between Worker Nodes using Arrow Flight (3). The Arrow record batch is sent without any intermediate memory copying or serialization, and the receiver can reconstruct the Arrow record without memory copy or deserialization. The efficient relationship between the remote processes eliminates two things: processing overhead for sending data and the efficient Arrow record format that eliminates wasted bandwidth.

At the scale common in Spark applications, the effect on network latency and bandwidth can add up quickly. The network transport savings really keep your data moving, even when volumes reach into terabytes and petabytes. Research (*https://oreil.ly/rve9i*) performed by Tanveer Ahmad at TU Delft showed a 20 to 30 times efficiency gain using Arrow Flight to move large volumes of data.

Versioned Object Storage with lakeFS

Object storage is becoming the standard for cloud native data persistence. It lowers the complexity for services but also points to a different way of thinking about data mutability. Instead of opening a file and providing random access, file storage is precomputed, written once, and read many times. Instead of updating a datafile, you write a new one, but how do you distinguish which datafiles are current? For this reason, object storage presents issues with disk space management. Since there is no concept of managing an entire filesystem, each file is an object in a virtually infinite resource.

Object storage APIs are fairly basic with few frills, but data teams need more than just the basics for their use cases. lakeFS (*https://lakefs.io*) and Nessie (*https://projectnessie.org*) are two projects trying to make object storage a better fit for emerging workloads on Kubernetes. Let's examine how lakeFS extends the functionality of object storage for cloud native applications.

Data Integrity to Let You Sleep at Night

With Adi Polak, VP of Developer Experience, Treeverse

In working as a full-time engineer building big data infrastructure, there were many times I had to manually change data in object storage in our production environment. This task became even more challenging when using complex data formats such as Parquet. On one occasion, I needed to delete some datafiles to resolve a production issue. Unfortunately, I accidentally deleted the wrong data. That meant 20 hours in the office with a very grumpy DevOps team trying to recover the data from backup because, of course, it was customer data. At least in this case, we were aware of the issue. What's even more concerning are the silent failures that impact data products without us even being aware.

These problems occur frequently today because our systems are too fragile. We are biased toward action, but we're human and therefore have a tendency to make mistakes. The result is that bad things happen to good data.

How does lakeFS help with situations like the one I've described? The simplest way to describe lakeFS is that it enables Git-like capabilities for object storage. It allows engineers to perform familiar actions like branch, commit, merge, and revert. This creates new options for the way you use data and enhances workflows.

For example, a typical use case for using lakeFS is continuous integration/continuous deployment (CI/CD) flows. Data engineers frequently need to reproduce some portion of a data pipeline over different versions of the data, which requires branching. When running on Kubernetes, multiple containers can potentially run the same code over different versions of data. Branching data on the object store creates an isolated environment for experimentation. If there is a mistake in the branch, you can simply revert. This provides the ability to experiment at low cost without harming the original data, which builds trust and allows teams to move faster with safety.

Another example is trying out a new application to see how it fits into the bigger data flow. Git semantics on data can make a massive difference in complicated scenarios that are typically hard to test. In "Analytics on Kubernetes Is the Next Frontier" on page 223, Holden Karau addressed the difficulty in testing big data applications. It's almost impossible to mimic production flows in development or staging environments because of the variety and production data volume. With lakeFS, you can use branching to test with multiple data versions, duplicating the variety and volume seen in production and building confidence in what is being built.

To integrate with your environment, lakeFS exposes an S3-compatible API endpoint through a stateless service. However, it doesn't actually serve as storage. LakeFS forks data commands from your application. Loading data to lakeFS is a metadata operation that creates your main branch in lakeFS by creating pointers to the physical data in your S3 bucket. Any additional branch is an atomic metadata operation pointing to the same data as main when created from it. The metadata created by lakeFS is saved to your S3. As long as the user application is using the lakeFS API endpoint, all Git functionality is available. If users want to stop using lakeFS at any point, the original data storage is unaltered and can be used directly by changing the endpoint address used by your application. To roll up any changes while using lakeFS, an offboarding script is available to synchronize any changes before taking lakeFS out of the path. This makes it easy for users to try lakeFS and then adopt or move on without the need to move existing data. The design of lakeFS enables seamless integrations with other parts of your data infrastructure such as Apache Iceberg, Apache Hudi, or Delta Lake, providing the added features of branch, commit, rollback, and merge.

lakeFS addresses the lack of atomicity, consistency, isolation, durability (ACID) transactions (*https://oreil.ly/mjGnN*) across multiple systems by providing the ability to have versioned object storage. The consistency level guarantees passthrough from the originating application. However, when multitable operations are performed on an isolated branch, the merge function across all tables is atomic, achieving cross-table consistency.

We are at an interesting intersection point for data workloads on Kubernetes. Many developers who have been working with distributed data workloads for years think in terms of the Hadoop ecosystem. Now we're actually bringing in a different type of developer: the application developer who works with Kubernetes. A potential for more friction and errors exists since these developers are not always aware of the infrastructure and the way things have traditionally worked in the big data world.

Kubernetes is now being used to orchestrate the systems that process data and turn it into products for sale. If the data is not protected, your business is at risk. Organizations need to be able to audit, save, and deliver data reliably, even if it is at a lower SLA. lakeFS is a great fit for Kubernetes deployment because it assumes that the complexity of distributed systems and distributed data will lead to many mistakes around data. That assumption is met with the assurance that any mistake is easily fixed and never devastating, leading to a great night of sleep for your DevOps teams.

Using lakeFS in Kubernetes is a great fit because of its stateless design and declarative deployment. A Helm deployment consists of configuring (*https://oreil.ly/GhZMB*) the lakeFS service, which then serves as a communication gateway to and from other services.

Communications into the server emulate S3 object storage, enabling interaction with any data store that supports the S3 API. Incoming communication is bound as a ClusterIP to serve HTTP traffic across one or more stateless lakeFS server Pods managed by a Deployment.

lakeFS uses PostgreSQL to manage metadata, so users can either provide the endpoint for a running system, as shown in Figure 10-6, or lakeFS can run an embedded PostgreSQL server inside the lakeFS Pod for its exclusive use. PostgreSQL is the state management for the stateless lakeFS servers when deployed as a cluster.

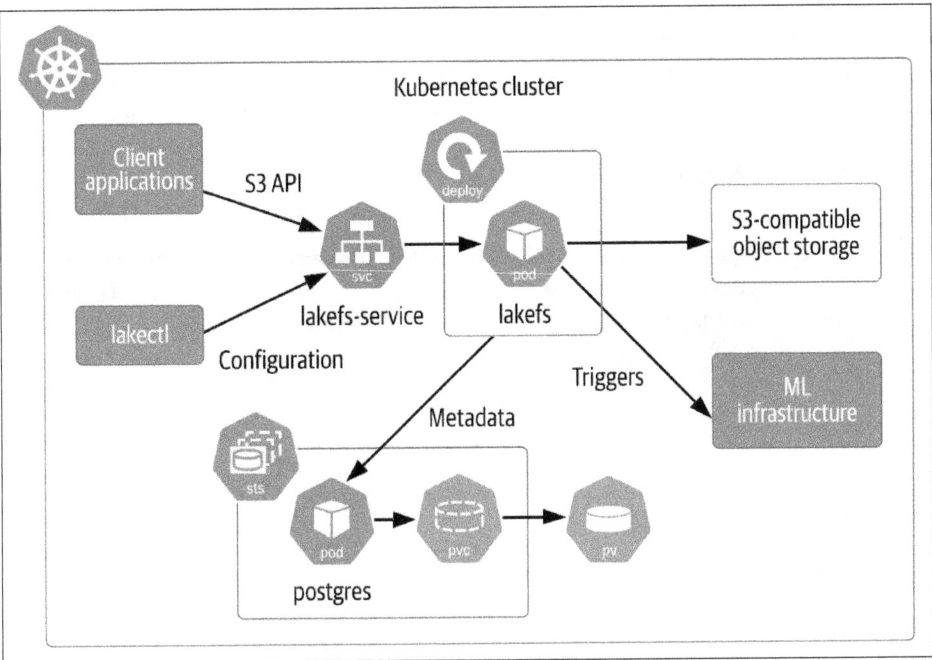

Figure 10-6. Deploying lakeFS in Kubernetes

The most important connection is to the object storage endpoints that will store the actual data. When users persist data to lakeFS, the actual datafile will pass through to the backend object storage, and versioning metadata is stored in PostgreSQL.

The additional outbound connection is for providing orchestration with other ML infrastructure. Webhooks allow for triggers on action that alert downstream systems when something such as a commit is issued. These triggers serve as a key ingredient to automated ML workflows and other applications.

Summary

As you can see, the pipeline of new and exciting ways to work with data in Kubernetes extends well into the future. New projects are addressing the challenges of advanced data workloads according to the cloud native principles of elasticity, scalability, and self-healing.

These tools give you the ability to manage the critical resources of compute, network and storage. You can better manage compute-intensive workloads such as AI/ML with KServe for the delivery, Feast for model management, and Milvus to operationalize new search methods. Network resources are ruled by the simple laws of volume and speed, and at the volumes of data we can create, every little bit helps. Apache Arrow reduces this volume by creating a common reference frame across applications. Unifying around object storage provides further efficiencies, with tools like lakeFS making object storage easier to consume in ways that are sympathetic to application data storage needs.

At this point, we've examined data infrastructure on Kubernetes from mature areas like storage all the way out to cutting-edge projects for managing AI/ML artifacts such as models and features. Now it's time to take all the knowledge you've gained so far and plan to put it into practice.

CHAPTER 11

Migrating Data Workloads to Kubernetes

In the first chapter, we presented a vision for combining all of the infrastructure needed for your cloud native applications into one place: Kubernetes. Our argument was simple: if you're excluding data and its supporting infrastructure from your Kubernetes deployments, you haven't fully embraced cloud native principles. We've covered a lot of ground since then, examining how various types of data infrastructure work on Kubernetes and demonstrating the art of the possible.

So, where do you go from here? What are the steps to fully realize this vision? At this point, you may already have some parts of your applications in Kubernetes. More than likely, you also have several previous generations of infrastructure such as containers, VMs, or bare-metal servers, whether running in your own datacenters or in the cloud. In this final chapter, we'll leverage everything you've learned so far to help you create a plan to fully manage your cloud native data in Kubernetes.

The Vision: Application-Aware Platforms

Throughout the book, we've heard a diverse range of voices in the community present their wisdom about data in Kubernetes and practical advice for this monumental undertaking. No matter where you are in the process, whether you're a Kubernetes beginner or a seasoned multiyear operator, we all have things to learn from their expertise. Now it's time to zoom out and consider how the move to Kubernetes intersects with other trends in the software industry. Craig McLuckie was part of the team that created Kubernetes at Google and eventually shepherded it into open source. He's been very active in the cloud native infrastructure community and shares some possibilities and challenges as we move toward data on Kubernetes.

What the Kubernetes Duty Cycle Means for Data

With Craig McLuckie, Kubernetes OSS cocreator

In electronics, the term *duty cycle* describes the time period when a signal is active in a system. In the IT domain, there are duty cycles associated with systems and technologies, and in some cases these cycles can be extremely long. For example, many people are surprised to learn that IBM continues to sell mainframes as a huge part of its business. In recognition of the evolving landscape of cloud native, we should anticipate a long duty cycle for Kubernetes as well. It's projected that by 2024, more than half of workloads running in public clouds will be hosted in Kubernetes, representing a growth rate of 24% year over year.

As an early proponent of not running stateful workloads in Kubernetes, I was always cautious to say it wasn't ready for data…yet. Now, things are beginning to change. Kubernetes began as a relatively simple way to orchestrate containers, but Kubernetes represents key concepts that help build higher layers beyond just infrastructure. For example, Kubernetes began as an ideal logical infrastructure abstraction and a way to frame systems thinking. It provides a set of logical primitives decoupled from the infrastructure that you can use to construct distributed systems. Now we're seeing applications like data infrastructure being built specifically for Kubernetes, which opens a more interesting future.

Another key concept being adopted outside the Kubernetes core is the controller-reconciler pattern. The Cluster API project (*https://oreil.ly/6kmTt*) uses Kubernetes-style APIs and the controller-reconciler pattern to automate lifecycle management of Kubernetes clusters. Starting with a CRD, a well-formed Kubernetes cluster can be assembled from infrastructure based on a declarative expression. This is a great example of the power of the controller-reconciler pattern applied to custom resources that can be followed for other infrastructure.

Following the convention of expressing as much as possible in a declarative context can help us address the problems associated with data management. We can then apply the pattern of choreography to handle fleet management of distributed data infrastructure, one of the historical challenges of running data at scale. The use of custom resources will be as disruptive as Kubernetes itself. There will be tremendous utility and value in having controls and capabilities built on Kubernetes expressed as an API. Bringing this platform-as-a-service (PaaS) mindset into enterprise organizations will enable developers to access data services in much the same way as they interact with public cloud services.

The inversion of control (IoC) pattern provides us with a powerful technique to build this type of infrastructure. Starting with a declarative description of the desired service, a controller implementing the description will read the manifest, and render and connect the components. Now combine that with the work done in Knative with duck typing (*https://oreil.ly/ANlHt*), which allows a resource to declare a dependency on another resource using a well-defined syntax. An intelligent system can examine each resource as it is provisioned to see if it matches any unbound dependencies and perform dependency injection and binding. If we do our job right, we will start to build application-aware platforms, a game-changing switch. In a world where applications can express their data infrastructure needs declaratively, we can move away from building infrastructure-coupled applications.

This level of automation doesn't mean that infrastructure will be completely hands-off, with nothing for SREs to do. Data infrastructure providers should strive to provide high-level abstractions first, but also provide lower-level access. When constructing systems, situations inevitably arise requiring users to be able to break glass and look at the number of Pods configured, or tune resource allocations based on insights into application behavior.

The world isn't getting any less complicated for people building applications. Data sovereignty laws are becoming more and more prevalent, and we are starting to think in terms of "sovereign clouds" and even "national clouds." When you layer on things like edge computing, it gets even more complicated as you want to run compute workloads closer to your users. Of the three main infrastructure resources—compute, network, and storage—networking will become more and more important as highly distributed use cases emerge.

Kubernetes offers a solution to these looming challenges—creating a unique opportunity to deliver an "as a service" experience into infrastructure that you control. The real potency will come via highly optimized "as a service" experiences delivered via a connected control plane into any infrastructure destination. Whoever can figure this out will create a tremendous amount of usability and, ultimately, win the game.

Craig offers an inspiring vision for a future where infrastructure conforms to the application instead of the infrastructure-coupled applications we have today. As you've seen in the technologies we've explored in this book, the idea of declarative infrastructure that reconciles via the Kubernetes control plane is everywhere. Now we can begin to flip the script by building applications from the top down instead of from the bottom up. This is an opportunity to change the way your organization leverages data technology. Are you ready to start? It's time to map out your journey.

Charting Your Path to Success

In preparing to migrate your stateful workloads to Kubernetes, you'll probably have a few questions in mind, like "What technologies should we use?" and "How will we roll out the changes?" and "How do we make sure our team is ready?" Most of these questions will map nicely to the classic IT framework of people, process, and technology (PPT). Since every organization's journey will be different, we'll provide recommendations in each category instead of a detailed roadmap. An important part of your exercise is choosing what migrates into Kubernetes and what doesn't. Every migration should have a strong case.

You will likely have some of these recommendations in place already, so the actual work needed is to ensure that your efforts in all three areas work together toward your desired outcome. One word of warning: this is not the time to "run fast and break things." You'll have plenty of time to do that after you have the core elements in place. With a strong foundation, you will achieve levels of agility and speed you haven't seen before.

People

The core of any IT organization is its people. Migrating any workload to Kubernetes represents a massive shift in mindset for your organization and requires proper training and preparation. You will need people who understand the technology already or are willing to learn. This requirement is even more true in preparing to migrate to stateful workloads. Beyond the apparent tasks of training up on Kubernetes and reading books like this one, we'd like to draw your attention to two areas: specific job roles that successful organizations execute well and leveraging open source communities as a force multiplier for your teams.

Critical people roles for cloud native data

We could list many roles that are key to a successful migration, but we'll highlight three that are central to managing cloud native data and discuss how they relate:

Cloud architects
: Architects provide technical direction to the development of cloud applications, influencing everything from the clouds and regions where you'll deploy your applications, to the data infrastructure you'll use. This includes when to rely on self-managed open source projects versus managed services. An effective cloud architect carefully selects technology to meet current business needs while leaving room for future extensibility.

Site reliability engineers
: In Chapter 1, we talked about adopting an SRE mindset. While this mindset is something that every engineer in your organization should be working toward, DBAs have an incredibly strategic opportunity to make the transition into an SRE role. Instead of just deploying a database and walking away, a data-focused SRE takes a holistic view of the data infrastructure and how it supports the system's overall goals, with an eye toward the best performance for the cost.

Data engineers
: Whereas data scientists are concerned about extracting the value from data, data engineers are responsible for operationalizing data. They build data processes,

assemble systems, and think about the end-user consumption of data products. Data engineers should be versed not only in Kubernetes-based technology but also in what cloud services can be used in concert for an optimized outcome. Data engineers will play a significant role in selecting and deploying technology that supports the AI/ML workloads we discussed in Chapter 10, composing multiple components to create flows that deliver real-time insights into your applications.

To think about how these roles work together in an organization, consider the analogy of a farming operation:

- The architect is like the planner who determines what crops to grow, and in what quantities in each season.
- The SRE is like the farmer who plants and cultivates the crops to ensure they are healthy and productive.
- The data engineer is like a distributor who harvests the crops and ensures they reach their proper destination.

If you don't already have these roles defined within your organization, don't worry. In many cases, it is possible to retrain engineers in your organization who are currently in a different role.

Communities to fast-track your innovation

To paraphrase the sword-wielding old man in *The Legend of Zelda*, it's dangerous to go alone. Bring friends. Communities are a core part of working in technology, and we work together, learn together, and share successes and failures. When embarking on a new technology journey, look for the communities that form around that technology. The following are a few notable communities in cloud native data. You can seek them out for information, join the conversation, and hopefully contribute:

Cloud Native Computing Foundation

Also known as the CNCF (*https://www.cncf.io*), this organization is a part of the more extensive Linux Foundation (*https://www.linuxfoundation.org*), a nonprofit organization devoted to open source advocacy. The CNCF is the home for Kubernetes and many projects that run in Kubernetes, including several featured in this book. You can see the amount of energy put into Kubernetes native projects from the graduated and incubating projects list. Members of CNCF pay a fee that goes to support the advocacy and administration of the foundation and its projects.

The Technical Oversight Committee (TOC) approves and maintains the technical vision for CNCF projects. With so many projects to maintain, Technical Advisory Groups (TAGs) (*https://oreil.ly/KSxmL*) have been formed to handle cross-project concerns. Each TAG maintains its autonomy within an initial charter to create a place for similarly grouped projects to maintain interoperability standards. Each maintains its own Slack workspace and mailing lists for community discussions.

All development activity for a project is centered around its GitHub repository. To get involved in contributing code, search for the "good first issue" (*https://oreil.ly/xt2QR*) tag in GitHub Issues for each project. If you have broader interests, you might consider joining the conversation happening in TAGs to help shape future direction. Twice a year, the KubeCon + CloudNativeCon user conferences (*https://oreil.ly/Ijlki*) are held by the CNCF in North America, China, and Europe, with an enormous session list. Some of the best sessions are the user stories about deploying specific cloud native technologies.

Apache Software Foundation

The ASF (*https://www.apache.org*) is a nonprofit organization for software conservancy. ASF members provide governance, services, and support for accepted projects. After going through an incubation process, projects graduate to become top-level projects where they earn the Apache name (e.g., Apache Cassandra, Apache Spark, and Apache Pulsar). Each project is run independently by a project management committee (PMC), and users with the right to make project changes are known as *committers*.

It's important to note the distinction between the project and user communities around Apache projects. The project community is concerned with building the project, and the user community is downstream and primarily focuses on using the project in their applications. This separation of concerns is evident in the two mailing lists available for most projects: *dev@<project name>.apache.org* and *user@<project name>.apache.org*.

If you are interested in contributing code, jumping right in is the best way to start. Apache projects use Jira (*https://oreil.ly/Odauf*) to track changes and bugs. Look for "low hanging fruit" or "good first project" tags on the Jira issues. In the user community, participating in the mailing list or Stack Overflow is a great way to start contributing by helping others. Giving presentations about Apache projects is the lifeblood of awareness for each project and one of the best contributions.

Data on Kubernetes Community (DoKC)

A different kind of organization than the CNCF and ASF, DoKC is a knowledge community composed of industry vendors and end users. DoKC isn't a place for hosting software projects but a central gathering place for people in a growing field within infrastructure. Technology vendors sponsor the community, but the charter is to remain vendor neutral in all activities. Those activities include in-person and online meetups, blogs on the *dok.community* website (*https://dok.community*), and a companion event to KubeCon, DoK Day.

In addition to gathering the community, DoKC also produces useful resources to guide users as they make decisions about data technology on Kubernetes:

- Given the number of data technologies available, the DoK Landscape (*https://oreil.ly/HgYlL*) has been created to help compare and evaluate the various options. You can search by attributes such as open source versus commercial licensing, or whether an operator or Helm chart is available.
- An annual DoK survey (*https://oreil.ly/ZmaQu*) is also conducted to gauge industry opinions and provide guidance on common problems. The report is free and can be used in your presentations.

As a knowledge community, the best way to participate in the DoKC is sharing knowledge. When the community was being formed, the amount of information about end users running stateful workloads in Kubernetes was scarce. Creating a space to focus on data topics has led to a growing set of common interests and concepts. Most of the interviews in this book came from people we met in the DoKC.

Throughout the book, we've seen the benefits of contributions from each of these communities toward making data technologies run effectively on Kubernetes:

- The PersistentVolume subsystem we discussed in Chapter 2 has provided a solid foundation for a wide variety of open source and commercial storage solutions on Kubernetes.
- Operator frameworks we discussed in Chapter 5, including Operator SDK, Kubebuilder, and KUDO have proven to be a great enabler toward developing operators for a variety of data infrastructure from the ASF and other open source projects.
- Kubernetes StatefulSets (first introduced in Chapter 3) are an interesting case. While they have proven quite valuable for managing distributed databases, the community has also identified some opportunities for improvement that we look forward to seeing addressed in the future.
- Similarly, Spark and other projects in the analytics community have identified challenges with the Kubernetes default scheduler, as you learned in Chapter 9. Thankfully, Kubernetes provides APIs for extending the scheduler that projects like Apache YuniKorn and Volcano can leverage.

As you can see, plenty of work remains to be done in this ecosystem of interconnected communities, and it will take contributions from all corners of the cloud native world to get us to the next stage of maturity as an industry. Remember, community participation isn't limited to providing code to a project. One of the most important contributions to any community is sharing your story. Think about your experiences of learning new technologies, and you'll likely recall good documentation, great examples, and the most valuable of all: "how we built this" stories. Please consider sharing your story any way you can. Your community needs you!

Technology

For many of you, this is the most exciting part. Cool toys! As you consider your journey to cloud native data, you'll have important decisions in terms of the technologies you choose to use and the way you integrate them into your applications. You'll recall from Chapter 1 the critical guiding principles for deploying cloud native data in Kubernetes:

- Principle 1: Leverage compute, network, and storage as commodity APIs.
- Principle 2: Separate the control and data planes.
- Principle 3: Make observability easy.
- Principle 4: Make the default configuration secure.
- Principle 5: Prefer declarative configuration.

As it turns out, these principles are useful for technology selection and integration, which you'll see next.

Selecting cloud native data projects

The years of building massive scale infrastructure, especially in data, have yielded an enormous supply of tooling to pick from, provided by various vendors and open source communities. For our examination here, we've made a deliberate choice to reason in terms of selecting projects instead of selecting technologies. Projects encapsulate the needed technology while integrating with the processes we need, created by the people who will drive the success. You're here because you believe Kubernetes is one of these enabling projects, but how do you make your next set of choices? Here are some principles we recommend:

Ready for Kubernetes

Chapter 7, outlined requirements for a Kubernetes native database, including:

- Maximum leverage of Kubernetes APIs
- Automated, declarative management via operators
- Observable through standard APIs (such as Prometheus)
- Secure by default

While not every project you use has to be Kubernetes native, the criterion for being Kubernetes-ready is a bit broader. At a minimum, projects you use should have an operator or Helm chart. The next level is a step toward the Kubernetes native idea of built-in awareness of Kubernetes for deeper integration. An example is Apache Spark, with the Kubernetes cluster deployment option that uses specialized containers. The highest level of maturity is populated by fully realized cloud native projects that can run only in Kubernetes because they depend on components in a Kubernetes cluster. An example of this type of project is KServe, which has no way of running outside of Kubernetes.

Open source
: Using an open source project in the age of cloud native is about choice. You can deploy what you need, where you need it. If you choose to use a managed service based on an open source project, it should be completely compatible with the open source version, with no restrictions in moving back to a self-managed solution. Choosing the right license gives you the confidence to use a project and maintain your choice. We recommend projects with the Apache License 2.0 (APLv2). All ASF and CNCF projects use this license, so projects from either source guarantee you a permissive license. Many other licenses (*https://oreil.ly/61pjy*) offer differing levels of permissiveness and restrictions, and you should carefully consider how they will affect your deployment and requirements.

Of course, project selections aren't something you can do in isolation. Upstream decisions influence each subsequent decision, and in turn can constrain what choices are available. This is why, in many cases, it makes sense to look at combinations of projects that work well together, either by deliberate design or by standard interfaces.

New architectures for cloud native data

The future of cloud native data should focus less on new projects and more on new architectures. This means using the projects we have today in combinations that make the best use of each. As we've discussed previously, the software industry has a history of leveraging ideas from prior generations lasting a decade or more to innovate from a new point of view. In the cloud native world, the past decade has been spent building scale infrastructure, and the next 10 years will likely be about how we can combine these projects for our needs.

The infrastructure community has historically demonstrated a fondness for integrated infrastructure stacks that solve a common set of problems. One example is the LAMP stack popularized for web applications in the early 2000s, consisting of the Linux operating system, the Apache HTTP Server, MySQL, and either PHP, Perl, or Python, depending on who you asked. The 2010s brought us the SMACK stack for big data applications, with the Spark engine, Mesos as the resource manager, Akka, Cassandra, and Kafka.

While it's tempting to describe such a stack for cloud native data, the reality is that the variety of use cases and available projects are simply too large to come up with a one-size-fits-all stack. Instead, let's consider a candidate solution architecture for a simple weather application case, as shown in Figure 11-1. This architecture demonstrates the principles and recommendations discussed throughout the book, leveraging our data infrastructure categories of persistence, streaming, and analytics. This is a conceptual vision that we can discuss, critique, and improve as a community. Each choice we've made here has alternatives and should be considered a starting point for the sake of discussion.

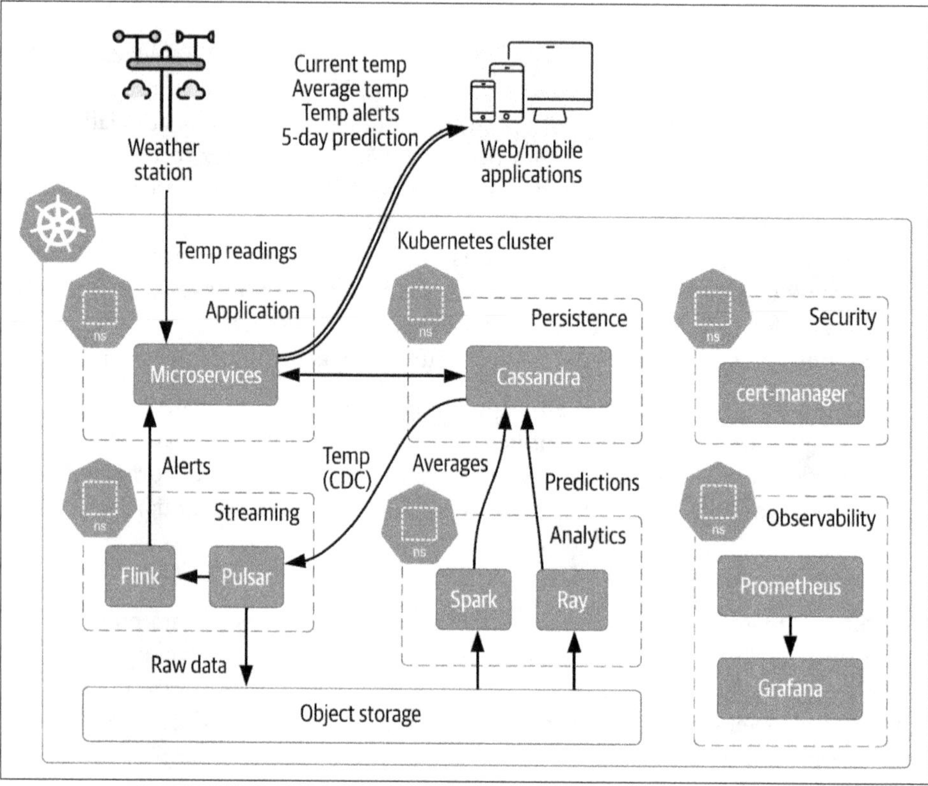

Figure 11-1. Sample architecture for a weather application

Let's walk through the flow of data to understand how this architecture satisfies the needs of a weather application with multiple data requirements. We'll assume that the entire server-side infrastructure stack is contained in a single Kubernetes cluster. More advanced forms of this architecture could include multicluster deployments or inclusion of networking capabilities such as load balancing or Ingress. For now, this will serve to illustrate the data architecture.

Weather data is collected from weather stations and posted to a waiting API with an Ingress port into your running Kubernetes cluster. The business logic and server-side application code are containerized and run as microservices in the `application`

Namespace. Client-side web and mobile applications also use the microservices via API calls, so all external data communications pass through the microservices layer.

Real-time data is sent to Cassandra for immediate use in the `persistence` Namespace. Once the data is committed at the desired consistency level, change data capture (CDC) emits the fully committed data to a Pulsar topic in the `streaming` Namespace. A Pulsar sink exports the raw data into a Parquet file put in object storage. At the same time, a Flink consumer subscribed to the topic analyzes new data for user-defined limits such as high or low temperatures. If a boundary condition is triggered, the temperature and station data is sent back to the microservices, which will send push alerts to the user application.

In the `analytics` Namespace, two separate processes will use the Parquet data in object storage. Spark Jobs are used to group temperature averages across geographic data. This application code needs a wide view of the data stored for multiple locations and times. Ray applies analysis code written in Python to accomplish the predictive analysis of weather forecasting. The following five-day forecast is built daily by looking at recent data and applying against models built over historical trends. Both the Spark and Ray jobs populate new tables of fast transactional data in Cassandra.

This candidate architecture also demonstrates some recommendations that aren't specific to a weather application that you should consider for all your deployments:

Use Namespaces to separate domains within applications
: Deploying hundreds of Pods into a Kubernetes cluster can create organizational issues you won't encounter with a small cluster on your laptop. Our recommendation here is simple: use Namespaces liberally to create order in your complex deployments. In the weather application example, we used simple Namespaces for each functional area of infrastructure: `application`, `persistence`, `streaming`, `analytics`, `security`, and `observability`. This approach will provide clear boundaries and naming when addressing services or managing Pods.

Automate certificate management
: In Chapter 8, we asserted that the best security solutions are the ones you don't have to think about. Automating your certificate management with cert-manager is an excellent example of a solution that makes that a possibility. Use TLS for all inter-service communication. For Ingress routes, ensure all traffic is HTTPS. Both cases use ACME plug-ins to rotate and assign certificates and never suffer another outage due to an expired certificate. When a security audit comes around, you can check the box that says you enforce all policies and guidelines and that all network communication is adequately encrypted. Just do it.

Prefer object storage
: When choosing storage for the stateful services in your Kubernetes cluster, you should prefer object storage where possible. As discussed in Chapter 7, several

reasons behind this recommendation will put you in a better place for deploying cloud native data. The primary one is the impact of immutability on separating storage from running processes. Block storage is generally tightly aligned with compute infrastructure and has a higher level of complexity. The tight coupling between compute and storage must be broken to build truly serverless data infrastructure. Object storage has proven to be a key enabler. You can choose to implement your own object storage inside Kubernetes or via a cloud service.

Standardize on Prometheus APIs for metrics
: Observability is mandatory for the complex infrastructure being built and run in Kubernetes, and the Prometheus API is the most widely adopted for metrics. Ensure that all services expose metrics in Prometheus format and that you collect them in a single place. The Prometheus API is implemented on various backends such as VictoriaMetrics and InfluxDB, giving you options for managing your own Prometheus deployment or connecting to a cloud service. Finally, collecting metrics is only one part of the challenge, and using those metrics to build dashboards and alerting completes the package.

As this architecture demonstrates, you can now deploy all of the infrastructure needed to support a complex application in a single deployment in Kubernetes. It's a flexible architecture in which new components can be tried and rejected or replaced as your requirements change: are you using the database that best fits your application needs? Should data be analyzed in the stream or after it is at rest? Architecture represents a series of choices based on capabilities, limits, knowledge, and philosophy.

We look forward to future conversations and conference talks sharing the patterns that work and the antipatterns to avoid.

Deploy services, not servers

One pattern we recommend is to start delivering capabilities at a higher level of abstraction: as services instead of servers. To help frame this discussion, think about the architectural design of a building. An architect must understand a structure's requirements and then apply knowledge of materials and style to create a plan for builders to implement. When an architect considers where to place a door, it must be in a useful location, but one that will not weaken the overall structure. At no point do they specify minute details such as whether the door has to have brass hinges.

In the software industry, we've historically required a lot of minute details about individual compute, network, and storage resources well before we get to the deployment stage. For example, in the days of bare-metal infrastructure, the idea of installing a server was a significant event. Each server represented a physical device with a network connection that needed a whole bill of software, including operating system and applications to fill its role in the system. Procuring, configuring, and deploying a web server or database server was a process that could take months.

Along with the migration to cloud computing came the aphorism that we should treat servers as "cattle, not pets." Despite this helpful emphasis, the care and feeding of individual servers persist in plenty of cases. Where a network server accepts requests and then responds with data, it still requires people installing these systems to get much further into the details needed for today's cloud native applications. These details create friction.

Kubernetes has encouraged a lot of progress in this area, emphasizing managing fleets of both stateless and stateful services with Deployments and StatefulSets, instead of focusing on individual Pods. It's time to take this kind of thinking to the next level, and Kubernetes gives us the tools to make it happen.

Consider how the architecture in the previous section can be described as a vertically integrated service—a weather service—consisting of an assembly of microservices and data infrastructure built from Kubernetes primitives for compute, network, and storage. Recalling the "virtual datacenter" concept from Chapter 1, Figure 11-2 depicts the contents of a vertically integrated service that exposes a simple API. While such a service could encompass a wide range of business logic and infrastructure, that complexity is hidden behind a simple API.

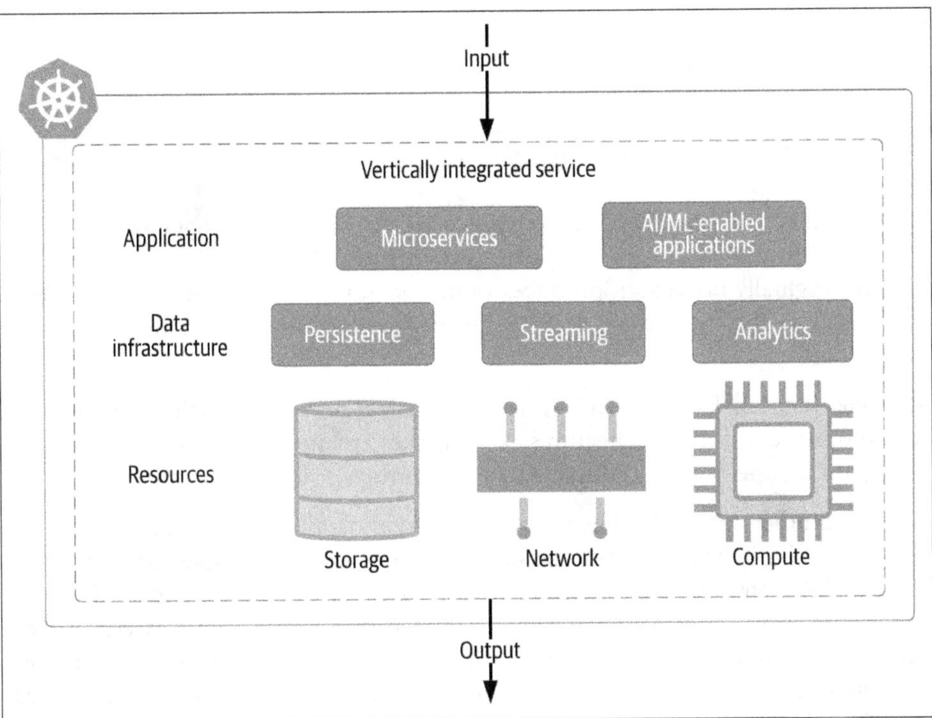

Figure 11-2. Vertically integrated Service

Returning to the example of the preceding weather Service, let's examine how this represents a lot of power behind a deceptively simple API. When you zoom out, the collection of deployed infrastructure looks like a function machine. Rather than a simple microservice that merely gets and puts data records, this function machine takes multiple inputs and produces multiple outputs, as shown in Figure 11-3.

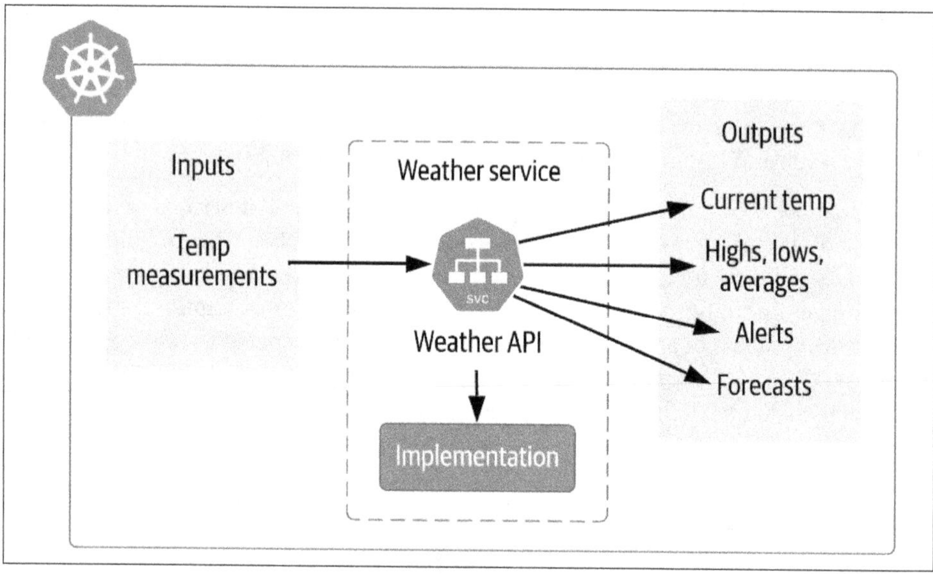

Figure 11-3. Weather Service as a function machine

As a function machine, the weather Service takes a stream of temperature measurements and produces multiple outputs. Beyond the ability to retrieve the individual records originally inserted, it produces value-added information like statistics, alerts, and forecasts that help users make sense of the data and how it relates to them personally.

A single traditional server won't service the variety required, which is why modern data infrastructure and architectures exist. It takes architectural work to assemble the right parts, connect them, and create new data from the single input value.

Users and other applications expect service endpoints that respond to the data they need. What happens inside the function machine is left to the implementation meeting the API contract. When thinking shifts to outcomes, it's clear how deploying services replaces the focus on deploying individual servers. Data services that can operate at various scales, built with resilience, using automation to keep us from worrying about minute details of the tools deployed. Using Kubernetes, you can specify what the function machine will do by using compute, network, and storage the same way you use any other consumable resource.

Process

Now that we have discussed the people and technology aspects of moving stateful workloads to Kubernetes, let's look at the practical process steps required to successfully execute this transition. To be clear, *process* doesn't mean more meetings or people involved in decision making. The dictionary defines a process as "a series of actions or steps to achieve a particular end." For a cloud native deployment process, let's append the word "automated," and that's the right spirit. The goal is to define and codify an automated process that enables you to deploy constantly with confidence. You'll know you've succeeded when you have not only a complete cloud native application stack managed in Kubernetes, but also a repeatable set of steps to reproduce that stack.

Where are you in your cloud native journey? You can be at the starting line or somewhere further along. For either starting point, we recommend the stages shown in Figure 11-4 for adopting cloud native data in Kubernetes.

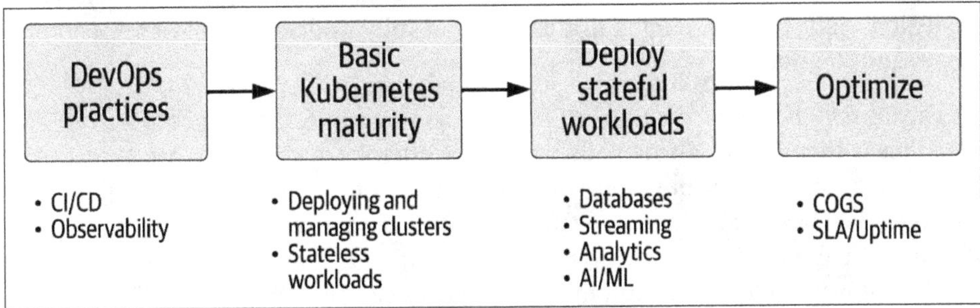

Figure 11-4. Stages of moving data workloads to Kubernetes

Each stage contains core competencies developed by organizations that successfully made this transition. You'll want to adopt and stabilize these competencies before moving on. Take your time and use the many resources available to become proficient in each stage. We'll explore each stage in greater detail next.

DevOps practices

Before you even begin the adoption of Kubernetes, you should completely embrace two areas of managing cloud native infrastructure:

Continuous integration/continuous delivery (CI/CD)
: DevOps teams have already widely used CI/CD for years. Correctly implemented, the outcome is a system that gives you the agility to make changes multiple times in a day with high confidence. For cloud native infrastructure, this has also been described as GitOps (*https://oreil.ly/p20Gt*). Using source control as the starting point for infrastructure changes that a system like Argo CD (*https://oreil.ly/fdj2s*) will use to automate deployments. Made a mistake? Roll it back.

Observability

You may have heard the phrase "Trust but verify," and nowhere is that more important than a highly complex cloud native deployment. You need to see what's happening and make adjustments, especially when using CI/CD. In the process of building services that perform to meet SLAs, every step must be observed. This builds confidence that the changes you make are working; if not, you can roll back and try again. Every step is being watched and recorded.

While specific implementation details of your CI/CD and observability practices will inevitably change as you begin to adopt Kubernetes, having a firm foundation in these areas will set you up nicely for success.

Basic Kubernetes maturity

If you are just starting with Kubernetes, this is a vital stage. Setting up a basic Kubernetes deployment on your laptop or cloud is an excellent way to learn, but your first production Kubernetes projects will stress the capability of your operations. It's realistic to take several months in this phase to fully understand all of the potential issues and solutions:

Deploying and managing clusters

This is the most fundamentally important experience you can have. While there is great learning in building your own Kubernetes clusters and installing your own databases, as we noted in Chapter 3, you can make progress toward production capability more quickly by using a managed Kubernetes service or tools like Terraform that can help automate Kubernetes cluster deployments. You'll get the most value from learning how to deploy and connect services both inside and outside the cluster, tasks that many new users find surprisingly tricky. You'll also want to understand the metrics collected for various elements of a cluster and what they can tell you about performance and capacity.

Moving stateless workloads

Once you are proficient at working with Kubernetes and understand some of the complexities, you can begin moving stateless workloads. The resource requirements for these workloads tend to be more straightforward to understand, and the body of prior art of deploying stateless workloads is deep. You'll likely need to manage external networking to stateful workloads and data infrastructure that you aren't yet moving during this stage. After a few successful migrations, you should feel comfortable with managing production workloads in Kubernetes and begin to see improvements in your operational tempo.

Here are a few competencies we recommend building as you start to move stateless workloads:

Leverage continuous delivery
: Using `kubectl` on the command line is great for learning, but terrible for daily operations. Get used to managing groups of resources as services instead of individual Pods and let the Kubernetes Operators do the work of maintaining your systems.

Network routing and Ingress
: Bad things happen when you fight the way Kubernetes works, and one place that people new to Kubernetes fail is with network communications. You should prefer service names over IP addresses and understand how the LoadBalancer and Ingress APIs work.

Default security and observability
: Deployed services should default to a secure state and expose observability interfaces such as metrics endpoints with no manual configuration required. Ensure that every new service is deployed with network-level encryption. To manage systems effectively, SREs must have the metrics available to diagnose problems without gaps in coverage.

These competencies will serve you well as you move into the following stages.

Deploy stateful workloads

The next stage is to migrate stateful workloads to Kubernetes, including their supporting data infrastructure. In this case, we recommend a phased approach in roughly the following order:

Persistence
: We recommend migrating databases as your first stateful workloads. Databases have been running in Kubernetes for far longer than other stateful workloads, with a higher level of maturity and documentation. Chapters 4 and 5 provide guidance on deploying with Helm and operators, respectively. Start with your development environment and parallel the same production traffic loads outside Kubernetes. Get proficient at backups and restore operations. Make sure your test cases include the loss of database compute and storage resources and move into staging and production when you feel your recovery response is sufficient.

Streaming
: The Kubernetes readiness for streaming workloads is becoming much more mature, but we still recommend you migrate these workloads after persistence workloads. As we discussed in Chapter 8, streaming workloads have some unique properties that can make them easier for migrations: most use cases don't need long-term message storage, so switching from one streaming service to the other typically doesn't require data migration. Since streaming is network intensive, proficiency with Kubernetes networking is a must.

Analytics

The complex nature of analytic workloads makes them the next logical choice for migration into Kubernetes after persistence and streaming are in place. A good starting approach is to deploy analytic workloads into a dedicated Kubernetes cluster so that you can learn the Kubernetes deployment modes and special considerations for job management and data access. Ultimately you should consider using a different scheduler to support batch workloads such as YuniKorn or Volcano, as we discussed in Chapter 9.

AI/ML workloads

You may consider your AI/ML workloads for extra migration bonus points. As we discussed in Chapter 10, this is one of the least mature areas organizations have concerning data infrastructure. Projects like KServe and Feast are well suited for Kubernetes, so this isn't the concern. The real question is whether your organization is proficient in MLOps and data engineering. You may be ready, but as a general recommendation for most organizations, this is an area you should address after other analytic workloads.

The details of your specific adoption plan will vary according to your Kubernetes readiness, the maturity of each workload, and the underlying data infrastructure on which it is built. The Kubernetes native definitions in Chapter 7 provide a valuable way of assessing the readiness of your infrastructure and where you may encounter additional work to properly deploy and manage it on Kubernetes.

Continually optimize your deployments

In the early days of the internet explosion, known as the "dot-com" years, startups were vying for venture capital and presenting plans. Almost every pitch deck would include a slide showing the planned datacenter build-out. It was there for a good reason: datacenters were a significant capital cost, and when asking for money, that had to be in the budget.

Things are different today. Startups now rent what they need from a cloud provider, and larger enterprises that still manage datacenters are reducing their footprints quickly. In this cloud native world, we have a lot more flexibility over the infrastructure we use, which gives greater opportunity for managing elements like cost, quality, and the trade-offs between them:

Optimizing cost

In any business, you have things that add to the ledger and subtract. People in finance call that the *cost of goods sold* (*COGS*). If you are building cars, COGS may account for costs like steel, the factory, and labor. Selling cars covers COGS and brings profit to the company. Controlling costs and making them predictable is a way to create a sustainable business.

In application software technology today, there are four main components of COGS: human labor, compute, network, and storage. These metrics have been tracked for a long time, and a lot of progress has been made to reduce costs and make things more predictable. DevOps has reduced the amount of human interaction needed, and cloud has normalized infrastructure costs. As mentioned in Chapter 1, Kubernetes wasn't a revolution. It was an evolution and a place to converge to help solve the problem of COGS with application software technology, a solution that doesn't compromise on quality and creates predictability.

Elasticity is one aspect of cloud native data that can lead to significant cost savings. If services are initially deployed with fixed capacity, optimize your deployments with the ability to not only scale up but also scale down when needed. When possible, use automation such as HorizontalPodAutoscaler (*https://oreil.ly/AoiRm*) for hands-off scaling with the added benefit of scaling under load to maintain performance. Choosing projects that can support elastic workload management is the most crucial way to be sure you are getting the best performance for the cost.

Optimizing quality (availability and performance)

Reducing human toil reduces the number of people needed to run your Kubernetes deployments. Automated deployments and sane defaults go a long way to reducing labor, but self-healing infrastructure will reduce the number of people that need to be on hand for when things go bad. Optimize your self-healing deployments by testing the recovery of services by injecting failures into your cluster. Kill a Pod or a StatefulSet. What happens to the surrounding services? If that scenario makes you nervous, you need to optimize your Deployment until you are comfortable with failures.

Reducing costs should never be optimized by sacrificing quality. Continuously optimize for price and performance. As you constantly look to optimize your Kubernetes deployments, you should ask yourself these questions:

- Are you maintaining SLAs?
- Is the need for human interaction reduced?
- Can you scale to zero with no traffic?

Given the current trends in operations, *AIOps* is a term that will soon enter your vocabulary, if it hasn't already. AIOps doesn't mean operations for AI/ML workloads; it refers to the use of AI/ML to manage infrastructure intelligently. With a strong baseline of observability, the metrics and other information you're collecting can be analyzed and used to generate recommended adjustments to your infrastructure. Automated scaling up and scaling down of Deployments and StatefulSets is just the beginning. We hope to soon see advanced AIOps capabilities, for example:

- A system that detects increased usage of a vertically integrated service in a given region and responds by deploying microservices and supporting infrastructure into that region, and proactively replicating data to optimize latency for client applications.
- A multitenant system that detects when a particular tenant is demonstrating increased usage and migrates traffic for that tenant to dedicated infrastructure.

These are just a couple of examples of what we might be able to achieve. We already have the foundations in the controller-reconciler pattern implemented by the Kubernetes control plane. Today's operators are heavily procedural, but what kind of decision flexibility could we build into future operators in order to achieve a desired quality of service? Stay tuned, because the cloud native world is constantly evolving.

The Future of Cloud Native Data

Over the course of a career in information technology, you're likely to see several generational shifts. A subtle evolution occurs over five- or ten-year periods as changes slowly build on a previous generation of technology, until the day you realize that the way you work is fundamentally new. Perhaps you've spent part of your career installing operating systems on physical servers. In a more recent generation, we've started using scripts to provision cloud instances with operating system images ready for software to be installed. Kubernetes represents the latest generation, where engineers define everything they need in a text file, and the control plane converges the state while performing all of the tasks every previous generation of engineers had to do manually.

What kind of progress will we continue to see from generation to generation? The following is a fictional story about a very possible near future. This story provides an example of where we could go as a community of data infrastructure engineers. The changes will be subtle but profound.

A Vision of a Not-Too-Distant Future

The kickoff meeting

I arrive Monday morning in the office and see an email invitation to a meeting from one of our product managers. Our company has been growing at a fast pace, and to stay ahead of our competition, we constantly release new products. The meeting will be a kickoff with everyone from user experience to the backend infrastructure. Somebody dreamed up a new app, so here we go.

Product management shares a one-pager with an ambitious, groundbreaking idea requiring everyone to make it work. The room is divided into groups of people you see in any product build: user experience and interface design, microservice developers, data engineers, and my team, responsible for the backend infrastructure. We collaborate closely across teams to move quickly and keep our customers happy.

In the meeting, it's clear that nobody is sure of how big of an idea this is and thus we have no idea of the needed capacity. While we used to expend a lot of energy on infrastructure planning and wasted a lot of money by provisioning too early, we don't have to do this anymore because our systems will adapt to what's needed. Things happen, and plans change. If we're lucky, an idea will take off like a rocket and then we'll scale to a global user base. Our job is to build the right product with quality and be ready for whatever comes.

Confidence booster

One aspect of my job I love is getting requirements and designing the right infrastructure to do the job. I'm inspired by the building architect I. M. Pei, who worked with clients to translate their vision into a functional reality, and one of his famous quotes: "Success is a collection of problems solved." He maintained the beauty and elegance of the original requirements and built things with a purpose, like the Grand Louvre and Kennedy Library. I'm not saying that I'm the I. M. Pei of data infrastructure, but his example is inspiring.

The first task I have is reasoning through each piece of the data infrastructure like a puzzle. It reminds me of the LEGO projects I created as a kid. I'll need a square piece, a rectangular piece, a specialty piece with a hinge, and that round dot that always seems to get lost. I help the development teams identify the data infrastructure components that will support this particular application: there's a mix of transactional data managed by various microservices, and we put together the right combination of databases, object storage, transformations, and streams to store, enhance and move data where it's needed. The data engineers highlight the data sets they will need to analyze business results and produce intelligent recommendations that will make the application work better for our users.

The initial architecture decisions aren't final; in most cases, the infrastructure we're building will automatically evolve. The basic parameters are defined by the application's needs according to its API contract. I set boundaries around costs and location and let Kubernetes and my operators figure out the rest intelligently. The system makes adjustments by analyzing usage to lower latency while remaining at or below budget. The solution I want is the one that gives me the lowest cost while still meeting our SLAs.

No plans survive contact with the enemy

We decide to roll out the new application with an initial pilot in North America. We deploy a Kubernetes cluster and install the application and supporting data infrastructure using automated scripting we've built up in previous projects and then run a few automated performance and compliance tests. The CI/CD pipeline reduces the time to deploy fixes for a couple of minor defects we found in testing to just a few minutes. Since we've automated the data collection and observability tools, it takes only a couple of hours for the quality and security teams to sign off on the application, and we are live!

At the product launch, things are looking great. From the first meeting to the final product approval, our time span was a few days, and everything is working as designed. The user experience and development engineers weren't waiting on us to provision infrastructure, so they could spend their time focusing on what made the product a delight for our customers. The application is working as designed, and we are continuing to refine and improve. I'm sure we'll get the go-ahead to start expanding into new regions soon.

On my way to work, I see on the news that storms threaten to shut down large parts of the eastern United States. I check my alerts and see the notifications from our service providers: "Due to the worsening storm conditions, the following locations will be flagged for evacuations…" They aren't just talking about human evacuations; these are infrastructure evacuations. Since our applications can route around datacenter failures, our providers don't have to put people in harm's way. Heroic efforts to fulfill fuel contracts and keep the generators running aren't needed now.

Years ago, this might have caused a Tier 1 emergency, but now our systems are resilient against both natural and human-error disasters. When providers post an evacuation warning, our intelligent operators ingest the new parameters and start reconciling a solution: finding new capacity, negotiating the price, and shutting down the affected areas. Even without a warning, like when human error is involved, our application will still be online. Intelligent geographical redundancy insulates us from localized problems, like somebody accidentally cutting a network or power cable. I feel bad for the people who are stuck maintaining legacy applications. Those systems have no way of managing an emergency, and it's left to the humans to figure it out. Somebody is going to have a late night, and I'm thankful it isn't me.

It's a hit!

A few days later, I get an email about how our new application has taken off in Europe. Our management has questions about our infrastructure capacity and potential effects on our SLA. We want to provide a good user experience, no matter how users find us or where they are. I reply with confidence that we have things covered because our infrastructure has already detected the new usage pattern and anticipated the needed changes. There's not much for me to do other than verify that our SLAs are being met and watch it work.

When I examine the updated deployment, I see adjustments to my initial architecture. In addition to the expansion in storage capacity and compute processing I expected to see, I notice that the faster and more expensive streaming pipelines I started with have been changed out for slower but more cost-effective rollups in batch analytics. This is the result of continuous analysis of the traffic patterns by our intelligent operators in response to observing user interaction. I can see that the application's response rate will be improved without the need to have the streaming pipeline results immediately. This provides a better user experience for a smaller cost, with no application code changes required.

Shortly after, our data engineering team reaches out. After analyzing the application usage patterns, they've identified some improvements to the recommendation engine the application uses. Working together, I add a new stream to push more operational data to an analytic store while they add analytic jobs to generate new feature data. The microservice developers do some quick A/B testing with the new recommendation data to verify that customers can make decisions more quickly, so we roll the changes out to the entire fleet. Our PR team shares an unsolicited article about how people are starting to notice the application. Is this our viral moment? We're not sure yet, but the management team is definitely excited.

No worries

Weeks later, I meet with the product manager to discuss changes for the next product rollout. They are delighted that things worked so seamlessly. I remind them that this is how people build cloud native applications these days. We don't deploy infrastructure; we declare it. My job isn't dominated by editing configuration files and spending time in a terminal. I spend my time listening to teams and working with them on what they need. Like I. M. Pei, I enjoy the creative process of defining elegant architectures. My focus is to design something that makes it easy for developers to be productive on the first day while giving our end users an amazing experience. With a modern Kubernetes native approach, I define what I need and worry a lot less about the how. Because most of what's deployed is open source, I can even take time to fix little things and contribute back to a project.

The area I never worry about is having to deploy something. I never have to ask if it will work or if there are a lot of trade-offs. I define what the application needs, and it will emerge. Having development timelines of days or hours instead of months is a great place to be.

This story aims to help you look beyond the drudgery of configuration files and the shiny distraction of hot new projects and focus on how embracing cloud native data opens the door for a more fantastic tomorrow. When the toil of infrastructure is reduced or even removed, think of the new abilities we have and how this could translate into tangible daily outcomes. This isn't science fiction, and you don't have to wait for the next generational breakthrough. All of this is feasible today with the correct application of existing technology.

Summary

You made it! We have taken quite a journey together and covered a lot of ground, not only in this chapter but in the entire book. At the outset, we presented an ambitious goal of putting stateful workloads on Kubernetes. As we learned from Craig McLuckie, this is very much in line with the original goals of the Kubernetes project. Ultimately, we will reverse the trend of infrastructure-aware applications and have application-aware platforms and building applications with speed, efficiency, and confidence.

Hopefully, we've convinced you that this is achievable technically and extremely compelling from a cost and quality standpoint. In this chapter, we've focused on helping you chart the course to make this transition by focusing on the people, process, and technology changes you'll need to make to be successful:

- Help people in your organization skill up on Kubernetes and data technologies, including those we've covered here. If you are in leadership, help place people in roles that give them direct responsibility and accountability for infrastructure choices. Empower them to interact and contribute in open source communities and be the catalyst for change in your organization.
- Select data infrastructure technologies that embody cloud native and Kubernetes native principles. Use Kubernetes custom resources and operators to raise the level of abstraction in your architecture to begin thinking about managing services that implement well-defined APIs instead of managing individual servers.
- Update your processes to automate "all the things"—from integration and delivery (CI/CD) to observability and management (AIOps). Leverage these mature processes as you strategically migrate stateful workloads to Kubernetes. Carefully balance the trade-offs between cost and quality to sustainably deliver the best experiences for your end users.

Now, the narrative of this journey shifts to you and where you choose to take us next. While this book has provided a broad overview of the world of data infrastructure on Kubernetes, each chapter could easily fill a book on its own. We encourage you to continue learning where your specific interests take you and share what you learn to continue to fill the gaps in our collective knowledge. As you successfully manage your cloud native data on Kubernetes, we hope to hear your story.

Index

B

C

D

E

F

G

H

N

O

P

Q

R

S

T

About the Authors

Jeff Carpenter has worked as a software engineer and architect in multiple industries and as a developer advocate helping engineers succeed with Apache Cassandra. He's involved in multiple open source projects in the Cassandra and Kubernetes ecosystems including Stargate (*https://stargate.io*) and K8ssandra (*https://k8ssandra.io*). Jeff is coauthor of *Cassandra: The Definitive Guide*.

Patrick McFadin has been a distributed systems hacker since he first plugged a modem into his Atari computer. Looking for adventure, he joined the US Navy, working on the Naval Tactical Data System (NTDS), which cemented his love of distributed systems. He then spent the 1990s working on infrastructure as the internet started to take off and barely survived the ensuing dot-com crash. Along the way, Patrick picked up a computer engineering degree from Cal Poly, San Luis Obispo, and has been focusing on high-scale internet infrastructure ever since. His latest obsession is distributed data systems, and he has been a steady contributor to the Apache Cassandra project since 2011.

Colophon

The animal on the cover of *Managing Cloud Native Data on Kubernetes* is the Indian golden oriole (*Oriolus kundoo*), a species of oriole found on the Indian subcontinent and in Central Asia. They belong to the order of Old World perching birds, which are not closely related to New World orioles.

Male Indian golden orioles are bright yellow, except for a black patch on the wings, black tail feathers, and a black eye stripe that gives them a masked appearance. Females are a duller shade of yellow-green, with brownish-green wings. Both males and females have red irises and pink bills.

Both parents participate in nest building and caring for young. After an incubation period of 16 to 17 days, the young hatch and are fledged in another 16 days.

The oriole has a wide range of habitats, including forests, mangroves, open country, parks, and gardens. Their diet primarily consists of fruit and insects.

The conservation status of the Indian golden oriole is Least Concern. Many of the animals on O'Reilly covers are endangered; all of them are important to the world.

The cover illustration is by Karen Montgomery, based on an antique line engraving from *Lydekker's Royal Natural History*. The cover fonts are Gilroy Semibold and Guardian Sans. The text font is Adobe Minion Pro; the heading font is Adobe Myriad Condensed; and the code font is Dalton Maag's Ubuntu Mono.

CPSIA information can be obtained
at www.ICGtesting.com
Printed in the USA
JSHW061912270223
38279JS00005B/83

9 781098 111397